"It's been said that the mark of real genius is the ability to reduce something to its purest and simplest form. For example, Einstein with e = mc² or Michelangelo, who, when asked to demonstrate his skill as an artist drew an absolutely perfect circle freehand in one stroke. Well, there's no question in my mind that Ray has done the same thing with backpacking. The philosophy, gear, and skills mesh perfectly and have been taken to a new level." Mike W.

"The cover price of Ray's book is about 2000% below what the information contained is worth. My whole outlook to the world and to the outdoors in general have changed for the better because of it. There are several titles out there but the Jardine way of doing things is the stuff of legends." Geoff G.

"This is greatest ever backpacking book. A masterpiece. It discusses ideas and skills that not only revolutionize the backpacking experience, but allow the reader to analyze other areas in life and make huge changes to those too. There is much more to this book than meets the eye - after several readings one realizes that it's not just about backpacking! Ray has written this book on various levels, so when thumbing through a chapter for the umpteenth time, there is invariably a new gem that pops out and makes the reader reconsider something that had previously been taken for granted." Mike G.

"The magnum opus of adventure guru Ray Jardine – rock climber, hang glider pilot, scuba diver, around-the-world sailor and long-distance paddler extraordinaire." Ethan B.

"Just to mention those parts of the book that I find useful: from the first page to the last, and pretty much everything in between." Michael D.

"This is a book you will not tire of re-reading. I have read my copy multiple times and acquire new ideas from it every time I reread it. Using Ray's tips and techniques I have been able to increase my outdoor enjoyment tenfold." Ken C.

"I bought Ray's book and devoured it, laughing all the way through in joy at his ingenuity, common sense and my own sheep-like, following the crowd without a second thought behavior. His ideas have opened up worlds of possibilities." Paul K.

"I a[...]king
bud[...]iven
me[...]and
adv[...]That
pict[...]ago.
Tha[...]

"My knees and feet were beginning to show the cumulative effects of 40 years of carrying 60-70-pound packs, so I decided to try going light. Bought this book, made the gear, and did a trial run. The results far surpassed my expectations. The change to light gear has added 30 years of backpacking to my life." Dick G.

"I found Ray's philosophy and techniques to be inspiring, refreshing and smart. The book gave me the extra encouragement to break away for a few months from my rather ordinary life and pursue an experience that was so big that I still cannot find any words to describe it." Stephanie B.

"I read this book after 5 days on the AT with my 'bone-crusher' pack and, jaw wide open, could not believe how much sense Ray's ideas made. Thanks to him for saving my back, knees (boy, did they hurt) and lots of cash." Mark P.

"One does not have to be a rocket scientist to know lighter is better." Tom J.

"After reading the book I am more excited than ever to 'hit the trail.' Also, the idea of dropping the weight gives me confidence that I will now be able to continue backpacking for many more years. Thanks to Ray for keeping the wilderness open to me." James M.

"Our outings have provided my kids with a sense of accomplishment and independence unobtainable in any other activity. Finding Ray's books has had a tremendous effect on this, and we are using many of the methods to great advantage." Jim W.

"I have really enjoyed Ray's books. Traveling light is so obvious but nearly always discounted due to 'conventional wisdom.' So thanks to Ray for his free and forward thinking." Mike Y.

"I read this book about 10 times in the past couple of months." Paul G.

"We liked the book so much we bought another copy for my niece. She said: 'This is exactly what I needed to learn about, and the book is about so much more than backpacking--it's about life!' That sums it up for us!" Hermann G.

"The overriding life philosophy presented in this book - think and find what works best for you. I love it!" John T.

"After reading this book I experimented with virtually every idea and found them all to be extremely useful, efficient, and safe. In short, Ray's methods allowed me to enjoy the outdoors at a level that I had never before experienced. The book is very well organized, clearly written, and presents ideas in such a way that makes one wonder 'Why didn't I think of that before?' This is a must read for both experienced and beginning adventurers and is already a classic among experienced backpackers." Richard M.

"This is the most phenomenal book on outdoor travel I have ever seen. After reading it I did a backpacking trip with 8 pounds of gear (excluding food and water), and it was by far the most enjoyable backpacking trip I have ever done. It made the trip seem like a pleasant stroll in the wilderness rather than hours of labor under a huge pack. It is often misunderstood that Jardine recommends these methods in order to go faster. I believe he recommends these methods because they are more fun, easier, and less expensive. This book would have saved me a lot of money, had I bought it sooner." Ryan H.

"Thanks to Ray for reminding us to think instead of buy." Mark N.

"Lightening the pack can be a spiritual path. I think this is why Ray's book is raging. He gently brings lightening the pack into the realm of conscious evolution. People are secretly starving for info like this. He brings backpacking into the realm of art. People love this. He's got everyone thinking and questioning assumptions. This is his gift to us all. He is a paradigm buster." Doug W.

"My enjoyment of the outdoors has increased exponentially since reading this book. Thanks to Ray for all the wonderful contributions he has made to the lightweight backpacking community." Josh B.

"I feel this is an excellent text obviously written from experience. It systematically and completely addresses all parts of a backpacking trip and is very useful at dispelling concerns novice campers or hikers may have. The tone of the book is very positive as well, as Jardine refrains from casting different methods in a negative light. The book also has an appealing 'outside the box' thinking process with innumerable bits of tips and wisdom and that can lead to more enjoyment of anyone's wilderness experience." David A.

"I haven't tried everything in Ray's book yet, but everything I have tried has worked. Ray's innovative challenge to conventional backpack thinking is nothing short of revolutionary." Troy H.

"Mr. Jardine's book is the most useful book on the topic of backpacking that I have read. It's greatest value is that it encourages the reader to think for him or herself. It asks the question, 'is the way we have been backpacking the most efficient, the most enjoyable?' The answer is found through direct experience with Jardine's ideas. I have begun experimenting with these and found it very rewarding. This book is much more than a guide to lighter gear. It is a how-to manual for enhancing all aspects of the wilderness experience. Very inspiring!" John B.

"We were interested in Ray and Jenny for a number of reasons: their achievements as long distance hikers (PCT 3 times; Triple Crown etc); their importance as innovators (Ray's designing of Friends for climbing in the 70's; their own design of kayak for their recent trips in the Arctic etc). But perhaps most importantly for the philosophy, motivation and commitment that lies behind these achievements - from our point of view their whole concept of ultra-lightweight backpacking together with their philosophy of going with nature. From a U.K. perspective we see them in a long line of U.S. based wilderness thinkers and philosophers - Muir, Emerson, Thoreau, Abbey etc. We view them as immensely important and they were right at the top of our list for this second series of Wilderness Walks." Richard Else, BBC.

"Revolutionary thinking for revolutionary results." Derek M.

"Bottom line – Ray is a genius." Clay B.

Trail Life

Ray Jardine's
Lightweight Backpacking

25,000-Miles Worth of Trail-Tested Know-How

Jenny on the PCT in the Goat Rocks Wilderness; Mount Rainier in the background. We used this photo on the cover of an earlier edition of this book, *The Pacific Crest Trail Hiker's Handbook*, published in 1996.

Trail Life
Ray Jardine's Lightweight Backpacking
25,000-Miles worth of Trail-Tested Know-How

Trail Life, First Edition
Published in the United States by
AdventureLore Press
www.AdventureLore.com

Library of Congress Catalog Card Number: 99-72758
Ray Jardine, Lightweight Backpacking
AdventureLore Press, AZ
ISBN 978-0-9632359-7-8

Welcome to Trail Life

"I hoped that the trip would be the best of all journeys: a journey into ourselves."
— *Shirley MacLaine*

PCT-3

Prior to 1991 when the first edition of this book was published (under a different title), recreational hiking with lightweight equipment was practically unheard of. Back then, hikers carried massive backpacks loaded with all manner of camping "luxuries." And they plodded along in heavy leather boots. This was backpacking. Never mind the aching shoulders, the pain in the knees, blistered feet and deep fatigue; these were considered a part of the experience.

Despite the cumbersome gear, I loved backpacking back then, and like most people I enjoyed at least some camp luxuries. But while on the trail, I found that carrying the typical heavy load was uncomfortable. To me, the profusion of heavy-duty equipment associated with the all-inclusive "everything-but-the-kitchen-sink" approach only detracted from my outings. So I started looking for ways of facilitating the hiking without sacrificing the comfort and safety.

For several decades (actually since the 1960's) I have devoted my energies mainly to adventuring; and this has given me plenty of opportunity to apply my aerospace engineering background to the design and construction of my own lightweight outdoor gear and clothing; and to refine my hiking and camping techniques accordingly.

From 1987 to 1994, my wife, Jenny and I logged over 15,000 miles of hiking, including five summer-long journeys each in excess of 2,000 miles. With each long trek I reexamined our gear and methods with an eye toward refinement. In effect, each journey became something of a multi-month field test, as we put my ideas into practice. These ideas had to work because we depended on them. But sometimes they did not work very well, and I always seemed to return home with new ideas for the next trip.

I was not interested in minimalism, but simply a reduction in what was not necessary. And we found that this reduction, when thoughtfully and skillfully applied, actually enhanced our safety and comfort on the trail.

The process of refinement has been evolutionary, and has led to a lightweight system of backpacking gear and philosophy that has been tried, tested, modified, and tested again.

We had a lot of fun on those hikes, and we still have fun backpacking today, especially with our lightly loaded backpacks. But in the wilds, our focus is not on our gear. Instead, it is on our enjoyment of the natural world, and on the adventures. Our equipment is only a means to help us enjoy the trips more.

This brings me to a fundamental aspect of our approach that adds even greater meaning to our wilderness adventures. We view our treks as more than just physical walks along trails, and our camping more than just pitching a tent and zipping ourselves inside. More important to us is our presence in the wilds: how we carry ourselves, how softly we move upon the landscape, how aware we are of the patterns of life around us and how we interact with them. This was a common theme with Native Americans and other aboriginal peoples around the world. Putting this concept into practice brings us a greater awareness and appreciation of the natural world around us, of our relationship with that world, and of our own inner nature. This is the *modus operandi* behind all our trips, and also our lightweight gear, techniques and methods.

This book is about our trail life: our experiences during those backpacking journeys and other wilderness adventures, and what we have learned from those experiences. Yes, this book is also about our gear and techniques, but only from the standpoint of what has worked well for us. If the reader gleans a few ideas from this book, so much the better. But an even better plan is to discover what works best for you by making your own choices and interpretations.

So think for yourself and keep your hikes enjoyable and safe. Take care of the wild places and leave them unspoiled for future generations of backpackers to enjoy. And perhaps along the way, see if you can discover for yourself paths that take you to a greater awareness and appreciation of the natural world.

Penstemon and paintbrush; PCT-2

Nature tugs at the soul

PCT-1

*"The purpose of a wilderness journey
is not to get from one end of the [trail] to the other,
but to enjoy the landscape,
and adapt to its ever-changing moods."*
— *Bill Mason*

What is the meaning of trail life? Certainly the lure of the wilds is different for each person, and the reasons for hiking and camping vary widely.

Many hikers appreciate the temporary respite from structured, citified living with its everyday stresses and distractions (the snarling traffic, blaring commercials, ringing telephones) and the schedules and responsibilities.

Backpacking also gives a person a chance to discover innumerable out of the way places, inaccessible to mechanized travelers. And in the process it might engender a kinship, as it were, with the ancient peoples who must have known these same places well. Life on the trail can be a time of rising early, of traipsing wet footed through meadow grass, and later of feeling the luxurious warmth of the morning sun. It can be a time of ambling through quiet forests, breathing fresh air and drinking pure water while listening to a splashing waterfall. It can be a time of admiring hillsides of wildflowers, and perhaps in the same day, laboring to gain a high vantage, then gazing across the vast landscape.

Nature has a way of reawakening one's senses and speaking to the heart.

Trail life affords opportunities to move quietly across the land and encounter wildlife. Then at the end of a long day of hiking, to savor a well-deserved meal (a spicy batch of spaghetti, in my case). And as the colors fade into the shadows of eventide, to consider the awesome star studded skies and note the changing phase of the moon.

I find such a life invigorating and rejuvenating.

Modern society exerts tremendous influences on a person; shaping, molding and changing the personality. In reacting continually to outside pressures, a person tends to take on a life not his or her own. But when that person steps into the wilderness, he or she might find freedom from those influences, at least temporarily, and may begin to see life from a new and different perspective.

So too, many hikers find that when surrounded by nature, they can more easily differentiate their wants from their needs. And of course, the adventure of it all: the seemingly boundless pathways stretching ahead, full of challenge, discovery, and lessons to be learned.

Trail life is a return to Nature; and for me it is a journey in search of what parts of myself might lie within its deserts, forests, and far-flung mountains. Granted, the way might be garnished with toil and fatigue, but they are the right kinds of toil and fatigue. And of course there are the usual adversities of snowpack, mosquitos and so forth. But such adversities only strengthen those people who learn to accept and adjust to them; in other words, who are open to personal growth.

So a long hike can be a test of abilities: not only of physical strength and stamina, but of adaptability as well. It can be truly a test of self and a journey of discovery.

One of my favorite trees along the PCT. It has so much color and character, and reminds me of how one can prevail over unfavorable circumstances.

Henry David Thoreau wrote: "*I went to the woods because I wished to live deliberately, to front only the essential facts of life, and see if I could not learn what it had to teach, and not, when I came to die, discover that I had not lived.*"

Part 1

PACKWEIGHT

North Cascades, PCT-2

Trail Life

Myth of Heavy-Duty Gear

*"Those who prepare for all the emergencies
of life beforehand may equip themselves
at the expense of joy."*

— *E. M. Forster*

Grandma Gatewood's legacy

The wilderness can seem to hammer us with fatigue, rain and insects, or it can enrich us with the joys of adventure and discovery. The determining factor is our attitude. A negative or fearful mindset will enervate even the strongest-bodied hiker; whereas a positive, more self-confident frame of mind will allow almost anyone to enjoy almost any trail.

A negative or fearful outlook often calls for a magnum-sized backpack full of heavy-duty gear to protect a person, supposedly, from the full range of nature's deterrents. A positive attitude, however, allows one to safely and comfortably adopt lightweight gear, and to dispense with the extraneous. The choice is whether to armor for battle, or to take a lighter, friendlier approach.

———

Emma "Grandma" Gatewood (1888-1975) did not look like much of a hiker. But sometimes looks can be deceiving.

During an illustrious hiking career that spanned eighteen years, she thru-hiked the Appalachian Trail (AT)—not just once, but twice—and she section-hiked it a third time. She also hiked the Chesapeake and Ohio Canal Towpath from Washington, DC to Cumberland, Maryland; the Long Trail in Vermont; the Baker Trail in Pennsylvania; and the Buckeye Trail in Ohio. And on the 100th anniversary of the Oregon Trail she walked its entire 2,000-mile length in fifteen days less than what most of the historic wagon trains had taken.

Grandma Gatewood (as Emma was popularly and fondly known) started hiking at an age when most people retire to their armchairs. And even then, her accomplishments were outstanding. During her second AT thru-hike she took no rest days, and completed the rugged journey in only 4½ months, finishing just a few days before her 70th birthday. Her secret? "I had always lived on a farm and was used to hard work," she told one reporter. "I was in good physical condition, so I decided to hike that trail, and I just started out." And in her spunky style she quipped, "Most people are pantywaists. Exercise is good for you."

What set Grandma Gatewood apart was her avoidance of the latest and most robust equipment. Backpackers wore sturdy boots to protect their feet; Grandma wore Keds™ sneakers. They used expensive parkas and "lightweight," bug-proof tents. She used a rain cape and a plastic shower curtain. They carried expensive external-frame packs that distributed their heavy loads evenly. Grandma didn't carry a heavy load. Her items of extra clothing and gear were few, and she carried them, along with her food, in a homemade bag simply draped over one shoulder.

I think Grandma's legacy encourages people in their own abilities, and reminds them of today's excess in heavy-duty paraphernalia. She was obviously a strong and gutsy woman, but I doubt whether she would have hiked even a fraction of those miles lugging the standard elephantine load. And what is more, I cannot think of a single item of modern clothing or equipment that would have added to her success.

The bulk of advertisements and articles in today's outdoor magazines are telling us quite the opposite: that we need a wide selection of the very best in heavy-duty gear in order to survive out there, let alone have a good time. But Grandma Gatewood proved otherwise. Then as now, her example stands as convincing evidence that a simpler, lighter-weight approach is just as workable.

I am not suggesting that hikers and backpackers abandon their gear and adopt a minimalist approach. But I do think that the bulk of today's heavy-duty equipment is hardly essential to one's hiking and camping enjoyment and safety.

If we do not need our gear to be heavy-duty, then why is most of today's gear so heavily constructed? Why do the "best" backpacks weigh 5 to 7 pounds rather than one? Why do the latest tents weigh 5 pounds rather than two? Why does the footwear weigh 6 pounds rather than one?

I see three reasons for this. The first concerns the outdoor industry's unwritten policy of keeping consumers (hikers and backpackers) in the dark, as a way to bolster profits. The second relates to the inconvenience to the manufacturer when gear is returned for repair or replacement. The third has to do with the marketing pressure driven by today's fiercely competitive climate.

Motivated by profit

The outdoor-equipment industry is just that: an industry. The professionals who manufacture, market, and sell this gear are motivated mainly by profit.

I have nothing against anyone in the industry. I am simply making an observation of how the system works, from the perspective of one who has been familiar with the outdoor industry for 40 years. I know that most of the players thrive on marketing, not what the consumer needs, necessarily, but on what will net the most money.

This helps explain why few outdoor stores sell gear that is simple and economical. From the perspective of the store owners, why sell one-pound backpacks for cheap, when they can sell five- to seven-pound behemoths with all the latest features for many times the price? Selling more expensive gear, the store owners pocket more money. So when a customer walks though the door interested in packs, the sales person will naturally show them to the more feature-laden backpacks. Keeping customers in the dark—by not telling them about the many advantages of backpacks that are simpler and also lighter, cheaper, and more efficient—will reap the most profit.

This principle applies also to the manufacturers, who send their sales reps to the retail trade shows to elicit business from store owners. The entire business thrives on the "new look," the allure and fanfare of showing new products with new features. So the manufacturers would make little profit in simpler and cheaper gear.

The outdoor magazines control the flow of money, serving as the link between manufacturers and consumers (and their money) and everyone in between. Yet the magazines rely on the manufacturers who pay mega-dollars for publishing and distributing their advertisements. So from the perspective of the magazine staff, it is good business to write impressive (if biased) reviews.

The online backpacking stores also win big, by charging the typical mark-ups of 45% to 60%, and by employing writers, each having a variety of writing "voices," who submit enthusiastic (if biased) "feedback" on the heavy-duty products.

It all boils down to who makes the most money on what kind of gear. Never mind the needs of the backpacker.

The principles and gear described in this book are beyond all this hype, simply because our type of gear represents no appreciable gains for the industry. But while the industry is concerned with maximizing its profits, Jenny and I are more interested in maximizing our outdoor experiences.

Product returns = more weight

The second reason today's gear is so heavily constructed has to do with manufacturing convenience.

Let's say that someone buys an expensive backpack, first verifying that it is fully guaranteed. If a seam subsequently rips out, or a strap tears off, the disgruntled customer will return the product for repair or replacement, probably having to pay the postage, and of course enduring the loss of valuable time if they happen to be on a long trek.

This is bad news also for the manufacturer, who thinks in terms of profit and public image. And it is particularly inconvenient for those who import their products, as most do. They cannot repair the item because they have no on-site sewing repair facilities. So they must send the customer a replacement (which usually has those same defects).

The manufacturer may enhance the design of future models not by reinforcing the overstressed area, in most cases, but by simply increasing the weight of the affected component, be it the fabric, fastener, or whatever. In time, after dozens of packs have been returned for repairs—each with a different problem—the manufacturer will have made the product massively stronger, and of course that much heavier.

This ultra-durability and its associated weight might be convenient for the manufacturer, and to the mainstream consumer who insists on "bombproof" products. And while this type of gear might be acceptable for expedition use in extreme environments, we have found it decidedly overkill for hiking in relatively accessible areas in all but the harshest conditions.

The backpacks that Jenny and I used on our third PCT thru-hike weighed less than a pound. Actually, mine weighed 13½ ounces, and Jenny's two ounces less. And even though we made them of lightweight materials, they handled those 2,700 miles perfectly. Not only that, but we have since carried them for thousands of miles more, and they are still holding up.

PCT-3 in Oregon

In every likelihood, many hikers might be happier with lighter weight gear, as long as it is well-designed and constructed, and treated with care. But the marketeers[1] would have us believe otherwise. And in order to convince us of our need for their heavy-duty wares, they sometimes resort to some rather fanciful tactics.

---

1 "There is a fine line between marketing and larceny." – Mark Twain

Your life depends on our product

Thumb through a few outdoor magazines and you may find advertisements pitting a hostile environment against you and some piece of clothing or gear. Here are a few examples:

* Fabrics: "Out here, Mother won't wipe your nose. She'll rub your nose in it. When it's just you and Mother Nature, you better be prepared. Cause Mother can have a bad attitude."

* Clothing: "OK, now technically we can't guarantee that you'll end the day with as many limbs as when you started. But when you consider what we put into our (clothing) you gotta like the chances. (Wear our clothing), thereby improving your odds of making it home in one piece."

* Boots: "How can you expect to touch the face of god when your feet are firmly planted in hell?"

* Fabric: "Sometimes even when the wind is with you, it's against you."

* "I hope I don't get mauled by a mountain lion. Good thing I ate a (popular energy bar)."

These ads use a common tactic: they attempt to arouse a person's fears of nature, and then come to the rescue with the company's wares as the ultimate defense against the big, bad natural world. My intent is not to discredit any particular product or company, but merely to highlight the advertising tactics.

Here are a few more examples:

* Clothing: "Rocks have eyes and they are mean. They aim for skin. Right for where it stings. Hoping to lift off pieces of you to keep with them on the ground."

* "It's nice to know that even when you're not breathing, your jacket is."

* Tent: "The wind howls because it can't get to you."

* Shorts: "You never know what dangers you'll have to face out there. So we've provided some (shorts) that can take on just about anything."

* Fabric: "One million sweat glands are conspiring against you. Retaliate." (Not only is nature out to get us, but our bodies are conspiring against us also.)

But are we really as alien to the natural environment as these advertisements would have us believe? Is nature so hostile and dangerous that we dare not venture forth without the most durable and heaviest gear? Accidents do happen, but I think they are more related to carelessness and lack of knowledge than to any lack of heavy-duty gear.

Any type of gear, heavy or light, requires competence in its use. But the marketeers are trying to convince us that the heavier gear is safer, more durable, and of higher quality. However, even heavy-duty materials can be cheaply put together. And just because a product uses those materials does not mean that it is well designed. The best designs are those that address the hiker's needs; and that calls for light and strong materials, expertly put together.

Perceived obstacles

The idea of nature as adversary has a long history, and we find plenty of examples in today's magazines and books. I came across one that described the Appalachian Trail as "one seriously tough mother." The author went on to say "(the AT's) peak bagging philosophy manifests itself into one grade-A butt-kicking experience. Then there's the heat, humidity, and rain to consider as well as the bugs and snakes."

This type of attitude reflects the advertising slant examined above. And yes, if a person ventures into the wilderness with the assumption that nature is out to get him or her, then that person is likely to encounter the envisioned obstacles, one after the next. Not genuine obstacles most of the time, but perceived ones. So I think our perceptions of nature are cultivated by our attitudes, and that our attitudes hinge upon whether we choose a negative mindset or a positive one.

To illustrate, here are a few words from another AT thru-hiker, Emma Stephens, who at the age of 55 thru-hiked that same AT:

"My trek left me feeling very proud of myself. I hiked through 14 states. That means I walked it like the pioneers did, but instead of a mule carrying my supplies, I carried them. (I am not comparing myself to a mule, but a little stubbornness is sometimes a good thing!) I hiked alone for about two of those months and thoroughly enjoyed it. I liked making my own decisions about when and where to stop and how long to hike each day. Throughout the hike I would wake up in the morning to the birds singing, and very often at night go to sleep with the sound of a creek or waterfall as a lullaby. Can you do that in the city? Each day was a new adventure. What would I find? Hills, rocks, creeks, deer, bird nests, bear, turkey, old foundations, huge old trees that designated a homestead many decades ago, wild berries, moose, a new friend...I would not trade this experience for all the rocking chairs in Texas!

"I guess my final advice would be: Do it! The pride and sense of worth and accomplishment you will come away with will be very hard to beat. Oh yes, it will be hard, you will be wet, cold, hot, tired, and sometimes scraped and scratched, but almost never will you be discouraged. This will be six months of my life that will live on in my memory forever. And I don't think my family will forget it either. They are so proud of me."

———————

Grandma Gatewood had no need for fancy gear and gadgets, so she ignored the marketing mainstream. Yet she enjoyed a lengthy and successful backpacking career on par with the best of them. How? By exercising her strong will to succeed, and relying on resources within. "It's about as nice a thing as anybody can do – walking," she said. "And it's cheap, too!"

We enjoy another day of hiking along the beautiful Appalachian Trail. Carrying water to camp.

Pack-Weight Evolution

"Go forth under the open sky,
and list to Nature's teachings."
— *William Cullen Bryant*

Objectivity regained
through trial and error

Evolution of Thought and Technique

I began backpacking as a youngster, following my dad into the remote mountains of Colorado in quest of the perfect trout lake. My pack was reasonably large for a young kid. It was actually more like an army-surplus rucksack, and my sleeping bag occupied all its space. In the early 1950's we did not have goose down and nylon sleeping bags. Ours were cotton, with cotton batting insulation. These were heavy and not very compressible; about all we could do was roll them up. My dad carried a pack-board lashed with what seemed like a ton of gear. He hiked in his rubber hip waders because his pack-board had no room for them.

Dad gave me a larger pack every few years, while handing down my smaller ones to my two younger brothers. And of course with each new pack, he encouraged us to share more of his load. This meant that as we grew up, our pack-weights were always maxed out. But we loved those trips nonetheless.

By the time I left for college I had backpacked many hundreds of miles, with family, friends and on my own; and almost always with a large pack. After college I divided my spare time between rock climbing and mountaineering. On the mountaineering trips, my friends and I would drive to the mountains on a Saturday and carry our heavy packs into "base camp." Sunday we would rise early, climb our chosen peak, return to camp, pack up, then hike back out to the trailhead and drive home. After a couple of years of this I decided the trips would be more adventurous if we dispensed with the camping gear and simply climbed the mountains alpine style – bivouacking high on the peaks if necessary rather than tenting at a base camp. This was the first time I had considered the idea of reducing my packweight, and it cost me my mountaineering friends. They were not about to give up their conventional base camping methods, despite the heavy loads associated with them.

So I found new partners and started scaling the mountains alpine style. For a sleeping bag I used a thin, three-quarter length bag of goose down and nylon, augmented by a down jacket. My pack was still very heavy with climbing hardware, but by minimizing our baseline pack-weights my partners and I were able to climb the mountains by their more technical routes.

Slashing pack-weight

In 1970 I began instructing for a well-known wilderness program, and started cutting my pack-weight in earnest. Between 1970 and 1978 I taught 19 of these classes, each running from 23 to 28 days, and with resupplies coming every 5 to 7 days. I needed to be careful how much gear I loaded into my pack, because the remainder of the load had to be food enough to see me to the next resupply. Also, these trips were fairly ambitious. I usually hiked with the students, but in the latter stages of each program I would shadow them. This required that I circumvent their more direct routes. And because I needed to reach our pre-arranged waypoints ahead of them, I had to hike more expediently. This called for mobility, and in turn it encouraged me to refine my pack-weight even further.

I carried a tarp rather than a tent. I wore running shoes rather than boots. I carried no stove but cooked on a small fire. In fact, I would invariably get so caught up in the minimalist approach that I would intentionally short myself two or three days' food.

Preparing for our first PCT hike

Years later, as Jenny and I began preparing for our first long thru-hike in 1987, we were aware of our need to minimize our pack-weights. Yet as much hiking and backpacking as I had done—and Jenny had done a fair amount herself—we still felt intimidated by the prospects of hiking the Pacific Crest Trail's two and a half thousand miles in a single season. It was the classic "*Omne ignotum pro magnifico*" syndrome (Everything unknown is taken as grand; i.e.: fear of the unknown). Especially because neither of us had done much hiking for several years. This insecurity about the prospects of hiking such a long distance sapped our objectivity. We read stacks of catalogs, studied reams of equipment reviews, and visited backpacking stores to try out the most "advanced" and durable gear.

We pulled together a lot of advice, but the problem was, it all sounded much the same: "You will get used to the weight." And "Anything lighter will fall apart."

For backpacks we chose magnum-sized, internal-frame models of the latest design. Then at home we proceeded to modify them.

We cut off every unneeded strap, tab and buckle. We removed the internal seam binding (the long nylon strips that hide the raw edges and stitching). In fact we disassembled the packs and re-shaped the nylon pieces for improved function, before sewing them back together. In the process we also coated the seams with sealing compound in a futile attempt to waterproof the packs. We even shaved down the aluminum stays with a grinder to minimize their weight. As a result, we reduced the packs by a few pounds. Still, we accepted the packs' weight, because we felt that they had to be large and robust. For after all, we had a lot of gear and clothing to load into them.

We were training on the snowbound flanks of Colorado's Pikes Peak in winter, so naturally our selection of clothing was slanted toward the cold. We purchased the latest polypropylene shirts and pants, Gore-Tex® rain jackets, and a load of expensive socks. And we bought a

Near the conclusion of our first PCT hike.

single goose-down sleeping bag with a full-length zipper, for use like a blanket.

We also sewed many items ourselves. These included waterproof stowbags, a homemade gravity-feed water filtration system of my invention, and clothing such as shirts, pants, fleece jackets, mittens and hats. We made a tarp also, but ultimately decided to use a commercial tent. The marketing for this tent was so convincing that, save for running a clothesline across the ceiling, and fitting loops for hanging our eyeglasses at night, we made no other modifications – an oversight that was to take its toll later.

We began our thru-hike with ungainly loads, and with them hiked for a month through southern California. But when we loaded the packs with mountaineering boots and a *three-week* supply of food for the trip through the snowbound High Sierra, my pack must have weighed 75 pounds and Jenny's around 60.

The boots we wore through the Sierra were the latest models but they performed poorly, mainly because they were always wet, due to the snow. And the wetness made them heavier still. After struggling through the high country with them, we sent them home. From then on I wore running shoes, and Jenny lighter fabric boots.

We also began to realize that much of our clothing and gear was redundant and nonessential, and in fact its weight and bulk were working against us. For example, we carried a variety of clothing, and of course we never used all of it at once. One day we wore this, and another day we wore that. We found we could reduce the number of garments without compromising comfort. So we started sending home extra shirts, pants, shorts, sweaters; things that we liked to wear now and then, but that we could do without.

This was more of a mental shift, differentiating our wants from our needs. We did not mind the lessened variety in shirts and pants as long as we kept them

laundered. And by washing socks every day or two, we did not need to carry a five-day supply. By sending the superfluous items home, we reduced our baseline pack-weights considerably.

The four-pound tent we used for most of the way was the latest and lightest design, but it failed us during one particular rainstorm in Oregon, due to severe condensation. I describe this in the "Tarp" chapter.

On reaching the Canadian border, we found a note written by an unknown thru-hiker: "I began this journey with many hopes and many fears. Glittering expectations blinded me as I crossed my trailheads. What I wanted to find and what I found never matched, yet the final experience has granted me profound illumination." This hiker had expressed our feelings also.

Our summer's hike was hugely successful, and of course richly rewarding. But it sure was a lot of work! In fact, it was our most arduous hike by far, simply because we carried such heavy packs.

PCT-2

In 1991 we decided to hike the PCT again. For gear, we chose the same packs, but made new clothing all around. We modified our sleeping system to make it more serviceable. We bought new rain jackets to replace the ones we had worn out, and we also bought and modified umbrellas. We sewed a rain awning to the fly of our original four-pound tent, and extensions along the sides to rebuff the splashes. We also made a great many other modifications to our clothing and gear.

When we set out from the Mexican border this time, we weighed our packs at the nearby town of Campo. We had not yet filled our water bottles, but were carrying a 2½-day supply of food and all the gear needed for the first month of the hike, including cold-weather clothing and gear for the mountains. Our packs weighed 22 pounds apiece.

At a food weight of 2½ pounds per day per person, this

meant our baseline packweight[2] was about 15¾ pounds. This was still fairly heavy, but about 12 pounds lighter than on our previous PCT hike.

And for the first time, our equipment was beginning to work for us. As before, we subsequently endured a great deal of rain, but the umbrellas shielded us nicely, allowing us to carry on hiking in comfort, many times when other hikers remained gloomily tent-bound. The new rain awning permitted us to keep the tent's doorway open. This provided more ventilation, keeping us, and our clothing drier. Jenny wore lightweight fabric boots for about half the distance, while I wore this type of foot-wear only through the snowbound High Sierra. Other-wise, we wore running shoes, with excellent results.

Reaching the Canadian border, we returned home and I wrote the first edition of this book, describing our new light-weight approach. The date was 1991 and book was entitled *The Pacific Crest Trail Hiker's Handbook*. This was the first book that described an entire, work-able system of lightweight hiking.

The next spring, PCT hikers began using the book's methods. One of these hikers, Scott W., wrote after his hike: "We talked constantly about various aspects of The Ray Way, as we called it. In the early stages a few hikers criticized the book's more 'radical' techniques. Later in the summer, though, I was amused to see these same people not only using the very techniques they had condemned, but praising them…after they saw how well they were work-ing for the rest of us."

CDT

In that spring of 1992 Jenny and I made new clothing and gear for the Continental Divide Trail; Canada to Mexico spanning Montana, Wyoming, Colorado and New Mexico. Once again we used our old, weather-beaten packs, which meant that we were still burdened with their 4½ pounds. However, the remainder of our gear was evolving. For example, we removed the zippers from our new sleeping bag and cut away the entire door of our tent to increase the much-needed ventilation. We relied instead on the awning sewed to the fly to keep the rain out. We did not realize it at the time, but our shelter was slowly evolving into a tarp.

CDT in Glacier Park

---

2 I define "baseline" to mean: not including food and water.

AT

The following year again, 1993, we prepared for an Appalachian Trail thru-hike, Georgia to Maine. This time we felt the need for an even more radical reduction in pack-weight, because of the severe up-and-down nature of this trail. Simple physics suggested that the more weight we carried, the more work it would be to climb each steep hill – of which the AT has many hundreds. And after our previous long distance treks, we were extremely reluctant to carry any unnecessary weight. This next hike would be so much more enjoyable, we reasoned, without having to lug any excess.

The AT in Georgia

Just as importantly at that point, we had been undergoing a mental shift. With thousands of trail miles behind us, we were much more confident in our abilities. No longer shackled by our own doubts and fears, the marketeer's hype lost its grip. This was when we regained our objectivity. As such, we began to shed our psychological urge for heavy-duty type gear. We finally realized that we were far better off without it.

We set aside our 4½-pound mega-packs and shopped for lighter models. Finding nothing even remotely suitable, we made our own. (These packs became the initial, prototype versions of our current light-weight packs.) We bought a new tent; the same model at four pounds, and again cut away the door and sewed a rain awning above it. And we outfitted ourselves with a selection of running shoes.

As an experiment in saving weight, we dispensed with the stove, and planned to buy food along the route and eat it cold. However, this proved a mistake because many of the trailside stores were small and offered only junk food. We also reduced our "kitchenware," to almost nothing. No cooking pot, bowls or cups. For water bottles we used empty soda bottles.

To avoid the cost of buying yet another new goose-down sleeping bag, we made a lightweight sleeping system that we dubbed the "quilt." This was probably the world's first backpacking quilt; and in relation to backpacking, we coined the term. And because of its synthetic insulation, it proved surprisingly easy to sew.

June 8, 1993 found us on Springer Mountain in Georgia, and the southern terminus of the great Appalachian Trail. We had fashioned our home-made backpacks with thin aluminum internal stays along with hip belts and quick-release buckles. But by the end of the first day we realized that the hip belts were not necessary, nor even beneficial. This was due to the lightness of our "loads." In fact, the hip belts were interfering with our gait. So we cut off the belts, and at the first way station we dispensed with them, along with the aluminum stays.

As we trekked northward, nearly everyone we met expressed skepticism when we said that our goal was Katahdin, the trail's northern terminus. Our too-late start and too-small packs essentially ostracized us from the backpacking community, both on the trail and off. Some people would mistake us for day-hikers, and when we told them we were thru-hikers, they looked at us askance; or sometimes informed us that we had no chance of finishing the hike that year. But our lightweight packs and running shoes worked well, and we reached the summit of Mt. Katahdin in 88 days, or just under three months.

PCT-3

The following summer we planned to hike the first 700 miles of the PCT from the Canadian border, south to our home in central Oregon. Preparing for this trek, we again re-made most of our gear, but this time even simpler and lighter. We finally dispensed with the tent, and hauled out that nylon tarp I had made seven years previously. The tarp would offer far more living space and rain protection, we reasoned, at a fraction of the weight and bulk.

We also abandoned most of our heavier garments, since we had rarely worn them on previous hikes of the mountain trails. Even in the coldest weather we had found the exercise of hiking sufficiently warming. And when not hiking, we were usually settled comfortably beneath our tarp and quilt.

The first couple of weeks of that trip were in heavy snow, yet the tarp worked beautifully, as did the quilt. Mainly this was because we sought out sheltered sites with snow-free ground.

Our plan changed along the way, for we found that we were enjoying the summer. We decided to continue hiking the remaining 1,960 miles to Mexico. Reaching Elk Lake, we detoured home and worked for 2½ days on business, and one more day preparing for the additional 2,000 miles of hiking.

The remaining trek to Mexico went extremely well, and I must say that the overall journey was by far our easiest and most enjoyable PCT trek to date. It was also our fastest, at three months and four days, border to border, total elapsed time including the 3½-day stopover at home. It was also a walk every inch of the way journey with no vehicle support, no flip-flopping, no short-cutting and stick with the trail 99% of the way.

And it was during this second phase of this trek that we brought the many aspects of our 8½ pound baseline packweight system to fruition.

Late summer in the Sierra, easy creek crossings, PCT-3

Slashing Packweight

"On a long journey
even a straw weighs heavy."
— *Spanish proverb*

The philosophy of wilderness enjoyment

Humankind spent untold thousands of years clawing out of the wilderness and establishing kernels of civilization. But only within the last several generations have people begun returning to the wilderness for recreation. The present mindset has become so ingrained that a person might lug along as many impediments as possible. The usual

Our 8.5 lb. backpacks at the end of a 2,700-mile hike, 1994.

intent is to reduce any unforeseen difficulties and hazards, and to insure the comforts.

Yet I think that the type of gear that hikers need depends almost entirely on, not what they actually need, but what they merely believe they need. Jenny and I certainly proved this to ourselves during those multi-thousand mile journeys afoot. Before we could reduce the loads on our backs, we had to lighten the loads in our minds. In other words, by trial and error we had to discover that our self-designed lighter-weight gear, and less of it, would work better for us. This realization was the key to our eventual success. When we opened our minds to at least the possibilities, we set the stage for extending our horizons.

Had we never tried to hike and camp with lighter gear, our beliefs would have remained unchanged. Or if we had tried an item or two, and designed and used them incorrectly, then the experiment might have been unsuccessful, and we may have reverted to our old, heavier gear once again. Either way, we would have remained stagnant.

Synergy in motion

We were hiking in Oregon during our third PCT thru-hike, traveling southbound, when late one afternoon we found ourselves hurrying along in an attempt to reach our next resupply point. Our supplies were waiting for us at the store inside the Timberline Lodge on Mt. Hood, and that store was about to close for the day. The late evening and early morning hours are among our favorite for hiking, and we knew that if we did not hurry, we would have to forfeit them and make an early camp somewhere near the lodge. So at my suggestion Jenny handed me her backpack, pocketed some cash and her ID, tied her shell jacket around her waist, and took off at a trot. We figured she could reach the store in about an hour. This left me carrying two backpacks. Since I normally carried mine on one shoulder, I simply slung Jenny's pack onto my other shoulder and continued ahead – carrying what I quipped was my 17 pound "pack-pack."

Farther along I overtook a pair of backpackers. They were obviously on journey, so I walked with them a ways. The woman and her husband said they were hiking the section of PCT from the Columbia Gorge to central Oregon, and had left the Gorge five days ago. I mentioned that Jenny and I had started in Canada, and had left the Gorge yesterday. After a few minutes of pleasant chat, we bid each other good-bye, with hopes of meeting again at the lodge.

We were sorting supplies inside the lodge when our friends arrived. It turned out that they had read the first edition of our *PCT Hiker's Handbook*, describing some of our earlier lightweight methods, but these people admitted that they simply "didn't believe any of it." Now they were brimming with questions.

The reaction of these backpackers was typical of the many we met that summer. On paper, our lighter-weight methods might seem "radical" and idealistic. But these people here at the lodge had become less skeptical when seeing how easily we were doubling or even tripling their daily mileages. The irony was that we were exerting ourselves no more than these backpackers. We were simply using our energy mainly for forward progress, rather than for load hauling.

Nevertheless, I see mileage as an effect rather than a cause. Not something to be strived for, but merely a by-product of a lighter load and a more efficient style. Our main focus is on the natural world, our place in it, and how that relates to our enjoyment and lessons learned along the way.

Pack-weight and daily mileage

Humans are wrought with limited capacities, particularly regarding hauling loads over long distances. In fact, studies have shown that doubling the load far more than doubles the effort required to carry it. The progression is geometric.

During our first thru-hike, with loads that were ponderous to us (34 pounds, but far lighter than what most other hikers were carrying) we averaged 17 miles a day. On our fifth journey, with baseline pack weights of 8½ pounds (not including food and water) we averaged 29 miles a day. The reduced pack weight made that much difference. Without the huge load, the hiking was no longer such a chore.

In many ways, a thru-hike is a series of day hikes. So I think the advantages of lighter-weight packs would be equally beneficial to most hikers, regardless of trip duration.

During each PCT hike, we kept track of our daily mileages, as well as hours on the trail each day. And we could easily remember the locations of each camp. With this information I was able to make some quantitive comparisons. While hiking southbound and nearing a resupply point with packs empty of food (meaning less weight) we far outdistanced our northbound daily mileages coming out of those same stations loaded with food (more weight). I extrapolated the data and plotted the results to give an interesting correlation between pack weight and daily mileage. This graph assumes constant

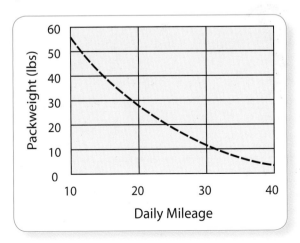

energy expenditure, hiking at a comfortable pace of 2.5 miles per hour. So the graph can also indicate one's expected daily mileage, relative to the weight of his or her pack. This is total average pack weight, including food, water, stove fuel and gear. Obviously the graph gives only an indication, due to the variables in terrain, weather, physical conditioning, motivation, type of footwear, and so many other factors.

Despite these variables, keep in mind that at any point on the graph, **the hiker exerts the same amount of effort**. For example, the hiker carrying a 58-pound pack expends about the same amount of energy in 10 miles, as the hiker carrying 10 pounds does in 30 miles.

If I am setting out on a day hike, with no intentions of traveling more than 5 or 10 miles, then a pack weight of 8 or 10 pounds will have little effect on my ease and mobility. If my plans are more ambitious, and I will be covering more than 10 miles while carrying more than 10 pounds, then I will benefit by conditioning my body ahead of time, gradually building up to my target pack weight and distance. Loads over 15 pounds are rare among day hikers, unless they are carrying gear for a specific purpose such as photography, or unless the conditions necessitate carrying a load of water.

Philosophy of wilderness enjoyment

In the next section "Equipment" I detail each item of our gear. And for those planning a longer journey and who would like to increase the daily mileages, I suggest the chapter "Supercharging Mileage." With the right techniques, a lighter pack can make the journey more expedient, if one's summer plans call for it.

Behind each piece of our gear and clothing is a philosophy for using it to best advantage. But again, we are not focused on the philosophy of light-weight hiking. Instead, we are focused on our wilderness enjoyment. And our ideas of wilderness enjoyment are based on the premise that the equipment is only a means to enjoy the end. For us, lighter equipment and less of it brings the most enjoyment. For other hikers, the opposite might be true. We have met many people who do not mind using heavy weight gear. They, too, have enjoyed their treks.

But to us, the weight and bulk of the heavy-duty gear detracted from our enjoyment, especially on the longer treks. So we chose a path less traveled, and began to experiment with new ideas using lighter gear. What follows, then, are a few of our guidelines and methods.

Phases of pack-weight reduction

Whether Jenny and I are planning a 5-mile loop, an overnight outing, or a months-long trek, experience has taught us that every additional pound (and ounce) we carry will magnify itself. So we avoid overburdening ourselves with items of luxury and comfort designed to

PCT-3 in Oregon

resemble what we left at home. Carrying these things for any distance would make the hiking uncomfortable. So we have learned to make it easy on ourselves by carving pack-weight.

I should note once again that we do not care for the minimalist approach. To us, this word implies long, exhausting days of self-denial and suffering, and shivering nights. Our gear lists near the back of this book show that the number of items in our packs is fairly consistent with what most other hikers carry. But each item of ours is perhaps more carefully thought out, specially built in many cases, smaller and lighter, and with fewer redundancies.

Phase 1: We concentrate on heavy items first

Traditionally, hikers have cut a few inches from the handles of their half-ounce toothbrushes, trimmed the margins from their maps, combined all their candy bars into a single bag and dispensed with the individual wrappers, and with a sense of accomplishment called the job done. As a result, they trimmed their 41-pound packs to 40.9 pounds.

When reducing the weight of our packs, Jenny and I concentrate on the heavier items first. Replacing a 6-pound backpack with a 1-pound pack saves 5 pounds! Replacing a 5-pound tent with a 1¾-pound tarp saves another 3¼ pounds. Wearing lightweight and functional clothing rather than heavy and bulky "all-conditions" attire saves again. The weight on our feet makes a difference too: switching from heavy boots to lighter-weight shoes saved us even more.

Of course, we do not compromise function. A tent that is too light could also be too flimsy. But consider the tarp that we carried on our third PCT trek. It weighed 1¾ pounds and was capable of withstanding gales that would have blown most tents away. This was because when necessary we could pitch it low lying, and because we could choose support sticks that were far stronger than the flimsy aluminum poles that come with most tents.

Phase 2: Leave superfluous gear behind

Every item placed into our backpacks will add to our load. Conversely, every item eliminated reduces its weight by 100%. This idea led to our second phase of pack-weight savings: avoiding the superfluous.

Our hiking wardrobe was notorious for taking up room in our backpacks. At first, we enjoyed a variety of clothing. But we found that we could get along just as well—in fact much better—with only the basic attire.

We also decided against the typical set of cookware and utensils: the nesting pots and lids, the handle tool, the frying pan, spatula and the cooking oil, the baking device, mixing bowls and mixing spoons, the plates and silverware, the insulated coffee mug and the Sierra cup. It is a nice thought, dining in elegance in the wilds. But in reality, all this camp cookery would have made the hiking more difficult due to its extra weight and bulk; and the camping more of a hassle while trying to keep all that cook-wear clean, free of flies, and organized. We have cooked many tasty and nutritious meals in a single, lidded pot. In lieu of silverware, we eat with a plastic spoon for each of us, and use a small, folding knife for any foods that require cutting.

Gadgets can add weight: the nifty multi-pliers tool, the camp chair, and items of entertainment such as paperback books, cell phones, radios or music players, decks of playing cards, and backgammon sets. We have even seen machetes, butane curling irons, and lawn chairs.

By leaving these things behind, we are well on our way to a lighter and more comfortable trip.

Phase 3: Select the lightest and most functional

In this phase we select the lightest and most useful of the usual profusion of small items, such as the knife, flashlight, compass, cookpot, camera, water bottle, eating utensils, first aid kit, personal hygiene kit, and so forth. Each fractional ounce saved is not much by itself, but in quantity they can add up fast.

I have seen hikers with headlamps that weighed a pound. I have known thru-hikers to use large metal spoons to scoop peanut butter from glass jars. We look at our gear with a more critical eye. A small plastic bag containing only the basic first aid items weighs only a fraction of a comprehensive kit that comes in its own nifty zippered case. How about the water bottle? An empty soda bottle with a screw-on lid works as well, and is lighter than the standard, heavy duty, wide-mouth bottle.

Phase 4: Cut and whack

Most commercial products come with guarantees or warranties that become void if you modify the product. This may leave you feeling that the company still owns the products long after you have paid for them and taken them home. But in truth, your purchases belong to you, and you may modify them any way you like. And by doing so, they are far more likely to serve your specific needs.

Heavy-duty backpacks are notorious for their superfluous features such as straps, loops and hooks, bells, whistles and doodads. After we purchased our original backpacks for our first thru-hike, we attacked them with knife, scissors, and seam ripper. We were assertive with this, because we knew that if we trimmed too much, we could always sew things back together. After all, the backpack is not magic, as the manufacture would have a person believe; but only a collection of materials in various sizes and shapes, sewn together.

Reading the map on the CDT in New Mexico.

We do the same with most of our commercial gear, cutting and removing things to our hearts' content. We cut away whatever portions of our maps we will not need, not just the borders. We may cut the bandana in half, and chop a small wedge from the bar of soap. Instead of carrying an entire guidebook for the trail we will be hiking, we cut out only the pages needed for each section, same with our trail journal.

Phase 5: Tabulate

We use a kitchen scale that shows ounces and tenths of an ounce. With this we record the weight of every piece of our gear, every item of clothing, our pack, shoes, the items in our first aid kit –everything. When we catalog this gear in letters and numbers, black and white, we tend to see it more objectively. This exercise might bring to light a few questionable items, or even a few glaring ones.

Phase 6: Reason and reject

The final phase takes place after we have selected and tabulated our gear, but before actually loading it into our packs. We scrutinize each item, and ask ourselves: Do we absolutely need it? We do this at home prior to departure, and again at the resupply points. This phase is particularly effective on longer journeys because it allows us more opportunities to experiment with our selection of gear, and to determine which items are essential and which are not. Our thinking is: even if we might need a particular item someday, this might not justify carrying it for perhaps hundreds of miles. Except for emergency items, if we are not using something, and are not likely to do so fairly soon, then we consider ridding our packs of it.

And whimsically, we do not set off carrying spare change; we spend it on snacks.

Works as a system, or independently

I designed our gear and methods to work as a system. That is, each item and method for using it fits together and complements the others like pieces of a jigsaw puzzle. For example, we reduced the quantity, size, and weight of the items that fit into the backpacks, then we designed smaller and lighter backpacks. If aiming for an 8½-pound baseline pack-weight, this is the recommended approach.

The IUA

However, for the person interested in reducing pack-weight more modestly, each of my recommended items would work well in combination with a selection of more traditional gear. The light-weight backpack can be used on day or weekend hikes, loaded with a modest supply of heavier gear. The quilt can be used in place of the sleeping bag, all other items remaining the traditional type. Or the tarp can be carried in place of the tent. Each item saves weight, and of course the more items adopted, the more the savings.

But the items do not have to be switched out all at once. In fact, a person might try only one or two new items at a time. This will give him or her a few trail miles to become familiar with those items, before trying something else new. For the long-distance hiker, this will mean practicing with the new gear ahead of time, during the conditioning hikes.

Sharing gear with a partner

Sharing gear with a partner can save some weight and bulk in the backpacks. How much gear can be shared will depend on the nature of the partnership – on how tolerable each person is to the intrusion of personal space, and the extent to which each person is willing to rely on the other. Even the closest of alliances can separate, whether intentionally or not. Partners who venture ahead or lag behind are well known for selecting the wrong fork in the trail. With this in mind, each member of a group might be wise to maintain a certain autonomy by carrying items for safety and well-being. At the very minimum these would include a sealed packet of matches, food, a relevant map, money and identification, and at least some type of shelter.

Sharing the tarp or tent will save weight and space in the backpack. But the partners would use this method on a long hike only if certain they would remain together for the duration. Sharing a quilt saves a great deal of weight, and adds shared body warmth; obviously this is a couples' approach. If sleeping beneath a single shelter, two people could share a double-size groundsheet. Should they decide to separate, they could cut it in half. Two people camping together could share a single stove, fuel bottle, and cookpot. Should they split, the stove-less person could revert to the cook-fire method (described in the "Campfire and Cook-fire" chapter) but might have to make do without a pot until reaching a store that sells one. Hikers in close partnerships might also share guidebooks, camera and batteries, first aid kits, pocket-knife, compass and many other small items. With the right mindset and relationship, this would hardly be an inconvenience, especially in light of the potential weight savings.

Timing a trip

By timing our outings to the most favorable seasons, Jenny and I will usually enjoy the best weather. A high country trek during the month of May is bound to be cold and sodden, whereas that same route in August will usually be warmer and drier. This kind of planning will reduce our need for cold-weather clothing and all sorts of other winter-related gear, including climbing ropes, crampons, snowshoes, expedition tents, heavy mountain boots, and extra fuel to melt snow. On a bona fide winter mountaineering trip, we might include some of these items.(A note of caution: winter mountaineering requires advanced skills in order to use the associated equipment properly and safely.) But by delaying the start of our hike until the snow has melted, we can do without the winter gear. Springtime snow usually melts amazingly fast, and often just a week or two can make a big difference. Still, we may need to carry certain items to handle any adverse conditions, such as ice axes and extra warm clothing. But by timing our outing properly, we will reduce our chances of encountering those conditions.

Tuning in to the environment

This is probably the most important concept in all our hiking and adventuring. The more we bend and flow with nature, rather than battle it, the lighter we can travel without sacrificing our margins of safety. For example, in strong wind, rather than camp out in the open while taking the brunt of the wind, we look for natural objects to pitch our shelter behind, such as protecting trees, bushes or rock outcroppings.

Benefits to families with children

Backpackers with children are often eager to share the joys of the outdoors with their kids. However, traditional gear tends to be so heavy that it limits the possibilities, especially for parents with younger children. What usually happens is that the entire family remains at home during the formative years, waiting for the youngsters to grow strong enough to carry

On the CDT in Montana

their own things. Lighter-weight equipment can change this. Each member of the family can carry his or her own gear. Or if the children are very young, then mom and dad can carry their gear as well, with little extra strain. This means that the whole family can enjoy these outings together. I think this is particularly beneficial for the kids themselves during their early years.

Children will appreciate the lighter gear, the smaller packs, comfortable lightweight shoes and clothing. They might have fun under a tarp of their own, pitched adjacent to the parents, and they may enjoy sleeping in their own small quilts. The joy of the wilds is contagious, and this simple, lightweight equipment can turn the overnight trips into such positive experiences for the children that they might eagerly look forward to subsequent outings.

Weight exemptions

For Jenny and me, our hiking food is generally exempt from our weight reduction campaign. The quantity of our food, and its quality, are important in terms of the nutrition and vitality it provides. This is especially true with our high-mileage hikes, when our energy needs are much greater. And we know that the food will diminish day by day as we consume it. So its weight is highly variable.

Water comes under the same plan. We learned some hard lessens by scrimping on drinking water to save pack-weight.

In trips past we experimented with making our tarps and quilts much narrower to save weight and bulk. These experiments were universally unsuccessful. What we learned is that by saving weight in these areas, we were edging too close to minimalism (i.e.: lack of comfort in the night and insufficient protection from the elements). We can design our tarps extra wide without adding much weight, because these modern fabrics are very light. Our

quilts are the same. Far more important than weight is that we sleep warmly.

A few basic emergency supplies are also exempt from our quest for weight savings. For us, these include: a small first-aid kit, a fire starter kit (see "fire starter kit" in the "Campfire and Cook-Fire" chapter), a small, sharp knife, and a set of cold weather and weatherproof clothing (a rain parka, an insulating sweater or jacket perhaps, and possibly mittens and a warm hat).

Pack-weight myths

In this chapter I have elaborated our methods of reducing pack weights. In contrast, I would like to highlight some of the standard arguments in favor of the traditional heavy-weight gear.

Myth: The longer the hike, the more gear it requires.

My reply: The longer the hike, the less gear it requires by far. This is because the more weeks and months we spend on the trails, the more skills we develop. The more skilled, the more self-confidence and the less we need to rely solely on equipment, and so the less equipment we need.

Myth: Those who traverse deserts and high snowy ranges need lots of heavy-duty gear and very large, sturdy packs to carry it in.

Reply: This argument is a favorite with companies selling these products, with those who are paid to market and "review" them, and with the occasional backpacker trying to impress others with fanciful escapades. For the person who traverses deserts, lightweight gear is essential. And when necessary, a lightweight but well designed and properly constructed pack will carry a heavy load of water. The person traversing snowbound mountains finds similar benefits in lightweight gear, mainly because it greatly facilitates the progress. Cold weather clothing does not have to be massively built.

Myth: The day or weekend hiker can carry a lot of gear

and not worry about the weight. These trips are short, and the extra load will not affect the hiker physically or mentally. The hiker can handle the load, and wants an enjoyable, laid-back trip with all the luxuries.

Reply: Lightweight methods and gear are well suited to day and weekend hikers because they reduce the chances of injury caused by lugging a heavy load. Gear-laden short trips tend to discourage a person from making longer trips, because the hiking is so much work.

Myth: A person's equipment must be rugged and durable. It has to be heavy.

Reply: Indeed, we should choose gear that is reliable and durable, but it certainly does not have to be heavy. Well-constructed gear can be made of lighter materials, and such gear can hold up extremely well.

One ploy with advertisers is to obscure the relative heaviness of their products. For example, they will describe an item weighing 8-ounces as "featherweight." Imagine a bird having feathers weighing half-a-pound each! Who benefits from this nonsense: the backpacker struggling along under a ponderous load of "lightweight" gear, or the manufacturers selling it?

Myth: The backpacker needs a full load of equipment for a safe and comfortable trip.

Reply: A bloated selection of hiking and camping gear is very heavy. Lumbering beneath a heavy load is anything but comfortable and enjoyable for most people, even those in excellent physical condition. A heavy load detracts from the trip's safety by increasing the person's chances of injury, and by reducing his or her ability to descend expediently to lower and more protected terrain in the event of a sudden storm. A load of heavy-duty gear is no substitute for good judgment, mobility and skill.

Myth: The backpack may feel very heavy at home while preparing for the hike, but once a person gets started and gets into shape, it won't be so bad.

Reply: Initially, a 60-pound pack might feel merely heavy. After the first few days of actual hiking, though, it will begin to become an unwieldy, ponderous burden. And 100 miles along the trail, such a burden will feel more like a crushing burden, and an insult to the hiker's flagging body. A heavy pack will steepen every hill and lengthen every mile. It will sap enjoyment and increase the chances of injury. Never will the hiker accustom to carrying it, and always will removing it from one's back bring immense relief.

Myth: To live the good life, we must ensure our comfort, both at home and in the woods.

Reply: The tendency is to simulate the comforts of home. Never mind that at home a person does not have to carry those things mile after mile over hill and dale.

Myth: Strong hikers don't mind carrying heavy packs.

Reply: Brawn and brute strength is one approach, but careful thought and planning are almost always more effective.

Myth: The standard backpacking practices have come to us from a long line of very respectable people and organizations, such as parents, friends, the Boy or Girl Scouts, or the military, to say nothing of hundreds of books on the subject, as well as magazines and websites.

Reply: In every advanced civilization, every practice that the people considered infallible has eventually given way to something better.

The Standard Backpacking Reasoning: It is better to have an item of gear and not need it, than to need it and not have it.

The Jardine Approach: If I need it and don't have it, then I don't need it.[3]

_____

3 Except for emergency supplies.

Camping and hiking with lightweight gear requires new attitudes and a willingness to experiment, until a person discovers what works best for him or her. Few of us learned to ride a bicycle by reading a book; we had to learn by actually doing. And so it is with the lighter-weight approach. Instead of merely reading and discussing, philosophizing and debating, why not give some of these ideas a try?

The joys of a lighter backpack

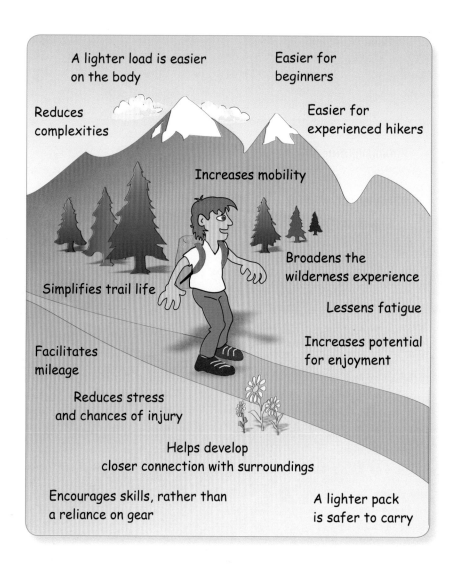

A lighter load is easier on the body

Easier for beginners

Reduces complexities

Easier for experienced hikers

Increases mobility

Broadens the wilderness experience

Simplifies trail life

Lessens fatigue

Increases potential for enjoyment

Facilitates mileage

Reduces stress and chances of injury

Helps develop closer connection with surroundings

Encourages skills, rather than a reliance on gear

A lighter pack is safer to carry

Safety of Light Hiking

"Safety is something that happens between your ears, not something you hold in your hands."
— *Jeff Cooper*

A safe and workable lightweight approach to backpacking does not just happen overnight. In fact, our system took us many years and thousands of trail miles to develop. But because we took things slowly, trying only a few new items of gear on each trip, we minimized any risks.

During that time we learned how to design our gear so that it would hold up. And more importantly, we learned how to use that gear safely and effectively in varying weather conditions.

So with each trip, we increased our experience gradually, step at a time, year at a time. And we refined our knowledge accordingly.

Nevertheless, the question of safety might still arise: Would a person new to backpacking, or with minimal, or even average experience, be able to hike and camp safely with lighter weight gear?

For starters, I feel that any type of gear carries much the same risks, whether super-heavy expedition weight or light-weight, store-bought or homemade. Any backpacking equipment requires proper use.

To use a piece of gear properly,

one must become familiar with it, and more importantly, practice with it beforehand. One also must know the gear's limitations, and avoid using it in places or climates that it was not intended or designed for.

Safe backpacking requires certain skills

Imagine that someone decides to take a short backpack trip. The person has not done much hiking or camping in a long while, and has not had time to prepare for this trip. At the end of the day's hiking, the person proceeds to set up camp. Out comes the new tent (didn't have time to look at it, at home before the trip). Now the head-scratching begins: these are obviously the poles, these are the stakes, and the rest of this is the tent. Why are there two pieces? Which pole belongs where? And how does it all fit together?

I have watched such befuddled scenarios a few times, and can report that the tent-pitching process was neither fast nor efficient. In fact, without outside help, it may take an hour or more. I have also seen moderately experienced mountain climbers at high altitude taking two

PCT-3

33

hours to pitch a tent in a storm. Why so long? Apparently they had not pitched a tent in such uninviting conditions before, so had underestimated the difficulties. Certainly the safety of that scenario was questionable.

While skiing to the South Pole in 2007, we were exposed to the elements for nearly two months. Each evening while making camp we had to be careful to protect our hands from becoming too cold. Otherwise they would quit working; at which time pitching the tent would have been next to impossible.[4]

Much the same could happen to someone in the mountains of the U.S., even in summer. If a person were to develop hypothermia, he or she might have great difficulty pitching a tent.

So any kind of gear, light or heavy, is safe only when a person knows how to use it, and when the conditions permit.

Knowing what gear to use, and when

I developed our lightweight hiking system for use in the summer months, in the temperate zones of the contiguous United States. However, for someone with the appropriate skills, this type of gear might be suitable for use during other seasons with more challenging weather. But for the un-skilled, no amount of equipment (either lightweight or heavy-duty) will guarantee a person's safety, for example in the high mountains during the off-season. A sudden storm could degrade the conditions fast.

Practice with the gear beforehand

Before taking a tent or a tarp into the wilds, a person should learn how to pitch it correctly, and then practice setting it up. A suitable location might be in a large empty room, or in a garage, a back yard, at a nearby park, or in an open field. If practicing on a hard floor, I tie the guy-lines to weights rather than stakes.

If experienced with a tent but new to a tarp, a person might take both on the next outing. The idea is to hone one's tarp pitching skills while keeping the tent close at hand, for use only if needed. Also, if one is new to a tarp, I might recommend my Tarp Book. It has much more detailed information on making and using a tarp than what is covered in this book.

Another good way to practice with new gear, whether it is a shelter, a quilt, a pack, or specialized clothing is to take them on a short camping trip. Not an overnight hike, but a simple car camping outing where the main focus is getting to know the gear in a safe and benign outdoor setting.

Tarp or Tent

In wintertime in the mountains, or in summer in the Arctic, sub-arctic, or Antarctica, we use a highly-modified, four-season tent. Conversely, in the western and eastern states in late spring, summer or early fall, we have found a tarp works best – by a wide margin.

As a general rule, then, we use a tarp when we expect the conditions will not be too limiting. For example, on the PCT, CDT or AT in summer. We have experienced a great deal of stormy weather on these trails to be sure, and our tarps have never yet failed us. And also we have endured a few tent failures in situations where a tarp would have functioned much better.

The deciding factor for most people, as to whether a tarp or tent would be safer, I think would depend on their skill level and the degree of familiarity with that particular shelter. Most hikers and campers are more familiar with tents, only because tents are the traditional approach. So a tent might be the best option for them. Or they might learn and practice their tarp pitching skills before heading into the wilds.

---

4 See "the Rubicon" in the Cold chapter.

Quilt

During our adventures, we use a two-person quilt. I cannot think of a situation where a sleeping bag would be safer or warmer, assuming an equal thickness of insulation in both.

Backpacks

The backpacks we carry during a normal hiking season are described in the "Backpack" chapter. Even though these packs are light-weight, we have hiked with them for many thousands of miles, and have found them to work much better than any heavier model. But someone new to backpacking and unfamiliar with the techniques outlined in this book, might want something larger. Beginners are well known for bringing everything but the proverbial kitchen sink. Even so, all those items are unlikely to bolster one's safety if the person does not know how to use them properly.

Of course, in the mountains in winter, or in the very high mountains in summer, for example in the Andes, we use larger backpacks to carry the extra clothing, gear, food and fuel.

Running shoes or boots

If we know that our trail will take us into snow-covered regions, we carry lightweight boots. At extreme altitudes we wear specialized climbing boots. Otherwise, for summertime hiking below, say, 18,000 feet on a snow-free trail, we wear running shoes. I tend to question the traditional belief that hikers on bare trails are safer in boots. See the "Footwear" chapter for details.

With all this in mind, I consider the arguments for the superiority of heavy-duty gear in terms of safety to be worn-out and invalid. Yet these arguments are still used as marketing ploys because they help sell products. And they are further perpetuated by many backpackers who have little or no experience with lighter-weight gear, so have no inkling how well this gear can perform.

Our lightweight gear and methods described in this book have worked extremely well for us, and while using them we have never felt unsafe. But as described above, any gear, heavy, light, or in between is subject to misuse. Heavy-duty gear is not magic, like the advertisements often suggest, but neither is light-weight gear. What might be magic is a person's enjoyment of hiking and camping in nature, regardless of the type of gear chosen.

IUA

Part 2

EQUIPMENT

Wind Rivers, CDT

Trail Life

Emphasis on Home-Made

Calvin: I wish my shirt had a logo or a product on it.
A good shirt turns the wearer into
a walking corporate billboard!
It says to the world, "My identity is so wrapped up in
what I buy that I paid the company
to advertise its products!"
Hobbes: You'd admit that?
Calvin: Oh sure, endorsing products is
the American way to express individuality.
— *Bill Watterson*

Freedom

Jenny and I make most of our own clothing and outdoor equipment, such as backpacks, tarps, and sleeping quilts. This saves us money and allows us to design and customize these items to suit our needs. Also, we can make them right, without using any cheap materials or manufacturing short-cuts.

In fact, this switch from buying consumer items to sewing them ourselves revolutionized our trail lives and brought us into a whole new level of meaning and enjoyment. The shift also brought a sense of freedom from today's consumer mentality, where goods are heavily advertised, expensive, and yet cheaply mass-produced. As such, it brought us more independence from the corporate influence.

Overseas manufacturing allows a gear company to use unbelievably cheap labor, commonly known as "sweatshop labor." The company can then turn around and sell the goods for up to 50 times the actual cost of the materials and fabrication. These companies often rationalize their sweatshop labor practices by saying that they are providing jobs where there were none previously. But in fact, the sweatshops only enslave the workers, while the executives hide behind their token donations to worthy causes to make themselves look good. When consumers purchase gear manufactured offshore, they are only supporting the affluent executives; the workers gain very little.

> Most commercial backpacking gear is sewn by people working for pathetically low wages

Jenny and I sidestep this particular issue by sewing much of our gear ourselves. By sewing clothing, backpacks, tarps and quilts we are gaining more freedom from this type of rampant consumerism. We still need to purchase the raw materials, but the labor behind those is the same whether we buy the finished products or make them. And we will have to make other purchases too. But at least we think carefully about what we are supporting with those purchases.

We say "no" to corporate logos

A century ago, companies hired people to wander around town wearing sandwich boards. These were essentially two large boards hinged at the top and worn over the shoulders, one board in front, and one on the back. Painted on the sandwich boards were boldface advertisements.

Today's companies actually get their customers to advertise their products for free. They do this by sewing logos conspicuously to the clothing, backpacks, and other gear.

In some cases, the person wearing a logo might not

realize he or she is being used in this manner. Or perhaps the individual wears the logo on the pretense that he or she is somehow associated with the company. Or the person uses the logo as a medallion of imagined bravado; like military medals or a tin sheriff's badge that children like to wear pinned to their shirt. Or the individual might think that wearing the corporate logo makes him or her look cool: fashionable and attractive. Or, as Calvin sardonically points out, as a way to express one's individuality.

Regardless of the reason, we think people who wear logos are being duped. Here is why:

In theory, a company's brand name or logo affixed to a garment or item of gear is meant to identify the item's manufacturer. At least that is the common misconception. Its real purpose is to increase the company's market strength and potential. The larger the "target audience," and the more that audience is exposed to its logo, the more tacit persuasion (brainwashing) accomplished.

Hikers may not see it this way; but the executives certainly do, and they are the ones who devised the system to their immense advantage.

To me, these logos are nothing but symbols of subjugation and avarice. I feel that they are out of place especially in the backcountry, be they on billboards, jackets, tents or water bottles. Basically, someone wearing a company logo is providing free advertising. But at the same time, they are also perhaps tainting the experience of someone else who enjoys freedom from the distractions of commercialism, at least while hiking and camping.

For example, I would not play a blaring radio that someone nearby would have to endure. Bold logos are the visual equivalent of blaring radios. They "shout"

Sewing on a patch to "remove" a logo

advertisements to everyone within sight. So in effect, their emphasis is on the consumer's connection with merchandising, rather than on the hiker's connection with nature. This is the exact opposite of my philosophy.

How we remove a logo

On rare occasions Jenny and I will need to purchase an item of gear. Of course I have come up with all manner of ways to remove the offending logos.

In some cases a logo will be sewn onto a ribbon or patch. This we can usually remove by simply slicing the stitching that attaches the patch to the product.

Some types of logos are printed, stamped or monogrammed directly onto the fabric. At first we tried blacking out this type of logo with an indelible pen. But the ink faded and the logo remained visible. Fabric paint had much the same shortcomings. So instead we now cover a logo by sewing a hemmed patch over it. If the backside of the fabric is not accessible, we hand-sew the patch onto the front side. Or if we can get to the backside, we may sew the patch on the front side by machine, then cut out the logo portion of the original fabric beneath our sewn patch. And we do not worry about the color of the patch matching the original fabric. A contrasting patch says, "Free your mind."

Logos on fuel bottles, water bottles, and cookpots can usually be removed with sandpaper. Or in the case of bottles, covered with duct tape. Should we ever need the duct tape for a repair in the field, we can peel off some from the bottle. We have also used rags moistened with a spot of acetone on plastic, and paint remover on metal.

And finally, some products come with logos that cannot be easily removed. By this we know that these companies do not want to give their customers a choice of advertising their products or not. In which case, we give those companies and their products a miss.

Avoid pirated designs

Designing our gear has been a lengthy process, but for other hikers who might want to make much the same type of gear for themselves, see our website www.RayJardine.com for our current offerings.

Our designs are meant to be experiences in sewing. Any commercial product that even resembles the gear described in the next few chapters has been pirated. I have no agreements or interests with any company.

You may be surprised at how easy it is to sew your own gear. And fun and rewarding too.

Some people believe they lack the ability to use a sewing machine

Some individuals tend to believe in their own limitations. But those beliefs only prevent the person from becoming who they really are, rather than who they only imagine themselves to be.

For example, a person might believe they cannot sew because they are "all thumbs," or they "lack coordination." Yet these same people can easily drive cars, which often require a great deal of coordination. Everyone has various wrong beliefs to some extent. But a person can easily abandon them and move ahead.

We have received a great deal of extremely enthusiastic feedback from those who have tried sewing their own outdoor gear, and succeeded. Many of those people also expressed amazement that they were able to make such nice looking gear, saying that they had not imagined it possible.

Some believe they are too busy to for sewing

A fair percentage of the population consider themselves too busy to sew. Yet these same people often spend hours browsing the internet, reading newspapers and magazines, and watching TV. And what do they have show for all those hours? Not much. But if a person were to devote even a fraction of that time to constructive projects, for example sewing, he or she would have many good-looking and useful projects to show for it, and some very fine skills learned and practiced. One approach is essentially a waste of time; the other is enjoying quality time and using it to best advantage.

Along similar lines, some hikers spend a great deal of time studying commercial gear in magazines and on the internet. What do they get for that? Heads full of hype, closets full of superfluous gear with logos, and squandered bank accounts. Again, were they to spend part of that time making their own gear, they would spare themselves the hype and the loss of hard-earned money, and would produce gear that is every bit as serviceable, and much more satisfying and rewarding.

The power of envisioning

Certain individuals have attitudes that might be termed "no-win," worrying that if they were to begin a sewing project, they would make a total mess of it, wasting all the materials and their time. They might imagine that the sewing experience would be a "battle" and that they would "butcher" the project.

Throughout life we have been taught—again by poor examples from parents, teachers, friends, scout masters, bosses, radio, television and movies—to think and talk in this type of self-defeating manner, to greater or lesser extent. Often this sarcastic, self-deprecating banter is supposedly only a type of joking. But the negative results it can produce are no joke.

Any type of thinking is a form of envisioning. And whatever a person envisions, that will tend to manifest in one's life. The brain's creative process uses mental pictures like blueprints. If those pictures are of battling and butchering, then the person is attracting that.

Often a person's thinking is like a radio that plays the same old songs. That is not the person's true self doing the thinking; but one's mental programming. So when demoralizing music starts playing, one can change the channel. For example, the person might think: "I hope I don't butcher this project..." Then catch themselves mid-sentence, realizing that they are merely playing the same worn-out song, and begin to think more positively: "You know, I am going to do a great job with this quilt!" Then that is what this proactive philosophy will likely manifest.

Taking this concept a step further: Let's say a person buys the materials, insulation and so forth for a quilt, and envisions him or herself doing a great job with the sewing. And the person also sees in their mind's eye family and friends looking at the finished quilt, raving about it, and saying: "You made this yourself? It's beautiful!" This process of envisioning is incredibly powerful, in terms of the results it can, and will produce.

Sewing your own backpacking gear opens up vast possibilities

The clothing and gear companies, big and small, are banking on the non-sewing majority. But in doing so, they are only offering hikers and campers a tedious future in which the executives pocket even more money, the exploited poor become even more destitute, and where the average middle-class man or woman may, one day, be so indebted to the system that he or she might not be able to afford much time off for hiking and camping.

As personal motivators often say in their books and lectures: "If you keep doing what you're doing, you'll keep getting what you're getting."

―――――――――

From a global perspective, Jenny and I have not changed the world much by sewing our own gear. But on a personal level, all sorts of possibilities have opened up. "Thinking outside the box" and acting accordingly has allowed us to consume less and enjoy the natural world more.

Thousands of backpackers have also discovered the magic of sewing their own gear. And in many cases they have found that same shift in attitude has carried over into other aspects of their lives.

We hope this trend towards self-discipline and self-sufficiency continues; and we like to think that people such as these are engendering hope in a brighter and more fulfilling future for us all.

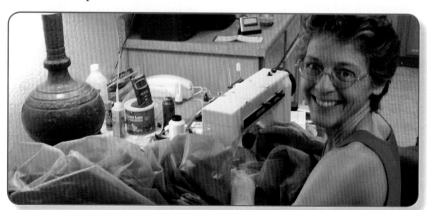

Backpack

Most hikers consider the backpack to be one of their most important items of hiking gear. Yet Grandma Gatewood did not carry one. She used a homemade bag, as we saw, closed at one end with a draw cord. It had no shoulder straps; the entire bag simply draped over her shoulder. With this she hiked many thousands of miles. Contrast her duffel-type bag with the massively built backpacks found in backpacking stores and catalogs today. These are over-complicated, overbuilt, and not as functional as the marketeers would have you believe.

Trends are beginning to change, but still we find the market dominated by internal frame packs weighing five to seven pounds, and more.

We hikers are trying to carve ounces from our gear, and the backpack manufacturers are adding them back in pounds. How do they get away with this? By including all sorts of complex gimmicks, such as devices of ergonomic fit, adjustable and even interchangeable suspension systems, stylized and garish panels, eye-catching loops of contrasting webbing, rugged, outdoorsy-sounding brand and model names, and much more – all of which effectively diverts the customer's attention away from the pack's weight.

Of course, the manufacturers assure us that these packs will carry the loads in comfort. Why does a hiker need this comfort? Because the load is so heavy. But what good is ergonomic fit to someone struggling beneath a heavy load? Is there such a thing as suffering in comfort? The way to make hiking more energy efficient is not to design a backpack to carry a heavy load more comfortably, but to reduce the load.

Example from a (biased) review: "A clever shock-absorbing rod extruded from aerospace-quality 7075-T6 aluminum stabilized the massive load side to side and channeled it down into the custom-moldable hip belt. There were times when we almost forgot we were wearing it." The insinuation is that this back-

Water stop along the IUA. The backpacks we carried on this trip are the same ones that we used for our third PCT hike. Here they are full of food for a long stretch of wilderness hiking.

pack turned the reviewer into superman, carrying a massive load with ease.

Lightening the load: the five-pound object

Imagine pulling a four to six pound object from your backpack and leaving it at home. That would lighten the load considerably. You may not have anything in your pack that weighs that much. But what about the pack itself? Most large backpacks on the market weigh from five to seven pounds, and more. Yet the pack adds nothing to the journey, other than acting as the container for the equipment, clothing and food. To me, it makes no sense that the container should be the heaviest article of gear.

As mentioned, the backpack that I carried on our third PCT thru-hike weighed 13½ ounces; and Jenny's was 11½ ounces. The reduced weight of these backpacks carved pounds from our loads, not mere ounces. And the packs worked great. Because we designed and constructed them properly—minimizing the stress points and optimizing the reinforcements—and because we treated them with reasonable care during the trip, they returned home in like-new condition. And with about 3,500 trail miles now on them, they are still going strong. (See the "Sewing" chapter for guidelines on making such a pack. Also see our website www.RayJardine.com for more information.)

With a lighter load, the pack does not need to be nearly as robust, nor does it need a frame or hip belt. However, this does not mean that these packs are limited in what they can do. During that PCT trek I carried up to 50 pounds in mine (mostly water) while traversing the desert regions of southern California.

One of the main benefits of these packs with their lightweight gear, is that virtually anyone can pick one up, put it on, and head on down the trail. We do not have to be muscle-bound athletes, which is good news because that would exclude most of us. At any rate, no longer must we struggle beneath the standard elephantine load. And now that we can carry less weight, I think many people will be more inclined to venture into the wilds, and more often – since the hiking is so much more fun.

Pack size

Hiking with a smaller and lighter pack requires a certain shift in thinking. One would not expect to fit the usual pile of camping gear and clothing into a smaller pack. Reducing the size of the pile is necessary, and in the chapters to follow I describe ways of doing that.

Actually, my pack is not as small as it might seem. When loaded, it is 11½" wide, 9⅓" deep, and 20½" tall, not taking into account its extension collar. The pack has a volume of 2,200 cubic inches. The three outside pockets add another 400 cubic inches, and the extension collar another 1,100. The all-up capacity, then, is 2,600 cubic inches (42.6 liters) or 3,700 with the collar, which is not bad for a 13½ ounce thru-hiking backpack.

I consider these packs suitable for any length of hike. If people can take them on overnight hikes with a smaller assortment of lightweight gear, then they can also travel for months carrying that same selection. This is because the gear needed for camping one night in the wilds is about what is needed for camping a hundred nights. The same holds true for the clothing, rainwear, and so forth. The only real variation is the supply of food. If a person is setting off with a large supply of food, then he or she can put some of the load into the pack's adjustable extension collar. More on that to follow.

Measuring pack volume

Published specifications for pack volume are not reliable, since the methods of measurement are not standardized among manufacturers. To measure pack volume, we visit our local shipping store and ask to borrow a large sack of recycled plastic "peanuts." Then taking these home, we fill the backpack with them. We use only a light pressure with the open hand to settle them into the backpack, being careful not to jam the peanuts in tightly, since that would give a false reading. When the backpack is full to the brim, we pour the peanuts from the pack into a cardboard box, and use the same light pressure of the hand to level them. The volume of the pack is now represented inside the cardboard box. We measure the box's length and width in inches. Then we slide a yardstick down the inside of the box, without disturbing the peanuts, and measure how many inches tall the peanuts are. Multiplying these three numbers together (length times width times height) gives us the backpack's volume in cubic inches.

Extension collar

The extension collar is a tube of extra material that pulls out of the pack's main body and extends above it, to create more carrying capacity when needed; for example if we are starting off from a trailhead with an extra large supply of food. In this case we re-load the pack with the heaviest items at the bottom and the lighter things in the extension collar. This way, the backpack does not become precariously top-heavy. In most situations we will consume the extra food in a day or so, if not hours. And at that time we will fold the extension collar back down, out of the way; and so reduce the pack to its normal cruising size.

Pack features

Backpacks used to be simple affairs, hardly more than bags fitted with shoulder straps. These uncomplicated rucksacks worked quite well – until people started carrying heavier loads in them. Responding to the demand, and in many cases actually creating that demand with various advertising methods, designers and manufacturers have been producing ever more complex backpacks.

My feelings are that this complexity has gone far beyond a person's needs. This is why I have simplified my backpack's design and reduced its features to the most basic and functional.

Frames and hip belts

The idea of frames and hip belts is many years old. Would you believe at least 5,000? The Iceman, whose frozen corpse dates back to the Stone Age, carried a frame pack. And from evidence that researchers have pieced together, it appears that he used a hip belt attached to that frame. The hip belt even had a front pouch for keeping small items handy. The story of Iceman, how he was found, and the fascinating details of his life are recounted in the book *The Man in the Ice*, by Konrad Spindler, 1994. See also *Building The Ice Man's Pack Frame* by John Mills, in Volume 4, Issue 3 of Wilderness Way magazine.

Pack frames, whether they are internal or external, aluminum, plastic, or stiff foam, are designed to take a portion of the crushing load off the shoulders, and transfer it down to the hip belt and onto the hips. Does this sound like fun, carrying a load so heavy that one's shoulders alone cannot bear it? With a much lighter load, the shoulders can cope very well, and we do not need the frame or the hip belt. And when we remove the hip belt and frame, we cut a fair percentage of the pack's weight.

Another function of the pack frame is to cushion the hiker's back from any pointed objects inside the pack, such as a camping stove, a pair of crampons thrown in haphazardly, a massively spiny Coulter pine cone, and possibly a large, craggy meteor found in some field. But the stove we can position on the side opposite the back, the crampons we can safely leave at home, the Coulter pine cone we can leave lie, and the chances of finding a meteor are very slim. So rather than rely on a frame for padding, we can pad our back with our available soft

Coulter
pine
cone,
PCT-2

goods, namely the spare clothing, tarp, groundsheet, foam pad and quilt.

You might experiment with carrying a lightly loaded pack with its hip belt unfastened. If the shoulder straps alone tire the shoulders to extreme discomfort, then you are probably carrying too much weight. If you need to carry more weight, then build up to it gradually, over the course of several outings.

Hikers accustomed to carrying heavy loads, and who switch to lighter gear and hip-belt-less packs, (and to lighter footwear) will often find themselves walking with surprising buoyancy. In fact, they may fairly jounce along the trail, with the small pack banging them in the back with every step. With a lighter load one should smooth the stride, making it less aggressive and jerky.

Hip belt stabilizing straps

Let's take another look at the industry-standard backpack and examine it in terms of bio-mechanics.

As we walk, our pelvis moves in three ways. It swivels as though we are dancing the "twist," opposite the arms as they swing forward and back. It see-saws, one side up, the other down, then vice versa. And it shuttles side to side as our body weight shifts from one leg to the other. The motions of our shoulder-girdle mirror those of our pelvis, but in opposite phase. Our spine connects the shoulder girdle and hips, and it accommodates these

opposing motions by bending and twisting. An internal or external frame pack with its hip belt cinched, acts as a brace, limiting the natural movement of the spine, and restraining these motions. Over the long haul this saps energy. Furthermore, by constraining the spine, designed for suppleness in absorbing shocks, both the hip belt and the frame increase one's chances of injury – for example should one step off a root or rock without thinking, and land too hard. Crunch!

All this harness-restraint works great for jet fighter pilots, securing them in their seats as they make radical G maneuvers. But this restraint is detrimental to hikers ambling along the trail. At the very least one might cut off any hip belt stabilizing straps (read: pelvis immobilizing straps), since these only cinch the load tighter about the hips, and render the hip belt even more inflexible. A person will walk more efficiently without this kind of restraint. Of course, for even better results, carry a lighter pack with no frame and hip belt at all.

Shoulder strap adjustments

In order for the frame to properly transfer the load down to the hip belt, the whole assembly must fit the hiker's body like a glove. Five thousand years ago, Iceman's hazel and larch pack frame and leather hip belt probably fit him perfectly. Today we can no longer custom fit a complex backpack by making adjustments to it with a knife and bit of lashing, such is the price of progress. Instead, the pack manufacturers must devise ways of accommodating the broad range of hiker sizes. They do this by making the packs in a few select sizes, and by contriving various adjustments in the height of the upper shoulder straps' attachments. One such adjustment is with "lifter straps." These attach to the pack straps several inches down from the upper attachments, and allow the user to raise or lower the shoulder straps according to torso shape and size. Another method is with complicated assemblies for adjusting the upper shoulder strap attachment points themselves. However, once the hiker makes all the adjustments to achieve a proper fit, these adjusting mechanisms are of no further advantage, even though the hiker must carry the extra weight of these contrivances from then on. A pack that lacks a frame and hip belt does not require the added complexity of adjustments.

My light-weight pack has one small adjusting buckle on each shoulder strap, where the strap attaches to the bottom of the pack. These buckles enable me to adjust the length of the straps, depending on how many layers of clothing I am wearing. I find, also, that the more weight in the pack, the more I tend to cinch the shoulder straps, keeping the pack riding higher on my back, at the correct level. Loose straps allow the pack to ride too low and to tip back away from the body, both of which can feel sloppy and cumbersome.

Compartments

Some types of commercial packs have horizontal partitions between the main loading area and a lower, sleeping bag compartment. The sleeping bag compartment is then accessed externally with a heavy zipper. This arrangement supposedly allows for better weight distribution, accommodating the lighter sleeping bag below, and the heavier food items above. The old, monster packs that Jenny and I struggled under for so many miles started life with such compartments. The zippers were heavy and difficult to open, especially with cold hands. Worse, the weight of food bearing down on the

sleeping bag seriously compromised its loft – despite the divider. After the first season we cut the partitions out, and stowed the heavier food items in the bottom.

The need to balance a pack properly, placing the heavy items in such and such a place, and the less heavy ones just so, is a requirement of the elephantine backpack. A lighter assortment of gear does not need to be carefully balanced. And with a little extra forethought in stowing things into the pack, we spare ourselves of the frustration of forever having to dig down into the pack looking for something. The idea is to stow each item according to its priority, and place the things we will need during the day near the top. (See Loading Sequence, below.)

External pockets

My pack has three external mesh pockets. One is located on the right side of the pack, for my water bottle, kept there for accessibility. This pocket is made of mesh to allow the bottle's condensation to evaporate. On the other side is a pocket for the fuel bottle, also mesh to permit the fumes to evaporate. And on the rear is a large pocket for stowing the tarp or tent fly when wet with the

Signing a trail register at a lean-to shelter along the AT

morning's dew. Each of these pockets is fitted with elastic in the top hem, to help secure the contents.

Back in the days when I carried a backpack heavy enough to warrant a hip belt, I stitched a home-made camera bag to the belt for easy access. This kept my little camera out of the way when not needed, but handy when it was needed. I now carry the camera in one of the mesh pockets on my small pack. Because the pack is compact and mobile, and because I carry the pack on one shoulder only, I can easily swing the entire pack around and reach into the pocket when I need the camera.

Frontpack

What about using a separate "frontpack" for added carrying capacity? This is a small pack worn "backwards," with the pack riding against the chest, or some kind of specially designed frontpack that attaches to the backpack's shoulder straps. Supposedly this helps balance the load of the backpack. But in the process it also increases the klutz factor, hampering one's mobility and restricting the visibility down at one's feet. The more paraphernalia hanging all over one's body, the more cumbersome, and the more a person will trudge along instead of enjoying a pleasant ramble.

Furthermore, most hikers do not need frontpacks to balance their loads. They balance them simply by leaning forward. In fact, one can gauge the weight of someone's load by looking at his or her degree of forward lean. With a heavy backpack this lean is pronounced; with a lightweight one it is hardly noticeable.

So rather than looking for ways of adding carrying capacity, a better plan is to rethink the gear selection, and find ways of reducing it.

Thumb loops

As a person hikes along a trail, the arms swing like pendulums in cadence with the gait. But because one is not using the arm and hand muscles, their vessels enlarge and the blood tends to "pool" in the fingers and hands. Several hours of this can swell and stiffen these extremities. To alleviate this, one can raise the hands occasionally and hook the thumbs behind the backpack's shoulder straps, at chest height. Or one can insert the thumbs into makeshift thumb or wrist loops secured to the shoulder straps at chest height. Not only will this help reduce the swelling in the fingers and hands, but it will relieve the shoulders and encourage the chest cavity to expand more fully with each breath.

Sternum strap

If there is one technical innovation that I call breathtaking, it is the sternum strap. This "chest corset" is a common feature on today's backpacks; it even appears on most of the smaller day-hiking models. Never mind that it constricts hikers where they need it the least – directly across their lungs, which in the normal course of hiking are laboring to expand with each breath. Technically, the sternum strap's only function is to pull the shoulder straps together, keeping them from sliding off the shoulders. And indeed, the straps can slide off the shoulders of someone wearing a pack that is sized for someone much larger. In effect, then, the sternum strap allows a wider range of fit. And while this may benefit the manufacturer's sales, it does little for the hiker's breathing. The sternum strap also makes the pack more difficult to remove in an emergency.

You could try hiking with the sternum strap unfastened. If you find that the shoulder straps slide off the shoulders, then maybe the pack is too large for your body size. Or maybe the straps are not designed properly. Either of these would be all the more reason to make your next backpack yourself, tailoring it to your needs. Or you could buy a pack that fits properly. Those who feel comfortable wearing a chest corset, might position it as high as possible on the shoulder straps.

Compression straps

Many commercial packs come with compression straps. Cinched tight, these act like a boa constrictor, squeezing and reducing the size of the pack. Theoretically this makes the pack ride with better stability as a person jogs along the trail. But how often does one jog along a trail? If that kind of speed is needed, on rare occasion, then one could try the cruising mode, which is free of jouncing (as described in the "Hiking Pace" chapter). Compression straps bring the pack's center of gravity closer to the body. This is important with heavy packs, but not with lighter ones.

Compression straps also reduce the size of the pack when the extra volume is not needed. With a smaller selection of lightweight gear, we do not need the extra volume to begin with, so why not simply carry a smaller and lighter pack? And when we need more carrying capacity for a fresh load of provisions, we use the extension collar.

Fear of pruning

Most companies specify that if you buy one of their products, and if you modify it in any way, then you void the warranty. I remember a pair of shoes that burst a heel-cushioning bubble after only a few hundred miles on the trail. I sent the shoes back for replacement, but was denied it on the basis that I had cut the tongues out. I seriously doubt whether the tongues had anything to do with the bubble failure, and suspect that the company was using that as a boilerplate excuse for not backing up their product. This was in the earlier days of that particular model, and no doubt the company has corrected the problem. But the fact remains that many times a manufacturer will use such an excuse to its own convenience.

The non-modification clause in the guarantee tends to leave you reluctant to cut the tongues out of a pair of shoes, or cut off compression straps, or remove company logos, or make the scores of other modifications that could be beneficial to your backpacking trip.

My feeling is that I pay my money and take my chances. First I inspect the product, looking for any defects or weaknesses. Then once I make the decision to purchase, I buy the product and take it home, confident that it now belongs to me and that I may modify it in any way I like. If I modify it in such a way that weakens it, then that is my fault, not the company's, and I would not expect a replacement. Instead, I break out a needle and thread, and make the repairs myself. Or if the product does later prove defective through no fault of my own, then maybe the company will accept that fact and make the replacement. If it does not, then that would not be the end of the world.

For many people, the idea of taking a pair of scissors to a commercial backpack is unthinkable. But remember that a pack is nothing more than a collection of simple pieces of material all sewn together. There is nothing magic about it. And just because a person might need the extraneous features someday, that does not mean he or she has to carry them needlessly for 20 miles or 2,000. Think about pruning them. In the unlikely event that you later find that you need them, sew them back on. And just because you trim something off, that does not mean that the pack will suddenly fall apart, or become useless. Rather, the pack will likely become more serviceable, as its weight and complexity decrease.

Loading sequence

Generally, my hiking belongings can be grouped into three categories: food, clothing and equipment. And each of these I can further separate into what is needed while hiking and resting—placed higher in the pack for accessibility—and what is needed at camp – placed lower in the pack, out of the way.

When filling my pack for overnight trips or longer, I load the bulk of the food into the bottom. Next comes the quilt in its waterproof stowbag, then the tarp if it is dry, again in its stowbag. On top of this I load the cookpot and stove. To keep these from digging into my back, I place spare clothing behind them, stowed inside their waterproof stowbag. Depending on the conditions, I keep my shell jacket and pants, sweater, mittens and warm hat near the top, along with the day's snacks, lunch, water filter if any, and perhaps a ditty bag containing the compass, foot care kit, and so forth. I carry the fuel and water bottle in the exterior mesh pockets. And if the tarp is wet with rain or dew, then its place is in the central, large mesh pocket.

My pack has no foam padding to cushion the back, since I find it unnecessary. If one thinks about what is carried in the pack—quilt or sleeping bag, clothing and so forth—most of it is soft. These are my padding.

Actually, my 36"-wide sleeping pad would fit nicely inside the empty pack. That is how Jenny carries hers. She rolls the pad loosely, places it into the pack, then allows it to unroll and fill the pack's interior. In effect, it acts as an internal foam liner, adding stiffness and cushioning.

Donning the backpack

When Jenny and I hiked the Appalachian Trail, we noticed that almost every chair-size rock or log near the track had a beaten path in front of it. Backpackers carrying massive loads were apparently using these objects to rest on, thereby reducing the distance they had to stoop when sitting down. These makeshift benches also made it easier for them to stand back up.

I have carried many a large load, mainly while climbing and portaging. So I know how it feels. But in most hiking scenarios I see no need to carry a load so gruesome that it requires a trailside object for use as a seat. Of course, a big load of food and water can increase the pack-weight dramatically. So when shouldering a heavy pack, one must be careful not to injure the back. This is especially true when dehydrated, because at such times the spinal discs are far more susceptible to injury.

If we both are traveling with heavy packs, we reduce the chances of injury by helping each other lift the packs to our backs. But when hiking solo, here is my method: I grasp the pack by its haul loop and one shoulder strap, and hoist it to bended knee. I support it there momentarily, then heft the pack to shoulder height

Home-made backpacks at one of our outdoor classes. The students made their quilts and tarps also.

and quickly turn my back into it, inserting one arm into its shoulder strap. The pack is now hanging from that shoulder. I take a few steps, turn around to check for anything left behind, then insert the other *elbow* into the remaining strap loop. Shouldering that strap, I then bring the arm through.

The single-shoulder carry

For decades I carried my pack on both shoulders, but when finally I reduced the size and weight sufficiently, I found it far more comfortable and less restrictive to carry the pack on one shoulder only. While this may seem like an unusual method, it has practical advantages.

First and foremost, it improves ventilation and reduces the sweating. Carried on both shoulders, the backpack acts like an ultra-thick layer of insulation, causing the hard working back muscles to sweat-soak both shirt and pack. This is far less problematic with the one-shoulder carry.

Also, my shoulders do not become nearly as tired as might be expected, since I can switch shoulders every ten or fifteen minutes and allow the opposite shoulder to relax completely.

In the unfortunate event of someone sliding pell-mell down a snow slope, or being swept downriver, a backpack attached securely to that person's back would essentially immobilize them, in most cases compromising their safety enormously. The single-shoulder carry is much safer in such an event, since the pack would normally drop away. However, before you try the one-shoulder method while traversing snowfields or fording rivers, make sure you are well accustomed to it, with a little practice on flat and safe terrain.

I do not design my packs differently to accommodate the single-shoulder carry; the positioning of the straps does not change. And actually I do use both straps, although not at the same time – except in rare instances, such as when I need to lug a heavy load of water, or when I want the pack to stay put as I clamber hand and foot over rugged terrain. The Appalachian Trail's Mahoosuc Notch, nearly a mile of boulders, comes to mind here.

You may have used the single-shoulder method without giving it much thought, perhaps during school days when toting a "book bag." It is the same idea. In any case, the single-shoulder carry is a viable option with a lighter-weight pack.

Pack cover

For information about pack covers, see the "Rain" chapter under "Keeping things dry inside the backpack."

Backpacks come in many different makes and models, and choosing the right one can be perplexing. We see internal frames and external frames, hip belts and lifter straps, lumbar pads, stabilizing straps, compression straps, daisy chains, loops and buckles galore. But do we really need all this? More importantly, do we need to carry huge loads? I think that most of us could get by quite nicely with a simple rucksack fitted with a couple of straps. Grandma Gatewood probably would have suggested that we do not even need the straps.

Tarp and Tent

"Where there is an open mind,
there will always be a frontier."
— *Charles Kettering*

A night spent sleeping under the stars can be a night of wonder and beauty. My first experience with this was as a youngster "camping" in the backyard of my parent's home. My brothers and I would throw our sleeping bags down on the grass, and sometimes a few of our neighbor friends would join us. This was independence and freedom; camping at its best! We even built a little brick fireplace and fried eggs over an open fire in one of mom's old skillets. We poured ketchup over the eggs, and to us it was the best breakfast in the world.

That was over fifty years ago, and since then I've done a lot of camping. I still remember those trips into th   e Colorado high country with my dad and brothers; those crisp evenings before the campfire, the craggy, snow-clad peaks towering all around. The tents we used were two-person army surplus pup tents made from two pieces of canvas joined along the ridgeline with buttons.

My grandfather owned a ranch, and we Boy Scouts camped there often, using the pup tents. During the summer months my family sometimes lived on the ranch. By day I drove the tractor, working the crops. At night I slept in my own private camp in the forest. When I awoke one morning and startled a gray jay off my sleeping bag, I realized that I was starting to develop a special kinship with nature.

During my early twenties I worked as an aerospace engineer, spending my weekends climbing mountains and technical rock. For about three of these years I slept in my home-made nylon tent.

After retiring the necktie, I taught wilderness classes, mostly in the Colorado Rockies. During this time neither I, nor my students, used tents. Instead, we used tarps. In later years our tarps were made of nylon, but at first they were nothing more than sheets of hardware-store clear polyethylene. At the start of each summer we would simply reel off what we needed from a roll. These plastic

Our first camp along the IUA

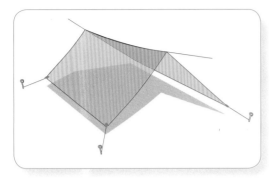

My first nylon tarps

After two seasons of camping with poly-tarps, I made my first tarp of nylon and used it all summer. The next year, 1973, I made a nylon tarp with lifter patches and prototype beaks. All three of these innovations (tarp of nylon with lifters and beaks) passed the test of time; I still use these concepts today.

tarps were cheap, easy to use, and durable. We draped them over cords strung between trees, A-frame style, and secured the corners to guy-lines fastened with sheet bend knots (see the "Knots" chapter). These knots are remarkably strong; I never saw one tear out.

Simple though these poly-tarps were, they had many advantages and very few disadvantages. They cost a fraction of what a tent sold for. They had no zippers or poles to break. They weighed less than half of what tents weighed, yet they provided far more sheltered living space. But most importantly to us, they permitted the best possible ventilation. We, our clothing, and our equipment stayed much drier. These tarps proved themselves eminently suitable for days and weeks of continued use, even during inclement weather. And in those high Colorado Rockies there was plenty of that.

Another advantage to the tarps was that in mild weather we were not so inclined to use them. They were not like tents where the tendency is to pitch them, rain or shine, and the perceived security draws a person in and compels him or her to shut out the world. Where possible we slept in the open, and this was a marvelous experience for everyone. With the starry canopy overhead and the earth's gentle embrace beneath, we found that our simple, low-tech style allowed us a more meaningful interaction with the natural world.

This photo was taken in 1973, in the Holy Cross mountains of Colorado. The main attraction is not me, but the tarp of my design. Note the lifter patches and prototype beaks. The students and other instructors used polytarps, but my home-made tarp was nylon. My father took this photo during a visit to a wilderness course that I was teaching.

Regression from tarp to tent

In 1986, when Jenny and I were preparing for our first thru-hike, I made a tarp, based on how well this type of shelter had worked for me in the past. Yet after studying backpacking books and magazines, and being swayed by the voluminous reams of hype, we opted instead for a commercial tent. We thought that the very best gear would improve our chances of success. So we purchased a 4-pound, 3-season tent of the latest design.

Subsequently, we carried fairly heavy loads that summer – typically 30 or 35 pounds including food and fuel. So when it came time to make camp, we found ourselves too tired to enjoy day's end. All we wanted was to crawl into the tent and collapse.

In the mornings we would usually find our sleeping bag dampened with condensation. This meant that we had to spend extra time drying things out. And it was not uncommon to see other hikers doing the same. I remember one fellow stopping to chat, and during our conversation he matter-of-factly pitched his free-standing tent inside-out, to dry.

The all important ventilation

During the night, a person's body gives off 2 to 4 *pounds* of moisture. Some comes from the breath, which is always saturated. And some comes from the skin, in the form of insensible perspiration – vapor produced by evaporation from the epidermis (skin). And if the person is too hot, the moisture loss is much greater because the sweat glands secrete water in the form of sweat.

The breath and insensible vapor is warmer than the ambient air, so it rises to the ceiling of the tent. And there it is trapped, in much the same way that warm air is trapped inside a hot-air balloon. Most double-wall tents have so-called ventilating gaps all around the lower perimeter of their rain flies. In much the same fashion, hot air balloons have gaping holes in their bottoms. Neither ventilates the interior, since the buoyancy of the warmer air keeps it from escaping.

To this day, I know of no tent that ventilates adequately. Large, open ports would help, several at the top to expel warmer, moist air, and several close to the ground to take in fresh, drier air. But these ports would need to be huge, and they would not work all that well anyway. I have seen marketing claims of how well certain tents ventilate, but in my experience the only time they do is during gale-force winds. Otherwise, their doorways (of both fly and tent body) need to be kept wide open.

The problem with keeping the doorway open is that, with most tents, it allows rain to enter. So when selecting a tent, prospective campers might look carefully at the design. With its door wide open, would rain fall directly into the tent? Or would rain drip or run into the open doorway? Many tents cannot pass this simple test, as though their designers were unfamiliar with the realities of camping in extended rainy weather.

The reality is this: After the first day or two of rain, the interior moisture will build to the point where you will need to keep the doorway open. If you cannot do this without admitting rain, then of course you will have to keep the door closed, in which case the interior dampness will pervade your clothing and sleeping gear. This extra moisture will add pounds to your pack-weight. More seriously, it will reduce the value of your insulation. In cold weather this could send a person into a survival-type situation. This is not a weather attack, but an equipment failure.

Tent failure

The build-up of moisture is one way a tent can fail its user. There are others. Jenny and I were on the trail in central Oregon during that first PCT hike, when a severe storm moved into the area. It began with several inches of snow – and this was mid-July, then it turned to rain, which began cascading from the sky. We hiked through it for half a day, then made camp. This was before we had learned to carry umbrellas, so we were ill-equipped to hike in such a heavy and prolonged downpour. Or to camp in it either, we soon found out.

During this storm we spent forty-two hours in the tent.

Whenever we opened the door for ventilation, the rain ricocheted in. When we closed the door to shut out the rain, we soon found ourselves inundated with condensation. Moisture given off by our breath and bodies condensed on the tent walls, dripped down, and absorbed into the sleeping bag. Outside, rain rebounded under the fly, soaking the tent's interior walls even further. Groundwater also worked its way between the tent floor and the underlying groundsheet, and oozed up through the floor.

No matter how we tried, we could not stop the pervading, warmth-sapping moisture. Every hour our clothing and goose-down sleeping bag grew more damp, and lost more of their ability to keep us warm. Waiting out the relentless storm, we began to realize that time was working against us; that our tent was slowly but inexorably failing. Eventually we packed up and made our soggy way out of the mountains and down to the nearest town.

On the theory that we needed a more substantial tent offering better coverage, we mail-ordered a new one, and of course spent the next several days waiting for it to arrive. Setting off again with the five-pound tent, we felt more confident – until the next rainstorm a few nights later when the new tent leaked, and also exhibited the same problems as before.

The Jardine Tent Awning

These difficulties with tents inspired us to make some changes while preparing for our second PCT hike. We sewed a simple awning to the tent fly, extending over its doorway. This awning allowed us to keep the tent door fully open in any kind of weather, even during the heaviest of rain. It also sheltered our backpacks. I describe how to make such an awning in the "Sewing" chapter.

The awning worked well, but still we needed more ventilation. So while preparing for our thru-hike of the Continental Divide Trail, I cut away the entire vestibule

from the tent fly. This modification created a huge open doorway. During the trip, we always tried to pitch the tent with its foot pointing into the wind, and with its doorway facing away from the wind. Where this was not possible, due to the ground's slope, we simply lowered the awning so that its front edge was close to, or against, the ground.

This tent and awning combination was reminiscent of the old time canvas tents, which had open, sheltered doorways. In rainy weather, the campers built a small fire out

On the CDT

front, allowing the heat to radiate into the tent's interior and dry their damp belongings. For an excellent example of this, see Bill Mason's "Campfire Tent" featured in his book *Song of the Paddle*. In a dire situation, my awning design could provide much the same benefits, when used with extreme care. Actually Jenny and I have used it this way only once. Note: If you build a drying fire in front of your tent awning (or in front of your tarp) keep it at a safe distance, and keep it small. A tent catching fire could be disastrous.

The tarp prevails

While preparing for our fifth thru-hike in 1994, south-bound on the PCT, I finally abandoned the tent idea. Those thousands of miles of trial and error finally convinced me that a tent does not ventilate its interior properly, even with one end wide open. Clearly, our tents had not worked as well as the tarps I had used in the 1970's, at least in summertime conditions here in the "Lower 48." So during that hike we used a tarp, with excellent results.

That tarp measured 8 feet 8 inches square, and weighed 28 ounces. We made it from urethane-coated nylon, which is very durable and makes an excellent tarp. But we now use the lighter silicone-nylon, which became available a few years later.

The Tarp Book

Our *Tarp Book* describes the history and evolution of our tarp in much more detail, along with correct use of the tarp, step-by-step pitching techniques, and detailed

sewing instructions for making both the Tarp and our Net-Tent. For more information visit www.RayJardine.com.

Tarp and tent compared

Most lighter-weight commercial tents weigh four to five pounds. Yes, there are lighter shelters out there, like bivy sacks or flimsy little one-man tents, but they tend to be cramped and extremely restrictive of ventilation.

Our two-person Ray-designed tarp made of 1.37 oz/yd2 silicone-nylon weighs 14.86 oz, plus 1.9 oz for the lineset, plus the seam-sealing. This is one-fourth to one-fifth the weight of even the lightest two-person tents currently available. Our one-person tarp weighs even less: 11.89 oz, plus 1.9 oz for the lineset, plus the seam-sealing.

Of course we enjoy the tarp's lightness, but we also like its roominess.

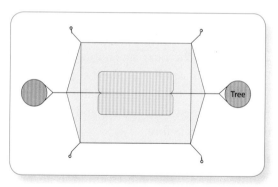

Our two-person tarp shelters an area 106" long by 92" wide when pitched with a roof slope of 30°. (see figure) In this configuration, note the size of the two foam pads, each measuring 20" wide by 72" long. This tarp offers outstanding coverage!

Our one-person tarp shelters the same length, and is 75" wide. As an example, for someone 20" wide at the shoulders (which is my own measurement) this tarp would give them 27" of additional coverage to either side.

> On a cold night, a tarp is warmer than a tent. This is because a tent traps moisture in one's clothes and quilt or sleeping bag, and this moisture lessens their warming ability.

This shelter would be more than three times their width. If a person cannot find a camping place this wide, which would be very rare, he or she would simply pitch the tarp with a steeper slope to its roof.

Cramped inside a small tent, we have to keep most of our gear out in the vestibule, where it is much less accessible. Our tarp offers at least twice the living space, and beneath it, our gear is right there beside us. If using a stove, we sometimes cook beneath the tarp, particularly in rainy weather. This can be a big advantage in the rain, in terms of comfort and convenience.

Beneath a tarp, we also remain more aware of our surroundings. We can see and hear everything around us, even while in bed. And we tend to sleep much better under a tarp than inside a tent, and awaken more refreshed. This is because the tarp allows for wonderfully fresh air.

Condensation and warmth

Even though the tarp is open all around, I find that in the majority of cases, a properly pitched tarp is warmer than a tent. And in persistent rain, I find it is much warmer. This is because of the tarp's superior ventilation. A tent traps moisture in one's clothes and quilt or sleeping bag; and that moisture saps body heat. A tarp reduces condensation, so one's clothes and bedding stay much dryer and warmer throughout the night.

Here is how the principle works:

The moisture coming from our skin (the "insensible perspiration" mentioned earlier) is in vapor form – invisible molecules of H_2O

in the gaseous state. This vapor mixes with the air, and the heat of our skin warming this air tends to buoy the vapor upwards. It rises into our clothing, not wicking because it is still vapor. Emerging from our clothing, it continues to rise into our quilt or sleeping bag, passes through condensation, called the "dew point," at which time the molecules of vapor condense into tiny molecules of water.

If this condensation happens outside our sleeping gear, then all is well, particularly if we are sleeping beneath a tarp. The ambient ventilation (outside breeze) carries this excess moisture away, although some of it condenses harmlessly on the tarp's underside, as dew – in the same way that dew collects on the surrounding vegetation. However, if we are sleeping inside a tent, which by its nature restricts ambient ventilation, then the moisture accumulates. And the vapor of our breath only adds to the accumulation. Some of this vapor condenses on the tent walls, and the rest of it works its way back into our bedding and clothing. Suffice it to say that the humidity level inside a tent is much greater than that beneath

The tarp we used for our third PCT hike was urethane-coated nylon. It weighed less than half of our "lightweight" tent, and afforded twice the living space.

The tarps we now use are silicone-nylon, and weigh less than a pound. Shown here is the tarp we used for our IUA hike of 2003.

a tarp. And high humidity inside a tent works against a person.

On very cold nights, as the vapor of insensible perspiration passes through our clothing and quilt or sleeping bag, it reaches the dew point somewhere inside that sleeping gear. The vapor then condenses into moisture and becomes trapped in the insulation, moistening it. If the ambient humidity is low, and if we are sleeping beneath a tarp, then much of this moisture will wick to the surface of the quilt or sleeping bag, evaporate, and be wafted away. Air at a certain temperature can contain only so much water vapor, and this amount decreases as the temperature falls. So if we are inside a tent on a cold night, then the tent's air soon reaches 100% humidity (saturation). In other words, the rate of evaporation is counteracted by an equal rate of re-absorption. In any

> The majority of nights we spend in the backcountry are mild. We are not automatically headed for an encounter with the ultimate storm the minute we step out the back door with lighter-weight gear. But should we meet with stormy weather, a properly pitched tarp would handle it.

case, the moisture trapped in the quilt or sleeping bag will stay trapped.

The net effect is that on cold nights, a tarp is warmer than a tent. The tent traps moisture in our clothes and quilt or sleeping bag, and this moisture lessens their warming ability. The moisture also adds considerably to the weight of our clothing and sleeping gear, increasing our pack-weight the following morning. In regions of higher humidity and low nighttime temperatures, the above problems are amplified, and the tarp becomes even more favorable.

Pitching in the rain

Supposedly the tent's most desirable feature is its protection it offers from rain. But if you have ever pitched a tent in the rain, then you know how discouraging the job can be. First you preen the site of sticks, pine cones, and small rocks, while fully exposed to the rain. Then you lay out the groundsheet, which starts acting as a rain catcher. Quickly you pull your tent from its stowbag and spread it on the groundsheet, at which time the tent begins soaking water from the groundsheet, and from the sky like a sponge. Hurriedly you fumble with the poles; they become wet and slippery; and hopefully in your rush you do not step or trip on one. A broken pole could render the tent unusable.

Nevertheless, by the time you get the tent erected, the whole thing is soaked. You throw the fly over the tent, attach its corners to the tent poles, and peg out the vestibule – provided your tent has a vestibule. If so, then you stuff your wet pack beneath it. You yourself are soaked;

you remove your rain jacket, place it in the vestibule atop your pack where it cannot possibly dry, and you slide into the tent. Welcome to a wet and decidedly uncomfortable home. But not to worry, you begin mopping the interior with a hand towel, wringing it out the door when necessary. And soon your abode has become at least tolerable.

Cooking in the rain

In the afternoon's heavy rain, you probably did not stop to cook dinner. Now that you are in your tent, you may feel like cooking. But alas, for safety's sake you cannot cook inside the tent, tempting though that might be. Fumes could accumulate and asphyxiate you. Or in the close confines, the stove could ignite or melt the sleeping bag or tent, or it could tip over and scald you with boiling liquid, and soak everything. You could reach out and cook in the vestibule and hope that the carbon monoxide does not waft into the tent and accumulate to dangerous levels. Except that your backpack is probably occupying the vestibule. Maybe you could shove the pack out into the rain, and light the stove in the vestibule, and take your chances with the fumes. But for safety's sake, you venture back outside in the pouring rain, and crouch beneath the partial shelter of a tree. And there you sit, hunkering over your sputtering stove for what scant warmth it provides, soaking wet and becoming more chilled all the time. This is high technology? Frankly, I doubt whether our primitive ancestors lived as miserably.

Jenny and I can pitch a tarp in the rain, shielded by our umbrellas, without the worry and rush of keeping things dry. Once pitched, we crawl beneath the tarp and bring in our backpacks, setting them to one side. After gently preening the ground of any sticks, pinecones, and small rocks— while fully protected from the rain—we lay out our groundsheet, dry side up. Next, we remove our damp garments, wring them out if necessary, and hang them from the clothesline strung lengthwise along the underside of the tarp's ridgeline. Right away we put on dry clothing, spread our foam pads, and crawl into the quilt. Welcome to a warm and dry home.

The luxury of being able to cook in the rain, under a tarp, while reclining in dry comfort is another of the tarp's many benefits. We simply reach beyond the groundsheet, ignite the stove, and cook a hearty meal. But if we are using a type of stove that might flare up at the start, we reach beyond the shelter of the tarp to ignite it, then once the flames have settled we bring the stove under the tarp to cook. Of course we keep the stove away from the sides of the tarp where they are lower, and also well away from our clothing, bedding, and all other flammable gear. This is not a problem because the tarp has so much room. We also locate the stove in such a place that should it tip over, it will not spill hot liquids onto us, or our groundsheet.

Runoff

Heavy rain rebounds into the tarp's interior just as it does into the gap around a tent fly. But because the tarp is so

Tarp camping in early spring on the high divide between Idaho and Montana, during our IUA summer's journey.

much larger than a tent, this rebounding does not come close to us, or our gear. And unlike a tent where this splatter inevitably wets the fabric, beneath a tarp it either soaks into the ground or evaporates. The same happens with the water running off the tarp's perimeter. Any ground water will flow away from us, as long as we have selected a site that is slightly elevated above the surroundings, or at least naturally absorbent.

While camping on sloped ground, if the rain starts pouring so hard that it courses downhill, we might have to use a stick to scrape a V-shaped trench in the ground, a few feet uphill of our tarp, and with the point of the V facing uphill. This would channel the groundwater away from our living quarters. Only in extreme need would we have to dig such a trench, and of course we would fill in the trench afterwards, and eradicate all signs of it.

If we cannot find a slight rise or a slope, we might have to camp on level ground. Should the rainwater start running into our living quarters, we simply dig a few holes for it to drain into.

Striking camp in the rain

On those mornings pouring with rain, most tent campers remain in bed. They know that breaking camp will get them and their gear soaking wet.

Not so, when using a tarp.

Still beneath the tarp, we load our backpacks. Then we deploy our umbrellas, step outside and set the packs beneath a sheltering tree if available. We then take down the tarp, give it a few vigorous shakes, and stuff it into the external mesh pocket of a backpack. We can do all this beneath our umbrellas. If the rain slackens during the day, we might take the time to spread the tarp to air-dry, then stuff it into its waterproof stowbag. Or if the rain is persistent, we simply carry on, knowing that the tarp is a little heavier with the wetness; but this will not affect the tarp's performance the following evening.

> Should a tent pole break in strong wind, a tent can become immediately uninhabitable. In other words, in conditions so severe that one's life depends on the tent, this is when the tent is most likely to fail. Not so with a tarp. If a tarp support breaks, we would simply replace it with a stronger stick from the forest.

Strength

In my experience, a properly pitched tarp is stronger than most tents, particularly the lighter-weight tents. This is because the tarp is an integration of straight lines and triangles, and these are in tension. The tarp has no weakness of curved members in compression, which accounts for its superior strength over tents. And thanks to its all-tension geometry, it can be constructed of thinner and lighter materials.

And speaking of strength, should a tent pole break in strong wind, the tent can become immediately uninhabitable. In other words, in conditions so severe that one's life depends on the tent, this is when the tent is most likely to fail. Not so with a tarp. If a tarp support breaks, we would simply replace it with a stronger stick from the forest. And if one cannot be found, then the tarp will still work with only one end elevated.

Tarp in strong wind

One summer in the San Juan Mountains of Colorado, my students and I spent two weeks hiking and camping directly atop the exposed Continental Divide. This was not the Continental Divide Trail but the actual high and rugged divide. I would not recommend trying this; we were doing it more as a challenge, and during that period the weather was free of thunderstorms. We did experience powerful winds, however. In fact the winds were so strong that they might have flattened most backpacking tents. Yet our plastic tarps worked very well, and we found that pitching them low to the ground was quick and easy.

To do this, we simply spread our plastic groundsheets, set our backpacks on their sides, in the center of the groundsheets to act as short supports, covered everything with a tarp, then placed smooth rocks all around the tarp's perimeter. In so doing, we created the ultimate in low-lying aerodynamic structures, no more than 18" tall. To enter, we crawled through a gap on the downwind side. And of course no matter how tightly we secured the tarp's perimeter, the gale-force winds provided ample ventilation.

> Look for natural protection from the wind: trees, rocks, tall bushes, etc.

Look for natural protection

When Jenny and I are using our nylon tarp in *strong winds*, we look for natural protection from the wind, such as trees, rocks, logs or tall bushes. At the same time, we avoid pitching the tarp directly against any of these objects, because they could abrade the tarp fabric as it vibrates in the wind.

Lower the windward edge

Having found a site somewhat protected from the strong wind, we pitch the tarp with its ridgeline broadside to the wind, and its windward edge lowered to the ground. To pin the windward edge to the ground, we insert the stakes directly into the tarp's guy-line webbing loops,

without using the guy-lines themselves. Or if not using stakes, we tie each windward guy-line to a rock, log, etc., several inches away from the edge of the tarp. Then we place another heavy rock on top of the guy-line an inch away from the edge of the tarp. We would not set this rock on the tarp itself, since it could abrade the thin fabric and make holes in it.

Even in a strong wind, ventilation under the tarp is still important. If we have the windward edge staked low, we keep the opposite edge (the downwind side) staked higher. If the wind begins angling into one end, we deploy an umbrella at that end.

Only in an extremely strong wind would we also pitch the tarp lower to the ground, but not so low that is would contact our quilt and cause condensation.

The beaks

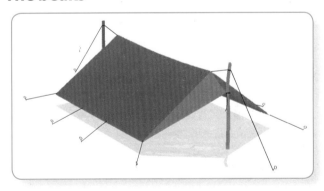

My tarp design includes a very useful feature, in that both ends of the tarp are drooped. I call these drooped ends "beaks." And the angle of these beaks is variable. The lower I pitch the tarp, and the wider the two halves of the tarp spread apart, the more the beaks point downward. In doing so, they partially close off the ends of the tarp, and help block both wind and rain. Once the tarp is pitched, the position of the beaks is fixed. But while pitching the tarp, I can point the beaks nearly horizontally (by pitching the tarp high, and angling the walls steeply), or I can point the beaks straight down vertically (by pitching the tarp very low, and spreading the edges wide). Or I can pitch the tarp so that the beaks are anywhere in between those two extremes.

The tip of each beak is fitted with a short guy-line. This we tie to the nearby support pole or tree, but only tight enough to support the beak, since this line does not support the main tarp body.

A student's tarp at one of our outdoor classes.

Using a tarp in snow

The tarp is not meant as a four-season shelter, but I have camped beneath tarps during fairly heavy snowfall without incident. If we are caught in an unexpected snowstorm, we pitch the tarp tighter and with the roof more steeply inclined to encourage the snow to slide off. When the snow begins to stick to the roof, we tap it with an open hand from underneath. This will dislodge the snow and prompt it to slide off the tarp. If the snow is accumulating rapidly, we will find it piling up along the sides, and this will help seal off the sides and add to the overall protection. But at some point the snow may pile so high along the edges that it begins pressing in on the tarp, at which time we might need to dig away some of it.

Using a tarp in snake country

How does one avoid nighttime encounters with snakes while sleeping under a tarp? Aren't these warmth-seeking reptiles drawn to us? While a person does generate a great deal of infrared heat, he or she is much too large to constitute a prospective meal. And while asleep, one certainly does not constitute a threat. Snakes use their warmth-seeking abilities only on creatures more their meal size, such as mice. Never mind the "true life" stories of some unsuspecting camper waking up with a rattlesnake in his sleeping bag. If snakes were attracted to the heat of sleeping people, then tent campers would often find snakes outside their tents and even underneath them, which is unheard of. And what about the countless numbers of people who slept out in the open in times past? I think that the chances of a nighttime encounter with a snake under a tarp are extremely slim.

Tall tales aside, we still use a bit of caution when selecting a place to pitch a tarp or a tent when in snake country. For example, we would not pitch our shelter near a pile of rocks. And if the surrounding brush is thick, then we probe it with a long stick before setting our packs down near it.

Transition from tent to tarp

Pitching a tarp is not difficult, but the methods differ from those of pitching a tent.

One of the best ways to familiarize yourself with a tarp and to avoid problems is to practice pitching it in your backyard, at a nearby park, or some other convenient location. Then during your first few overnight outings with the new tarp, you might consider carrying a backup tent as well. If the weather is favorable, keep the tent handy. If the weather is threatening, pitch both the tarp and the tent, but sleep under the tarp. If for some reason your tarp setup fails, and you are forced to move into the tent, figure out what went wrong, and make the necessary corrections the next time.

Three common tarp pitching mistakes

Generally, there are three situations to avoid when pitching a tarp.

❋ **Pitching on dished ground**. In a heavy rain, the water might run under the tarp (or tent) and invade the living quarters. The solution is to camp on ground that is slightly elevated above its surroundings, or ground that is sloped. In most cases finding such a place is easy if we simply take a few minutes to look around.

❋ An improperly pitched tarp can invite problems if a chilling **wind blows through the interior**. As mentioned previously, we pitch the tarp sideways to the wind, and in a strong wind we pin the upwind edge of the tarp to the ground. This offers even better protection than most tents with their non-closeable gaps beneath their rain flies.

❋ The third pitching problem is **human error**: a knot coming untied, a poor choice of support sticks, not enough tension on the guy-lines, or the wind pulling a stake out of the ground.

Pitching a tarp

Pitching a tarp is easy, even for one person. Especially after you have practiced it a few times.

The A-frame mode

The tarp is usually pitched in one of three modes: 1) with the ridge-line stretched between two ridge poles or sticks, 2) or two trees, 3) or one stick and one tree. Often, the ground at the base of a tree is slightly raised, thus providing excellent drainage. However, trees are known for dropping branches during storms.

In general, Jenny and I use two sticks about 50% of the time; one stick and a tree 40% of the time; and two trees 10% of the time. The two sticks method allows greater freedom in the choice of a site, so that is what I will describe in the next few pages.

Common mistakes

Whenever you find someone using a tarp, you might see the following mistakes.

▶ **Ridge-line staked short.** Each ridge-line should be 12' in length, and the stake should be tied at its far end. Never stake a ridge-line short because that would be much weaker. Remember that the security of the entire pitch depends on the strength of the ridge-lines and their stakes.

▶ **Ridge-line stake not pressed or tapped fully into the ground.** The ridge-lines must be staked with maximum security, more than all the other stakes combined. Unless the ground is exceptionally solid, do not leave a ridge stake partially extending. This does not normally apply to the other stakes.

▶ **Corner stake tied closer or farther from the tarp than 18".** On a windless day, tying them closer restricts the all-important ventilation; internal condensation will likely result. Only on a windy day do we tie the stake closer, for better support. The more wind, the closer, and of course the strong wind will prevent condensation.

We never tie a corner stake significantly farther from the tarp than 18", because this would reduce the corner support. The line's extra length is for tying around rocks or larger objects when desired.

The two sticks pitch

Start by laying the tarp on the chosen area. Do not spread it out. Instead, simply straighten the ridge somewhat, and align it in about the desired direction.

Attach a stake to a corner line, about 18" from the tarp. To attach any tarp line to its stake, I use a clove hitch with a quick release.

With one hand, lift the ridge to the estimated height. With the other, press the stake firmly into the ground with a twisting motion. The reason we hold the ridge up is to estimate the best location for placing the stakes.

Clove hitch the opposite corner line to a second stake. Again holding the ridge up with one hand, place this stake with the second hand.

With the two stakes in place, walk to the other end and raise a support stick. Wrap the ridge-line once around the stick - at the proper height to suit the conditions. Keeping only enough tension on the ridge-line to prevent the stick from falling over, back away from the tarp to the line's end. There, clove-hitch the line around a stake, and press it firmly into the ground. Note that the stick remains upright. This is because it is triangulated between the three stakes.

Walk back to the first end of the tarp, and raise the second stick. Wrap the ridgeline around it once, step back and place the stake.

Now place the two remaining corner line stakes, while adjusting the corner line's position and tension to eliminate wrinkles.

At this point we are basically camping. All with only six stakes, two sticks, and a few minutes of one's time.

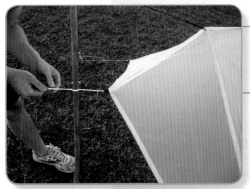

Beaks
Pull the beak-line horizontally and wrap it around the support stick twice. Secure with a two-half-hitches, finishing the hitch with a quick release for ease of removal.

The tip of the extended beak should be one to three inches from the support stick. To move the stick closer or farther, simply twist the stick.

The lifters are optional; they create more headroom and add stability. The lifter sticks do not need to be very stout, since there is very little pressure on them. Wrap the line around the lifter stick once, then stake the line down at its end with only enough tension to create a bit of extra headroom. Note: the stick is positioned against the "V" where the line splits into two directions.

Side guys
In addition to the four corner guys, we can further secure the tarp against strong wind with the side guys, two on each side. Tension these only lightly, otherwise they will lower the tarp's mid-section.

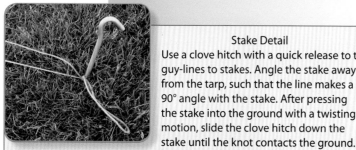

Stake Detail
Use a clove hitch with a quick release to tie guy-lines to stakes. Angle the stake away from the tarp, such that the line makes a 90° angle with the stake. After pressing the stake into the ground with a twisting motion, slide the clove hitch down the stake until the knot contacts the ground. In ground as solid as shown here, one would not need to pound the stake fully in. As long as the angle is correct, and the knot slid to the ground, a firm, twisting press should do fine. How to tell? Simply by pulling on the line. If the stake moves, it needs to be pressed farther in.

▶ **Stakes not angled back, away from the tarp.** Placing the stakes vertically reduces their holding power enormously. The stake should always make an angle of 90° to the line attached to it.

▶ **Knots attaching lines to stakes positioned above ground level.** This places an unnecessary bending stress on the stakes, greatly reducing holding power. Always slide the knot down the stake right to the ground.

▶ **Lifter stick not against the "V" in the lifter line where the line splits into two directions.** The "V" supports the stick from wobbling side to side.

▶ **Beak line too loose, causing the beak to sag.** This will cause the beak to flail noisily in any kind of wind, and it reduces the designed weather coverage. The beak line should be tied straight horizontally, and just snugly enough to give the beak its proper shape, without over-tightening.

The following problems are not universal like the ones above, but they do occur with some regularity.

» Camping on dished ground. As already mentioned, look for a place that is somewhat elevated above its surroundings, so any rain will flow away from your shelter. Flat ground that is on a gentle slope also works well, because the slope does not allow rainwater to puddle. In pouring rain you can trench sloped ground. Trenching from inside a tent is not possible; from beneath a tarp is easy. Don't trench until you absolutely have to, which is almost never; and be sure to restore the landscape before moving on. In 35 years of tarp camping I have trenched only three times.

» I have seen people camping under large dead branches or leaning dead trees. I suppose the theory is that if it hasn't fallen yet, it won't tonight.

» Speaking of objects that could topple in the night,

make sure your tarp support sticks are not injuriously large. Always use the thinnest sticks that will do the job. If too long, break off the excess.

» 90% of the tarps I have seen were pitched too low. Psychologically, lower seems more stormproof. But look at the sky and ask yourself, is this a storm? Probably not. A heavy rain with a bit of wind is no call for a too-low pitch. A strong wind is, and if you need to lower the tarp in the middle of the night, this is actually quite simple. Slacken the lines just a bit, slide the ridge-lines down the support sticks a ways, then re-tighten the lines. How to slacken and tighten the lines? Simply by moving the stakes. You can usually do this from under the tarp.

» Finding condensation under the tarp when awakening in the morning. This is an indication that the tarp was pitched to low, restricting the needed ventilation.

Support sticks

Normally we start looking for ridge sticks well in advance of reaching the evening's camp. Where trees are sparse, we start looking for the sticks an hour before making camp. Where trees are entirely lacking we carry a couple of sticks with us. In the desert we have used dead stalks of agave plants as ridge sticks. We have also used a length of cord to spiral wrap much smaller sticks together to make a longer and very strong support stick. And as a last resort we have even used our umbrellas. Trekking poles would work, and if the poles are too slippery to hold the ridge-lines, then a person could wrap the poles with a bit of adhesive tape for a better grip. Metal trekking poles might not make the best tarp supports in a lightning storm.

In strong wind, we use stout ridge sticks, and tension the ridge-lines tightly.

Normally we would choose ridge sticks of about the same height, but if necessary we could use a shorter stick at the foot end, such that the tarp's ridge slopes down from the head to the foot.

At any rate, the situation to avoid is laying the tarp directly on the quilt or sleeping bag. This would greatly restrict ventilation, and will usually make one's clothing and sleeping gear sopping wet with condensation.

Practice sticks

For the tarp owner, a set of practice sticks would be handy for pitching the tarp at home. That means, two support sticks, and two lifter sticks. On your next outing to the wilds, look for the strongest but lightest sticks you can find, and bring them home. Or look for sticks around your neighborhood. You could even buy them at your local hardware or department store, in the form of hardwood dowels: 1/2" for the tarp supports, and 5/16" for the lifters, two of each. The 1/2" dowels might not be quite long enough for the supports, but they should work fine

Our tarp pitched in a grove of trees, with no sticks or internal supports; IUA.

for practice. Before buying, test them for stiffness. Avoid the soft types identified by the creamy color and lack of grain. Good hardwood is usually darker. Another option is bamboo, often available in the lawn and garden section of large hardware or home improvement stores.

Tarp lines

My tarp has extremely thin lifter lines and side guys. This is because these points of attachment are not heavily stressed, compared with the others. But with very thin lines, one must avoid tying knots that will later need to be untied. I use a clove hitch with quick release on stakes, or if tying to a stump, rock, or log, I use a two-half-hitches with a quick release.

Anchor points

As the wind speed doubles, the pressure it exerts on a tarp or tent quadruples. This is why I attach the guy-lines to objects that are very secure. Stakes are suitable only in firm ground.

If using stakes, I secure the guy-lines to them with quick release clove hitches. The clove hitch can be tied anywhere along the length of the guy-lines, it is adjustable, and it automatically unties itself when you pull the quick release.

Where the ground is not firm, I tie the guy-lines to hefty flat-bottomed rocks, to logs placed endwise to prevent them from rolling, or to the base of bushes. Even small bushes can be very strongly rooted, and guy-lines tied to them properly can be quite secure. To do this, I wrap the guy-line twice around the bush at its base (twice prevents the line from sliding up the stem) then secure the end of the guy-line back to itself with a two-half-hitches. If I am concerned about the line cutting into the bush's bark and harming the plant, I wrap the base of the

Place your best tarp stake to windward

bush with natural materials—dry grasses, pine needles, or leaves—to make a protective padding.

Clothesline

Every tarp and tent should have a clothesline overhead, running the length of its interior. With a tarp, the clothesline runs from one end to the other, under the ridgeline. If the clothing is soaking wet, we wring it out before hanging it on the line. Clothes hung to dry overnight under a tarp will dry at least partially by morning. Same with a clothesline under a tent awning. On the other hand, clothes hung to dry inside a tent will rarely dry, but this is still a good way of separating wet clothing from the sleeping gear.

Holders for eyeglasses and wristwatch

When planning to tent camp, we fit the tent with holders for our eyeglasses and wristwatch. These holders are small loops of cord or thin webbing that we have attached to the tent fabric overhead; not to the waterproof fly, but to the breathable tent wall or ceiling. From these loops we hang our eyeglasses at night, out of harm's way yet handy when needed. We usually sew the loops to the fabric, but another way to attach them is to use a hot ice pick, or a hot nail held with pliers, to melt small holes in the fabric in two places, half an inch apart. The cord runs through both holes, and is tied on the outside of the tent body where the knot will be out of the way.

We sometimes use a wristwatch alarm to awaken us in the early morning. For this we install a similar loop to hold the wristwatch. With the watch hanging near our heads, we are much more likely to hear its alarm.

With the tarp, we sew these small loops on the underside of the tarp, at both ends, and seam-seal the stitching on the outside. We have also hung our eyeglasses and watch from the overhead clothesline.

In the chill of early morning, the eyeglasses will normally fog when first putting them on. One solution is to pre-warm them. To do this, while still lying under the bedding, I place my glasses on my chest for a couple of minutes. Speaking of eyeglasses, I make a habit of checking and tightening the tiny connecting screws before leaving home. I also apply Loctite Threadlocker 242 or the equivalent to prevent the screws from working loose.

Stabilizers

The stabilizers are optional tabs and lines attached to the beak ends of the tarp, at mid-height. They are used to stabilize those end panels in strong wind. I rarely use them because they get in the way and add to the guy-line tangle. But when the wind is blowing strongly they add stability. To use them I would attach the lines, bring these lines together at their far ends and secure them to a single stake.

More uses for the tarp

The tarp complements my 8½-pound system nicely, but it also works well in combination with more traditional gear. A person could, of course, carry a tarp instead of a tent, especially in fine weather; or carry it in addition to the tent. The tarp is lightweight and compact, and both can be carried on a short trip. At camp, the tarp can serve as a "garage" for sheltering the pack and supplies. One can also use it as a lightweight but spacious cooking shelter. If rain starts pouring from the skies, a person can pitch the tarp over the tent for added protection. This would be particularly useful should the tent start leaking. Or one could pitch the tarp over the tent's doorway to create a wealth of add-on living space. In a heavy rain, this would shelter the tent's entryway, and allow one to keep the door wide open for better ventilation, even in a deluge.

Tarp and tent color

In terms of performance, I think the least desirable color for a tarp or tent fly would be black. It would gain more heat by day, and lose more by night. Other very dark colors share these disadvantages. Light colors, such as white and bright yellow or gold, can be glaring under them, at least when the sun is still in the sky. But at our outdoor classes we have noticed that of all the tarp colors, the lighter ones accumulate the least amount of condensation in the night. I therefore suspect that they lose the least amount of radiant heat, meaning that they are a bit warmer to sleep under. Of course, the best colors in terms of low-profile camping would be something that blends in with the surroundings, helping the shelter remain unobtrusive. But of course, the best color is the one you like the most.

Using a tarp in bug season

The tarp does not offer substantial protection from biting insects. Back in the mid-1970's I experimented with sewing a width of netting around the tarp's perimeter, but found that this idea had a host of disadvantages. First, it did not rid the enclosure of mosquitoes, blackflies, ticks and other insects. Many of these insects were on the ground, in the grass or forest litter, prior to my pitching the tarp over them. All the netting did was to cage them, and make me available to them at night while I slept. The netting added a certain amount of weight to the tarp, and this increase was not justified when the bugs were largely absent – which was most of the time. And the netting greatly restricted the needed cross-ventilation on hot days. The netting sewn all around the tarp also prevented me from pitching the tarp higher in fine weather, and it got in my way when I pitched the tarp very low in stormy conditions. And when I pitched the tarp low in rainy weather, the netting got soaked and muddy, creating more of a mess.

Netting sewn to the quilt

In swarming mosquitoes, netting sewn to the tarp wasn't the answer. But we have had good results with a simple piece of netting sewn to the head of the quilt. For details, see the "Quilt" chapter under the heading "Netting sewn to the quilt." And what if the night is buggy but too warm to be under the quilt? Enter my Net-Tent:

The Ray-designed Net-Tent

Abandoning the idea of sewing the netting to the tarp, I designed a separate "Net-Tent" that hooks to the underside of the tarp. The one-person Net-Tent weighs only 9.0 ounces. The two-person Net-Tent is only a few ounces more. And because it has a floor, it is very effective at keeping the bugs at bay. The floor serves also as the ground-sheet on all but the wettest terrain, saving the weight of a separate groundsheet.

On the IUA

But the best feature of the Net-Tent is that we can leave it behind in reasonably bug-free conditions.

For more information on how to make one, see my *Tarp Book*.

Note, too, that the Net-Tent can be used as a ground-sheet—with or without the tarp—when the bugs are not a problem. We simply spread it on the ground, floor side down, fold the netting on top of the floor to keep the netting clean, and lay our insulating foam pads on the netting. This gives us an additional layer under our pads for a little more comfort and warmth. This option can be especially attractive when carrying a minimal foam pad.

———

A tent can offer a false sense of security. Its walls might encourage its occupants to relax and shut down their senses. But these walls are no barrier to any kind of threat.

Security comes from staying alert; watching, listening, and reacting when necessary.

Without a tent enveloping us, Jenny and I are more attuned to the wilderness around us. Comfortably reclined beneath our tarp, we can watch the sunset if we are retiring early; and well into the night we can listen for animals roving about, and any changes in weather. Awakening at dawn we can watch the sky as it begins to lighten, signaling the new day.

In our experience, a tarp provides the best of both worlds: an effective and efficient shelter, yet one that provides a wonderful sense of openness.

Quilt and Sleeping Bag

*"Man's mind once stretched by a new idea,
never regains its original dimension."*
— *Oliver Wendall Holmes*

No matter what trail we are hiking or how long the trip, a good night's sleep is important. And two of the basics of a good night's rest are shelter and a warm quilt or sleeping bag.

I was in high school when I bought my first down-filled sleeping bag. The year was 1960 and the company that made the bag was Holubar. In fact, Mrs. Holubar sewed this particular sleeping bag herself. It was filled with the highest quality prime northern goose down, and was a big improvement over my old cotton-batting filled bag. Even so, after several years of rigorous service, the down lost its loft.

Jenny shows our 2-person quilt that we used for two months while skiing to the South Pole (9,100', coldest night -40C). For this quilt we used two layers of 1" thick insulation. This same quilt went with us (and me, solo) on several other trips including two weeks sledging and kite-skiing on the Greenland ice cap; and climbing Vinson Massif the highest peak in Antarctica.

Our Greenland and Antarctica quilt

In the decades that followed, I went through a number of mummy-style sleeping bags, both down and synthetic filled, but never quite got used to them. They always seemed claustrophobic and usually too warm. Eventually I solved the problems by opening the sleeping bag and using it as a blanket. This method worked so well that by the time I met Jenny, I had not slept in a zipped-closed sleeping bag for ten years, even though I had used sleeping bags most of that time. So during our outings we shared a single sleeping bag, draped over us like a blanket. This saved us half the weight of two individual sleeping bags, half the bulk and half the cost.

The PCT: goose down bag

On our first PCT thru-hike, we bought a top-quality goose down sleeping bag with a full-length zipper. Then we sewed a couple of full length, closed-cell foam pads, 3/8" thick to a thin groundsheet of nylon, and fitted them with a full-length zipper to match the sleeping bag. Zipping the pads to the bag kept the cold air from wafting in around the sides, and prevented the bag from shifting during the night. In effect, we created a two-person sleeping bag with a goose-down upper and a foam pad lower.

This system was reasonably successful, but during the trip the sleeping bag itself failed us twice. Both times, the goose down became wet and lost its loft.

One of these failures occurred during that heavy deluge in the mountains of central Oregon. As described in the "Tarp" chapter, the main problem was not with the rain, but with our tent that trapped the moisture and soaked everything inside, including the down sleeping bag. For the first 24-hours we endured. But as time slowly passed, and the temperature slowly dropped, our ever more wet and cold sleeping bag could no longer keep us warm. On the verge of hypothermia we packed up—in the pouring, near-freezing rain—and resumed hiking.

Hiking in a storm with a soaking wet goose-down sleeping bag is risky. This is because the margins of safety are so small. Should the storm intensify and require making camp, the wet and flattened sleeping bag would sap body warmth rather than preserve it. Many people have died in wet down sleeping bags, and I knew of a few of them.

Fortunately, Jenny and I were not too many miles from a road, and managed to catch a ride into town.

In the final few weeks of that 4-plus month hike, the goose down had lost so much of its loft that it would not stay on top of us. It had so much room to move around inside the nylon layers that every time we shifted, so did the down – from off the top of us. This left large, cold areas, empty of down, even when bone dry. We spent a lot of time shaking the down back toward the center. And even then, the sleeping bag was no longer warm.

PCT-2: another $350 down bag

Back at it again in 1991, we hiked the PCT a second time, again with a new goose down sleeping bag. It finished the trip in the same inglorious fashion as the first one; but at least during this trip the goose down failed us only once.

We were hiking in a storm in northern California, miles from nowhere. Here again, the tent trapped moisture and soaked the sleeping bag, causing it to lose most of its loft. Nevertheless, we broke camp and hiked all through the next day. Towards evening we stopped to

Drying the down sleeping bag; PCT-2

make camp, and in the rain we pitched the tent. The weather was very cold, but our sleeping bag was no longer warm so we could not crawl into it.

Luckily we were able to start a campfire with our emergency fire starter kit. (See our Fire Starter Kit in the "Campfire and Cook-Fire chapter.")[5] And we had sewn a large awning to our tent. So there we sat under the awning, (which resembled a tarp) holding the bag out of the rain but towards the fire and its radiating warmth. Of course we kept the fire small and at a safe distance, six or eight feet from our shelter.

In a few hours we managed to dry the sleeping bag

---

5 In a storm situation already fraught with predicaments, one might be tempted to try warming oneself and drying the sleeping bag or other wet gear with a camp stove used inside the tent. This is rarely a good idea. All fossil fuel stoves generate large amounts of moisture (and asphyxiating carbon monoxide) as a byproduct of combustion. So rather than drying things, the stove would make them wetter.

just enough to safely fall asleep. The night was anything but comfortable, but the weather began to clear the following day.

CDT: another $350 bag

The next year, 1992, we again bought a new goose down bag for a hike of the CDT. But this time we removed the full-length zipper. We had found that we slept warmer without the bag attached to the foam pad. The zipper, attaching the edge of the bag to the edge of the foam pad, was holding the edge of the bag away from our bodies, creating an undesirable air space. Without the zipper, the edges of the bag rested comfortably against us. Gravity held it in place nicely, and we now had more control over the temperature under the bag. In cold weather we could pull the sides of the bag close to us for warmth, and in mild conditions we could drape it more loosely.

This trip certainly had its moments, weather-wise, but the sleeping bag at least survived, even though in typical fashion it, too, lost about half of its loft.

AT: our first home-made quilt

This method of sleeping under, rather than inside, a single sleeping bag was working reasonably well for us. However, we were no longer inclined to buy yet another new $350 sleeping bag. So we decided to make our own.

However I had made a 2-person goose down sleeping bag many years ago, and found the job somewhat complicated due to the internal baffles. We had also learned first-hand that a wet goose down sleeping bag is decidedly unsafe.

And too, in the course of carrying, stowing and unstowing the down bag month after month on those summer-long journeys, the down's loft had degraded, leaving cold spots. Therefore, what we needed, it seemed to us, was a modern synthetic insulation that required no baffles. We knew that synthetic insulation degrades in loft also, but

certain types come with the filaments linked together, so they cannot shift and create cold spots.

While preparing for the AT, then, we constructed a wide-open sleeping bag out of this type of synthetic insulation. And because we made the bag ourselves, we could tailor it to our needs by cutting the bag narrower and tapering it, to save even more weight and bulk.

The final product was little more than a layer of synthetic insulation sandwiched between two layers of nylon fabric, sewn closed around its perimeter, and terminated with a foot pocket. And because we quilted it with yarn across its width and length to keep the shape intact, we adopted the term "quilt." [6]

This quilt proved remarkably easy to make, and inexpensive. Yet it performed a hundred times better than any sleeping bag I had ever used. Many times we experienced heavy and prolonged downpours on that trip; and we knew from experience that the pervading moisture would have flattened a down sleeping bag. But even though our synthetic quilt became quite moisture-laden on several occasions, it stayed warm. This was a big difference!

PCT-3

In 1994 we hiked the PCT a third time, using another home-made quilt of continuous filament polyester insulation. Once again, the quilt was a big success.

Since that fifth long-distance hike we have enjoyed many long paddling journeys in the extreme conditions of the Arctic, in addition to our IUA hike & bike, rowing across the Atlantic, kite skiing on the Greenland Ice Cap, skiing to the South Pole, climbing Vinson Massif in Antarctica, trekking in the Himalayas with a 2-week stay at Everest Base Camp at 17,300', mountaineering in Argentina, all with home-made synthetic insulation quilts.

We use these quilts exclusively, in part because we find them just as warm as sleeping bags for considerably less

6 We first documented our quilt concept in this book, Feb 1996 edition.

weight and bulk. But also we have learned—through much trial and error—the true disadvantages of down insulation; and we are not taking any more chances with it.

Moreover, we like to think that thanks to our quilts made of synthetic insulation, there are a few geese out there with their precious down still attached to their bodies rather than plucked as a commodity for commercial gain.

The quilt design

Prior to the advent of sleeping bags, people slept beneath blankets. In fact, the use of animal pelts for blankets probably dates back to the dawn of prehistory. Later, blankets were woven of many different natural materials. Until the late 1800's most outdoor enthusiasts camped with wool blankets. But when sleeping bags were introduced, most campers left their blankets at home and started using the new sleeping bags. This was because sleeping bags were lighter and less bulky for the same warmth.

We use quilts for the same reasons. They are more efficient than sleeping bags in terms of warmth and reduced weight and bulk.

As a camper lies in a sleeping bag, the body weight compresses the insulation beneath him or her to nearly to nothing. These modern insulations depend on their thickness for warmth, so the crushed part does almost nothing to keep the person warm. That is why the camper must also use a foam pad. Without the pad, the cold would come up from the ground, and pass through the sleeping bag's crushed insulation.

Making our second quilt, this time for the PCT-3

Our quilt design eliminates the needless part of the sleeping bag flattened beneath the person, and therefore it saves the unnecessary weight and bulk. To use the quilt, we lie on our foam pads, and drape the quilt over us like a blanket.

Granted, the idea of unzipping a sleeping bag and draping it over a person was nothing new. But what was new was my concept of making the quilt contoured. Unlike a blanket, the quilt molds to the shape of our bodies.

This contouring took us many years to work out, in order for the design to offer the greatest warmth for the least amount of sewing. But in late 2003 we hit on what we feel is the optimum configuration, and began selling our Quilt Sewing Kits.

Our two-person quilt is rated at 20°F, and weighs one pound, fifteen ounces. **In no pair of commercial sleeping bags could two people sleep comfortably in 20°F temperatures for less than a pound per person.** That kind of performance is unheard of in the sleeping bag industry.

In addition, we share each other's warmth. So our 2-person quilt is actually warmer than two separate bags with the people sleeping isolated from each other.

The 2-person quilt saves us from carrying a second sleeping bag. This is an important consideration on all of our journeys, because we have to carry our gear in backpacks, kayak, canoe, or rowing boat. So the weight and bulk of our gear is critical. And in Antarctica, the 2-person quilt saved us from carrying two expedition-weight sleeping bags, which would have been quite a bundle in our sleds.

Of course, in Antarctica the weather was much colder than 20°F. But I also realized a spin-off feature in these quilts that makes up for the difference. This feature works for either a 2-person quilt or a 1-person quilt. Before I describe this feature, let's look at some background information.

What the manufacturers do not want you to know

Certain manufacturers claim that a sleeping bag needs raw body heat in order to keep the occupant warm in cold weather. That is, the bag requires the heat generated by an unclothed, or nearly unclothed camper to provide the best warmth.

In actual fact, the clothing we wear inside a sleeping bag, or under a quilt, does not diminish warmth; it adds to it. And what the manufacturers and marketeers do not talk about, in some cases because they do not know this themselves, is that the sleeping bag is usually too warm. Most campers cannot sense overheating, so if they wear their clothes in their sleeping bags, their body temperature begins to rise, without them knowing it. The body then calls for cooling, so it activates the sweat glands. The sweat is meant to cool the over-heated body by evaporation. But the sweat cannot evaporate inside the clothes, so the sweat only dampens the clothes. The person does not feel the dampness because the clothes are warm. But as the clothes become ever more damp—over the next few hours—they start to become heat-robbing. And from then on, the person is likely to spend an uncomfortable night.

By telling us that we need to sleep in the buff, the people selling sleeping bags can sell us a heavier one. An unnecessarily thick sleeping bag is more expensive, heavier to carry, and it claims valuable space in the backpack. And with a more massive sleeping bag, a person also needs to buy a larger and more expensive backpack to carry it in.

This would mean that I would have to carry an excessively large, bulky and heavy sleeping bag during the day, and then to sleep alongside a pile of perfectly adequate, insulating clothing at night. Obviously, this idea has little benefit to us.

Another idea, also unworkable in most cases, is to use a somewhat thinner sleeping bag, and to sleep in ones clothes to compensate. For more than one hundred years people have been trying that, and failing. Why? Sleeping bags are too restrictive of ventilation. This means that either the clothes worn inside the thin bag are themselves too thin, causing the person to sleep cold; or the clothes are too thick, causing perspiration which moistens the clothes and bag and saps heat; so the person sleeps cold as well.

This brings me to my shelter/insulation analogy:

Quilts are to tarps, as sleeping bags are to tents

That is, both the sleeping bag and the tent restrict ventilation. The quilt and tarp are open all around, so they promote ventilation. More ventilation means drier clothes and insulation, and therefore more comfort. So the quilt/tarp combination is much warmer for the equivalent weight and bulk.

This concept allowed me to design our quilts for sleeping with our clothes on (the spin-off feature mentioned earlier). And the colder the night, the more clothes we wear. After all, in cold weather we are carrying warm clothes for the day. So why not put them to use at night also? With a quilt, we can.

That's how Jenny and I can use a 2-person quilt with only 2" of insulation on virtually all our cold weather trips. The colder the night, the more clothes we wear under the quilt.

Insulation thickness

Because the sleeping bag is restrictive of ventilation, is has a very narrow band of comfort at any given temperature. That is why sleeping bags come in so many different thicknesses. And each thickness has its own temperature rating. If the ambient temperature is much above or below the bag's rating, the camper will likely spend a cold and uncomfortable night.

Our quilt design offers superb ventilation. So it can handle a huge range of temperatures.

We have made dozens of quilts; prototyping, testing, trying out various thicknesses of synthetic insulation for use in varying climates. The more adventures we take these quilts on, the more we have come to the conclusion that we actually need only two different thicknesses.

The thickness of insulation we use the most is 2" (two layers of 1"). This works in the four seasons on the PCT, CDT, and most other western trails; also in the mountains worldwide in the summer below, say, 19,000'. It also works at home in winter.

The other thickness of insulation we use is 1". This is for warm climates: in our Arizona home in the spring and fall, and on mid-west or eastern trails such as the AT in summer.

If a person becomes too hot in a sleeping bag, he or she cannot adjust the bag for less warmth. The thickness of insulation in that bag is fixed. Granted, a person can remove a layer or two of clothing, which is what we do under the quilt. But the quilt is also open all around, or can be. So if we find either the 2" thickness or the 1" too warm, we simply let in a little more ventilation on one side. Or we shift our feet temporarily out. On exceptionally warm nights we might even sleep with the quilt only partially covering us.

Features of my Quilt design

Foot Pocket

Our quilt design begins with a foot pocket that comfortably envelops the feet. Its main purpose is to position the quilt over our feet, and to prevent the quilt from sliding off the feet and legs laterally during the night. It also prevents the quilt from shifting toward the head when inadvertently tugged on. Yet we can still easily pull our feet out of the pocket, and shift them out from under the quilt if desired on a less cold night.

The photo shows the quilt upside down for purposes of illustration only. We do not use the quilt this way. But the photo does show the foot pocket, and the draft stopper.

With the feet tucked inside the foot pocket, a simple tug re-positions the quilt over us, for example when we shift position. But also we have learned to roll over or shift position without a lot of extra movement, keeping the quilt in place. Both methods are effective.

With the two-person quilt, the foot pocket is for the taller person only. The shorter person does not need it. Jenny is about five inches shorter than me, and since we sleep with our heads even, her feet do not reach the foot pocket. This arrangement benefits us both. The quilt is secure over my feet, but because of the quilt's wide taper in the leg area, the quilt offers her feet and legs even better coverage. As a result, the quilt keeps us both comfortably warm.

Contouring

My contouring design creates a 3-dimensional profile, allowing the quilt to drape nicely over and about us, especially in the neck and shoulder areas. Without the contouring qualities, the quilt would remain open at the top. But with the contouring, the top edge of the quilt hugs our shoulders and the ground.

Draft Stopper

The Draft Stopper is a strip of extra material sewn around the quilt's perimeter. Its purpose is to close off any inadvertent gaps. Any kind of wind blowing on the quilt (and this should not happen beneath a properly pitched tarp) will tend to pin the draft stopper to the ground.

Alternatively, we can tuck the draft stopper under us. And if desired, we can even tuck the edges of the quilt under us. But usually this is not necessary.

> You can make the items described in this book, rather than buy them. For more information see www.RayJardine.com.

SplitZip

Our 2-person quilt uses about the same amount of fabric and insulation as an ultralight 1-person commercial sleeping bag. But imagine splitting that 1-person sleeping bag in half, and carrying only half of it. Our SplitZip allows the 2-person quilt to separate into two pieces, for packing into two separate backpacks. So in effect, each person carries the equivalent of one half of a sleeping bag. That is a huge savings in weight, bulk, and expense for a couple who sleeps together.

The SplitZip divides our 2-person quilt into two pieces laterally, with the zipper running side to side. The zipper is protected by a baffle that prevents cold spots.

We use quilts having the SplitZip for hiking and mountain climbing, or whenever we need to carry the quilt in our backpacks. The SplitZip allows us to spread the load and bulk. However, it also adds a few ounces in weight; so we make the quilt in one piece when planning a trip that does not require backpacks.

Holding the warmth

In a sleeping bag, when a person draws the opening tightly closed, the opening normally faces straight up. Even though the opening is small, it nevertheless allows much of one's body warmth to escape; since warm air rises.

When sleeping in cold weather, one might be inclined to hunker down into the quilt, and cover the head and face with it. That would keep one's body warmth in, but also the moisture from the breath would condense into the quilt (or bag) and reduce its warming ability while adding to its weight.

Instead, we sleep with the quilt covering our bodies and necks, but not our heads and faces. In addition, we also wear warm hats. Depending on the conditions, we wear either a "bomber hat" made out of the same continuous filament polyester insulation as the quilt, or a fleece-like hat pulled down over the face and mouth. This single-layer skullcap is simple to make, and is described in the "Sewing" chapter.

Ninety-five percent of the time Jenny and I use the quilt with it simply draped loosely over us, not tucked in. The quilt and draft stopper seal any gaps around the neck. But for even more warmth, we may tuck the edges under us, and cover our heads with the quilt in such a way that our breath is not trapped by the quilt. In this method, we keep our faces very near an open edge for the best ventilation.

In this view, Jenny has tucked the draft stopper under her, and pulled the quilt completely over her head. As her heat rises, the quilt captures it and holds it next to her.

Still, she has left her face exposed to permit the escape of her moisture-laden breath.

To achieve this configuration, she covered her head with the quilt, then with one hand pulled the quilt under her chin. When she wants to roll over, she simply repeats the process on the other side.

Wearing clothing under the quilt

Some people prefer more insulation than others. Partly the differences are physical. Their at-rest metabolisms drop lower than most, resulting in less heat production. But also they may be less tolerant, emotionally, of cooler nighttime temperatures. Either way, they need more insulation at night. However, this does not necessarily mean they need thicker quilts or sleeping bags. In most cases they can easily make up the difference by sleeping in more clothing.

In my quest for a lighter pack-weight, I have come to the conclusion that carrying a lighter-weight quilt and wearing our hiking clothes when the nights are extra chilly makes far more sense. This approach saves us pack-weight and bulk without compromising our nighttime comfort. And as a bonus, we find it quite convenient to rise on the coldest of mornings already dressed in warm clothes.

When planning to sleep in our hiking clothing, we need to keep this clothing reasonably dry during the day's hiking. This means that we must be careful not to sweat soak it. To accomplish this, we dress in layers and remove a layer or two whenever we begin to sweat. The layering and dynamic-wearing approach (see "Clothing" chapter) will not eliminate sweating. A hard-working body naturally perspires, whatever the temperature. But it certainly will minimize sweating, while allowing the sweat to evaporate. Also, as we hike in the cooler hours of late afternoon or evening, our perspiration will be much reduced, so that we are likely to arrive at camp in hiking clothing quite suitable for wearing at night.

We find clean clothes the most comfortable, for both hiking and sleeping. Dirty clothes are not as warm because the body oils, salts and accumulated "trail patina" reduce the fiber's loft while conducting away more heat. For this reason, we launder the clothing dundo-style (as described in the "Hygiene" chapter) every few days, and more often in hot, muggy weather. Clean garments last longer, too.

What if our clothes are muddy? In muddy hiking conditions, we normally wear shell pants, while being careful not to wear too many underlayers that would lead to sweat soaking. If our shell pants are wet or muddy when we make camp, we hang them under the tarp and sleep in the garments beneath. The shell pants will perform equally well the following day, wet or dry, clean or muddy. And because they are easily washed, we do not leave them muddy for long.

In fact, the shell pants are so fast drying that unless the rain is continuous, the pants are usually dry once we reach camp. When dry, they offer surprising additional warmth for wearing at night in the quilt, because of the extra insulating air they entrap.

On cooler nights we wear socks inside our quilt, but

we always change into a dry and cleaner pair before retiring. We have tried wearing wet socks on cold nights in hopes of drying them, but found that instead of drying the socks, this method only chilled our feet. Wet socks are better dried on a clothesline, or in demanding conditions against the stomach inside a shirt, after vigorously ringing them out.

Quilt used as a robe

During the day, the quilt makes an excellent robe for wearing at the rest stops in cold weather. It also makes a great comforter when sitting outside in the mornings, before the sun has warmed the day, and again on chilly evenings. Note, however, that one would not sit beneath a quilt out in the open after sundown when the dew begins to form. At the first sign of dew, it is time to place the quilt under the tarp, to keep it dry.

Netting sewn to the quilt

When Jenny and I hiked the PCT for the third time, we used a piece of netting sewn to the head of the quilt to keep the mosquitoes and blackflies at bay. This worked extremely well, even when the bugs were swarming.

The netting was 54 inches long, and 72 inches wide – extending about 10 inches to either side of the quilt. The netting was not flat, but tucked on both sides to form an enclosure, which we could support with an open umbrella beneath it, or suspend from the tarp overhead. But most often we simply pulled it over our faces at night. It was effective against the bugs, and on chillier, bug-free nights we found that it kept our heads warmer. When not needed, we rolled it down and tied it with special tabs, holding it out of the way.

On nights too warm for the quilt, we slept only in the mosquito-proof clothing, and head nets if the insects were bothersome. In the wee hours when more warmth was needed, we would then pull the quilt over us.

At one of our classes, Mike W. demonstrates his home-made quilt with attached netting.

But what about bugs crawling around at night? If the night is cold, then the bugs are dormant. On warm nights they are active, certainly, but apart from a few mosquitoes, the bugs, snakes, and mice would rather keep away from us, even when we are asleep. The "size ratio" is to their disadvantage. Jenny and I have slept under a quilt hundreds of times, both out in the open and beneath a tarp, and we have not been bitten at night by any creature other than the occasional mosquito. This is not to say that it could not happen, but I think the odds are quite against it.

However, the ants. These little fellows are fond of getting into everything, including our clothing at night – not to bite, but merely to wander around in search of dead insects, crumbs or whatever. They can be distracting when crawling on bare flesh. So, on warmer nights we usually sleep in our bug-proof "shell" garments.

Air-drying the sleeping gear

Regardless of whether a person carries a quilt or sleeping bag, it benefits by daily airing to rid it of the moisture accumulated during the previous night. Down bags require airing because they need to be kept dry in order to preserve loft. But even synthetic-fill bags and quilts will shed a pound or two as the entrapped moisture evaporates.

The sun does not have to be gleaming down from a clear blue sky in order to dry a quilt or bag. The clearer the sky the better, but even beneath a fully clouded sky a person can spread the sleeping gear to dry any time between mid morning and mid afternoon, in the absence of rain of course. Much of the sun's energy penetrates the clouds and will dry the sleeping gear surprisingly well. The cooler the day, the more important it is to avoid spreading the gear on vegetation, which tends to collect condensation. On dank days, look for a patch of rock or gravel that angles toward where you think the sun might be. This type of surface holds relatively little moisture and tends to be warmer than the surrounding terrain.

When stopping at day's end to make camp, we do not un-stow the quilt (or bag) and lay it directly on the ground where it would absorb moisture. Instead, we pitch our tarp, spread the groundsheet under it, then unstow and spread the quilt on the groundsheet. This allows the most time for the insulation to "loft up" before use. But in a light rain, we leave the quilt in its stowbag until ready for use. Or if the weather is good and we have extra time, we spread the quilt on top of the tarp for extra air-drying.

Quilt Stowbag (stuff sack)

To keep the quilt dry while stowed inside the backpack, we use a waterproof stowbag. Of course, our 2-person quilt with SplitZip requires two stowbags, one for each half.

The "Sewing" chapter describes how to make a basic waterproof stowbag. I used this type for decades, including on most of our hikes, long and short. They are inexpensive and easy to make, and can be constructed in any size to hold sleeping bags, clothing, food, or whatever. For a sleeping bag, I preferred a stowbag that was about two-inches taller than the width of my backpack. After loading the heavier food items into the bottom of my pack, I loaded the sleeping bag vertically, then turned it horizontally, side to side. This provided for a lightly compressed fit that occupied about one-quarter of my available pack volume, leaving no unused space below. It was a snug but perfect fit.

Someone not inclined to make or buy a waterproof stowbag could use a non-waterproof one and simply line it with a plastic trash bag. Place the plastic bag inside the stowbag rather than outside, to protect the plastic from abrasion. This approach adds some weight and fuss, but it works well.

Ants fascinate me. If you have never studied them, you are missing some great entertainment and education. And studying ants is something we normally have plenty of time for, during the rest stops. I wonder how many ant-miles one of these tiny creatures walks per day? Have you ever noticed the huge loads they often carry? Not only are they indefatigable workers, but they are also amazingly well organized. And many times we have watched scores of them come out of their hole all at the same time and only mill around, as if for exercise and fresh air.

So too, ants are nature's tireless house cleaners. We slap a mosquito, it drops to the ground—and the ants quickly haul it off. Without the ants, the earth would be a rubbish heap. All aspects of the natural world are fascinating, if we take the time to watch, listen and participate. Whenever an ant or two show up at my bedside, I let them go about their business. Knowing they mean no harm, I simply turn over and return to sleep.

My website gives information on the waterproof stow-bags we use today. These are somewhat more complex, but weigh less than one-third of the usual commercial varieties. These stowbags fit perfectly into our backpacks. They sit in the pack vertically, one on top of the other, and are adjustable in volume, expanding or compressing to occupy however much space is needed in the backpack.

If we are fresh from a resupply and carrying a quantity of food, we reduce the size of the quilt stowbags to make more space for the food. Or if we are several days out and carrying less food, we expand the stowbags to allow the quilt a little more breathing room.

We also use these stowbags to carry clothing and other items inside our backpacks. Typically, we load the heavy food items into the packs first, followed by the quilt in its stowbag, and then the clothing stowbag.

Stowing the Quilt

When stowing the quilt in the stowbag, we do not fold and roll the quilt, as we would the tarp and net-tent. Instead, we stuff it.

The stressful part of a quilt's life is not carrying or using it, but un-stowing it from its stowbag. When removing the quilt from its stowbag, I pull gently. To that end, I do not carry a quilt in a stowbag so small that it requires yanking to pull it out. Pulling mightily on a handful of quilt would be extremely hard on the synthetic fill. It can tear the individual insulation filaments and separate them from each-other, and can pull them out of the side stitching and quilting. Rather than pulling forcefully, it is better to release one's grip, and grab a different part of the quilt somewhere else within the stowbag.

Jenny and I make our stowbags of silicone-coated nylon, which is quite slippery and therefore offers less resistance to the item being withdrawn.

For a weekend hike we might stuff the quilt a little more

tightly; as long as we give it a few hours of relaxing out of the stowbag prior to using it. Once we have returned home, we then leave it out of the stowbag for a few weeks to allow it to loft back up. The tighter the stuff, and the longer it has been left that way, the more the quilt (or any sleeping bag) will lose its ability to loft back up over time. For storing a quilt at home, we use a large, breathable stowbag that does not compress the insulation.

On a long thru-hike, we have very little time for loft-ing, so we make our stowbags as large as practicable.

Compression stuff sack

A quilt or sleeping bag tends to lose loft over time. This is true with both goose down and synthetic materials. And compression stuff sacks only add to the problem.

I do not use a compression stuff sack to contain any item made with low density insulation. This includes quilts, sleeping bags, and insulated parkas, hats and mittens. These compression devices are very effective at reducing bulk, but they are equally effective at destroying loft. The first time a person cinches down on those compression straps, one snuffs out approximately 10% of a sleeping quilt or bag's loft; *permanently*. And each additional hyper-compression destroys about 2% of the remaining loft. And of course, the quilt or bag loses that percentage of its ability to maintain warmth. Even more damaging than using a compression stuff sack is to sit on a quilt or sleeping bag when it is contained in any kind of a stuff sack. Low-density insulation cannot withstand such crushing loads. The more carefully a person treats the insulating gear, the better it will work. This is especially important during a long journey that runs into the late fall season. During that time one may need the most from the gear's warmth. For best results, use the largest stuff sack practicable, refrain from stowing heavy gear or provisions on top of it, and resist the temptation to sit on it.

Certain manufacturers claim that their proprietary insulation materials do not lose loft. But even if a sleeping bag does not lose its loft, it might not be the best choice if it weighs five to seven pounds. So be sure to check the product's weight. The discussions in this chapter deal with the more efficient, lighter-weight types.

Breathability in the quilt or bag

Waterproof-breathable and vapor-permeable fabrics have some very useful applications, but I feel that they actually reduce the performance of any sleeping system made from them. They restrict the transportation of water vapor exuded from our skin during the night. Not entirely, but enough to increase the accumulation of moisture in the insulation. This entrapment of moisture reduces the thermal value and it adds weight. And during the day, these materials greatly hamper one's air-drying efforts.

Around-the-world-walker Larry Amkraut had this to say about a waterproof-breathable sleeping bag: "I once had a [popular brand name of fabric] sleeping bag that cost $520.00 nicknamed Lazarus, because it came out of the stuff sack in a lump and I had to stretch it out length-wise and width-wise and then fluff it up, bringing it back from the dead. Eventually I sent it home, in exchange for a different type."

The best plan is to place our protective, waterproof layer overhead, in the form of a tarp. Between that and ourselves should be a flow of ventilating, moisture-purging air. Against our bodies we need only breathable materials, allowing the transportation of our body moisture into that air. Simply put, the tarp is our shelter, the quilt or bag is our insulation.

Vapor barrier liners

Sleeping bag liners made of vapor-barrier (waterproof) materials might seem compatible with minimum weight camping. After all, they prevent the body's insensible perspiration from reaching the quilt or sleeping bag's insulation, and therefore they keep the insulation at its lightest and warmest.

But I am not an advocate of VB. I find it uncomfortable when worn next to the skin, even if wearing a thin garment underneath. And I think the human body was not designed to live in a plastic bag. A person's skin needs to "breathe." That is, the skin needs to emit moisture and small amounts of gas such as carbon dioxide, as well as certain soluble and in-suspension by-products. And it needs to absorb moisture and a small amount of oxygen and other gasses. This is why doctors sometimes call the skin our second liver, because it helps detoxify the body. When it comes to one's health and comfort, breathability in the garments is vital.

Shredded newspapers

Picture an expensive, premium quality sleeping bag made with prime northern goose down. Let's say that this bag has a thickness—measuring only that part of the bag that would cover the person—of two inches. As we will calculate below, this bag has an Effective Temperature Rating (ETR) of 20° Fahrenheit. Now imagine this: A sleeping bag filled with two inches of very fine steel wool would be just as warm. Another one filled with two inches of finely shredded newspaper would be equally warm. And let us not forget modern technology: a sleeping bag filled with two inches of the latest synthetic fill: 20° Fahrenheit once again.

How can all these fill materials provide comparable warmth? The fibers are not what provide the insulating ability. All the fibers do is trap tiny pockets of air. It is the air that provides the insulation.

Goose down and synthetic fill

Warmth is an important quality in a quilt or sleeping bag, but hikers have additional requirements. They need the sleeping gear to be reasonably light in weight. And to fit into small stuff sacks and come out looking about like new. So they need insulating materials that are low in density and high in loft-retention.

Among these, prime northern goose down offers the greatest warmth and compressibility for the least weight. Put another way: for a given loft, (thickness of covering) goose down weighs the least and compresses the best. However, technology is gradually closing the gap, and the performance differences between goose down and the best synthetics are no longer very great. This is good news because goose down has a few shortcomings that for most of us might outweigh its advantages.

Wet and cold

As stated earlier, a goose down sleeping bag loses most of its loft when allowed to become soaked. Sopping wet down turns into waterlogged clumps that have no insulating value whatsoever. And if you attempt to wring the water from it, you make it even flatter. In fact, the clumps of wet down will do a good job of extracting a person's warmth, what little might remain. What is more, that down is extremely difficult and slow to dry.

This is not to suggest that when goose down becomes saturated, all is lost. Left with no alternative, you might be able to restore its ability to insulate by drying the bag in front of a campfire. This can be effective, but slow and often risky because the heat can melt or even ignite the material, and sparks can burn holes in it. And what if the skies are pouring with rain? This is where a small campfire and a tarp come in handy.

Synthetic fill materials also lose their ability to insulate when wet. For after all, water absorbed into the insulation, whether that insulation is down or synthetic, replaces the tiny pockets of insulating air. This water conducts away body heat. But at least when synthetic insulation becomes wet, even soaking wet, we can wring it out and restore much of its loft. There is no need to dry it before a campfire to ensure our survival in cold and stormy weather. In the event of such a predicament, this wring-and-restore feature can make a huge difference.

If the ground is completely saturated from a recent rain, you can drape your damp sleeping gear over you and carry on down the trail.

Effective Temperature Rating formula

When a person relies on a sleeping bag as the main source for warmth, the colder the night, the more insulation he or she will need. But when one tries to quantify the matter, one runs into difficulties due to the many variables. Everyone reacts differently to nighttime temperatures. Some people do not mind being a little chilled, while others prefer incubation. Another variable is the type of fabrics used on both sides of the insulation, and their permeability. If those fabrics are overly breathable, then the warm and moist air will escape too voluminously, and much warmth will be lost. The color of the outer layer affects the amount of heat it will radiate away. Another variable is the ambient humidity. Yet another is the local wind-chill factor.

In practical terms, we can speak of the sleeping bag's "Effective Temperature Rating." This is the hypothetical lowest outside air temperature at which a sleeping bag would preserve one's body warmth. I have quantified the matter into an easy-to-use formula that gives a very useful approximation.

In this formula, the letter "T" represents the thickness of that part of the bag covering the person.

The formula: $ETR = 100 - (40 * T)$

Again, "T" is the sleeping bag's thickness, in inches, covering the person. When we multiply this by 40, then subtract the result from 100, we arrive at the ETR, the quilt or bag's Effective Temperature Rating, in degrees Fahrenheit.

Let's say that on a summer journey taking a person into the cool mountain heights, he or she carries a sleeping bag having 2 inches of insulation in the part that covers the torso. Plugging the 2 inches into the formula: $100 - (40 * 2")$ gives this bag an ETR of 20°F. In other words, when sleeping in this bag in the buff, the person can expect to remain comfortable down to 20°F.

The ETR is only a guideline, but a very useful one. It gives us an easy means of comparing commercial and home-made bags and quilts, independent of manufacturer's claims. And until an independent lab starts testing these items in some definitive and standard way, then I think the ETR can be applied universally.

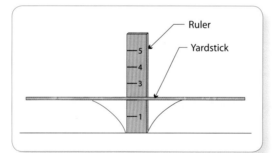

Measuring thickness

Here is an easy and reasonably accurate way of measuring thickness of insulation: Lay the quilt or bag on a flat surface. If measuring a sleeping bag, unzip it, and open it so that it is not doubled – measure only the part that would cover you. Lay a yardstick gently on the quilt or bag. Stand a ruler on the quilt or bag, alongside the yardstick, and press it down onto the underlying flat surface. Read the thickness measurement on the ruler at the yardstick.

Colors

We have made quilts in all manner of colors, and liked them all. Theoretically, the quilt's upper surface works best in a lighter color, to reduce radiant heat loss. The principle works the same in daylight and the blackness of night. If the quilt's under surface is also light in color then it will reflect one's body heat back to the sleeping person a little better. But I usually make the under surface of my quilts dark in color for an important reason. When I stop hiking in mid-morning to dry my gear, I air the quilt mainly dark-side up to speed drying. Also, when sleeping in the open in an area where I prefer not to be noticed, which is rare, I might sleep with the quilt dark-side up.

Washing a quilt

The best and safest method for washing a quilt is by hand in a clean bathtub, laundry sink or tub with warm water and a small amount of mild soap. Agitate by hand, then rinse several times. Rather than trying to wring out the excess water, drape the wet quilt over a picnic table outdoors, or a couple lawn chairs, or anything that will allow it to drip. As the quilt sheds the excess water you can then flake it out, turn it over, and fluff it up gently for more effective drying.

Alternatively, a person can safely use a front-loading washing machine, again with warm water and mild soap. One should not use a top loading washing machine because the action of its rotating center post could damage the quilt.

I also recommend against the use of an automatic clothes drier because the temperature controls of these machines are typically unreliable, and even moderately hot air can damage the materials. In a pinch, say on a rainy day in town during a long hike, you could use a clothes drier set to no heat, or to very low heat that you would check often. Otherwise, the safest drying method is to spread the quilt on a clean groundsheet, or a pitched tarp, and let it air dry.

Groundsheet and Pad

"We act as though comfort and luxury
were the chief requirements of life,
when all that we need to make us really happy
is something to be enthusiastic about."
— *Charles Kingsley*

As the name implies, the groundsheet is a thin, protective sheet of plastic or coated nylon placed on the ground under the shelter. If using a tarp, we pitch the tarp first, then spread the groundsheet under it to serve as the "floor." The groundsheet is waterproof, or nearly so, hence it acts as a barrier against ground dampness, as well as dirt and tree sap. If using a tent, we pitch the tent on top of the groundsheet.

Each evening as Jenny and I make camp, we are careful to place the groundsheet with the clean side facing up and the soiled side against the ground. In the morning when we break camp, we fold the groundsheet the same way every time: soiled sides together.

Tarp groundsheet

If the ground is wet, one might imagine that sleeping beneath a tarp would not work very well. But with a properly located tarp, and the right groundsheet material, tarp camping works surprisingly well. If the ground is the least bit absorptive (not solid rock) then a tarp pitched over it will shield the ground from the rain, and give the ground a chance to dry. Some of the wetness evaporates, but most is absorbed. A groundsheet spread over this ground will actually enhance the absorption, especially as our body heat warms the ground slightly as

we lie on it. And after sleeping there all night and breaking camp the following morning, we will often find the ground underneath the groundsheet dry, in contrast to the wet ground everywhere else.

Tent groundsheet

When used with a tent, the groundsheet helps protect the tent floor from abrasion. But it will not protect the tent's floor from punctures, since the groundsheet itself is thin and punctures fairly readily. That is one reason why we preen the site beforehand of anything sharp or pointed, such as sticks, stones, and needle-tipped pinecone scales. This gentle preening makes the area more comfortable to sleep on as well, reducing the need for a thick foam pad.

Most tent floors are made of nylon coated with polyurethane, or rarely, silicone polymer. Although touted as waterproof, these coatings are not completely impervious to water when pressed against something wet, like the ground after a good rain. So the manufacturers might use a double-coated floor, which is a bit more waterproof but adds weight, or even a triple-coated floor, which adds even more weight. The trouble with these coatings is that moisture can migrate through them, although minutely. So a person might wake up in the morning and find condensation inside the tent, between the tent floor and the sleeping pad.

Groundsheet materials

Ordinary 3-mil (3 thousandths of an inch) polyethylene is highly impervious to moisture from wet ground. It is sold in hardware stores as "poly" or plastic sheeting. It makes an inexpensive and very serviceable groundsheet; surprisingly durable but also somewhat heavy.

The person more concerned about pack weight could use a polyethylene sheet of less than 3 mil thickness, and carry a few extra inches of duct tape for repairs.

For even more weight savings we have used a groundsheet of silicone-coated nylon. This is durable, but very slippery. The ground must be level; otherwise the camper and groundsheet might slide a ways downhill.

A non-slippery, heavier, but much more durable alternative is polyurethane-coated nylon. This is the same material as most tent floors.

Another option is the "Space® brand *All Weather* Blanket." This is a four-layer laminate: one side is a reflective silver color, and the other side is a ripstop-like plastic in various colors. We used these types for our first four thru-hikes. One caution about colors: If a person chooses the bright orange or red, he or she should be careful about airing the blanket colored-side up, since an aviator could misconstrue the "signal" as a call for help.

The ultralight "Space brand Emergency Blanket" looks somewhat like aluminum foil, but is an aluminized polyester film with a highly reflective, silver-colored coating. It is impervious to moisture, and very lightweight. We have used these as groundsheets but found that they tear too easily. But we do use this material on our umbrellas. See the "Umbrella" chapter.

Holes in the groundsheet

With the exception of the polyester film mention above, all these types of groundsheet material are fairly durable. However, none of them are puncture-proof. So once we have used a groundsheet for a few days or weeks, we may begin to find various small holes in it, normally the result of inadequate site preening.

By the end of a long trip, our groundsheet is usually riddled with such holes. But we have not noticed any decrease in performance. Before we realized this, we patched the holes with small bits of adhesive tape. Of course, any larger holes, as well as tears in the material, are genuine candidates for taping.

Duct tape works about the best, and it is also effective on mosquito netting, the tent fly, waterproof bags, and even water bottles. Duct tape is fairly heavy, however, so we usually do not carry it. But we might include a few feet of it, rolled and flattened, in our resupply boxes. A more lasting method of repairing tears in a urethane-coated groundsheet, tarp or tent fly is to apply a thin coating of SeamGrip. For fabrics that are silicone-coated, no adhesive tape that I have found will stick to it, so we use a thin layer of silicone sealant.

Trimming the groundsheet to size

We cut the groundsheet to the appropriate size to reduce its weight and bulk.

If we are trimming the groundsheet for use with a tarp, we spread the groundsheet on the ground, lay the foam pads down and lie on them. Then we draw a line around us and the pads, leaving about twelve extra inches all the way around. We leave even more space when we want extra "floor space" for some of our gear. We then use scissors to trim the sheet along the line. The two-person groundsheets that Jenny and I have used on numerous outings are 48" wide in the shoulder area, tapering to 34" at the foot, and about 7' long.

If we are cutting a groundsheet for use beneath a tent, we pitch the tent on it, then draw a line on the groundsheet around the tent's perimeter. Then we cut about an inch inside the line, making the groundsheet that much smaller than the tent's footprint. The trimming not only eliminates excess weight and bulk, it also eliminates channeling. That is, any margins of groundsheet left exposed might collect rainwater running off the tent fly, and channel it unfavorably beneath the tent. This is when a camper might discover that the floor of the tent is not waterproof, contrary to the manufacturer's claims.

The sleeping pad

The self-inflating mattress is so popular with many backpackers that it is almost an icon of the traditional approach. Never mind its weight and bulk; it is expensive, susceptible to damage, and practically impossible to customize to a person's specific needs. Yet it is one of the last items that most campers would leave at home. Why? Because it offers comfort when camping on hard ground, and warmth on cold ground. The inference is that all ground is hard and cold. But is this true? In the established campsites it usually is, especially where decades of campers have scraped away the cushioning layers of forest litter and duff – right down to the dirt. And where that dirt has been heavily compacted by innumerable boots and steel-shod hooves.

Such is not the case with undisturbed areas far off the beaten track, where soft, cushioning leaves or needles, or deep and pliant layers of duff or leaf debris offer comfortable camping. Even bare dirt in many pristine, untrammeled areas is reasonably soft. Places like these do not require self-inflating mattresses. Neither do they call for scraping together the natural insulation from far and wide for the best possible cushioning and insulation. We simply use it as we find it – nature's perfect bedding.

But how can we be assured of finding such places every night? Simply by spending a little extra time each evening exploring the surroundings, looking for them.

The thin foam pad

We have found the natural insulation approach so effective that it requires only thin foam pads. On all our hiking journeys and overnight outings, Jenny and I have slept on pads of closed-cell, polyethylene foam with a thickness of about 3/8 inch. These are no sacrifice in warmth and comfort because we avoid camping on hard and cold ground at the overused campsites.

Also, to save even more weight and bulk in our backpacks, we cut our foam pads short. Ours are 36 inches in length, about the size of our torso-print.

These thin foam pads are available in many sporting goods stores and some of the large department stores. Before each journey we buy a new pad. It is generally 72" long and 20" wide, so we cut it in half, making two shorter pieces. Jenny gets one, and I the other. Then we trim each piece to shoulder and hip width. The pads need only match our "torso prints." Specifically, my pad is 20" wide at the shoulder, and at 24" from the top I begin tapering it to a width of 17" at the bottom.

The pads do not need to be under our heads, since we use makeshift pillows of jackets, stowbags filled with spare clothing, or sometimes even packs and shoes. These pillows lie on the groundsheet but extend beyond the top of the pads.

And the foam pads do not need to be under our feet or legs, because the site itself is most often insulated with natural ground materials. Or sometimes we might need a bit of spare clothing under the legs.

In fact, in warm weather and areas of good ground cover, Jenny and I might not use the foam pads at all. We are more comfortable without them.

Still, many people have doubts about the effectiveness of a thin, short pad, let alone using no pad at all. Perhaps the main reservation is the lack of a bedroom-like ambience. We find the concept of comfort has many levels of interpretation, from the hedonistic to the plain and simple. The more time we spend in the wilds, the more we have been able to differentiate between our actual needs and our wants. So the less it usually takes to make us comfortable. The end result is still comfort—we are not sacrificing that—we are merely making a few mental adjustments.

And this is not to infer that we have toughened ourselves to the cold. To the contrary. Extended wilderness trekking tends to deplete a person's metabolic reserves. The longer the outing, the more carefully we have to guard our body heat. And the best way to do that is to select sites that do not sap that body heat.

And too, should we feel a bit of chill working up

through the groundsheet and foam pad, we simply stuff a few items of clothing under us, or put them on.

In desert-like regions where the ground is bare, we look for non-compacted terrain, where, in most cases, the dirt is soft.

What about camping on snow? Early season hikers often encounter plenty of snow, but that does not mean they have to sleep on it. Jenny and I have hiked well over a thousand miles on snow, and we have always managed to find bare earth to camp on. We do this by ending our days at the lower elevations where the snow is not as pervasive. And when we choose to remain higher, we look for isolated pockets of snow-free ground. In late spring, these often exist right up to treeline.

What about camping inside a shelter, like the type found along the Appalachian Trail? If a hiker intends to sleep on those hard wooden bunks or floors, then yes, he or she will probably need the extra cushioning.

The sweet spot

In my teens and 20's I spent a great deal of time hiking and camping. The ground was quite different at every camp; sometimes very lumpy, sometimes only a bump or two, sometimes soft, or sloped, sometimes flat and hard. Each spot had a unique feel to it. I noticed that when I made camp each night, the ground was not too comfortable at any one place. But many times I would awaken the next morning feeling much more comfortable than when I had gone to sleep.

I thought about this, and realized that I had moved a few inches in my sleep, or a few feet, to a more comfortable spot. When I had first lain down, the lumps were not matching my body contours. But in my sleep, I moved over and found a ground contour that more closely matched my body.

I started calling these "sweet spots."

Most of that time I was sleeping under the stars, or under a tarp; and this gave me plenty of elbow room to rove about in the night. In a tent with its limited room I could not have made this discovery. But once I learned to recognize the sweet spots by sight, I could pitch a tent over them.

At the same time, I realized that flat ground is uncomfortable to sleep on because it has no possible sweet spots. It is the same with some beds; one spot is just as uncomfortable as another, causing a person to toss and turn. The body naturally wants to find a more comfortable spot.

In days of yore, campers would dig shallow holes or depressions into the ground for their hips and shoulders. Those depressions seemed to add greatly to their comfort.

To illustrate this theory, if a camper digs shoulder and hip depressions, but falls asleep on flat ground 8-inches

PCT-3

away from the depressions, he or she will likely awaken the next morning in the depressions. Why? In the night, the body found those depressions and stayed there because it was much more comfortable.

I discovered also that the entire body benefits from

sweet spots, not just the shoulders and hips. And taking the discovery a step further, I began to realize that the more un-flat the ground, the more comfortable the sweet spots.

In the 1970's I made several sea-kayaking trips to Baja. At night I would sleep on the beaches, of course, but many of those beaches consisted of smooth and round softball-size rocks. I actually found them comfortable to sleep on because by then I knew the secret. So while my partners slept on the flat sand nearby, I spread my thin foam pad out on the rocks, and a few moments of moving around was usually all it took to find the marvelously comfortable sweet spots.

Modern humans believe they need flat surfaces to sleep on, and would not think of sleeping on ground that is lumpy and filled with depressions. But were they to actually try it, they might be surprised. It might not feel comfortable when first falling asleep, because the person has not learned to fit the body into the sweet spots. But in the night, the body will naturally find them by feel.

So, before erecting your shelter, spread out your groundsheet and foam pad, and lie down on them. Then, shift a few inches, or a few feet, one way or the other, feeling for just the right spot – one that better matches your body contours. Then pitch your shelter there.

––––––––––

With a carefully selected location and a willingness to try a new idea or two, you may be surprised at how little you need to camp comfortably and enjoy a pleasant night's rest.

PCT-2

Umbrella

"Every path hath a puddle."
— Anonymous

I first saw the idea of hiking with an umbrella in Peter Jenkins' book *The Walk West: A Walk Across America II*. Peter and Barbara had attached umbrellas to their pack frames as shade in the hot and arid Southwest. Jenny and I adopted the idea for our second PCT thru-hike in 1991, and found the umbrellas so functional for both sun and rain that we have carried them on all our treks since.

The umbrellas are not our lightest option, especially because we must also carry rain jackets as back-ups, in case a storm brings rain-laced winds of gale force. But they do allow us to hike far more comfortably and efficiently in anything less: from drizzle to downpour to snowfall, and even intense sunshine. While shielding us from these elements, the umbrellas also provide superb ventilation. We like this ventilation when hiking with any degree of vigor – in any climate, hot or cold.

Blow-up of the Grandma Gatewood photo in the "Myth of Heavy-Duty Gear" chapter. In 2008 as I was restoring the Grandma Gatewood image for this book, I saw something that I had not noticed before. What looks like a walking staff is actually an umbrella lashed to a lightweight but strong stick. Grandma is holding onto the curved handle of the umbrella. One can also see the umbrella's trigger mechanism in this enlargement.

Day 2 on our third PCT journey, hiking south from Canada in early season

It helps keep us comfortable and free of the sweat-soaked clothing syndrome. We consider our umbrellas well worth the weight.

Rainy-day comfort under the umbrella

Most hikers know the pleasant feeling of crawling into a tent after a day of tramping in the rain. The umbrella offers much the same protection and comfort, without having to wait for day's end, or even having to stop. As we hike under the patter of raindrops, our umbrellas keep most of the wet off of us. And they cover the top portion of our backpacks as well. When we need to stop and withdraw something from a pack, the umbrella held overhead shields the pack's contents.

Have you ever seen hikers in rain jackets lounging around at rest stops, out in the open during a heavy rain? It does not happen. But the umbrella makes those rainy rest stops quite plausible, and therefore it makes hiking in the rain far more appealing, since a person needs to rest every so often.

If the rain is slanting with wind, we look for a rest stop beneath a sheltering tree; and if we cannot sit on the downwind side of the tree, we simply place the umbrellas close in front of us to block the wind. So, too, on a rainy late afternoon, we can sit cooking dinner using the umbrellas to shield both us and the stove.

When hiking in exceptionally rainy weather, at day's end we will still be wet, at least from the thighs down. The umbrellas do not keep us perfectly dry all of the time, but most likely they will keep us free of the hassles normally associated with rainy weather.

Also with the umbrellas we are free of the rain jackets' restraining hood, able to see ahead and all around while still protected from the dollops.

While hiking beneath an umbrella, my preferred attire is my usual spandex shorts and short sleeve polyester shirt (described in the "Clothing" chapter). If the day is chilly, then I add the shell jacket and pants. These retain considerable warmth, even when wet. And they breathe nicely. Then if the day is chillier still, I wear insulating garments under the shells, and a warm hat when necessary. And in cold conditions, I will wear my waterproof-breathable rain jacket over all these layers, while still sheltered from the rain by the umbrella.

Holding the umbrella overhead

The umbrella can be tiring to hold overhead for any length of time, which is why I do not hold it that way, except in very hot weather when I need the best possible ventilation. Most of the time I let the umbrella ride with the lower edge of its canopy resting on my backpack. In calm weather the "brolly" will stay there on its own. Even so, I hold onto the handle in case a gust of wind tries to send the umbrella flying. I learned the necessity of this after a few spirited chases. And

Day 5 on our third PCT journey; a storm is moving in, and the wind is blowing a gale. We retreated a few thousand feet down the slope and beneath the snow-line made a sheltered and comfortable camp. Next morning we climbed back up to the divide, and resumed our trek.

while holding onto the umbrella's handle, I often hike with a thumb tucked under my pack strap to save effort. I can reach up with the other hand to douse the brolly quickly if needed. In areas of dense vegetation, over-hanging rocks or low tree limbs, it is a simple matter to draw the umbrella partially closed until I have passed the obstacle.

The umbrella in wind

We point the umbrellas into the wind to block both wind and rain. When hit by a gust, we partially close the umbrellas and aim them into the gust. This keeps the wind from getting under the umbrellas and possibly damaging them. In brisk headwinds we might hold the umbrellas in front of us and hike along while peering over the tops. This arrangement provides full-torso protection while allowing us to see where we are walking.

Jenny and I have carried umbrellas on all our mega-hikes except the first one, as well as on the hundreds of training hikes preceding them. And we have carried them on a great many shorter hikes as well. Only once has one come apart, and that was during a storm experienced while hiking in the Three Sisters Wilderness in central Oregon. The incident actually turned out to be instructive: I was using the same umbrella I had carried all summer on a thru-hike, so it was pretty well worn. My

hiking partner that day was using a new umbrella, and, interestingly, his came apart also. These two umbrellas were made by the same company, and were the same size and model. And both, I soon learned, had the same structural defect: a weak wire securing the tines to the shaft.

The fact remains that any umbrella could blow apart in a vicious gust, structural defects or no. So we carry waterproof-breathable rain jackets also. See the Umbrella heading in the "Rain" chapter.

Wind and rain along the AT

Some people are fond of telling everyone about the high winds they have hiked in, and how the umbrella would be useless in such cases. But I think most of these people have not actually tried using an umbrella properly in such conditions. I have hiked in a great deal of rain with high winds using an umbrella. It is extremely rare for me to put the umbrella away in favor of a rain parka. What I do instead is point the umbrella into the storm and partially collapse it. For example, if the wind is coming horizontally from the right, I point the umbrella horizontally to the right. And by partially collapsing it, I take most of the strain off it. The stronger the storm, the more welcome the protection of an umbrella, when properly and carefully used. Hikers should carry storm clothing to wear in rain lashed by strong wind, but they also might find the umbrellas very useful in such conditions.

For sun protection

In addition to rain protection, Jenny and I use umbrellas to shield us from much of the sun's harmful ultraviolet radiation. The umbrellas also block a great deal of the sun's heat. And they will block a great deal more heat if covered with a film of reflective plastic material.

It took us a while to discover all this. While tramping through the Mojave Desert regions of the PCT our first year in 115°-120° F temperatures, we concluded that there must be a more tolerable way to deal with the extreme heat. At the time we were trying to adhere to the traditional methods of desert travel: rising at first light, hiking until the day grew intolerably hot, resting in the shade during the afternoon, then setting off again as the heat begins to subside. The strong sunshine is what made us uncomfortable, far more than the high temperatures. In fact, life in the shade was almost pleasant. Unfortunately, mid-day shade in the desert seemed to be a figment of someone's imagination. When the sun was directly overhead, the shade beneath the scrawny desert flora was far too small to squeeze into. What we needed was portable shade.

On our second PCT hike we carried our own shade in the form of umbrellas. These blocked the sun's ultraviolet radiation, allowing us to hike throughout the day, even in the hottest weather, as long as we carried and drank plenty of water. But the sun's heat still penetrated the umbrella's canopy, and this led me to the idea of covering them with reflective polyester.

The reflective polyester covering

As mentioned in the "Groundsheet" chapter, we use a highly reflective sheet (film) of plastic material to cover

Hiking in 100 degree temperatures, in the shade; PCT 2000

our umbrellas. Look for the "Space brand Emergency Blanket" manufactured by MPI. This is a thin plastic sheet made of polyethylene terephthalate, (PET) generically referred to as polyester film, and coated with a vapor deposited aluminum only one-millionth of an inch thick. Interestingly, this technology was developed for NASA in the late 1950's.

The film looks somewhat like plastic aluminum foil. A piece of this covering an umbrella blocks nearly all of the sun's ultraviolet radiation and about 80% of its infrared heat. Jenny and I now use this on our umbrellas whenever the sun beats down fiercely. (Not to be confused with the reinforced "Space brand *All Weather* Blanket" also described in the "Groundsheet" chapter.)

To fit a piece of this reflective film to the umbrella, we lay the umbrella head down onto a sheet of film, then carefully draw a line on the film around the umbrella canopy, but about an inch away from it. Using scissors, we cut along this line to create an octagonal piece about an inch larger than the umbrella all around. This piece will lie on top of our existing umbrella canopy.

At each umbrella tine (rib) tip, where the film wraps over the tip, we secure the film in place by wrapping it several times with a small rubber band. The most suitable bands are about ¼" in diameter, of the type often available from the dentist or orthodontist. But of course any small rubber bands will do. Between the tine tips we fold the reflective film under the canopy and secure it to the canopy's underside with several small pieces of duct tape.

With heavy use, the aluminized coating will eventually scuff away, leaving the film ever more transparent. This reduces its reflectivity and therefore its ability to block the sun's heat. We take care, then, to protect the covering from abrasion. For best results, we do not attach the film to the umbrella until we need it. Let's say, for example, that we are planning a hike that will take us, in part, through a desert region. Normally we would carry the reflective film neatly folded in a small plastic bag. Before putting it into that bag, we cut it to the appropriate size and include the rubber bands and a very small, flattened roll of duct tape, just enough for the job. When we reach the desert section, we attach the reflective film to the umbrella and carry on. Then when we have crossed the stretch of desert and are back into the shaded forest, we remove the film by unwrapping the rubber bands and carefully peeling away the tape.

When the umbrella is fitted with the film, we avoid shoving it down inside a backpack, where the other gear inside the pack would chafe against it, and over time would rub off the reflective coating. Instead, we carry the umbrella on the outside of the pack, head up and handle shoved down behind a side strap and nestled into the pack's side pocket.

The reflective coating on a piece of film typically lasts for several weeks of continuous use. On longer journeys we include a spare piece of pre-cut film for each umbrella in a resupply box, along with rubber bands and tape. For repairs of small rips or punctures, we use a bit of duct tape.

Modifying a commercial umbrella

The type of umbrella we have used has a 21-inch radius, and weighs 14½ ounces new. I select the type with the fewest complexities. The collapsible, or multi-folding type is not suitable because the extra joints mid-way along the tines are weak points. I then modify the umbrella extensively – taking its weight down to 9 ounces, and its length to 25 inches. I describe the modification process in the "Sewing" chapter.

Umbrella colors

Darker colors absorb more of the sun's thermal radiation. In the case of the umbrella, darker colors also re-radiate more of the sun's heat down to the hiker. Therefore, darker colors provide very little relief from the heat.

In hot, sunny weather, lighter colors are much cooler. The ultimate umbrella color in terms of its ability to reduce direct solar heating is of course the reflective film covering.

In cool, rainy weather, the umbrella's color is of little technical concern. In these situations hikers might like subdued, earth tones, or they might prefer something more colorful and cheery to brighten an otherwise wet and cloudy day.

Rain or shine, with or without the reflective film, the umbrella is an extremely functional piece of gear. I would not think of setting out on a long hike without one.

Hiking up to the snow-line on the IUA

Remaining Gear

"Build momentum by accumulating small successes."
— *Anonymous*

Preparing to sleep in the open on our 3rd PCT trip

Cooking on an open fire

The warmth and flickering glow of a campfire has always attracted people, sometimes in mystic ways, and inspired them to contemplation. And a campfire is a pleasing way to cook for those who have the know-how.[7] But today's dwindling natural resources, and increasing numbers of campers might suggest a person limit the campfires. Especially considering the potential for starting a wildfire.

Unlike the larger campfire that consumes wood like an incinerator, the cook-fire does not deplete the local supply of firewood, since it uses only pencil-size kindling. And because of the small size of its fuel, the cook-fire tends to burn that fuel to powdery ash. This ash is easily buried a few inches below the surface. Properly cared for and eradicated, the cook-fire has very little impact on its surroundings. The cook-fire is my choice for cooking meals *where open fires are permitted*. See the "Campfire and Cook-fire" chapter.

Stoves

There is nothing quite like the cheery hum of a gasoline-type stove. At dawn it quickens the heart with prospects of the new day. And in the evenings it soothes the spirit with its promise of a hot drink and a well-deserved meal. The problem is, the cheery hum might be more like an industrial roar, drowning out the more interesting and enlivening sounds of nature all around. Like an auditory fence surrounding a person, it can command one's attention to the exclusion of the surroundings. So in this section I also cover a few alternatives.

Alcohol stove

Stoves that burn alcohol are quieter than liquid gas stoves, and tend to be fairly simple in construction and relatively light in weight. A number of web sites and magazine articles describe ways of making alcohol stoves from various types of cans. I have made a few of these, and found that they work fairly well.

The alcohol stove heats water slower than a cook-fire, and compared to a stove that burns petroleum hydrocarbons, their heat output is lower, so they require more

---

7 See *Camping and Woodcraft*, or *Camp Cookery*, both by Horace Kephart.

fuel. For longer trips, their overall weight advantage is questionable.

Nevertheless, I like these for the simple reason that they can be home-made; and because of their convenience on a long trip. They burn ethyl (denatured) alcohol or isopropyl alcohol, and these "fuels" are often available in the hardware stores, sold as denatured alcohol, or at trailside grocery stores, convenience stores, and gas stations sold under such brand names as Heet (isopropyl) or Iso-Heet (ethyl). And too, alcohol can be carried in a lightweight container such as a plastic soda bottle.

Denatured or isopropyl alcohol might be legal to ship with one's supplies, or it might not, depending on whom you talk to. Check with your postal or parcel carrier.

In a pinch, these stoves might burn the drugstore variety rubbing alcohols (isopropyl with water) but with less heat depending on the water content.

A person must be careful, however, of not letting the alcohol stove become too hot, by inclosing it in a too-close and too-tight windscreen. If the alcohol in the reservoir becomes super heated, it could erupt suddenly and dramatically.

Gas Stoves (Butane-Propane)

Butane and propane are flammable gaseous hydrocarbons, with small differences in their molecular constituents. Specifically, butane is C_4H_{10} and propane is C_3H_8. They are held as liquids under pressure in the storage bottles, but vaporize as they arrive at the stove burner. Propane puts out more heat for its weight than butane, and it pressurizes better at low temperatures; but it is more volatile in small containers so requires a heavier-walled container. Most gas-fuel backpacking stoves, lanterns and lighters use butane, or at least a mixture comprising mainly butane.

Camping stoves that operate on canisters of compressed butane or propane are legal in most wilderness areas, and they have certain advantages in terms of convenience. They burn more quietly than the gasoline-type stoves. They are easier to ignite; and once lit, their valves regulate the flame better. They burn essentially soot-free, and properly cared for they rarely clog. The cartridges are not legal to ship by air, and they are rarely available in the trailside stores. We have used them, but always had the niggling concern that the empty cartridges were adding to the environmental impact of the landfills.

Gasoline and White Gas Stoves

White gas (Naptha) is a liquid hydrocarbon mixture blended from petroleum. Gasoline (petrol) is white gas with over 200 additives to help improve automobile performance. Unleaded gasoline is gasoline without the addition of lead, to help ease emission toxicity. Coleman fuel, MSR fuel, Blazo, and some others are little more than white gas with coloring dyes added.

Most published stove comparisons give the weights of the stoves, but this is only a part of the picture. When debating the pros and cons of various types, one must keep in mind the weights and bulk of the fuel and fuel bottle, windscreen, primer and cleaning kit.

For a stove with a separate fuel tank, a windscreen placed around the stove will conserve fuel by blocking the heat-robbing wind, and reflecting some of the radiating heat back to the pot. Placing a windscreen around a stove with a built-in tank is unsafe, for obvious reasons.

The longer the outing, the more one must consider fuel availability when choosing a stove. The white gas type fuels are widely available near popular camping areas, and of course unleaded gasoline is available at gas stations. Either type of stove will burn the other type of fuel, but not as well; meaning that its jet will require more frequent cleaning. When burning unleaded gasoline in a stove designed to burn white gas, a person could try placing a small piece of aluminum foil over the air intake, closing off about 25% of its area. This reduces the air-gas mixture ratio.

The stove's jet is the tiny hole that sprays the fuel vapor, under pressure, into the open combustion chamber. The size of the jet (hole) is mainly what determines the type of fuel the stove will burn most efficiently: kerosene, white gas or unleaded gasoline.

Jet cleaning

The impurities of combustion are well known for clogging a stove's jet and weakening its flame. Some stoves come with a "shaker jet," which is a weighted cleaning needle fitted loosely inside the jet's lower passage. Supposedly, all one has to do is invert the stove and shake it a few times, thus running the needle in and out of the jet and thereby cleaning it. Actually, this idea is not new. Decades ago, many of the white-gas stoves had internal cleaning needles controlled by the regulating valve itself. As the flow was turned to maximum, a simple gear shoved the cleaning needle out through the jet. It worked perfectly, and in ten years of cooking on such a stove I never had to disassemble it for cleaning its jet or anything else. My experiences with the modern jet stoves have not been as trouble free.

The job of cleaning a jet manually is an inglorious one, but after many hours of fiddling with white gas backpacking stoves in the Arctic, I developed methods for doing the job most effectively.

Regardless of whether my white gas or unleaded gasoline stove has a shaker jet or not, I carry a jet-cleaning kit. This kit contains a jet removal wrench as supplied with the stove, and a jet-cleaning needle that typically does not come with the stove, but is usually available at backpacking shops. These jet needles are far thinner than any sewing needle or pin. I also include a small piece of fine steel wool.

I start by unscrewing the stove's jet with the wrench.

Then I tear off a pinch of steel wool and twist it to a size that I can just force into the back cavity of the jet nipple. This is used to scour out the cavity. I tear off another small pinch and repeat the scouring until the steel wool comes out clean, and the inside of the jet is shiny. Then comes the important part. With the steel wool inserted loosely into the cavity, I prod the other side of the jet with the cleaning needle. This forces the jet's debris into the steel wool. Without the steel wool, the needle would poke the debris into the cavity and leave it there; then the next time I used the stove, the debris would re-clog the jet.

The cleaning needle is delicate and must be protected. The best way I have found is to duct-tape its handle (not the needle itself) to something flat and hard, such as the side of a small plastic bottle in our first aid kit. Along with the jet-cleaning needle, I also tape down our sewing needles.

Fuel bottles can leak

Many hikers have discovered that fuel bottles can and do leak. If carrying fuel inside the pack, one should keep it wrapped in a plastic bag and away from any food. And be sure to depressurize the fuel bottle after each use to minimize leakage.

Our backpacks accommodate the fuel bottle in an external mesh side-pocket, where any leakage can evaporate. If your pack does not have such a pocket you could sew one onto the pack.

Prohibited baggage

If traveling by air to your intended trail, be aware that camp stoves, fuel bottles and fuel are not permitted in either checked baggage or carry-on bags. Sometimes— but not always—you can bring with you a partially disassembled and air-dried stove, and possibly an empty and air-dried fuel bottle with its lid removed. If in doubt, call your airline representative. However, you should still plan to buy your fuel at your destination. You may also have to buy your stove and bottle there, or your could mail them using UPS Ground or Parcel Post, (checking with your UPS or postal authorities first) to a destination near your trailhead where you would then pick them up.

The dangers of carbon monoxide

Cooking inside a tent may be convenient in foul weather, but it is decidedly unsafe. The stove could explode, and while such incidents are uncommon, they are not unheard of. The stove could flair-up wildly, which is not so uncommon. The stove could ignite a too-close article of clothing, the sleeping bag, or the tent itself. One careless swing of the elbow could knock the stove over, spilling scalding liquid, soaking everything, and melting a hole in the tent's floor and groundsheet.

Another very real danger is that of the stove filling the tent with deadly carbon monoxide. As the hot gases of combustion rise to the ceiling, they accumulate – despite an open doorway and the ground-level ventilation around the fly's perimeter. The gases are odorless, and what makes the poisoning so dangerous is that it produces no appreciable symptoms. One minute all is apparently well, and the next minute the person is sprawled on the floor, unconscious – never to recover unless someone drags him or her outside to fresh air. In his book *Arctic Manual*, Vilhjalmur Stefansson wrote, "If you watch carefully, a feeling as of pressure on the temples can be detected for some little while, perhaps only a few moments, before you keel over."

The can stove

Can stoves burn natural materials—twigs, bark, pinecones—in an enclosed container. Where open fires are prohibited, a person might still be able to use this type of stove because the flames are contained in a metal enclosure. When in doubt, check with the local authorities.

I refer to these stoves as "can stoves" because I have made a number of them from cans. If constructed properly they work surprisingly well, although not as well as the cook-fire or a stove that burns gas or liquid hydrocarbons. But the real advantage is the availability of fuel (wood) all along the way.

To make one of these rustic stoves, remove the top of a large (46 fluid ounce) juice can, then cut a few sizeable air-intake holes in the can along the bottom edge. These holes should extend about a third of the way around the can's circumference. The fresh air enters the can through these holes, is heated by the fire, then is expelled out the top of the can. Therefore, when using the stove, it helps to position the intake holes into the wind. If you make the holes too small they will plug with ashes, but you can clear them from the outside by poking a stick into the holes. The best way to cut the holes is with a sheet metal nibbler, after drilling a starting hole, or punching it with a large nail. You can also use only the nail. Simply punch the outline with numerous holes until the tab breaks free. Use a block of wood under the metal to keep the can from collapsing. Whichever method you use, be careful of the sharp edges. In addition, cut a few holes along the top edge to act as pot supports. Without these, the pot would smother the flame. One feeds sticks into the can from the top.

Certain manufacturers are making much more complex can-type stoves with battery-powered fans. The fan supplies the burning materials with more oxygen, so the flame is spectacular. I have experimented with these stoves, but much prefer the simple can type, mainly because it does not need a battery, and because it is lighter.

Obviously, if you are using a can-stove or its battery-operated counterpart, you will need twigs and other natural materials to fuel it. These you can collect along the way, prior to cook time. If the woods are wet, then you will need to carry at least enough kindling to get the stove running, collected in advance. Once that is burning, it will dry what kindling you add that is moist, as long as you add it slowly.

As with preparing to build any fire, search for dry twigs at the base of trees and beneath overhanging rocks and logs. On a very wet day you can also carve slivers from the inner wood of larger dead branches. This inner wood will be dry in any kind of weather. Before packing up, make sure to extinguish the last of the embers.

Stoveless hiking

Jenny and I have experimented extensively with non-cook foods. And we have hiked for weeks without a stove, eating pre-cooked and dehydrated foods. So it can be done, but we have never found it satisfying, nor particularly energizing. In our minds, the energy and vitality provided by freshly cooked meals is well worth the trouble.

The main reason for not cooking would be the danger of attracting grizzly bears, such as in Glacier and Yellowstone National Parks. To us, this is a valid reason.

Cookpot

Traditionally, backpacking cookware was made of steel. Then aluminum became common, then stainless steel, and currently we have titanium. Cookpots made of titanium are more expensive than their aluminum and stainless steel counterparts, but they are lighter than stainless steel, and stronger but a little heavier than aluminum.

I have used aluminum pots for many years, but after researching the matter I now suspect that aluminum in contact with food and water may pose certain health risks. Some cookpots come with plastic, non-stick coatings. These coatings facilitate cleaning, and they prevent

the food and water from contacting the aluminum. Yet I wonder whether even these coatings are safe.

Our trips tend to be rather lengthy, so we like to start each one with a new, two-liter cookpot. When new, the bottom can be slippery, so I might use coarser-grit sandpaper or a rock to scrape the bottom repeatedly until it is no longer as slippery. Most everything here is based on experience, and the bottom-scuffing treatment is no exception. The first evening of a long sea-kayaking trip, Jenny and I watched our brand new cookpot slide off the stove and send our meal crashing headlong into the sand.

Some types of cookware come with the company's name and logo printed on the lids. I remove these with paint remover followed by a light scraping with fine-grit sandpaper.

Jenny and I share a 2-liter pot. When solo, I find anything smaller than 1.5 liters is too small.

The cookpot should have a lid of some sort – either a fitted lid or, to save a bit of weight, a sheet of aluminum foil. The lid conserves stove fuel by keeping the heat in, and any ashes from the cook-fire out. It also prevents any flying insects from sacrificing themselves into the pot, which for some reason they are apt to do.

A handle extending from the side of the pot is a convenience, but unless it folds flush against the sides, it would create unnecessary bulk and difficulties when stowing the pot inside the backpack. The separate handle, the type that clamps onto the side of the pot, is a good idea in concept, but it is another item to carry and to keep track of, and possibly to lose. If you use one of these, make sure that it is in serviceable condition. You would not want it to slip off a heavy pot of boiling water.

I prefer a simple wire bail. This supports the pot from above, and when not needed it swings down out of the way. The wire bail gets hot, so to lift the pot by the bail I use a stick. If the cookpot did not come with a bail, I drill a pair of holes in the pot, one on each side near the top, and run a wire through them. For specifics see the "Campfire and Cook-fire" chapter.

When we use a cook-fire, or a stove that burns natural materials, the outside of the pot will blacken with soot. This is actually beneficial because a blackened pot transfers heat to its contents better. To prevent the pot, in turn, from blackening the contents of our pack, we keep the pot in its own stowbag. If you use a gas stove and want to reduce its fuel consumption without adding another gadget to your inventory, simply fill the pot with water, suspend it over a wood fire for a few minutes, and let it blacken with carbon. A blackened pot will bring the water to a boil a little faster.

Cup, bowl and spoon

To reduce pack-weight, bulk, and the inglorious task of post-meal cleanup, we carry only the bare minimum of cookware.

A person can eat from a small, plastic bowl; and afterwards use it as drinking cup. And if that bowl has a tight-fitting lid, then one can shake and mix drinks in it, carry cooked food in it stowed inside the backpack, and fill it with prepared food from home or a trailside store or restaurant. During our first three thru-hikes, Jenny and I used three-cup capacity, cylindrical-shaped lidded bowls. On the AT we improvised, using small cottage cheese or deli tubs, or at times the bottom section cut from a soda bottle. Continuing with the weight saving measures, on our fifth journey we dispensed with bowls and cups altogether, eating our hot meals directly from the cookpot, and sipping the infrequent hot beverage from the pot as well.

On all our journeys we carry one plastic spoon each. Our preference is the tablespoon size made of polycarbonate, and sold under the brand name Permaware™.

See the "Hygiene" chapter for methods of sterilizing the utensils.

Water bottles

Having tried all sorts of commercial water bottles and hydration systems, we much prefer the ordinary grocery-store type bottled water bottles with 1½" wide screw-on lids. These are strong, lightweight, and inexpensive. The narrow-mouthed water and soda bottles also serve well, as long as they have screw-on caps. If the bottle does become damaged we can usually repair it with duct tape, and buy a new soda bottle at the next outpost along the way. Most importantly, by changing bottles every few weeks we avoid the accumulation of fungi.

Water bottles, bags and bladders are well known for cultivating stubborn splotches of fungi known as "water mold." This mold can impart an unpleasant, musty taste to the water. The type of water bags worn against the hiker's back tend to accelerate the formation of water mold, since the heat of the body warms the water and encourages microbial growth.

At any rate, the foul taste of the water mold can be difficult to remove from any type of container. One method we use is to fill the container half full of treated water, and add a scoop of clean, dry sand; taking care, of course, to keep the sand off of the threads, because it can score the seal. After screwing the lid back on, we shake the container vigorously to abrade away the mold. Then we dump out the mixture, and rinse the bottle and lid with more treated water. Then we use a small, sharp twig to clean the threads inside the lid.

Typically we each carry a single, one-liter bottle on the trail. And when traversing long, dry stretches we each carry a 2½ gallon water bag also.

Knife

Everyone has their preferences as to what type of knife they like to carry while hiking. I have seen everything from magnum-sized hunting knives with 8-inch blades, to the "toolbox" type Swiss Army knives.

My preferred knife is the diminutive Victorinox Classic. With its single, 1¼" folding blade we open food packages, sever cord, slice vegetables, and cut packaging tape to length. The scissors we use to cut adhesive tape and 2nd Skin, to cut fingernails and toenails, and to trim hangnails. With the knife's file we round our trimmed nails. And we use the tweezers to remove any splinters or ticks. All this utility costs us a mere 0.8 ounces.

Such a small but useful knife is easily lost among the leaves and pine needles at camp. To make it more conspicuous, both on the ground and while contained within the ditty bag, I affix a short length of bright orange parachute cord.

Any kind of blade can dull with use, especially when cutting cardboard. If you are planning a long distance hike that will require resupply boxes, you will probably find yourself sitting outside various post offices cutting cardboard boxes down to size for sending things home or ahead. Cardboard is very abrasive, and for this job you could use a small, disposable-blade utility knife. Rather than carry this with you, you could place it in your drift box (see the "Resupply" chapter).

If hiking in wet terrain we carry a fixed-blade knife with a 4" blade for carving into wet branches to make dry tinder. We use this type of knife also for making our bow-drill sets.

The Tub

The tub is a versatile addition for the hiker out for more than a few days. Jenny made the one we used on our first two thru-hikes, by cutting the top off a 2½ gallon collapsible water jug (Reliance™). We found all manner of uses for this tub, including collecting water, carrying water to camp and storing it there, settling sediment, containing water for filtering, pouring water into the Hiker's Friend water filter bag (see the "Sewing" chapter), laundering clothes, and pouring water onto ourselves when bathing. At 2.8 ounces, the tub was reasonably lightweight, and because it folded nearly flat, it occupied little space in the backpack.

Washing socks in the tub, PCT-2.

Wristwatch

When buying a wristwatch, I select a women's size small. Machismo aside, this fits my wrist better, and it is less bulky and lighter in weight. And I choose one that is waterproof to at least six feet, so that I do not have to be careful about getting it wet. The watch also has an alarm and a night-light. And it shows the date and the day of the week, since on the longer trips a person can easily lose track of them. In most cases, the day of the week is not important, except when heading for a resupply station. Post offices normally close on weekends, and in some small towns nearly everything shuts down. Knowing the day of the week helps us plan to arrive at the resupply towns on weekdays.

Stopwatch

During our training forays, we use the stopwatch feature of the wristwatch to time the duration of our outings. This data we enter into our training log. Also during the training hikes of our first two thru-hikes, (not on the actual journeys) we used the watch's countdown timer at rest stops. Set at ten minutes, it would remind us to be moving along. In this way we conditioned ourselves against the tendency to linger at those rest stops.

Dead reckoning

One of my more important uses for the wristwatch is for dead reckoning. This term comes to us from those who sailed the square-rigged sailing vessels, and the method was, and still is, an important component in any navigational plan. It works on the concept that speed multiplied by duration equals distance traveled. For example, if we hike at 3 mph for 2 hours, then we know we have covered 6 miles. I try to look at my watch at each known point, such as a signed trail junction, a high pass, a lake, or a road crossing. If later I become confused as to my whereabouts on the map, I look at my watch again and "DR" my distance hiked from the last known waypoint. On moderately graded trails I find that an assumed hiking speed of 2¾ mph in my calculations yields the most accurate results. Of course, on steep climbs or rough terrain this figure will be reduced.

As an example, say I have hiked for three hours from a road crossing clearly shown on the map. Looking at the map, I know that I am about 8¼ miles beyond the crossing.

Wristwatch holder

I like to rise at the first hint of dawn, and while on journey I use an alarm to wake me at that time. If I wear the watch on my wrist during the night, I might not hear the alarm. So each evening when retiring I remove the wristwatch and place it near my head. In the days when I used tents, I sewed a hook-and-loop tab to the tent wall, onto which I hung the watch. Or, as described earlier, I have sewed such loops to the underside of some of our tarps, and waterproofed the seams on the outside with sealing compound.

The watch band

A plastic watch band can restrict ventilation and irritate the wrist. I choose a watch that comes with a band made of breathable, quick-drying webbing.

Particularly on longer hikes in warm climates, a person's wrist can swell considerably during the day's walking. The watch band will have to be long enough to accommodate that. The difference in the size of my wrist, from when I rise in the mornings at home, to when I retire at night during a thru-hike, is four holes on the watch-band.

Compass

I prefer a basic, uncomplicated compass with only the features I need. These are: a rotating housing, and a minimal-friction bearing.

If you do not know whether your existing compass has a quality bearing, here is a simple test. Lay the compass on a table. After the needle has settled, rotate the compass base with imperceptible slowness. Note the angle at which the bearing releases and allows the needle to swing back to magnetic north. Repeat the test in the other direction. If the discrepancy is more than one or two degrees in each direction, the bearing is not a low friction type. The Silva 7NL (also known as Type 1-2-3) weighs 0.7 ounce including its lanyard, and is my long-time favorite.

A person proficient at taking field bearings by hand can achieve an accuracy of ±1½°. Those who are not

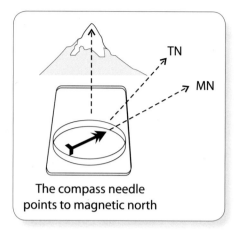

The compass needle
points to magnetic north

might prefer a type of compass having a sighting mirror. Sloppy navigation can cause unnecessary confusion, which could lead to a difficult situation. But it depends on the trail. On the CDT I used my compass so often that I frequently carried it in my shirt pocket. On the PCT I used the compass only rarely, but a few times it saved the day. On the AT I did not carry a compass.

Some types of compasses feature built-in adjustments for the local magnetic declination. This feature is of little benefit to the person who cannot remember whether the adjustment is supposed to be set to the left or right. The problem is that most hikers are never quite sure whether to add or subtract the declination. My mnemonic might help.

▶ Along the PCT and CDT, the compass needle points a little east of true north, as though honoring the AT.

▶ Along the AT the needle points a little west of true north, as though honoring the western trails.

Depending on whether you are hiking in the east or west, you will therefore know whether the needle points left or right of true north. If you are hiking in the Midwest you could examine a map showing magnetic lines of flux, and locate the line of zero declination relative to your own location.

Now that you know which way the needle points, you need to know whether to add or subtract the declination:

Field-to-Map – Add.

F—M—A (First Man Adam).

When taking a bearing to a distant mountain, then setting the compass down onto a map, you are going from field to map. Field to Map: Add. So you add the declination before setting the compass onto the map.

When reading a bearing on the map, then raising the compass and pointing it in the direction you want to travel, you are going from map to field. You are reversing the procedure, and therefore you would subtract the declination.

In the eastern states you would add the negative declination when plotting from field to map. For example, along the Appalachian Trail in Maine the declination is about 20 degrees west of true north, or minus 20. So you would add the minus 20 to the field bearing before plotting it on the map. Say my field bearing is 300 degrees; I would add the minus 20, to give me 280 degrees to plot on the map. When going from map to field, you would subtract the negative declination: if the bearing on the map reads 280 I would subtract the minus 20 declination for a field bearing of 300.

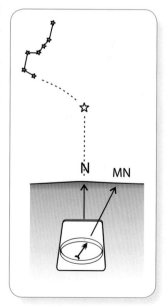

Most maps give the local magnetic declination of the area they depict. One can also measure declination directly by taking a bearing to Polaris, the north star.

Innate sense of direction?

Years ago, a climbing partner

and I were descending one of Colorado's 14,000-foot mountains in inclement weather, when a cloud moved in and reduced visibility to a scant hundred feet. Coming to a drop-off, we rigged a sling and used our rope to rappel down. Continuing down another three hours, we eventually came to something that stunned us momentarily senseless. Our rappel sling at that same drop-off! There was nothing for it but to rappel a second time. In another hour the sky began to clear, and eventually we found our way down to camp. In retrospect, we somehow must have walked all the way around the mountain. But this was incomprehensible, since we felt that we were descending in a diagonal fashion the whole way. I mention this to suggest how easily one can become disoriented.

Experiments have shown that a blindfolded person attempting to walk directly from point A to B on level ground will wander far off track, while believing that he or she is traveling in a straight line. The tendency to deviate is caused mainly by a difference in leg length and strength, left and right. I have witnessed the same effect when paddling with a group of sea-kayakers, crossing a large bay. With different arm strengths, some will veer far to the left, and some to the right. And after regrouping at the distant headland, everyone claims to have been the only one paddling in a straight line. In fact, I have seen paddlers veer so far away that they nearly disappeared from sight.

As I hike along a trail, or cross-country, I try to keep track of my direction of travel. And I check my external compass every so often and see how well my internal compass is doing.

Of course, if the day is clear or only partly cloudy, then I remain aware of the sun's position. I do not have to actually look at the sun to do this. Instead, I watch the direction of the shadows as the day progresses.

Flashlight

Jenny and I find a small flashlight useful on extended hiking journeys. Not because we cannot see our surroundings without one. In all but the thickest forests we usually can see by the subdued light of the stars. We use a flashlight because it allows us to night-hike at our daytime pace. In rattlesnake country, it also helps us avoid unfavorable encounters. When searching out a good campsite, the flashlight illuminates any poison ivy or oak. And after settling into camp, we like to spend some time writing by flashlight in our journal.

While hiking at night, we hold the flashlight much lower than eye-level, so it will produce the best shadows and therefore the best definition. Holding it at eye level washes out most detail. This is why everything looks flat when using a headlamp.

When a flashlight begins to fade, one can extend its life by using it only intermittently. Switching it on only momentarily will give you a quick glimpse of the way ahead, enough for you to "memorize" the scene. Then when you have hiked to the end of your memory, repeat the switching on-off process. You can use a disposable butane lighter in the same way, even one that has run out of fuel. Simply flick the Bic, and memorize the terrain ahead in the flash. I once found my way out of a mile-long cave this way, when my lamp ran out of carbide.

For the most efficient and lightest weight flashlight, choose one with high-intensity LED bulbs powered by one AA or AAA battery. Familiarize yourself with the battery changing procedure ahead of time, when you can see what you are doing.

At the time of this writing, lithium batteries cost two or three times as much as alkaline ones. They last about three times longer, however, and are lighter in weight. One should never dispose of batteries in the wilds; over time they damage the ecology. This is especially true of lithium batteries.

When not on journey I rarely carry a flashlight. Unless in known rattlesnake country, I much prefer to hike at night by ambient light alone. A flashlight blinds me to the surroundings, with the exception of a red light. Hiking at night without a flashlight necessitates a slower pace, but allows for a much better awareness.

Journal

When we journey into the backcountry, Jenny's and my senses expand and we start to notice more detail. We make observations, perhaps learn lessons, philosophize, and possibly find some answers. Being in the wilderness also lends itself well to contemplation, and this is why we find that keeping a trail journal is extremely worthwhile. Recording those bits of wisdom, the observations, and the many interesting details of our hikes may not seem important beforehand, or even at the moment, especially when we are tired. But months and years later we enjoy reminiscing, and reliving our experiences through our trail journals. Some people record only the basic daily data: the weather, where they camped and how many miles they hiked. Others record some of the details of what they saw, who they met, and how they were feeling.

Journal writing has no limits. As one long-distance hiker pointed out: "The more you put into your journal, the more you will get out of it." And as Oscar Wilde quipped: "I never travel without my diary. One should always have something sensational to read on the train."

Each evening Jenny and I write an average of three pages on both sides. As a weight savings measure we prepare our own writing pads ahead of time, containing only as many pages as we will need, since an excess of paper can be surprisingly heavy. Figuring the number of days hiking between any given pair of resupply points, and multiplying this number by the three pages per day, we know how many pages we will need on that stretch of trail. We remove that many pages from a narrow-ruled pad measuring 6" by 9", and either staple them together along their top edges, or tack them together with a couple of stitches using a hand awl.

We carry our trail journal in a resealable plastic bag, along with maps and any other paperwork, which again we try to keep to a minimum. And we send each section of journal home from the resupply stations.

Ditty bag

We each use a ditty bag to hold our assorted knick-knacks. We make these bags small, and usually of light-weight nylon fabric. For details on size and construction, see the "Sewing" chapter.

I have learned over the years that small items left lying about camp or a rest stop are all too easily left behind or lost. So after using an item, we make it a practice to return it into its ditty bag. If the smaller items are brightly colored, then we can locate them easier.

At camp we keep all our belongings centrally located. Those socks hanging to dry in the tree – over there. They might be left behind. Or a water bottle left on a stump; a pocketknife and spoon left on the ground; a hat left on a rock, and so on.

When setting off from camp, or from a rest stop, we walk a few paces then turn around and inspect the area for anything we might have forgotten.

Zippers

To extend the life of a zipper, and to make it easier to slide, we rub some wax on the teeth or coils. Any kind of wax will do: beeswax, paraffin, even an old candle. You can buy spray lubricants for zippers, but wax works just as well.

The sawing action of the zipper teeth—even nylon coil or plastic molded teeth—will eventually wear out the slider. A worn slider will slide, but it will not zip the two halves together. One way to improvise a temporary repair is to reduce the size of the slider's aft end by crimping it slightly. In lieu of pliers, try using one small rock as an anvil, and another as a hammer.

Ice axe

For your own safety, carry an ice axe wherever you might encounter steep slopes with snow covering the trail. You can expect to find such conditions just about anywhere in the high country, at least from October through June. This means that even the casual day hiker visiting these regions during any season except mid-to-late summer may require an ice axe.

The AT thru-hiker can generally get by without an ice axe. But along the PCT and CDT, an ice axe and self-arrest skills are essential. For more information on the hiker's ice axe and how to use it, see the "Snow" chapter.

Gaiters

Gaiters are a type of ankle covering, originally designed to keep the snow from entering the boot tops. Many hikers use knee-high gaiters while ambling along a bare trail. The intent is to keep the gravel and dirt out of the boots, and to protect the legs from poison ivy and oak, and insects such as blackflies, ticks and chiggers.

I find gaiters necessary only on endless miles of snow tromping. On snow-free terrain, anything covering the clothing and footwear restricts ventilation and causes overheating and sweating. Rather than try to keep the dirt and gravel out of my shoes, I tie the laces loosely so that I can stop when necessary and remove and empty the shoes without having to untie and re-tie the laces. But on a long day of hiking I might stop to do this only once or twice. At each rest stop I remove the shoes and bang the small amount of dirt and grit from them.

Back in the days when Jenny wore lighter fabric boots, she improvised a pair of gaiters by cutting the forefoots off a pair of old socks. She slipped the resulting tubes over her lower calves before putting on the boots, then pulled

On the CDT in Montana

the bottom part of the makeshift gaiters down over the top of the boots. These kept the grit out of her boots.

We wear the shell pants ("Clothing" chapter) in conjunction with the usual lightweight nylon socks to protect our legs from poison plants and biting insects. If the blackflies are particularly bothersome, we tuck the pant legs into the socks; or in some cases we might apply repellent to the calves just under the pant legs.

Climbing rope

First and foremost, a rope should never be used to assist

a river crossing. For a discussion of the dangers, see the "Creek Fording" chapter. In skilled hands, a rope can sometimes increase the safety on a snow slope. If one person slips, the other can stop that person from sliding off the mountain by holding the rope in a special way known as belaying. As with any piece of equipment, this requires know-how.

One person hiking solo would have no use for a rope when negotiating a steep snowfield, or for any other aspect of a hiking journey. Two people hiking together, both of them well experienced at snow travel, would not need a rope because they would be adept at the ice-axe self-arrest and at judging and avoiding the dangers of a snow slope to begin with.

Where the rope can be handy is when one person is experienced and the other is not. The experienced person can use the rope to safeguard the inexperienced partner. With two inexperienced people the rope can be doubly dangerous; for if one person slips the rope could wrench the other off balance too. So if you are thinking of carrying a rope for snow safety, be sure that at least one person in your party has plenty of experience with it.

For the weight-conscious, a 20 foot length of 7-millimeter Spectra rope might be best. Spectra is very strong and lightweight, but it is also slippery and does not hold some of the more basic knots very well.

Early one morning Jenny and I climbed up to snowbound Glenn Pass, in the Sierra. The ascent went well, but as we began heading down the other side we found the snow frozen hard. Stomp as we did, our boots barely indented the surface. This was not a problem for me because I was accustomed to edging aggressively with my boots. I was also used to the exposure of the mountainside dropping away far below. But not so, Jenny. She slipped and quickly self-arrested, but not before her weight came partially to bear on our safety rope. We were using a 20-foot length of polypropylene, which (as

I learned that day) is so slippery that it does not hold a bowline knot very well. In an instant my knot untied itself from around my waist, and I found myself hanging onto the rope with my hands. This meant that I could not drop down into a self-arrest; I would need both hands on my axe for that.

Fortunately, this was not an immediate concern. I was quite secure on my feet. Jenny was in no danger either, she was pinning herself securely to the slope with her ice axe. But the slope was frozen so hard that she could not kick footholds, so she had no way of standing back up. And because I no longer trusted the knots in the rope around her waist, I could not use the rope to assist her to her feet, lest it suddenly come lose and throw her off balance. So I stomped my way down and moved into position beneath her, and used my axe to quickly chop her a set of footholds. With these she easily stood up. I tied a figure-eight knot around her, secured with a couple of half-hitches and leaving plenty of free end. I did the same with my end of the rope around me, and together we proceeded down the slope without further incident.

Snowshoes

Snowshoes can be quite useful when negotiating soft and moderately sloped snow. But while most trails seem gently graded, they are often cut across steep slopes. When these slopes are covered in snow, the "trail" becomes steeply sloped in the lateral direction. In such conditions snowshoes are decidedly unsafe, since they cannot be edged into the slope like skis or boots, for security. They tend to slide off the trail sideways.

Most hikers who have carried snowshoes have not found them sufficiently useful to justify their weight and bulk. Proper timing can eliminate their need altogether. Snow that is soft enough to require the use of snowshoes has not yet consolidated. This condition indicates merely that the hiker is there too early in the spring season – or far too late after summer has passed into autumn.

In early season you may find yourself slogging in mush or postholing. This is especially true in the late afternoons when the sun has been softening the crud all day. At night, if the sky is clear (allowing radiant cooling) the surface will start to re-freeze. In the very early mornings, then, this frozen crust will probably support your weight, and this is the best time to make tracks – miles of barely indented ones.

Mid-June in Washington. In the afternoon, our shoes are sinking in a few inches into the softening snow. PCT-3

Skis

Skiing across the alpine heights in early season requires a very high level of proficiency. This is especially true in light of the consequences of a skiing-related injury in the remote backcountry. If a person is sufficiently skilled, and if the snowpack is deep and pervasive, then skis might be well worth considering. However, in late spring when the snow has coalesced, one can walk on the snow's surface most of the time. So in terms of making miles, I think waiting and walking is easier and more expedient.

Crampons

Strapping on a pair of crampons and venturing across a steep and frozen snow slope might seem like a safe way to proceed. But without the skill to use these implements, they can be dangerous. First, they allow a person to more easily climb into a very exposed position. And second, they can then fail that person. Crampon failures happen in a number of ways, mostly through error or misuse. In order for crampons to function properly, obviously the person wearing them must remain upright. But while negotiating a steep slope, one could easily lose balance

and fall. Among the possible scenarios, the person could catch a crampon prong on the other crampon or its strap, or on a pant leg or gaiter. A crampon clip or strap could work loose, or a tooth or other metal component of the crampons could fracture. The person could stumble on an unseen dip or rise. Or he or she could experience a moment of vertigo, due to unfamiliarity with the exposure, and lose balance. Moreover, if the snow is wet, it can stick to the bottom of the crampons and accumulate with every step until the hiker is walking not on perforating spikes, but on slippery snowballs.

As discussed in the "Snow" chapter, the proper way to stop a fall, for someone sliding down a slope, requires a three-point contact with the snow. The three points are the pick of the ice axe, and the toe of each boot. But the person wearing crampons cannot so much as touch the crampons to the snow's surface because the crampon points can grab the snow and possibly cartwheel the person wildly out of control.

If you need crampons to climb a frozen slope, then in most cases you are there too early in the day. The morning's warmth will probably soften that snow within a few hours, and allow you to kick perfectly adequate steps.

Bivy sacks

Most bivy sacks are lighter and more compact than tents, making them seem like an attractive option for lightweight hiking. I do not favor them because of their lack of ventilation. A bivy sack is also heavier than a tarp for a fraction of the living space, and it tends to be more expensive. It provides little or no shelter for the backpack and other belongings, no place to set the wet clothing, no convenient place to cook out of the rain. Its singular advantage is its small footprint, useful in areas with little open ground, such as high on rocky mountainsides. This type of adventuring is beyond the scope of this book.

Re-Centering

Choosing all the right gear can be a challenge in itself, but regardless of the length and nature of your outings, if you compile your gear carefully, taking only what is necessary, and leaving behind the superfluous, then you are likely to travel more easily, and with your mind focused more on your natural surroundings.

So as you peruse the many tempting racks of clothing and gear display cases, stop occasionally and re-center yourself. Think about how that gear is affecting you emotionally. Judge whether or not it will lead you to a more meaningful outing with a better understanding of the natural world and a closer connection to it. And do not let any of that gear become your main focus. Otherwise, the real beauties of the hike—the priceless gifts of nature—might be lost.

I like to think that life is more than money and merchandise. So I encourage the making of one's own outdoor clothing and gear. And no doubt a person could strike a compromise and do a little home sewing and a little shopping, and come out very well. But the experience is more important than the gear. If an item of equipment helps a person achieve a closer connection with the natural world, then that equipment is worthwhile. If it fails to serve this purpose, then maybe one could modify it, or discard it and try something else. But the important thing is simply to set out, and to enjoy your outings for all they are worth; which will surely be a great deal.

Part 3

ESSENTIALS

In the remote mountains of Idaho on the IUA

Trail Life

Clothing

"There's no such thing as bad weather,
only a poor choice of clothing."
— *Norse proverb*

The search for what works best

In our pursuit of the most functional wilderness ward-robe, Jenny and I have tried and tested what seemed like every imaginable type of outdoor wear, looking for what worked best in various conditions. With these garments we have taken day hikes, overnight trips, weeks-long wanders, and full-summer thru-hikes with their mega miles and preliminary months of conditioning forays.

In the process, we have put this clothing to the test in climates ranging from the desiccating hot with intense sunshine, to muggy hot, to freezing cold with snow. And we have tried these garments against insects, wind, inter-minable rain and brush.

We have sought out garments that were the lightest in weight and the least in bulk. We needed them to be warm on cold days and cool on hot ones. They needed to be breathable in order to minimize sweating, and easily laundered by hand and fast to dry.

We make our own outdoor garments

Of course, we tested a fair amount of commercially man-ufactured outdoor clothing. Yet very little of it worked well for us. We sometimes had the feeling that the design-ers were more intent on creating outdoor fashion state-ments. And while we appreciate appearances, the reali-ties of wilderness travel were teaching us that a garment's performance was far more important.

So too, the outdoor clothing manufacturers sometimes capitalize on a person's fears of the unknown, trying to convince them to carry a wide assortment of heavy and bulky items. As if the wilds can only be survived inside an expensive, all-weather fortress. Our experience has not born this out.

So we began making our own outdoor clothing. Free of commercial restraint, we spent many years creating, testing, and returning to the proverbial drawing board for further refinement.

Eventually we settled on a very modest selection of home-made garments that we feel offer the best possible performance in all but the most wintry conditions.

At first glance these garments might seem simplistic. But they work together synergistically in the widest pos-sible range of conditions. The reason we strive for effi-ciency in our clothing, and think of it as a system, is that we must carry it in a wide variety of conditions. And by now, the advantages of a lighter weight pack should be evident.

Our clothes are comfortable, durable, highly versatile, and very packable. And taken as a whole, we feel their efficiency is unmatched.

Garment descriptions

This list reflects our own personal inventory. Jenny and I have found these articles eminently suitable during a normal hiking season. Depending on your hiking style, you may wish to experiment with these or other options. My intent here is simply to offer the benefit of our expe-rience, and perhaps to serve as a catalyst in your own thinking.

Shell jacket and pants

These are intended to protect us from thick brush, to block the wind, and to rebuff ticks, which seem to find these garments too slippery to cling to. Also designed to thwart mosquitoes, blackflies and other biting and crawling insects. The shells also provide a moderate amount of warmth, especially when worn over the other garments.

I call them "shells" because we often wear them as a protective outer layer over one or several inner layers. But in warmer weather we might wear them alone, for example on a hot day as protection from bugs or brush. These garments are so versatile that we carry them on all our backpacking trips, regardless of whether we are day hiking or thru-hiking. We often sleep in our shells when out in the wilds. And we even wear them in the Arctic while distance-canoeing and sea kayaking, and when relaxing around the tundra camps.

Our shell jacket and pants are performance oriented, no-frills items. Made of nylon or polyester, they are single-layer, lightweight and loose fitting. We use an uncoated fabric for optimum breathability, allowing sufficient ventilation for the hard working muscles, even in warm weather. Yet the shell garments still block the wind very nicely. And the fabrics are woven with sufficient tightness to block stings and bites from mosquitoes, blackflies and other insects. Unlike mosquito netting, the shell jacket and pants can lie directly against the skin, for example at the shoulders and elbows, and the bugs cannot penetrate it. As mentioned, these garments are ideal wherever the trail is overgrown in brush.

I have added no extraneous zippers, flaps or designer features, since these only add weight and bulk. The jacket has a full-length, front-opening zipper for greatest ventilation when needed. It has a pair of zippered cargo pockets for stowing mittens and so forth. And it has a small breast pocket with a zipper for keeping small items handy, such as compass or keys. The sleeve cuffs and waist-band are elasticized and fit snugly to block insects.

The pants have an elasticized waist-band and leg-cuffs,

and a small chafe patch inside each ankle where the shoes may brush against the pant legs.

Polyester shirt

My hiking shirt is short sleeve, loose fitting, and made of lightweight polyester. In the right weave, this fabric is highly breathable, and amazingly fast drying. Other 100% synthetic fabrics such as nylon (Supplex and taffeta) would work reasonably well. As with all my recommended garments, the shirt is very simple. It opens fully in the front for ventilation, and it closes with buttons. It features a standup collar to help shade the back of the neck. In other words, it looks like a casual dress shirt, except that it has no cotton content. It can be worn alone in warm weather or as an inner layer in cold weather. It is also my garment of choice when hiking in very hot temperatures where going shirtless would be socially inappropriate. And when freshly laundered, dundo style (see "Hygiene" chapter) it is suitable for wearing in trail towns.

> Certainly the needs and preferences of other hikers and campers for different types of clothing may differ widely. What we are describing here is only what works for us.

Hiking shorts

These are less restrictive than long pants and of course cooler. This is important on warm days since the muscles of the legs will work more efficiently if kept cooler.

One option is loose fitting shorts made of nylon taffeta or Supplex. These are breathable and quick-drying. Side pockets add utility but reduce breathability and ease of drying.

Leg chafe can be a serious problem with some hikers, and ordinary loose fitting shorts will rarely prevent this.

Leg chafe results when the moist skin of the upper thighs rubs together while walking. The resulting irritation may prompt the hiker to apply a lubricating ointment, but this only clogs the pores and collects dirt. Or the person might stuff a bandana between the legs; this can help in an emergency but only marginally.

My solution is to wear shorts made of spandex, like bicycle shorts but without the padding. Spandex is a nylon-blend stretch knit commonly known under the Lycra® trade name. Spandex shorts fit somewhat snugly around the upper legs, especially on the inside of the thighs where we may need the chafe protection. Because they are sheer, and since they stay put, the material can rub against itself all day long with no discomfort to me. I like them snug enough to prevent chafing, yet loose enough for long-term comfort.

I have hiked over 18,000 miles in spandex shorts, and find that one pair will easily last me an entire summer. I choose black because this color is the least revealing. Still, I avoid wearing them in trail towns, although most townspeople are becoming more accustomed to seeing bicyclists and joggers wearing them.

Spandex shorts could serve as underwear, although in warm weather any extra layers would promote and retain more sweat. Some hikers prefer to wear spandex underneath to eliminate chafe, and a pair of looser fitting shorts over them for appearances.

Another option to shorts is the skirt. Jenny has hiked many thousands of miles in skirts. Made of polyester, they are comfortable, she says, and fast drying. I have heard of guys hiking in kilts; those would be the same idea.

Thermal shirt

This is a long sleeve, pullover shirt made of a thermal wicking fabric such as polypropylene or Thermax. It can be worn alone, in combination with the short sleeve polyester shirt, or as "long underwear" beneath other layers such as the shell jacket. This shirt is reasonably fast-drying, yet because the fabric is thicker than the lightweight polyester shirt, it is more insulating. I wear the thermal shirt for its added warmth, for example on cold days while hiking, at rest stops, around camp, and while sleeping during extra-chilly nights. In unseasonably cold weather one could wear two or more of these shirts in combination, same with the pants, below.

Thermal pants

Made of the same material as the thermal shirt, these pants keep the legs warm while hiking or resting in chilly to moderately cold conditions. They are rather loose fitting for ease of knee articulation, and can be worn alone or under the shell pants when the cold is accompanied by wind, and of course at night.

Insulated jacket

The typical fleece jacket may be comfortable to wear around camp, but it tends to be fairly heavy and bulky for its rather limited warmth. I prefer a light-weight jacket with a thin layer of synthetic insulation. Such a jacket is lighter than most fleece jackets, even with an insulated hood attached, yet it is much warmer. Our jacket features a full-length, front-opening zipper for utmost ventilation when needed, and a pair of zippered hand-warming pockets. A person could wear it while resting alongside the trail, and while lounging around camp. Normally one would not hike in it, as this would cause overheating in all but the coldest climes. One can also sleep in this jacket, or use it as a pillow, or as a cushion under the legs for added ground insulation.

Umbrella

This is our primary protection from rain, used instead of the rain jacket in all but the most blustery weather. The umbrella provides superior ventilation as it shields us from the rain. In so doing it can make the difference between a soggy, dreary day on the trail, and a pleasant one.

The umbrella also offers welcome relief from intense sunshine, such as in open, treeless regions. In extreme heat and sun, I cover my umbrella with solar-reflective film. While not essential, this affords even greater protection from the sun's intense heat and ultraviolet radiation. See both the "Umbrella" and "Rain" chapters for details.

Rain Jacket

Used in rain accompanied by wind too strong for the umbrella. Like our other garments, the rain jacket is a no-frills item. Made of a two-layer waterproof-breathable fabric, it is light in weight, loose fitting, breathable and packable. It features a hood and a full-length, front-opening zipper for improved ventilation when needed. In fact, my rain jacket is virtually identical in design to

A chilly morning on the IUA

my shell jacket; the only differences are that the rain jacket is made from waterproof-breathable material, and is fractionally larger. When fully unzipped it can be worn backwards, the advantages of which I describe in the "Cold" chapter. For more information on the rain jacket's features, uses and limitations, see the "Rain" chapter.

Rain Pants

While hiking in the rain, I do not normally wear rain pants, since they tend to restrict the needed ventilation. The problem is one of condensation inside the rain jacket and pants, described in the "Rain" chapter.

To me, the rain pants are an emergency item kept in the pack for an unexpected rain or snow storm. Rain pants can also be useful while ambling in rain and wet brush at a leisurely pace, and while sitting around camp on a drizzly afternoon.

The rain pants are made of the same material as the rain jacket and are very basic in design. They have an elastic waist with a drawcord, and leg cuffs that are left open (no elastic) for better ventilation.

Socks, thin nylon

For hiking in warmer weather I prefer thin nylon socks, sold inexpensively in clothing and department stores. These socks are highly breathable, meaning that they contribute only marginally to foot sweating. And they are easy easily washed by hand and quick to dry. In fact, I sometimes rinse them in cold water, dundo style, wring them out, and put them right back on. In my opinion these thin nylon socks perform better than expensive sports socks, and in cool to moderately cold weather I wear two or three pairs for added warmth. The right kind of thin nylon socks are extremely durable, typically lasting me thousands of trail miles. The wrong kind, namely the ultra-thin varieties, can wear out in a single day. I test my newly purchased socks for durability during my training hikes.

Socks, medium weight, wool-synthetic-blend

For cold weather hiking I sometimes wear medium weight (thickness) wool-blend socks. I say "sometimes" because where possible I much prefer wearing multiple layers of thin nylon socks, even in very chilly weather

– and especially in wet weather. Why? Because the thin nylon socks dry much faster, meaning that in intermittently wet weather my feet do not stay wet. That said, medium weight wool-blend socks are faster drying than heavy weight wool-blend socks, so in very cold conditions I might double up on the medium weight socks.

Wool provides reasonable warmth when wet, but wool by itself is poorly resistant to abrasion. So I select socks that have a blend of synthetics, preferably with more wool than synthetic; for example 70 percent wool and 30 percent nylon.

Even with the synthetic blend, these socks are not long lasting. Three hundred miles is about my limit with wool-blend socks, which on a longer hike is around ten to fourteen days. Even with everyday washing, the wool-blends slowly glaze and lose loft. And once softness is lost, the socks begin "fossilizing" into what feels to the feet more like sandpaper. If I anticipate long periods of cold and wet conditions that would call for wool-blend socks, I carry a few extra pairs or place extras in the resupply parcels.

Mittens, fleece

These are nice to have, even in only moderately cold weather. As a person hikes along, the hands are relatively inactive; but they do swing forward and back with the normal walking action. The swinging tends to pool the blood in the hands and hampers circulation. So once the hands become chilled, they tend to stay that way. Mittens prevent the hands from chilling in the first place.

I prefer synthetic fleece mittens because they are lightweight, warm and reasonably fast drying. Mittens made of wool are heavier, bulkier and much slower drying. My hands tend to sweat in thick mittens, particularly while hiking, so in most conditions I wear very thin mittens. However, if I know I will be hiking in cold conditions I bring along mid-weight fleece mittens in addition to the thin ones, so I can layer them as needed. If caught short, a person could improvise with spare socks.

Mittens are much warmer than gloves. Gloves have more surface area and most of this lies between the fingers where it robs them of heat. In mittens, the fingers share their heat.

Bomber hat

Made of breathable nylon enclosing a layer of synthetic insulation. We wear the bomber hats during cold days along the trail, at rest stops, and at night while sleeping. We use them also in wind too strong for the umbrella. They protect the head without restricting one's field of vision like the hood of a parka does. See our website for details. For use in cold and wet conditions, we sometimes make our bomber hats using a waterproof-breathable fabric for the outside layer. But usually a breathable fabric works best.

Skull-cap

In addition to the bomber hat, I usually carry a simple "skull-cap" made of a lightweight thermal fabric for use when the bomber hat would be too warm. I make the skull-cap long enough to pull down over my face at night while sleeping. The material is easy to breathe through, yet it keeps the face nicely warm. On very cold nights, one can wear the bomber hat over the skull-cap.

The bomber hat and skull-cap are essential components of my cold weather clothing system. This is because one's head tends to radiate a comparatively large amount of body heat. I often use one of these hats as my primary means of regulating body temperature while hiking. Which hat, depends on the temperature. The minute I begin to overheat, I remove the hat. Should I later begin to chill, I put the hat back on, before putting on more clothing, because often the hat alone restores the needed warmth.

Wide-brimmed sun hat

Used in moderately sunny conditions when the umbrella is not needed. Used also in strong sunshine when the wind is too gusty for the umbrella. My sun hat is made of nylon taffeta and has an encircling brim. The brim is stabilized by an internal wire, which I fit around its perimeter. This keeps the brim from flopping down in front of my face in gusts of wind. When the hat is not needed I stow it inside my pack carefully to prevent bending the wire, or I tie the hat to the outside of the pack. The hat also has a chin-strap made of thin cord, for use in strong wind.

Head net

Made of no-see-um netting, for use when the mosquitoes are swarming. Used on the trail, at the rest and meal stops, and at camp. In swarms of bugs we often wear the head-nets under the hoods of the shell jackets to reduce the sometimes irritating hum and whine of the ravenous insects. Otherwise, we wear the head-net over the wide-brimmed hat, which keeps the netting away from the face and off the top of the head.

Shell mitts and booties

Made of shell jacket material (breathable nylon) and worn in buggy conditions along with the shell jacket, pants and head-net. The shell mitts protect the hands by virtue of the fact that insects cannot penetrate them, even where these mitts contact the skin. In this regard, mitts and booties constructed of no-see-um netting are wholly inadequate. The shell mitts and booties spare us from the effects of chemical repellents. The shell mitts can be worn anytime; while the booties are very useful at buggy trail stops where we might want to remove our shoes and socks in order to relax in comfort. Both the shell mitts and the booties are suitable for use on bug-ridden nights when we are sleeping beneath an open tarp or under the stars.

Shower booties

Made of coated nylon, these protect the bare feet from athlete's foot fungus and other parasites usually endemic to the floors of public shower stalls and on motel room floors, showers and bathtubs. The booties have elastic around the tops, much like a pair of upside-down shower caps.

The layering approach

When the temperature drops, many hikers tend to over-protect themselves by putting on clothing that is too thick and heavy. This can cause overheating and sweating, even while hiking in the coldest of temperatures. And when the garments become sweat-soaked, they are far less serviceable.

Enter the layering approach to keeping warm (and cool). Here, we select garments that are thin and lightweight, and in harsher weather we wear these garments one on top of another.

As an example, say we start out on a beautiful, sunny morning wearing a lightweight polyester shirt and pair of shorts. A frontal system moves into the area, and we begin to feel the temperature dropping as the morning progresses.

So over the shirt and shorts we put on our shell jackets and pants; and for a few hours this is the most comfortable arrangement. Any more clothing would make us sweat. But as the ambient temperature continues its decline, soon we need a bit more warmth. So we remove the shell jacket, don a thermal shirt over the polyester one, and put the shell jacket back on.

Now wearing three layers on the torso, we continue ahead, once again in comfort. Then in a few hours, as the temperature decreases further, we remove the shell pants, put on the thermal pants over the shorts, and put the shell pants back on. And we pull on our warm hat and mittens.

If the wind increases, we don our wind-proof rain jackets. At the rest stops we may don the insulated parkas and pull their insulated hood over our heads. Or we might use the quilt as a wonderfully warming robe.

The layering approach is important in several ways. It affords a greater comfort range by enabling small adjustments, as we don and doff relatively thin layers. It keeps us comfortably warm without sweat-soaking everything. And it makes for faster drying of all our garments, since each is less thick than the heavy-duty types. The faster our clothes can dry, the less the storms will affect us.

The key here is comfort. Never do we allow ourselves to become chilled (or overheated). If we feel the need for more layers, we put them on.

Cotton and hypothermia

The ubiquitous cotton T-shirt – comfortable when clean, rather less so when dirty, and very slow to dry even in warm weather. In fact, a cotton T-shirt is so slow to dry that the hiker usually does not bother washing it. And with the passing of days and weeks, as the shirt grows ever more soiled and odiferous, it begins acting as a people repellent and a bear attractant.

On a cold day, when cotton becomes wet—from sweat for example—it can sap body heat. Cotton fibers are hydrophilic, meaning that they absorb moisture. This is why the hiker who wears cotton, and who sweat-soaks the garments in cold weather, will be socializing with hypothermia at every rest stop. Even as little as a few percent cotton in a garment is unfavorable.

Certain synthetics (like polyester and polypropylene) are hydrophobic, meaning that the individual fibers do not absorb moisture appreciably. (Nylon is fractionally absorptive, making it somewhat slower drying than the true hydrophobics.) Any synthetic garment will be as cold as cotton when wet. However, the synthetics are faster drying; so in essence they are much more forgiving, which helps explain their popularity in today's outdoor apparel.

Wool is an exception. It can preserve at least a measure of warmth when wet. However, because of its weight and bulk, most hikers find it of limited use. The only wool applicable to lightweight hiking we use is the wool-blend socks.

People sometimes experience reactions to synthetic fabrics. Generally, the fibers themselves are inert, but some of the chemicals added to them can cause sensitivities. Which is not to infer that cotton garments are chemical-free either. But for most people, synthetic hiking garments offer the best performance, comfort and safety.

Optimum color

Often the tendency is to choose the color of one's garments based on personal preference. But when hiking in various weather conditions, color plays a significant role in a garment's performance.

Light colored clothing blocks solar radiation better, meaning that it absorbs less heat. This is extremely important when hiking under a hot sun, especially during the height of summer. Light colors also radiate less heat away, helping us stay warmer on cold, cloudy days and at night. And light colored clothing is less attractive to flying and biting insects. Ticks, which are generally brown, are more conspicuous on lighter colored clothing.

Dark colored clothing absorbs more solar heat, and this works against us on a hot, sunny day. On a cold, sunny day, the dark color may generate needed warmth, but only for the parts of our body facing the sun. That same dark clothing will radiate valuable body heat on the shaded side of us. However, because dark clothing is again a good radiator of heat, we can use it in hot, shaded regions, at least when we need to cover ourselves fully because of mosquitoes or biting flies.

If I had to choose only one color, it would be a light one, since most of the hiking I do is in sunshine. Even in the Appalachian Trail's "green tunnel" a lighter color will not attract as many flying insects and will make the presence of any ticks more obvious.

Laundering

Washing clothes by hand is rarely convenient. But clean clothes are far more comfortable to wear and they are warmer and longer lasting than soiled ones. Also, they are less prone to attracting unwanted wildlife into a camp. So if we will be hiking for more than a few days, we wash our clothing regularly. And since these garments are light in weight, the washing will be easily done.

I try to rinse my polyester shirt and spandex shorts near the end of every day, along with my socks, usually at the dinner stop if water is handy. If I have soap, then I rub a small amount on the garments. Soap is not critical; rinsing alone will suffice. Whether or not I use soap, I am careful to wash and rinse the clothes well away from the natural water sources, to keep from polluting the water. Normally the best way is to use the dundo method, which I describe in the "Hygiene" chapter. This involves collecting water in a water bottle or cookpot, then moving well away from the water source and pouring that water over the garments. I hold the shirt or a sock in my hands and scrub the material against itself vigorously. Then I mix in a very small amount of soap if I have it, scrub again, and rinse well. The rinse is the most important step, since any remaining soap residue can irritate the skin.

On our first two thru-hikes Jenny and I carried a "tub." Filled with water and carried away from the water source, it served as a basin for hand laundering clothes. See the "Remaining Equipment" chapter for details about this 2.8-ounce option.

If planning an extended trek, our garments will probably wear out. Regular laundering will help forestall such problems, but still we may need a replacement shirt or two, along with a supply of extra socks. We plan ahead and include these in our resupply parcels.

Clothing stowbags

Dry clothing inside our backpacks is precious cargo. But since backpacks tend to leak in rainy weather, and pack covers often fail, our spare clothing may become wet unless we take precautions. To protect our garments, we keep them in a waterproof stowbag. See the "Rain chapter" on "Keeping things dry inside the backpack."

In an emergency or unexpected situation, a person can usually turn to nature for added warmth. Look for a natural windblock, and build a fire. Stuff your clothing with natural insulating materials such as grasses, leaves, pine needles and moss. These provide the same dead-air spaces that the insulating jacket and sleeping bags do, and depending on how much of these natural materials you use, their potential for warmth is practically unlimited. They even work reasonably well when wet. If you become cold at night, you can cover your quilt or sleeping bag with the same kind of natural materials.

Footwear

"It is better to wear out one's shoes
than one's sheets."
— *Genoese proverb*

I think of my footwear as the link between my feet and the ground; between my envisioned goal and the path that leads me there. So whether I am aspiring to an occasional ramble through the woods near home, or a multi-month thru-hike, I give my footwear some very careful thought.

Hiking barefoot

A person's feet are naturally light in weight, flexible and full of sensory receptors and transmitters. As we walk barefoot, the nerves in the soles of our feet provide our brains with a wealth of tactile information. This sensory data augments our sense of spatial orientation and balance, and it brings us more in tune with our environment. In fact, there is something Neolithic and sensual about hiking barefoot through a quiet, needle-carpeted forest, or a trail of soft dirt, or even on glacier-polished and sun-warmed granite.

PCT-2

The human foot contains 126 ligaments that interconnect 26 bones. These interconnections form working, flexing joints that allow the foot to better accommodate irregularities of terrain by shifting side to side, twisting, and flexing. Stiff footwear restrains much of this beneficial flexing and give-and-take action. And the stiffer the footwear, the more clumsy and difficult the person's walk, and the more fatigue and chances of sustaining a debilitating stress injury.

Practically every day while training for a long thru-hike, and during the hikes themselves, I remove my shoes and hike barefoot for half-an-hour or so. This keeps my feet tough, both internally and externally. And if I am experiencing leg pains after a month or so on the trail, quite likely they will disappear after I walk only a short distance barefoot. Therefore, it seems that those pains are caused, not by the interminable hiking, but mainly by the footwear.

This is especially true for the blister-footed hiker in the early stages of a longer journey. Walking a short distance barefoot is great therapy for ailing feet.

The methods for walking barefoot are completely different than for walking in shoes or boots. Mainly, the bare foot does not strike the ground with the heel. Heel stomping is unnatural and requires extra cushioning in the shoe. Rather, the technique is to land on the outside of the forefoot, roll to the middle of the forefoot, then lower the heel. In this way a person walks more gently and gracefully, and with less stress. And to avoid a stubbing or puncturing injury, I slow down and watch where I am placing my feet.

At the same time I would not want to hike barefoot for more than half-an-hour. Any more than that would slow me down too much, and create overly-thick calluses. Thick calluses are the result of the abrasion of walking combined with the excessive ventilation. Because of the dryness, thick calluses are subject to cracking. The cracks are unable to heal, because callus is dead tissue. Yet the cracks can cause considerable pain, since they work down into the underlying live tissue. More on this in the "Foot Care" chapter.

Moccasins

Jenny and I have hiked many miles in moccasins, and find them the next best thing to walking barefoot. We have even worn them on cross-country trips of a hundred miles and more. We make our own moccasins based on a hard-sole design of the Ute Indians. For more information on making moccasins, see the *Craft Manual of North American Indian Footwear* by George M. White, and the moccasin making section of *Blue Mountain Buckskin* by Jim Riggs.

Sturdier footwear

When hiking barefoot or in moccasins, we place the feet carefully, and with much less force than if wearing sturdier footwear. In shoes or boots, we can tromp along with considerable vigor. This allows us to hike at a faster pace, but it also increases our chances of incurring a stress-related injury, and of course it alerts the wildlife at a considerable distance. Still, sturdier footwear has its advantages. Shoes or boots protect the toes when accidentally kicking rocks, roots and pointed sticks. The carbon-rubber soles allow us to walk with little attention to the sharp rocks, cactus spines and needle-tipped pine cone scales underfoot. The soles insulate the feet from temperature extremes. And they act as barriers to parasites that could auger into the feet when stepping on manure in various stages of decay, something that is unavoidable on many trails.

Experimentation and experience

Growing up in the foothills of the Colorado Rockies, I hiked a great many trail miles and climbed scores of peaks in stout, leather boots. In the early 1970's, when I began instructing outdoor programs, I started hiking hundreds of miles each summer. For the first few years I hiked in leather boots, but I also carried a spare pair of running shoes for use around camp. The shoes, I came to realize, were much more comfortable. So in my third year I began hiking in them. This worked surprisingly well, except that I had to carry the boots in my pack, and they were much heavier and bulkier than the shoes. I quickly grew tired of carrying that extra weight, so I simply left the boots at home.

Hiking in running shoes was practically unheard of at the time. Most people believed that without the support of boots, the ankles would buckle under the load of a backpack. Yet my ankles did not buckle, or even complain. This was true even though I have steel pins in a lower leg from a spiral fracture during a skiing accident, and a flattened arch from a karate sparring mishap. In spite of these old injuries, or perhaps because of them, I found that with less weight on my feet I could cover the miles easier. Most importantly, the soles of the running shoes provided better traction. What I discovered back then was that the aggressiveness of sole tread is entirely secondary to the frictional properties of its rubber. The day I started wearing running shoes was the day I stopped slipping on wet rocks and crashing into creeks. Another benefit was that the shoes were more economical. This was important because the summer's earnings had to last me the entire year.

Years later when Jenny and I first hiked the PCT, the snowpack in the High Sierra was 120% above normal. We spent the entire month of May wallowing through it, en route from Kennedy Meadows to Tuolumne Meadows. We had planned on a wintry adventure, and most of our gear handled it reasonably well – except the sturdy leather boots. Once they became soaked, they stayed that way. And each time we applied waterproofing compound, we only made them heavier. Reaching Tuolumne Meadows we sent the boots home. I switched back into running shoes, and Jenny her lighter-weight fabric boots, and we continued on to Canada.

During our second PCT journey we again traversed

PCT-3

the High Sierra in early season, but this time late enough so that the snow had consolidated – meaning that we could generally walk on top of it without sinking in. Even though snow covered the ground most of the way, we hiked from Kennedy Meadows to Tuolumne in twelve days. This was less than half of our previous time. We both wore lighter-weight fabric boots on the steeper sections, and running shoes on less steep snow and the occasional stretches of bare ground.

On the Continental Divide Trail we wore running shoes the entire way, and with excellent results. Even on the steeper snow slopes in Glacier National Park we found the shoes perfectly adequate, but of course we carried ice axes and a short length of climbing rope. Because running shoes dry so much faster than boots, we did not worry when they became wet during the drenching spring rains and the scores of river crossings in Montana. Yet we did experience one problem near the end of the trip, among the prickly weeds of New Mexico. The

stickers dropped into the spaces between our ankles and the shoes, and made walking painful. Lacking gaiters that would fit over our running shoes, we used a bit of duct tape, and that solved the problem.

Running shoes proved ideal for our thru-hike of the Appalachian Trail; more on this to follow. On our third PCT hike, which took us southbound, we wore ultra-lightweight fabric boots during the initial few weeks through the snowbound North Cascades. In weight, these "boots" were only marginally heavier than a pair of lightweight running shoes. The specific make and model is no longer in production, but I mention them only to illustrate the possibilities. Once out of the snow we retired the "boots" and wore running shoes the rest of the way, along with sandals for a bit of variety.

Boot fallacies

During all these experiments with boots and running shoes, I tried to look at the pros and cons more objectively, rather than simply accept the standard practices. What follows is my reasoning, based on my own discoveries.

The ankle-support myth

Most hikers who wear stout boots believe they need them for ankle support. But if hikers need boots for ankle support, then logically they would also need crutches for hip support and braces for lower back support. Which of course is nonsense. What hikers need is not ankle support, but ankle strength. Weak ankles are a result of walking mostly on flat floors, sidewalks and stairs. By design, these level surfaces do not stress the ankles in the sideways direction. Civilized, yes, but they leave the ankles unprepared to handle the irregularities of natural terrain. Boots attempt to rectify this, but they only introduce a host of problems. A far better solution is to strengthen the lateral muscles and ligaments of the ankles and feet. A person's ankles were meant to sustain the weight of body and backpack, without external support, and to transport him or her over rugged ground for hundreds and even thousands of miles. And in every probability those ankles will do so, safely and without problems, if first they are strengthened by conditioning. See the "Physical Conditioning" chapter for details.

Hiking rugged terrain safely

One of backpacking's greatest fallacies is that sturdy boots allow a person to negotiate rugged terrain safely. The truth is, boot-clad hikers suffer leg and foot injuries practically every day of the summer, in all kinds of terrain and weather. I know several people who have broken legs or sprained ankles while wearing sturdy boots. The summer that we hiked the Appalachian Trail, four people suffered serious mishaps on the slopes of just one mountain (Mt. Moosilauke) all in sturdy boots. Boots actually contribute to such accidents in a number of ways.

Boots reduce a person's tactual awareness of the

Rugged terrain on the AT

terrain underfoot. In lightweight footwear I can feel the earth beneath me. This is a huge advantage. If I happen to step on something that might twist my ankle or throw me off balance, I immediately sense this. My feet rush the message to my brain, and the brain directs me to quickly lift that foot, and put it down somewhere else. This is known as autonomic reaction, and it is something innate in

121

everyone. Yet heavy footwear prevents the feet from fore-knowing of these missteps, and once the person places his or her weight fully down, it could be too late.

Heavier footwear reduces the accuracy of one's foot placements, while restricting mobility and dexterity. The person wearing boots or heavy shoes might aim to step between two basketball-sized rocks on the trail – and miss. Down for the count of ten. Why? Because of the difficulty of aiming a heavily-weighted foot in motion, and of regaining balance after a poor placement.

Can you imagine driving a cement truck on a twisting, winding race-course? No, a sports car would be better. And to me, that is the difference between heavy footwear and lighter running shoes. The more rugged the terrain—with rocks and roots, steep slopes, difficult tread and boulder hopping—the more maneuverability I need. The lighter the shoe, the more maneuverability it provides.

Protecting the bottom of the feet

But don't we need stiff-soled boots to protect our feet from bruising – for example when stepping on sharp-edged rocks, or when accidentally kicking trail-embedded rocks and roots? Massive boots protect the feet from these occurrences, but they also cause the hiker to kick and stumble on them in the first place. By virtue of their size and weight, they make the hiking clumsier.

During our second PCT journey, Jenny and I walked a ways behind a fellow who hiked with a unique style. Several times a minute he kicked roots or rocks, slipped on mud, or skidded a ways recklessly down intervening snowbanks. But each time he immediately corrected, and threw himself adroitly back into balance, as a matter of course and apparently without giving it any thought. Jenny and I were wearing running shoes, and were just as subconsciously avoiding those rocks and roots, and treading on the mud and snow more deliberately so as

not to stumble and slip. For this fellow, the terrain was full of obstacles that required sturdy boots. To us, the trail seemed mostly obstacle free, and our soft shoes performed very well.

One might argue that hikers in running shoes spend all their time "watching their step," and that they therefore miss most of the scenery passing by. But in actual fact, boots do not exempt anyone from the need to watch where they are stepping. Inattentiveness could lead to injury due to a slip or stumble. This is not to suggest I constantly watch my feet. Instead, I move my eyes in a continuous sweeping motion, from the immediate foreground to the scenery, back and forth, side to side. With practice, this sweeping pattern has become routine. And it helps me avoid kicking rocks and tripping on roots, while at the same time allowing me to enjoy the scenery.

The Appalachian Trail has a reputation for terrain so rugged that it requires stout boots. Following Grandma Gatewood's example and our own usual practice, Jenny and I hiked its full length in running shoes. We found the trail remarkably rugged in many places. In particular, veteran hikers told us that we would never make it through the notoriously rocky sections of Pennsylvania in our running shoes. But we had no problems with the rocks there or anywhere else. One might imagine that our running shoes slowed us down as we watched every step. Actually, they shortened our trip's duration dramatically. Not because they allowed us to hike faster—we always try to maintain a moderate pace—but because they made the walking easier, and therefore they allowed us to spend more of each day hiking comfortably.

Kicking steps in steep, hard snow

But don't we need stiff soles in order to kick steps in steep, hard snowpack? Yes, and this is why we travel through the alpine regions in spring and early summer equipped with two types of footwear: a lightweight boot

Kicking steps in steep, hard snowpack; PCT-3

where best to strike. The hiker's legs would constitute equally suitable targets unless covered by exceptionally thick pants or snake chaps. In snake country, boots do not lessen the hiker's need to watch where he or she is stepping.

Advantages of running shoes

Let's take a look at some of the advantages of running shoes.

Kinetics of the footstep

Imagine you are resting beside the trail, watching a hiker striding past. The hiker is moving ahead at a steady pace – say three miles an hour. But each foot is starting and stopping with every step. You might better visualize this by "walking" two fingers across a tabletop. When a foot is on the ground and the hiker's weight is on it, that foot does not move. Its forward speed is zero for that moment. Then taking the weight off the foot, the hiker's leg muscles accelerate it quickly forward while taking the next step. This quick acceleration requires muscular effort. How much effort depends on the mass of the leg, foot and the footwear. A person cannot reduce the mass of legs or feet, but he or she certainly can select less massive footwear. As an extreme example, imagine walking with your feet encased in concrete blocks. The heavier the footwear, the more difficult the walking. The lighter the footwear, the easier the walking.

More miles, no extra effort

I estimate that each 1¾ ounces removed from a shoe or boot (3½ ounces for the pair) can add about a mile to a hiker's daily progress. One-and-three-quarter ounces is not much. It is about the same weight as a pair of expensive cushioning insoles. But it is enough to degrade progress by one mile each and every day.

I might put this into even better perspective. Replace a

of moderate stiffness for trouncing steps in steep snowpack; and a softer shoe for making easier miles across hard crusted snow and open ground. We do not need our boots to be board-stiff in order to provide adequate purchase. They could be lighter-weight fabric boots that feature good "toe-bumpers" (the welt around the toe area) for kicking steps, and sturdy edges for biting into hard, steep snowpack. The skier on steep, hard snow "sets" or digs in with the edges of the skis for purchase and security. We do the same with the boots. On steep snow, we use the edges for security, much more than we rely on the stiff lug soles. When the snow is frozen too hard to kick steps with our lighter-weight boots, we have two options. We could chop steps with our ice axe. Or more preferably, since the spring snow typically freezes at night then re-thaws in the morning, we could simply wait a few hours for the morning sunshine to soften it.

Snake protection

Aren't stout boots good protection from snake bites? For the feet, yes. For the legs, no. And remember that pit vipers use their infrared (heat) sensors to decide pair of medium-weight leather boots weighing 3 pounds, with a pair of medium-weight running shoes weighing 1 pound, 5 ounces, and with no extra effort find yourself hiking 7½ more miles each day.

Imagine two people beginning a thru-hike of the PCT together. They are equally well conditioned, they carry packs of equal weight, and they eat the same kinds of foods. The only difference is that one wears stout boots while the other hikes in lightweight running shoes. On the first day the boot-clad backpacker covers, say, 11 miles. With no more effort, the hiker in running shoes walks 18½ miles. The running shoe hiker reaches the

PCT-3

first resupply station, 50 miles into the journey, 1½ days ahead of the other. And he reaches trail's end 1¾ months ahead.

All other factors being equal, the thru-hiker in running shoes is capable of covering that trail in seven weeks less time. But what usually happens is that this hiker

simply takes it easier, hiking the trail in 4½ or 5 months while spending less time on the trail each day. The lighter footwear makes the journey less work. On shorter trips, hikers can reap these same benefits, hiking further each day if desired, or at least covering the intended miles with less effort.

The handicap of stiff soles

Stiff soles place great demands on the hiker's calf muscles and Achilles tendons. Technically, I could discuss this in terms of the shoe or boot's longitudinal center of effort. This is the theoretical point about which the sole pivots with each step. The stiffer the sole, the further forward is its center of effort, and therefore the greater the effort of walking in that shoe or boot. As an extreme example, imagine walking with boards strapped to the undersides of your feet and extending in front of your toes. The farther the boards extend forward, the harder your calf muscles must pull, in order to lift your heels. The stiff shank of a boot or a stiff-soled hiking shoe acts in the same detrimental way.

Therefore, when trying on a shoe or boot prior to purchase, I test the stiffness by grasping the toe in one hand and the heel in the other, and bending the sole as it would bend when taking a step. A person could compare this stiffness to his or her everyday street shoe or trainer. If the hiking shoe or boot in question is quite stiff, it will add considerably to the stress in the legs.

Mid-foot cushioning

Another reason I prefer hiking in running shoes is the heel and mid-foot cushioning they provide. Foot ailments are common among runners, so the makers of running shoes have gone to great lengths to design their products for maximum comfort and cushioning. The makers of hiking boots think differently. In general, they are more concerned with heavy-duty construction and durability.

Running shoes easier to break in

New boots are often quite difficult to break in. In the process they tend to "break in" the hiker's feet instead. For after all, the boots are tough and durable, like the advertisements claim. If the boots fit properly, then all may be well. But if they do not fit properly, then they will continue to conform the hiker's feet to the shape of the boots. This can weaken the feet, and while such an arrangement may be tolerable for a few miles, it can eventually lead to pain and even injury. Running shoes are more soft and supple, and require very little break-in time, if any.

Tread softly for minimum impact

A stiff-soled boot providing maximum security on steep snow can be very damaging to the exposed alpine soil and its sensitive plant ecology. Hiking and backpacking are gaining in popularity, and the detrimental impact of the lug soles found on boots and trail-running shoes is becoming ever more pronounced. This is particularly apparent in places where the ground is soft or moist, such as in delicate springtime meadows and along high alpine trails. For this reason, when descending out of the snow, we change into softer-soled running shoes at the first opportunity.

Renowned climber Steve Roper originated the Sierra High Route, one of the more rugged and challenging treks in America. In his guidebook to this route, *The Sierra High Route, Traversing Timberline Country*, Steve recommends wearing running shoes to reduce the impact on the fragile alpine ecology. This is a strong statement in favor of both wilderness preservation and the suitability of running shoes for handling difficult terrain.

Footwear for cold and rainy conditions

The prospects of extended wet weather used to intimidate me. I knew that my socks and boots would become soaked, and that they would stay that way for days. When I freed myself of the boots and started wearing running shoes instead, I left behind the anxieties the boots were causing.

Boots in rain

We have all seen magazine ads showing boot-clad hikers stomping melodramatically through puddles. These ultra-wet conditions supposedly necessitate heavy boots. But are boots capable of keeping the feet dry? In my experience, leather boots might deter the pervading wetness for a day or two, depending on their quality and the amount of sealing compound recently applied, and as long as water does not simply run down into their tops. But eventually they will probably become waterlogged. And when they do, they are that much heavier. This is not a big problem on a weekend hike, when a person can take the boots home and set them aside to dry. Nor is it a serious bother for hiking hut-to-hut, where the person might be able to dry the wet boots overnight, at least partially. But during a longer hike, wet boots can be a genuine concern. Not only are they heavier than dry boots, which are heavy enough to begin with, but they take a long time to dry, even in good weather. In rainy weather they may never dry. Even in dry weather, waterproofing compound applied to leather boots reduces their breathability. So the compound only adds to the problem of dank, uncomfortable feet. And lack of comfort aside, sweaty, boot-bound feet are much more likely to blister.

But what about boots laminated with an inner ply of

waterproof-breathable material? Don't they permit the inside moisture to escape while holding the outside water at bay? In theory, yes. But when used in boots, these materials tend to break down rather quickly. Even if the materials could hold up, their breathability is minute, compared with that of the more permeable fabrics usually—but not always—used in running shoes. Also, the high-tech membrane only seems to obviate the need to apply sealant. The outer boot material, left untreated, will soak water like a sponge. The membrane then inhibits drying by restricting cross ventilation. One could apply a sealing compound in order to reduce external absorption, but this would further restrict breathability, and cause the intervening sandwich of leather to retain the entrapped moisture from sweat indefinitely. One could apply a breathable sealing liquid, but these tend to be short lived in harsh conditions.

On the CDT in Montana, we sometimes forded dozens of creeks per day, usually without stopping to remove our shoes and socks.

Running shoes in rain

When I hike in running shoes, I know they will not become massively heavy when soaked, and that they will dry fairly quickly at the first opportunity. This leaves me squishing along feeling almost impervious to the rain, sloppy snow and wet brush. My feet are naturally waterproof and do not mind being wet, as long as they do not become too cold, which they do not if I am hiking and generating metabolic heat. And as long as I spend my nights comfortably warm and dry under the quilt, which of course I do. What I need, then, are not boots to keep my feet dry, but lightweight shoes and socks that will dry faster once the rain stops. With these, I will spend far less time with wet feet.

During our CDT thru-hike, Jenny and I encountered frigid rain for several weeks in Montana. This was a good test of our running shoes, particularly since we often forded dozens of creeks per day, usually without stopping to remove shoes and socks. The creek water was only momentarily numbing; our feet re-warmed after walking only a short ways.

Dealing with wet shoes and socks at camp

After we have spent a long, wet day on the trail, we remove our wet shoes and socks as soon as we have pitched our shelter and finished our camp chores. Snug and dry under the shelter, we reach outside and wring out the socks, then hang them from the tarp's clothesline (or from a line rigged inside a tent or underneath its awning). If the nighttime air temperatures are likely to drop below freezing, we place the wet socks under the edge of our foam pads. They will not dry there, but neither will they freeze into stiff boards. In sub-zero weather we might also place our shoes under our groundsheet. Otherwise, we leave the shoes out, but protected beneath the tarp. By morning we will find them probably much less wet. And if the morning's weather proves fine, and if the dew is not on the trailside vegetation, then our shoes will likely dry within a few short hours of tramping.

Creek fording footwear

When it comes time to ford a creek, I sometimes remove my shoes and socks, and wear two pairs of spare socks. The socks provide some cushioning against the stones, they insulate my feet somewhat from the cold, and they receive a hasty laundering in the process. But if the water is more than 10 or 12 inches deep and flowing strongly, I wear just the shoes, minus the socks, for better traction and maneuverability.

Shoe requirements

The variety of running, hiking and cross-training shoes on the market is almost overwhelming. And in response to the competition, manufacturers are continually shelling the market with new models. I cannot recommend specific ones that have worked well for me because without a single exception they have gone out of production. But I can list the guidelines I use when selecting new shoes.

▶ Reasonable cost – midway between the cheapest and most expensive.

▶ Lightweight – 10½ oz. each. This is the average weight of a men's size 10½, the *current* industry standard. The ideal weight will be proportionally heavier for larger sizes, and lighter for smaller sizes.

▶ Ample tread for traction, but not massive tread that would cause excessive damage to the land.

▶ Adequate heel support, (not ankle support) keeping the shoe centered under the heel (see below).

▶ Excellent cushioning beneath both the heel and ball of the foot.

▶ Highly breathable uppers, allowing perspiration to evaporate.

And a few qualities I steer away from:

» Visible gas or liquid filled cushioning devices molded into the sole's *bottom* surface (that which contacts the ground). These can burst on contact with sharp rocks.

» Gaping indentations in the sole that reduce the footprint area. These soles are less stable, and since they create more pressure in contact with the ground, they are harder on the ecology. As an extreme example, picture a woman's high-heeled shoe. The "sole" of the heel spike has very little surface area. It would sink deeply into softer ground, and is very unstable.

» Stiff soles, and extra wide or flaring soles.

» Upper foam linings. These over-insulate and restrict ventilation.

» Built-in elastic sock. These also restrict ventilation.

Shoe construction: lasting

Before buying any type of hiking footwear, I remove the insole and inspect the lasting (the inside bed of the actual shoe itself). This will not be possible with a cheaply made shoe that has the insole (sock liner) glued into place.

▶ Inside a board-lasted shoe or boot is a sole-shaped piece of cardboard or other stiff material, glued in place.

▶ In a combination-lasted shoe, a piece of cardboard covers only the rear half of the foot area.

▶ Inside a slip-lasted shoe you will see fabric joined by a hand-sewn seam running the length of the shoe. This seam is actually the shoe's upper that has been pulled over the last and glued to the mid-sole.

Board-lasted shoes and boots are less costly to manufacture. The board (cardboard) last adds stiffness, and naturally it comes in various qualities. Some merely abrade and roughen when wet, while others actually begin to disintegrate. And the glue securing the boards in place sometimes dissolves. Bereft of its last, a board-lasted or combination-lasted shoe can be un-wearable. Given the choice, I usually choose slip-lasted footwear.

Insoles

The insole is the removable, foot-shaped pad that comes in most running shoes and boots. The heel and toe areas of the insole are normally molded in an upward curve. I pull out the insoles in my new shoes, and using a pair of scissors I carefully trim away the outermost edge of those curved portions at the toe and heel. This provides more space, and reduces the chances of blistering.

In my earlier days of long-distance hiking, I fitted expensive insoles beneath the factory-equipped ones for added cushioning. Eventually I realized that the extra cushioning was beneficial only because I was wearing the shoes too many miles and breaking them down internally – even though the shoes still looked fine on the outsides. The problem with trying to extend the life of a shoe or boot is that sooner or later it can begin harming one's feet. Pains can surface suddenly and without warning – for example, in the middle of a long section between trailheads. A better plan is to replace broken-down footwear with a new pair.

Orthotics

The karate sparring mishap that flattened my arch also left me with an over-pronating ankle. So before embarking on my first long hike I consulted a sports podiatrist. He cast a plaster mold of the bottom of each foot, and supplied me with a pair of custom plastic orthotics. Invented by the late Dr. George Sheehan, the well-known running advocate of the 1970's and 80's, these are removable inserts worn inside the footwear. My orthotics provided support not beneath the arch, but behind the arch on the forward part of the heel. I wore them during the pre-hike training and eventually determined that the non-injured foot was gaining no benefit. I wore the orthotic in the other shoe the full distances of our first two journeys. As the injured foot became stronger, it outgrew its need for the orthotic.

Pronating ankles are not necessarily incapable. But they can cause pain in the ankles or knees. Here is an easy test of whether your feet might benefit from orthotics. Place a sheet of paper on the floor. Wet your foot, then step naturally onto the paper. The moisture should leave a well-defined footprint. If most of the foot area is visible, but a small area is scooped out at the side, then your arch is probably normal. If the entire outline of your foot is revealed, your ankle might be over-pronating. Also, ask someone to stand behind you and watch as you walk away bare-footed and bare-legged from the knees down. They should be able to tell whether your ankles are flexing inward as you place your weight on them.

If your ankles over-pronate, the calf-stretching exercises (see the "Stretching" chapter) will help reduce any associated problems. During the stretch, do not allow the ankles to flex inward.

If you experience a knee pain that you think might be related to an over-pronating ankle, try this simple test: Walk on terrain sloped down and away from the painful knee. For example if the left knee hurts, walk on ground sloped down and to your left. If this seems to help, it might indicate a weakness in that ankle.

Supination is the opposite of pronation: the ankles turn outward with each step. Supination is rare, and seems to cause few problems among hikers. However, turning the ankle forcefully outward, when stepping clumsily on a rock or root with the inside of the foot, can result in a sprained ankle. This is best avoided by watching where you place your feet, and by strengthening your ankles during a pre-hike training program.

Heel support

Most hikers have "normal" feet and do not require orthotics. And hikers with properly strengthened ankles, the result of pre-hike training, do not require ankle support either. But almost everyone needs good heel support in his or her shoes. Heel support means that the shoe's heel-cup is fairly stiff. This keeps the heel of the shoe centered beneath the heel of the foot. This is important if the shoe is to work well on uneven terrain. When you walk on laterally sloped ground, your heel tends to slide off the shoe's foot-bed. But good heel support prevents this.

However, most shoes made for good heel support are also fairly heavy. Eleven ounces (average for a men's size 10½) is getting up there, and many such shoes climb into the twelve-ounce category. When studying running shoe catalogs, I pay attention to both the weights and the advertised extent of support provided by the various shoes. Better yet, I visit shoe stores and examine the models personally. To test a shoe for heel support, I simply squeeze the heel cup laterally. The stiffer the heel-cup, the more heel support it will provide. It is that simple. What is not so simple is finding shoes that have good heel support, yet which are light in weight and easy on the wallet. They do exist, but sometimes finding them takes a bit of searching.

Wide and thick soles

An overly thick sole raises the vertical center of effort, reducing stability. A too-narrow sole also reduces stability. With either problem, a person's foot can sometimes "fall off" the shoe. This happens when stepping inadvertently on the side of a rock or root. The sole twists to match the slope of the rock, and the foot slides off the sole. And because the fabric is flexible, the sensation is that of falling off, or out of, the shoe.

A far greater problem is that of the sole being too wide. In addition to a shoe's longitudinal (front to back) center of effort, a shoe has a lateral (side to side) center of effort. Wider soles might seem to provide more lateral stability, but this is true on flat ground only. More often, we hike on irregular ground. When a person steps on a protuberance with the edge of a too-wide sole, it can torque the ankle tremendously. And the wider the sole, the more apt the person is to step on something with its edge.

We can look at the wide-sole problem another way. Suppose you are traversing a steep slope. Narrow soles will allow you to walk on their edges, keeping your ankles more vertical. Wide soles stress the ankles so much that you cannot walk on the soles' edges. Instead, you have to walk with the soles flat against the steeply sloped ground. This torques the ankles sideways, and can stretch and weaken those outer tendons and ligaments.

Proper fit

When planning a long trek, we purchase our footwear larger than normal, to accommodate the swelling of our feet. While hiking only every other day during our training exercises, we might not notice the feet swelling. But once we start hiking many miles on a daily basis, our feet will begin to increase in size. This is especially true if we are hiking in hot and arid climes. Some of this enlargement is due to the feet strengthening to the task. The muscles are growing in size, and the blood vessels are expanding. And some of the enlargement is due to blood pooling and fluid accumulating. This is perfectly normal; healthy in fact. But to accommodate this swelling, we buy our shoes 1 to 1½ sizes larger than usual for hiking in cool to moderately warm climates, and 1½ to 2½ sizes larger in hot climates. Otherwise, as the swelling progresses, our feet are likely to become very cramped inside the shoes. Hiking in tight shoes or boots is a sure way to painfully blistered feet – and maybe to bruised toes and blackened toe nails as well. A person might be reluctant to buy footwear that much larger in size, especially in the presence of a "helpful" salesperson. But as our own experience has shown, and scores of hikers have affirmed, buying shoes or boots that fit properly in the city is a big mistake. They can become unwearable within the first couple of days on the trail.

However, unless your feet are exceptionally wide, I would not recommend buying extra wide shoes, usually denoted as 2E or 4E. No matter how enlarged your feet become, these extra wide sizes may be far too roomy in the rear-foot areas. Even when swollen, your feet are likely to wallow in them. Conversely, some brands of shoes are very narrow in the forefoot. These are best avoided also, even if your feet are quite narrow. Once on the trail you may find the extra space to your advantage. Many women hikers wear men's shoes on the trail because these shoes tend to be wider in the forefoot where the extra space is beneficial.

Modifying shoes

During our first thru-hike we started out with shoes that were not sufficiently large, and the tremendous heat caused our foot problems to multiply out of control. So we had to improvise a solution. It was time for surgery. Not on our feet, but on the shoes.

First, I cut out the tongues. I did this by cramming the tongue deep into the shoe's toe box, then carefully slicing the tongue-to-uppers stitching. With the tongue done away with, I slit the shoe's upper forefoot down its centerline an inch toward the toe of the shoe. This slit allowed the shoe's forefoot to expand laterally, creating more space for my foot. After hiking in the shoes awhile, I elongated the forefoot slit when necessary, but only in

> I do not recommend shoe modifications for all hikers. But on a long-distance hike they could save the day for someone suffering foot problems.

small increments. I avoided slitting all the way to the vicinity of my toenails, as they could then begin snagging the slit with each step. But I knew that if I sliced too far, I could always break out the sewing needle and thread, and stitch a cross-hatch pattern back along the slice, leaving it plenty wide.

Crossing the Columbia River; PCT-2

Removing the tongues and slitting the upper forefoot areas increased the shoe's ventilation tremendously, so helped my feet stay cool and dry. It also admitted more dirt, yet even this can be an advantage. I call it "dura-dirt" because it can be difficult to scrub off, but actually it helps toughen the feet, as long as I scrub it off at day's end.

The gap left by the missing tongue also admitted the occasional bit of gravel. I handled this by lacing my shoelaces so loosely that I could slip out of the shoes without having to untie the laces, and slip back into them in the same way. But of course I tightened the laces before crossing steep terrain and making the more serious creek crossings.

Since that first thru-hike, I have de-tongued and slit dozens of pairs of shoes on various long hikes. This makes them fit much better. At least those shoes that need it. About two thirds of the shoes I have hiked in did not need much modification, mainly because I now buy them much larger.

Sometimes a shoe will cause problems in a different area of the foot.

A shoe or lightweight boot might rub or exert pressure on the Achilles tendon, creating tenderness in the back of the heel. Trying to walk far with that kind of pressure is a sure invitation to injury. I typically relieve this pressure by slitting the shoe an inch or so down the back; not starting at the top of the heal necessarily, but only in the area of the soreness. If that does not help, I make the slit a bit longer, but again, only in the area of pressure.

Sometimes a shoe will chafe the side of the foot day after day. In this case I might slice the shoe to make it larger, or I might cut out a hole where the material is causing a persistent blister.

Reducing footwear-related injuries

Most types of running shoes offer excellent cushioning, and this cushioning is beneficial to the hiker. But it comes at a cost. With the passing of many miles, the cushioning materials slowly break down – even though the shoes might still look fine on the outsides. However, these materials do not break down evenly, and the result is a shoe that transmits unbalanced forces with every step. These imbalances can ultimately lead to a stress injury.

A budding stress injury is signaled by a sharp or burning pain with each step that manifests itself for no apparent cause. The pain can be in the foot, but usually it is somewhere in the leg, knee, or up into the lower back. Hiking pains can stem from other problems, such as a lack of pre-hike training, too heavy a load, severe and prolonged dehydration, inadequate nutrition, lack of calf-limbering exercises, and of course from stepping down crooked when hopping across a brook or slipping off a wet log. Most often though, the pains are caused by the footwear. So whenever I begin experiencing a pain that stabs with every step, I immediately suspect the footwear.

If the cushioning in running shoes is prone to breaking down and causing stress injuries, then why not wear boots instead? Because boots, too, are well known for causing stress injuries. This is not because their cushioning breaks down, since they usually have very little, but because they do not fit the hiker's foot too well. And this imperfect fit creates imbalances that can gradually grind away at the hiker's foot tendons and ligaments.

For every person who manages to hike a couple thousand miles in a single pair of boots with "no problems," several others are not so fortunate. The boot advertisements claim comfort for untold miles across all sorts of rugged terrain, but such is often not the case. Hiking-related stress injuries occur with both running shoes and boots, and I discuss the matter in the "Stress Injuries" chapter. However the matter bears looking at from a different angle here.

Imagine that you buy a pair of shoes or boots that, due to a quality control problem, has a sizeable lump under the ball of one foot. It could be a glob of hardened glue, or a fold in several layers of material. Either way, it is an internal problem, not visible. You notice something a little odd, but decide to break in the shoes or boots gradually over a few weeks' time. Later, you embark on a hiking journey in these shoes, and for the first few weeks all seems well. What is happening is that your foot is trying to adapt to the lump as best it can. But as this irregularity hammers incessantly at your foot, eventually you may start feeling a nagging pain at that spot – or just as likely somewhere else. It could just as easily be in the leg, knee, hip or back.

This scenario is not imagined; it happened to me once. The shoes were expensive, but I had to cut the shoe apart to find out what the problem was. I found a pea-sized lump of hardened glue.

Every shoe, boot, and sandal has its irregularities. These are not normally as pronounced as in my example, and they might not be lumps; they could be areas that twist or cramp the foot in some unnatural way. A person might not feel them; and if they are minor and the feet manage to accommodate, then one may experience no problems.

But if the feet cannot accommodate them, then in all likelihood they will eventually, over many miles of hiking, begin to cause a stress injury.

So at the first sign of pain, I take off the offending shoes, boots, or sandals, and never wear them again, at least while hiking. Then I change into a different pair.

Carrying spare shoes

From my own experience, a pair of quality running shoes lasts me anywhere from three hundred to a thousand miles. And when the shoes finally "hit the wall," they suddenly start causing pain. One minute all is well, and the next minute I am hobbling. At times like these, ten miles to the nearest trailhead can be a vast distance. Many thousands of hiking miles have taught me to carry spare footwear, and to include spares in various resupply parcels. I know the life of a shoe (or boot) is limited, so I plan accordingly.

I buy good quality running shoes, but for planning proposes I figure on hiking around 500 miles in them. This is a conservative estimate, for I have learned that the price and quality are only guidelines. The shoes might last the distance, but more than likely they might not. So for example if my hike will be 2,500 miles in length, I would need 5 pairs.

I also carry spare footwear. These could be another pair of lightweight running shoes, or an even lighter weight pair of shoes, or lightweight sandals.

Worn out shoes on the PCT-2

The spares cover the very real risk of incurring a stress injury many miles from the nearest trailhead. If the primary pair starts causing a stress injury, then I will have something to change into. And if nothing else, the spares allow me to change back and forth several times a day for variation.

The point is, I think ahead and know that my feet will be closer to the center of my personal universe than they are at home. So I give them plenty of choice in footwear all along the way.

Common arguments

Here is a common argument in favor of boots: "If the running shoe idea requires that we carry spare shoes to make it work, consequently increasing our overall load, why don't we just wear one, good-fitting pair of boots, and forget about the spares?"

Let me give a few reasons. First, the weight on your feet is critical. Second, boots sap the hiker's energy and decrease forward progress. They are clumsier to walk in; and they are more likely to cause an injury.

Along these lines, a thru-hiker-in-planning writes: "The main issue I'm looking at is economics. I would believe that shoes not designed for a lengthy trek would break down more rapidly, causing you to have to purchase more and more pairs. Why not buy just one pair of boots that will last the whole way?"

One pair of sturdy boots costs more than a few pair of moderately priced running shoes. But let's overlook the expense of the footwear for a moment and consider the costs of the journey as a whole. To start with, we must consider the worth of one's time spent planning, preparing and training, and the cost of lost wages during the actual journey. Then there is the cost of equipment, provisions, postage on the resupply parcels, transportation to the start and from the finish, and groceries, meals and perhaps a few motel rooms along the way. The price of the footwear, be it one pair of boots or half a dozen pairs of running shoes, is a fraction of these costs. Now let's look at cost effectiveness. The success of the journey will depend—entirely—on the footwear. Many hikers have set off trusting in a single pair of boots, and returned home prematurely with major foot problems. Trusting in a single pair of boots is neither wise nor cost effective. So if you decide to wear boots on a multi-month hike, make sure you have access to backup footwear.

Sandals

Jenny and I first saw people hiking in sandals on the Appalachian Trail in 1993. The following summer we wore sandals for about five hundred miles on the PCT, sometimes with socks and sometimes without. The extra ventilation and foot room were most welcome. The cushioning was quite good, at least in the types we wore; in some other types it is lacking. But with almost any type of sandal, the heel support is practically non-existent, and as with running shoes this requires strong ankles – especially for the person carrying a full pack. With the straps well secured, sandals work great for creek crossings. Some sandals have a raised lip around the sole, and this helps protect the toes when stumbling, or kicking rocks or roots. Sandals also expose the feet to more dura-dirt.

Slipping into a pair of sandals can be a welcome and therapeutic change for one's painfully blistered feet. However, the straps of the sandals can sometimes create new blisters, as they rub against the skin in areas that the

hiker's regular shoes do not. A thin pair of socks or a bit of tape applied to the feet beneath the straps can be effective remedies. And as time passes, the feet will become more resistant to strap chafe, since the extra ventilation encourages the skin to toughen. In fact, the ventilation is so good that the fungus responsible for the infection of athlete's feet does not stand a chance – although the mosquitoes certainly do.

Hiking in sandals requires a few novel techniques. Pebbles tend to work themselves under the sole of the foot, and usually we can remove them with a few shakes of the foot. The more obstinate stones require a few well-placed kicks of the sandal against a rock or log. Bits of gravel can also work through any small holes in a sock, and about the only way to remove them is to sit down and remove both sandal and sock. When hiking in sandals, a person must be particularly careful of sticks lying on the trail. Not noticing, you step on the far end, which raises the near end, and when your other foot swings forward it is speared by the near end. Ouch! I remember one that put me down for fifteen minutes of first aid. That was a good reminder to tread more carefully.

After about five hundred miles in those sandals I started feeling what I thought was a wood sliver in the ball of my foot. Closer inspection showed it to be a deep crack in the callus. I applied triple antibiotic ointment and carried on, but every day the crack grew larger, even though I continued to apply the ointment. In a few weeks the crack became positively gaping, and other cracks began forming as well. Realizing that the callus was becoming too thick and rigid, I tried grinding it down with rough stones, but to no avail. I would have applied a callus-dissolving solution, had I been carrying it. Or super-glue to close the cracks. But clearly, the sandals' ventilation was too great. So I started wearing more layers of socks, in an effort to reduce the ventilation. And sure enough, three pairs of thin nylon socks solved the problem. The cracks

On the IUA

did not heal shut, but at least they quit worsening. In the end I reverted to wearing running shoes, and wearing the sandals only occasionally.

Future technology in trail footwear

Before we published the first edition of this book in 1991, very few backpackers hiked in running shoes. In 1992 the trend started gaining momentum. Back then I wrote: "In the coming years we will undoubtedly see new types of footwear designed for hiking and active outdoor wear." This has indeed come to pass.

But regardless of the design of new shoes, they still need to meet the basic needs of our feet, as discussed throughout this chapter. Weight is important. If that new model that has attracted our interest weighs much over 11 ounces (men's size 10½), we think twice before buying it. Another important feature is heel and mid-foot cushioning. Another is adequate (but not excessive) breathability. Yet another is very mild tread, not lugs. A lug-sole shoe or boot does not provide any more traction, as hyped, but instead it only damages the landscape unnecessarily.

And until someone figures out a way to make a shoe mold to a person's foot and stay that way, we buy several pairs, of different makes and models.

Why different makes? Because each manufacturer tends to use the same basic molds for their "lasts," and to use these for making all their models. These lasts are designed to fit an average foot, so are unlikely to fit any one particular person's foot. And if the miss-fit is significant, it will impart unbalanced forces to the person's feet and on up into the body. So for the best variety, we choose from a wide selection of brand names. Runners are well known for their strong preferences for specific brands and models of footwear, and I think this is one reason they experience so many stress injuries. They subject themselves to the same unbalanced forces.

Ordering footwear by mail

While hiking a longer trail, a person might find themselves in need of a new pair of shoes, sandals or boots. At your next waypoint you could telephone a friend or home-base person and request a pair be express mailed to you there, or to your next stopover. Or with a credit card you could order new shoes online. Before placing the call, arrange with someone locally to receive your package, since these companies might not ship to General Delivery. If all else fails you might have to hitchhike to the nearest town and buy a pair. The problem of needing fresh footwear is very common, and is so much more easily solved ahead of time by including spare shoes in your resupply parcels. Those shoes you decide you don't need, you can mail home and use later; possibly on your next hike.

Reflective material affects photographs

The reflective material used on most running shoes is intended to alert night-time motorists. But it can wreak havoc with the photographs. In any situation where a person uses a fill-in flash, in day or night, the burst of light from the flash can rebound from the reflective material of the subject's shoes, and over-expose that part of the image. The same can happen with the sun's reflection when the subject is walking away from a sunset or sunrise. One could slice away the reflective material from the shoes, or cover it with paint, or simply remember to point the camera a little higher, keeping the reflections from the shoes out of the picture. Of course, the rebound might also be removed with digital editing software.

Protecting the stitching

All exposed stitching on a pair of shoes or boots is vulnerable to abrasion. In the past we coated that stitching with fast-setting 3 to 5 minute epoxy. Fast-setting epoxy is more flexible than the slower setting types. While mixing the epoxy, we add an equal amount of rubbing alcohol. This acts as a thinner, and encourages the mixture to soak into the fabric and the stitching. We use a toothpick to dab the epoxy on, and smear some also wherever the uppers might need extra protection from abrasion. We mix the epoxy in small batches, on tin-can lids for example. I have found, however, that most shoes break down internally long before the stitching wears out.

The technology represented in today's shoes is considerably improved over that of Grandma Gatewood's era. The present running shoes offer better cushioning, stability and motion control. I am not suggesting that running shoes are the ultimate for long distance hiking. But to us, lighter-weight footwear has been a major contributor to our many enjoyable, successful and trouble-free journeys.

The camera's flash rebounding from Jenny's shoes and from the pot lid. When the woods are wet, we have to build our cook-fires extra large to keep them burning. On the IUA.

Food

"Part of the secret of success in life
is to eat what you like,
and let the food fight it out inside."
— *Mark Twain*

"Don't rely too much on labels,
for too often they are fables."
— Charles H. Spurgeon

The subject of food is important to most hikers and backpackers. Most want their food to taste good and to be filling. Some may want their meals to be quick and easy to prepare. Others might want their food to be light in weight. Some are more concerned with long-lasting energy. And for others, nutrition might play the key role.

In fact, most of us would like our trail food to meet all these requirements. But which foods are best? **This is a matter of personal preference**. So in this chapter I describe only what foods have worked well for Jenny and me.

Food for a short day-hike

If Jenny and I are hiking only a few hours, we typically do not carry food, although we will drink plenty of water. However, we know we will probably be hungry by the time we return to the house or car, so we have a few after-hike snacks waiting for us. Our favorite is bananas or other fresh fruit, along with lots of water, and maybe some fresh-squeezed fruit juice. These will last us until the next full meal.

Food for a day-hike

We have racked up a lot of mileage on our long-distance trips. But we have logged even more while day-hiking. For these shorter jaunts we bring plenty of water, along with a few snacks and something for lunch. We prefer to keep our food simple; fresh fruit and vegetables, nuts and seeds. In the past we might have included trail mix and cookie bars. Lunch might have been whole-grain sandwiches and maybe corn chips with bean dip. In winter, we sometimes carried a vacuum flask of soup or hot chocolate.

On our overnight trips, we include dinner meals, and maybe breakfasts in addition to our lunch and snack items. We have enough room in our packs to carry fresh food, thus allowing us to eat the foods we find the most appealing.

A lack of a picnic table is no obstacle for making sandwiches on the AT.

For a long-distance trek, we think nutrition

When preparing for long distance hikes, a new set of food rules come into play. Weight is still a factor, as is taste and ease of preparation. But also Jenny and I have to plan for variety, longevity, (the food may be sitting in resupply boxes for a month or more) and especially for high nutritional value. We need lots of high quality foods that provide long-term energy and vitality. And more importantly, we need maximum regeneration from the previous day's fatigue. This helps insure that we will awaken each morning feeling good and looking forward to another day of good hiking.

We have enjoyed a great many strenuous and challenging adventures; and here is one key to success: We do not consider simply the whims of our taste buds, or the convenience of fast-cooking or ready-to-eat foods. Far more importantly, we think about the nutritional value in our foods, both on the trail and at home.

Because each person has his or her own tastes and food preferences, I am not making any recommendations in this chapter. Instead, I am only describing what has worked well for us.

Nutritional content

The nutritional value of a food relates to its capacity to provide a person with strength and endurance, to aid cellular growth and repair, and to facilitate mental acuity and stability. A person stores this nutrition in the cells of his or her body, to be used as needed. Exercise—hiking, in this case—withdraws from these stored reserves, and on a longer backpacking trip may actually deplete them. So unless the person replenishes the reserves regularly with good nutrition, he or she will usually begin to suffer various effects.

Manifestations of poor nutrition

Poorly-nourished hikers often find themselves low on energy and endurance. They usually assume that hiking is inherently tiring, and that the steepness and length of the trail is to blame for their weariness.

Malnutrition can also manifest itself in the hiker's mental outlook. The poorly-nourished brain is largely incapable of producing positive emotions. The sun, rain, snow, the hiking companions and even the trail itself might become intolerable. Endless miles of beautiful surroundings glide past, and most of it is disregarded. More severe cases can lead to a sour attitude, apathy, disharmony, intolerance… the list rattles on – and any one of these can sap the enjoyment from one's wilderness journey. And what is more, over the long term the person can also expect an inexorable decline in health and well-being. Such is the price of poor nutrition.

These symptoms of poor nutrition are epitomized in many distance hikers of both sexes, at any age, on practically every day of the summer in every year. Ironically, these symptoms are also avoidable, simply by changing one's food choices.

Not all "food" is food

Basing one's food choices solely on one's preferences must have worked reasonably well in centuries past, when foods were not so heavily processed. But today's foods are different. In fact, some types might no longer be food.

Also, some of a person's food preferences may not be his or her own. Many of the larger food companies bombard the person with advertising. This advertising pervades everyone's lives, and is continually suggesting preferences. One inference is that the products most heavily advertised must be the best. And a person's emotional responses often agree. Moreover, the high-tech processing ensures that these "foods" are quick and easy to prepare, and the modern packaging is aimed at making the package attractive on the shelves. These food companies are large and prosperous, and they use every resource in their arsenal to sell their products. The consumers are their prey.

So to explore what is causing any low energy and lack of a positive attitude, I have structured the first part of this chapter as a general guide to how we recognize overly processed junk foods in their various disguises. And in the second part of the chapter I detail the trail foods that we consider more wholesome.

Unwrapping the freeze-dried fallacy

In my early years I hiked a great many trail miles, even though only a few days at a time. Then in the early 1970s I started working full time as a wilderness instructor. A few years later, in 1973, I learned an important lesson about a certain type of food.

The previous few summers I had subsisted on freeze-dried food, as supplied by the company. But I began to suspect that these meals were not providing optimum, long-term nutrition, or anywhere near it. So as an experiment I relinquished my personal supply of freeze-dried meals, and bought more nutritious foods from the supermarket. My job entailed backpacking almost continuously throughout the summer, and despite the extra weight of fresh food, I found that I could now hike circles around my students who were eating the light-weight freeze-dried food.

Not only did my energy levels skyrocket, but so did my hiking and camping enjoyment. Before the switch, my 23 to 28 days per course seemed to drag on. After a while, I could hardly wait to return to the city. The other instructors and the students, who were also eating freeze-dried food, were in much the same state of mind. After my switch, not only did I have more energy, but I began to

feel more at home in the wilds. For one thing, when at camp and on the trail, I could quit "food tripping," that is, thinking of food I did not have. For after all, I was now carrying that food in my backpack.

My increased vitality led me to suspect that when eating freeze-dried food I was relying instead on the nutritional reserves previously stored in the cells of my own body. That is why I did not notice the loss of energy on the weekend hikes before I became a professional instructor. But hiking all summer on freeze-dried foods depleted my reserves. More on this subject to follow.

Freeze-dried foods are expensive, in part because the processing requires large-scale equipment. The food is deep-frozen to minus 50° Fahrenheit, subjected to a vacuum, then rapidly heated to 120° to promote sublimation while low-temperature condenser plates remove the vapor.

After all this processing, the product is sealed in extra durable packaging, to preserve "freshness." The empty packaging lasts for a long time in the wilds, should someone indiscreetly leave it there, hidden from sight under a rock for example.

Despite the expense and un-ecological packaging, freeze-dried foods are readily available in the backpacking stores and catalogs. So they are popular with many backpackers who like the low weight, the convenience, and the ease of preparation.

Some people also find these foods tasty. This might be because many types of freeze-dried food are laced with taste-enhancing chemicals designed to trick a person's brain into interpreting the foods as tasting good. These chemicals are called "excitotoxins," and although commonly found in almost all pre-packaged, processed foods, some freeze-dried foods might contain more of them. On a label from a popular brand of freeze-dried Chicken a la King, for example, I counted eight different excitotoxins on the list of ingredients.

Excitotoxins

Neuroscientists call these chemicals "excitotoxins" because they excite the neurons of the brain to the point of killing many of them, causing brain damage in varying degrees. When these chemicals appear on the label's list of ingredients, which they rarely do, their names are almost always disguised. Yet despite their well-documented health risks, the food industry finds them enormously helpful in bolstering profits.

One of the most notorious of the excitotoxins is MSG: Monosodium glutamate. And this comes in many guises. In his excellent book *Excitotoxins, The Taste that Kills*, Dr. Russell L. Blaylock lists a few hidden sources of MSG:

Dr. Blaylock's list of Hidden Sources of MSG

"MSG (Monosodium glutamate), Glutamate, Monopotassium glutamate, Glutamic acid, Hydrolyzed protein (from 12 to 40% MSG), Autolyzed yeast (from 10 to 20% MSG), Yeast extract, Calcium caseinate (8-12% MSG), Sodium caseinate (8-12% MSG).

"In addition, some ingredients always contain MSG: Textured protein, gelatin, yeast food, plant protein extract, yeast nutrient, hydrolyzed oat flour.

"And the following are ingredients that often contain MSG: malt extract, malt flavoring, barley malt, bouillon, stock, broth, carrageenan, maltodextrin (corn), whey protein, whey protein isolate, whey protein concentrate, anything enzyme-modified, xanthum gum (corn), pectin, flavor(s) & flavoring(s), natural flavor(s) & flavoring(s), natural pork flavoring, natural beef flavoring, natural chicken flavoring, 'seasonings,' soy sauce, soy sauce extract, soy protein, soy protein isolate, soy protein concentrate, anything protein-fortified, 'spices.'"

Dr. Blaylock also points out that "glutamate, aspartate and cysteine are found in nature," which is how the industry gets away with labeling them as "natural" ingredients. He also says that "the label designating 'natural flavoring' may contain anywhere from 20 to 60 percent MSG. The powerful excitotoxins asparate and L-cysteine are frequently added to foods, and according to FDA rules, require no labeling at all."

And he says: "More and more diseases of the nervous system are being linked to excitotoxin build-up in the brain. For example disorders such as strokes, brain injury, hypoglycemic brain damage, seizures, migraine headaches, hypoxic brain damage, and even AIDS dementia have been linked to excitotoxin damage."

Non-food

In 2007 I joined an expedition to climb the highest mountain in Antarctica. The group was served freeze-dried meals every day; however I could manage only one of these meals. Even though the other climbers continued wolfing them down, I could not stand to be around this food. To me it smelled positively nauseating. And after a while, the gas produced by the other climbers smelled much the same.

I was not experiencing an allergic reaction, yet my body and brain were rejecting something in, or about, the food. My reaction might not have been related to the excitotoxins, but more to the actual freeze-dried processing, which, it seems to me, might change the food into a non-food. From this I have concluded that the effects of eating freeze-dried food may be cumulative and permanent. Once a person has eaten a great deal of it, as I did back in the 1970s, the body may start objecting.

Processed flour (white flour)

Processed flour is the nation's most popular food staple. Americans eat more of it than anything else. Yet it is so lacking in nutrition that it hardly qualifies as food. Yes, it fills the stomach and satisfies the palate, but it also provides very little nutrition.

The backpacker's larder usually contains plenty of items made of white flour: bread, bagels, crackers, spaghetti, macaroni, flavored pasta mixes, couscous, and ramen instant noodles. We find these items acceptable in moderation, but certainly do not consider them a primary source of sustenance. Let me describe why that is:

In its natural form, the kernel of wheat is protected by an inedible hull. Even after winnowing to remove the hull, the kernel remains alive, waiting to germinate. In fact, in favorable conditions it can lie dormant for decades, thanks to its surrounding layer called the bran. The bran serves to protect the inside from invasive microorganisms, and the bran is also a nutritious part of the kernel. At the heart of the kernel is the germ, the part that would grow if the kernel were planted. The germ is also high in nutrition. And lastly, the endosperm lies within the bran, surrounding the germ. The endosperm is mostly starches, and contains little nutrition.

Bran 14%

Endosperm 83%

Germ 3%

Milling breaks down the grain's protective bran, and exposes its germ to air-borne microorganisms. These start feeding on the germ, and begin turning it rancid. To prevent rancidity, the milling machinery removes the germ. And for better texture and color, it also removes the bran. What remains is the endosperm. This starchy, lifeless part of the grain is then further processed, refined, bleached and treated to become the nutritionally desolate version of wheat known as white flour. It has a long shelf life because microbes cannot subsist on it very well. And neither can humans.

To compensate for robbing the products of their nature-given nutrients, the food industry "enriches" them with all manner of chemicals. The word "enrich" incorrectly leads one to believe that these chemicals are good for a person – even though they restore none of the nutrition and only a fraction of the vitamins and minerals. And most of these so-called vitamins are nothing but artificially synthesized chemicals. Under an electron microscope they appear quite different from the genuine vitamins found naturally in food. Some other "fortifying" chemicals are added to make the product taste better. Others are texture and color additives to make the product seem more like real food.

One of the best references on this subject is *Beating the Food Giants*, by Paul A. Stitt. In fact, this book is so informative that I consider it essential reading for anyone concerned about the quality of his or her food. The author details his work as a foods research scientist, citing a number of shocking studies and experiments involving, among many other things, the nutritional value of white flour. He says that the food giants do their best to stifle these types of studies because "too often these tests show their 'foods' are **incapable of sustaining life**."

Nutritional bankruptcy

How does one know whether a certain bread, for example, contains the nutrient-rich germ and bran? The product description certainly does not reveal this. Nor does the labeling "100% whole wheat bread." This means only that the bread is made from 100% whole wheat, before removal of the germ and bran and the introduction of the usual barrage of additives. And lest a person put too much faith in the list of ingredients, Paul Stitt informs us that "Bread can contain oxides of nitrogen, chlorine, notrosyl chloride, chlorine dioxide, benzoyl peroxide (acne medication), acetone peroxide, azodicarbonamide, even plaster of Paris and sawdust, and the manufacturer is not obligated by the Code of Federal Regulations to warn you of these. Nor is bread the only product that can have hidden additives…"

About the only way a person can know whether the germ and bran are present is to grind the grains yourself, and bake your own bread. Genuine whole-grain bread is coarse and crumbly (and packed with nutrition).

So why do people eat white flour breads? In part, because they contain a lot of gluten, which gives the bread its fine consistency. And the labels disguise the ingredients in all manner of ways.

But actually it all started back in the Middle Ages when white bread was first contrived. Back then it was called manchet, and later wastel bread. These were made of the "finest and most delicate flours obtainable," and were so expensive that only the aristocracy could afford them. Laborers, servants and other people of few means had to make do with darker, coarser, whole-grain breads. When the industrial revolution introduced machines that could produce white flour cheaply and in quantity, white bread became available to the common class, who wanted to eat the same foods as the wealthy.

Other popular but nutritionally plundered substances

Durum is a variety of wheat; semolina is the milled product of durum wheat stripped of its bran and germ. And what is left? Lifeless white flour. And while it might make a tasty meal on occasion, we certainly would not mistake white-flour-based (semolina) spaghetti and other pastas for highly nutritious food and eat it for every dinner during a long-distance hike. Consumed in such high quantities, it would sap a person's energy, and might turn the summer's journey from one of enjoyment to one of drudgery. We have seen many examples of this unfortunate practice.

Then there is macaroni and cheese. This, too, is durum semolina (white flour) and the "cheese" is usually artificial. Flavored pasta mixes are made from white flour with various flavorings, as are ramen instant noodles.

Couscous is a finely cracked durum wheat or millet that has been steamed, dried, and refined (stripped of its bran and germ).

Instant oatmeal is in the same category. To make oats "instant," the bran and germ are removed, and the endosperm is pre-cooked and rolled thin. Another so-called "instant" product is instant rice. This is the most heavily processed and least nourishing form of rice, even when "enriched." It, too, lacks the bran and germ.

Paul Stitt asserts that "Whole wheat and whole rice is produced in ample abundance in most places of the world. But when rice and wheat are processed, i.e., when the bran and germ are removed, the grains are stripped of all major nutrient value. The [malnourished] people don't get too little to eat. The tragic truth is that the food they do get has been ruined before it gets to their mouths."

"Energy" bars

Jenny and I want our snacks to provide the best energy, keeping us well fueled throughout the day. This brings to mind the so-called energy bars so prevalent today. Why do people normally associate health and energy with these bars? Mainly as a response to the advertising. But do these products actually provide a significant boost in energy? The way I see it, if energy bars supplied significant energy, then at the Olympic Games, all athletes would gorge on them prior to competition. These people need energy more than just about anyone, and what do they eat? Wholesome, natural foods, not on the morning of competition, but during their months of training. So what is a person to make of these supposed "energy" bars? I tend to agree with one description: "high-priced candy bars."

In a survey done by a popular magazine, the bar that won top place received such accolades as "loved the real food texture and awesome energy." Looking at the wrapper on one of these bars, I found the first ingredient was malted corn and barley. Malted corn and malted barley are sugars and may contain MSG. And as if these do not make that particular bar sweet enough, the fourth ingredient is honey. The fact is, simple sugars are ineffective at replenishing glycogen stores, essential for working muscles.

The second most popular "energy bar" in the magazine comparison is practically the de facto standard in the current sports "energy" market. This bar lists its first ingredient as "high fructose corn syrup with grape and pear juice concentrate." In other words: sugars. The third is maltodextrin, which often contains hidden MSG and excitotoxins. A few ingredients later we come to: "natural flavors (no MSG)." The protein content in this bar is derived mainly from powdered milk, which many hikers often carry anyway. And according to my calculations, the bar's vitamin and mineral content is the equivalent of a two-cent vitamin pill. If I had to choose from among a handful of these "energy" bars, I would opt instead for a package of Fig Newton type cookies. Or even better, I would make my own snack bars, as described later.

I am wary of the type of advertising that attributes magic-like qualities to products made of ordinary ingredients, or even made of exotic-sounding ingredients. Full page, monthly advertisements are phenomenally expensive, and they are paid for by unsuspecting customers. And because these ads appear in so many magazines, one gets the impression that the products are very popular. Why are they popular? Because they work so well, we are led to believe. Yet the market is flooded with tens of thousands of similar products promoted as sports foods, snacks and drinks. The multi-billon dollar sports foods and drinks industry is exactly as the name implies: an industry. And like most industries, its motives are profit.

The calorie myth and candy craving

Some hikers believe that their foods must be high in calories for sufficient energy. If calories gave a person energy, then he or she could eat a dozen candy bars a day and practically fly along the trail. Sugars are high in calories, but they do not provide a person with much usable energy. Nor do they encourage recuperation from strenuous exercise, cleanse one's muscles of their byproducts, help repair micro-damaged muscle fibers, or help strengthen the muscles and increase their stamina. Sugars are also quite useless at promoting mental acuity and encouraging what is perhaps the journey's most vital ingredient – a positive mental attitude.

Jenny and I ate a fair amount of candy during our first thru-hike in an attempt to bolster energy. But rather than energize us, the candy sapped our energy. Some people are familiar with the "sugar-high, sugar-low" syndrome. This is a chain reaction caused by the over-consumption of refined sugar. And it leads to the pancreas overreacting and secreting too much insulin; resulting in low blood sugar levels.

I think that if a person's journey degenerates into a battle in terms of lost energy and mental buoyancy, then the battle is usually won or lost in the grocery stores, rather than on the trails. And the good news is that the more a person avoids the overly sweetened and highly processed junk food and drinks, the easier they become to resist.

Coffee

During our first PCT hike, my wristwatch alarm would sound at 5:30 am. Jenny would reach out and ignite the stove, and set on the coffee pot. We would rise, pack our gear, then hastily chug two cups of café-campo (camp coffee) before shouldering our packs and setting off, usually by 6:15.

I had been drinking coffee all my adult life; ostensibly to stimulate alertness. In reality, I was addicted to the caffeine, as indicated by the low-level headaches I experienced for several months after I stopped drinking coffee. Jenny stopped also, and before long we both began to notice an increase in mental acuity. Free of the daily drug infusions, we found that we slept better and were generally in better physical shape.

During our second PCT hike the alarm sounded at 4:40 am. We would rise, pack our gear, and set off typically by 5:00. Whereas breaking camp used to take us 45 minutes, now released of the coffee rites we were afoot in 20 minutes.

By refraining from the morning coffee, we gained an extra 25 minutes every day. We used that time for hiking, but could have used it for sleeping in.

However, the main reason we quit drinking coffee was because we did not like being controlled by a substance. Also, we came to see the morning's coffee ritual as pointless. It had little to do with enjoyment; rather, we drank the coffee for the effects of its caffeine. And this artificial high added nothing to our wilderness experience.

Alcohol

Alcohol is a powerful diuretic. This is why responding to thirst by opening a can of beer might not be such a good idea. Just a few beers will severely dehydrate a person and greatly reduce one's energy levels. In fact, a hangover is mainly the result of plunging rapidly and acutely into dehydration. Hikers who enjoy drinking alcohol socially from time to time might also drink large quantities of water along with it. The same holds true for coffee and sports drinks. But for even better results, drink only the water.

Pack-weight and food weight

The "foods" I have discussed thus far are all relatively light in weight, and this partly accounts for their popularity. And granted, thus far in the book I have gone to great lengths to describe our reduction in pack weight. So it might seem logical that I would concentrate on lightweight foods when planning our trail menus. But in fact I do not.

I think of pack-weight in terms of the total load minus the food and water. This may seem incongruous, considering that a hiker has to carry it all. But I make this distinction for two important reasons. First, the food and water are consumable. Heading out from a trailhead or resupply, we might carry 2½ pounds of food per person for each day. Along the way we eat most of the food. But as the food weight drops from say, a dozen pounds to nearly zero, our baseline pack-weight—the equipment and clothing—remains more or less constant. Our supply of water also varies considerably throughout the day; so like the food, its weight is outside the baseline. This is one reason I discount the weight of food and water, but the second reason is the important one. Even though reducing my pack weight is extremely beneficial, reducing my food weight is entirely counterproductive. Jenny and I never scrimp on quality food. Ultralight (and nutritionally empty) meals are about as useless to a hiker as a pogo stick would be to an astronaut. Neither provides sufficient energy.

Continuing with the analogy, rocket fuel is incredibly heavy, but also packed with enough energy to propel both it and the spacecraft skyward. Take it from me: rocket engineers work only with those propellants capable of delivering the payload the highest and farthest, in the most practical manner. And Jenny and I do the same when on a self-propelled journey.

When I consider our hiking gear inventory, I know that the weight of each item, while a major concern, is less important than the item's function. In my experience, most lightweight "foods" are not functional.

I remember my first week-long climbing trip into an area of sandstone towers in the deserts of Utah. This was in the days of heavy steel pitons, and my pack was loaded with about 70 pounds of hardware. My partner and I

Along the CDT in Idaho

Burning the reserves

During a weekend of strenuous activity, most backpackers can subsist on freeze-dried and other nutritionally "empty" foods without noticing too many ill effects. But in realty, they are relying instead on the energy and nutritional reserves stored in the cells of their own bodies. However, there comes a point on a longer journey when the exertion begins to deplete those reserves. This is because the nutrition stored in the body is withdrawn faster than it is being replaced. The most noticeable result is usually a profound sense of fatigue. So to make the person feel better, he or she might binge on junk food at the stores en route. That leads to even greater fatigue.

Specifically, I estimate that the effect of dwindling reserves will begin to take hold after eight to twelve days of strenuous hiking. Most people have never been out long enough to experience the acute loss of energy due to depleted reserves. Or if they have, they may not have associated the fatigue with the cause.

Nevertheless, during a longer hike, as the person's reserves start bottoming out, the brain senses that survival is becoming at risk. Subconsciously the brain knows what it needs – better food. And it knows where to get it – back at home. The subconscious mind then starts prompting the person to return home by suggesting various excuses. Ironically, these excuses usually have nothing to do with the real problem: the nutritional deficit. Instead, some external aspect becomes a scapegoat, and

could not lighten our gear, so we decided to lighten our food. For one continuous week we ate packaged instant oatmeal. During the first few days all seemed well, but soon the rigors of climbing overwhelmed what little energy the oatmeal could impart. Nearing trip's end we were reduced to lying listlessly in our tents. We failed to climb our chosen towers for want of strength. In fact we probably could have done better by fasting.

Traditional backpackers face a similar dilemma. Their packs are so heavy that they can hardly afford to carry the additional weight of heavier food. But with lighter-weight gear and therefore with a much lower baseline pack weights, they could afford heavier and more nutritious foods; like fresh vegetables and fruits, and whole grain meals to name but a few. These are likely to deliver them to their distant objective in much better condition – physically and mentally.

with the passing of days or weeks the scapegoat grows more intolerable. The trail might seem dreadfully full of rocks and roots, and the hills impossibly steep. Blisters might seem to be destroying the feet. The trail's propensity to wander might become more outrageous with the passing of every mile. The sun might be too hot, or the rain too drenching. Or perhaps the person develops a rekindled passion for a former hobby such as collecting license plate numbers.

These are mental ploys, contrived by a brain trying to direct the body to a supply of nutrients. The problem might seem enigmatic at the time, but the solution is straightforward: start eating quality foods in quantity.

Nutritious foods suitable for hiking

Fresh, wholesome (live) foods are the most capable of sustaining a person at higher levels. At the top of our personal list are fresh fruits and vegetables. Next come whole grains, seeds, nuts, and legumes. Some people might include meat, fish, eggs, and cheese on their list. Obviously, fresh and perishable food will spoil if kept too long in one's pack, although in many cases not as quickly as one might imagine. But since people have different diet preferences, what follows are the guidelines that we have used. Obviously, **each person will make their own choices**.

Fresh fruits and vegetables

In terms of nutrition, Jenny and I consider fresh fruits and vegetables to be worth every ounce in our backpacks. At various times we have carried potatoes, carrots, onions, celery, corn on the cob, tomatoes, lettuce, cucumbers, cabbage, apples, oranges, limes, lemons, grapefruit, nectarines, bananas and plums. On shorter hikes we bring these fresh foods from home; and on longer hikes in places where stores are available, we buy whatever fresh fruits and vegetables they offer. Even slightly wilted, these are well worth their weight in terms of the restorative

effects and sense of well-being they provide. We can boil the vegetables alone or in a stew, but they are even more nutritious when eaten raw. Corn on the cob is particularly so. If we load these foods carefully into our packs, and cushion and insulate them, they will likely keep for several days. Citrus fruit, apples, carrots, potatoes and cabbage are particularly long lasting.

Fresh potatoes

Potatoes are an important option for us if hiking for more than a day. Fresh potatoes are sometimes available in stores along the way. Prior to departing on a long hike, Jenny and I might place a couple of potatoes in each resupply parcel going to a place where there is no grocery store. Previously, at the supermarket we select the potatoes individually for robustness, making sure they are blemish free. Usually they will arrive at the resupply stations, months later, in fine condition. Some will have budded, and the buds we cut off because they are said to be toxic. Inside the resupply box we store the potatoes loose, rather than in plastic bags which would restrict ventilation and accelerate spoiling. Once as an experiment we vacuum-sealed a few potatoes in an attempt to preserve their freshness. When we collected the resupply box months later, we found that the rotting potatoes had burst their bags, and that a foul liquid had ruined everything. While this experience was less than pleasant, it does illustrate that real foods—unlike nutritionally plundered substances—are alive. They grow, mature, and yes, eventually die.

To cook potatoes while on the trail, we dice and boil them. Otherwise, we eat them raw. "New potatoes" taste the best this way. These are not a separate variety, but are simply harvested early. One can recognize them by their small size and their thin, tender skins usually reddish in color.

Fresh meat and dairy products

Meat eaters can sometimes buy fresh or frozen meats in the stores at trail towns. A few chunks of stew meat, or a small boneless steak, is easily cut into bite-sized pieces and boiled. One might keep the boiling brief to avoid destroying vitamins, cooking only until the pieces are brown on the outside. One might drink the broth as well; it makes a tasty and satisfying hot beverage, and is said to be full of vitamins. Of course if you are a bona-fide meat eater and also a cook-fire enthusiast (see the "Campfire and Cook-fire" chapter) the cooking possibilities become more varied and interesting. However, you might save the BBQs for outside of bear country. Another meat option is to make jerky on a food dehydrator at home. Watch out for commercially processed meats and their nitrates and nitrites, and do not eat spoiled meat due to the danger of botulism.

One issue for consideration by those who eat meat and dairy products is the questionable and often atrocious methods used in the meat and dairy industry, using growth hormones, assorted chemicals, and types of feed too revolting to mention. Rather than spell out the sorry details, let me recommend the book: *Mad Cowboy, Plain Truth From the Cattle Rancher Who Won't Eat Meat* by Howard F. Lyman.

Preparations for our first long hike

When Jenny and I returned from our three-year, around-the-world sailing voyage in 1986, we wanted to immerse ourselves in forests, mountains and deserts. So we decided to hike the PCT. But first we needed to get ourselves in shape. Starting from scratch, we spent seven months training for this hike, and preparing our food and gear.

We studied the subject of food extensively, because we wanted the best energy. And during our training hikes and overnighters, we tried out many of the more interesting food-related ideas. Of course some worked better than others.

Corn spaghetti

Every other day of training we slogged up the snowbound flanks of Pikes Peak in Colorado, testing our energy levels and stamina in relation to the types of processed foods we were trying out.

> Because each person has his or her own tastes and food preferences, I am not making any recommendations. Instead, I am only describing what has worked well for Jenny and me.

One day we found ourselves covering the miles more easily and buoyantly, and we thought back to our previous dinner – corn spaghetti. This was the first time we had tried this type of pasta, and we thought the energy boost was coincidental. However, the more we experimented with it on subsequent hikes, the more we began to realize that it was working for us.

During our first PCT thru-hike, we ate corn spaghetti twice a week.

On our second long hike (PCT-2) we ate corn spaghetti two out of three dinners. Not once did it fail to provide the energy we needed, and never did we tire of eating it. Had we included more in our resupply parcels we would have eaten it. In fact, during the latter stages of that trip we were actually rationing our supply, eating the corn spaghetti only in the late afternoons when we needed an energy boost for the remaining hours of hiking.

Why and how it works for us, we do not know. We can only report that after we have been on journey for several weeks and have **depleted our reserves**, this food provides us with the most energy.

During our third long trek (CDT) we again ate corn spaghetti two out of three dinners. Then on our fifth summer-long trek (PCT-3) we ate it for almost every dinner. Since then, we have eaten it for most dinners on nearly every trip. This has included our IUA hike & bike, our many sea-kayaking and canoeing trips in the Arctic and far north, our row across the Atlantic, even our ski trip to the South Pole.

On some of our earlier trips we carried corn elbows, rather than spaghetti, because the elbows are faster to cook. But we found that they do not provide as much energy. Now we carry corn spaghetti exclusively.

While on journey, we each tend to eat about seven ounces of corn spaghetti, dry weight, per meal. However, when the energy requirements are more extreme, we eat as much as ten ounces each per serving.

Where to find

Corn spaghetti looks like the more usual durum wheat spaghetti, except that it is yellow in color. It is manufactured in much the same way, but supposedly consists only of corn flour. Its shelf life is measured in years if protected from sunlight and moisture. We have used corn spaghetti that was up to five years old, with no diminished effects.

We sometimes find corn spaghetti in a health foods store, but we like to buy it in bulk. And in order to save postage on an internet order, we buy it from a supermarket where the grocer is willing to special order it for us. Bulk orders usually come in cases of individually wrapped packages, either 12-ounce or 8-ounce.

Cooking corn spaghetti

Into a two-liter cookpot, we pour an estimated five cups of water, and cover with the pot's lid or a sheet of aluminum foil.

While waiting for the water to boil, we break 14 ounces of spaghetti into pieces three or four inches long. (When cooking for myself, I use 2½ to 3 cups of water to cook 7 ounces of pasta.)

When the water boils, we remove the lid and place a handful of spaghetti into the pot. Only when the water resumes boiling do we add more. Adding too much at once cools the water and tends to make clumps. As the water begins to boil again, we add another handful of spaghetti then lightly stir it. Too much stirring tends to break down and dissolve the pasta, but not enough stirring will leave clumps. Once we have added all the spaghetti to the pot, we bring the water back to a boil, then shut off the stove and fit the lid. The hot water will continue to cook the pasta nearly as fast; no sense in wasting fuel. But if we are using a cook-fire, we leave the pot on the fire. Either way, we lift the lid occasionally to stir the spaghetti gently to discourage it from clumping together.

A hearty pot of corn spaghetti on the PCT-2

Corn pasta is fairly delicate and must not be over-cooked. When the time seems about right, we fish out a few pieces and sample them. When the spaghetti has reached the *al dente* stage—firm and not yet mushy soft—we decide whether we want to drain the pasta or not. If we need the most energy, we do not discard the starchy liquid, for it contains some food value. But at those times when we prefer the most flavor, we discard most of the liquid. To do this, we keep the lid partly on to retain the spaghetti in the pot, and tilting the pot over to about 75 degrees, we pour the liquid into a small hole in the ground that we have dug with the heel of our shoe. As the hot liquid drains out, the pot lid will become too hot to hold with the fingertips, so we use a short stick instead. Afterwards we fill in the hole. Then before adding the seasonings, we add about a cup of cold water.

Whichever method we have used, it is time to add the various seasonings.

Jenny's Spaghetti-Sauce Leather

My favorite spaghetti sauce is Jenny's tomato leather. She makes it with a small can of tomato paste and one of tomato sauce. To these she adds Italian seasonings, or a store-bought packet of spaghetti seasoning, selecting the type that contains the fewest chemicals. She then chops and sautés a few mushrooms, onions or bell peppers, then blends them into the sauce.

To make this sauce lightweight and long lasting, she dehydrates it.

Jenny made a simple dehydrating rack of 1"-by-2"s that had three trays which she made out of window screen kits from the hardware store. She assembled the aluminum frames, cut the fiberglass screen to the right size, then constructed the wooden drying rack to fit the screens.

Before use, she covers each tray with a sheet of plastic wrap, enough so that the ends overhang the sides of the tray by an inch or two. Then she tapes the plastic's four corners to the under side of the tray to prevent the plastic from curling back onto itself. When the trays are covered, she spreads the sauce on them with a spatula to about a quarter of an inch thick.

During warm months, she sets the rack outside, and covers it with mosquito netting. The hot sun and wafting breeze dehydrates the sauce nicely. In the winter she placed the drying rack indoors near the wood stove, with a fan that circulated air through the trays. However, with no wood stove in our present home, she uses an electric food dehydrator in winter.

When the leather has dried to the pliable but not yet brittle stage, she leaves it adhered to the plastic wrap, rolls it up tightly and cuts each roll in half. Then she seals the pieces in storage bags. Each piece of "leather" is about 12" by 6" when unrolled, and it will season one corn pasta meal for both of us.

However, sometimes she dries the sauce until it is brittle, then freezes it. Then she shreds it in a blender. This makes it somewhat faster to prepare on the trail. Then she packages the leather flakes in resealable bags to protect them from moisture.

On the trail she adds the leather (torn-into-small-chunks or blender-shredded) to the pot. She also might add any embellishments such as dry salami or cheese, or dehydrated items such as meat, tomato, mushroom, onion, or bell pepper.

When the meal is ready to be served, she sprinkles on some Parmesan cheese. Then we share the meal by eating directly from the cookpot.

Corn meal mush

Instant oatmeal is said to be about as nutritious as the box it comes in. Based on my experiences, I think this is a bit of an exaggeration. Nevertheless, we much prefer corn meal mush, which cooks just as quickly. Most store-bought corn meal is de-germed. But if we grind the grains at home, we know that they are complete. Either way, to cook the corn meal we add it to cold water and stir occasionally while bringing the porridge to a boil. Then we reduce the heat and let it simmer for one or two minutes. After allowing it to cool a little, we add powdered milk. We also make small packets of sweeteners with brown sugar, chopped nuts, and raisins. Sometimes we have other tidbits at hand, such as huckleberries, blueberries, or cranberries. This corn "gruel" makes a nutritious and satisfying breakfast and even the occasional dinner.

Way-of-Life Porridge

Granola has long been a standard breakfast with backpackers. And while it may fill the stomach, most commercial varieties are highly processed, and contain heavy doses of sugars, stabilizers, preservatives, etc.

While preparing for our first thru-hike, we experimented with a variety of whole grains and eventually came up with a whole-grain porridge that we call "Way-of-Life."

Our basic Way-of-Life mixture contains equal portions of barley, oats, millet and corn. We are careful to buy organically grown grains, available in most health foods stores. These types are free of pesticides and herbicides, and most likely have not suffered the degrading influences of bio-genetic engineering.

We also buy whole grains that are in their sproutable condition – meaning that they are "alive" and waiting for the right conditions to germinate. We check whether a certain batch of grains is sproutable by simply trying to sprout a small handful of them. To do this, we place them in a jar with

Grinding grains with a hand mill

a mesh lid and let them soak in water overnight. Then a few times a day we rinse and drain the grains. In two or three days we should see the initial stages of growth. This method works with any type of grain, pea or bean. And by the way, after they have germinated they are even more nutritious. If the grains fail to sprout, they may still be suitable for consumption, but not as nutritious.

Most types of processing kill the grains and reduce their long-term nutritional value. But to speed the cooking time, we crack the grains using a hand mill. This reduces their long term food value, but we are still far ahead of the packaged mixes whose ingredients were processed many months, even years ago, and which contain additives of unknown descriptions. With hand milling, the idea is to split each kernel into only a few pieces. A blender or poor quality hand mill will grind some of the grains to powder, while leaving the others nearly intact.

To our basic Way-of-Life mixture we often add smaller amounts of other cracked grains, such as triticale (trit-i-KAY-lee), rye, or brown rice. Then we add various enlivening ingredients, which might include sunflower seeds, sesame seeds, chopped almonds, pecans, cinnamon, or nutmeg.

To cook two hungry-hiker servings, we pour one cup of grain mixture into two or three cups of water. After bringing to a boil, we reduce the heat and simmer for several minutes while stirring frequently, then turn off the stove and place the lid on the pot to hold in the steam. Just like cooking the pasta, the hot water will continue to cook the grains. In terms of cooking times, we find that under-cooked is better than over-cooked; slightly chewy is preferable to glutinous.

Our usual sweeteners of choice include raisins, or home-dried fruits such as apple, pear, peach, apricot, pineapple or papaya, and sometimes a bit of powdered milk. And when on the trail we again add wild berries where available, or sometimes honey or jam. We wait until the grains have cooked before adding these sweeteners, to prevent scorching the bottom of the cookpot.

Pre-soaking the breakfast grains is one way to shorten the morning's cooking routine. We do this by letting the grains sit in cold water overnight. But instead, we often cook them the evening before; that is, immediately following the dinner meal. Leaving the cooked grains in the pot, we place them carefully in one of our backpacks, then carry them for the remaining hours until making camp. The next morning we may hike with them for a few hours, then stop and eat a cold grain breakfast. These grain meals also make good lunches and dinners. They are nutritious, long-lasting and inexpensive.

Well-stocked natural food stores offer many other grains, including kamut, spelt, amaranth (which grows as a weed in many backyards), sorghum, buckwheat and quinoa. These are usually more expensive than the basic oats, barley, and millet, but they add variety. Which grains are best is a matter of preference. If they will sprout, then they are nutritious.

The fastest cooking whole grains are millet and quinoa: three minutes after the water reaches a boil will suffice, with an additional five minutes off the stove while covered with a lid.

Grain and legume dinners

We ate many cracked grains dinners during our early days of backpacking, either by themselves or in combination with cracked peas, beans or lentils. The amino acids found in legumes are said to largely make up for those lacking in the grains.

Some of the more common dry legumes are black beans, black-eyed peas, chickpeas (garbanzos), great northern beans, kidney beans, lentils, lima beans, mung beans, navy beans, pinto beans, soybeans, split peas and whole peas. The legumes suitable for backpacking are those that cook the quickest, and that the hiker likes best. Like grains, they can also be prepared whole; they simply require more cooking time.

Nuts and seeds

Raw nuts and seeds are excellent foods. However, one must watch them because their natural oils can turn rancid after many months. Look for a yellow or brownish hue to the nut or seed, along with the tell-tale odor. Rancidity causes the nut or seed to become bitter and in some cases possibly carcinogenic. So we buy them fresh, and use them before they begin to perish. The most common are sunflower, sesame, pumpkin, flax, almond, cashew, filbert or hazelnut, pine nut, walnut, pecan and peanut (which is actually a legume). Sunflower seeds, hazelnuts, walnuts and brazil nuts contain the most oils, so are the most prone to rancidity. We buy nuts and seeds raw, rather than roasted, salted, sweetened or otherwise processed. And we tend to avoid the commercially packaged nuts containing the usual plethora of chemicals.

Home-made snack bars

Most commercial granola bars and "energy bars" are packed with sugars and chemicals including excitotoxins. We much prefer to make our own healthy, wholegrain snack bars. A simple version might be stone-rolled oats, barley flour, chopped almonds, coconut flakes, raisins and organic honey; baked at 350°F until done.

One could look in various cookbooks for recipes of "cookie bars." Also a person could examine the list of ingredients on the wrappers of some commercial snack bars, then purchase those ingredients at health food stores, mix them imaginatively, and bake. The results would be nothing like the commercial products because one can experiment with different ingredients and proportions.

I think Jenny's home-made creations are far superior to the store-bought varieties, and we know what is in them. If a person wants to bolster protein content, he or she could add powdered milk. And if one wants to equal the synthesized vitamin and mineral content of the commercial techno-wonder-bars, he or she could take a multi-vitamin/mineral supplement every few days.

Snack bars do not have to be sweet; one can make them more like a heavy bread, using freshly milled whole grain flours. Some cookbooks have recipes for hard tack, trail bread, and pemmican.

Home packaging

For our first thru-hike, we packaged our corn pasta and fresh-milled grain and legume meals using a vacuum sealing machine. This extracted most of the air from the plastic bags, and sealed them closed. The resulting packages were hard like blocks of wood, such was the vacuum's pressure. Our intent was to preserve the food's freshness. During shipment, however, about 80% of the packages lost their vacuum. This happened because the packages jostled against one another, and the rough contents punctured the plastic bags like needles.

Preparing for our second thru-hike, we again used the vacuum sealer, but with much less vacuum pressure. In addition, we used a simple non-vacuum sealing machine, and this also worked well. What packaged foods we did not eat on the trail, we sent home for consumption during the winter months.

However, while out on the trails we experienced a different kind of problem with the packaging. The weight and bulk of the plastic bags were not so noticeable when the bags were full, but as we emptied them we found it hard to ignore the size and weight of our accumulating trash. This we had to carry to the next resupply point,

from where we sent the reusable plastic bags home for later use. Clearly, we needed to minimize our food packaging materials.

For our next trip we packed the individual meals in paper, which we could then burn when empty. Specifically, we placed the contents of a grain, legume, or corn pasta meal on a sheet of brown paper, such as that cut from a grocery sack. We rolled and folded the paper to envelop the contents, and taped it closed. Another option is to use small paper lunch bags. Then we identified the contents in writing on the package. This system is still our preferred method today.

Plastic bags with zip tops (resealable) are neither waterproof nor moisture-proof. Heat-sealed bags are better, and one can make them quite small to contain seasonings, etc. When cutting one open the first time, we only cut a corner off, diagonally. To reseal, we fold the corner down and secure it with a small bit of adhesive tape.

Other ideas we've tried

Trail mix

I suspect that gorp (Good Ol' Raisins and Peanuts) and all its variations will be around as long as hikers themselves. I have certainly eaten my share of trail mix, and during our first few long distance hikes Jenny and I always carried a bag of it in our packs.

We made our trail mix from dried fruit, raisins, chopped dates, shredded coconut, sunflower seeds, peanuts, almonds, cashews, walnuts, and sometimes small candies. For even more variety we added chips, snack-type crackers, and dry breakfast cereals made from corn.

The reason we paid so much attention to variety was to make the mix more appealing. We tried making it an art form. We tried making it colorful to look at and fun to eat. We avoided items laden with chemicals. But no matter how varied with ingredients, half way through the hikes we found ourselves high-grading the bags (picking through them and eating only the most appealing items and tossing the rest to the imaginary chipmunks). Clearly, all this no longer appealed to us.

Today we seem to have come full circle, returning to the basics. We sometimes carry small bags of basic trail-mix: nuts, seeds, and raisins.

Powdered potatoes

Potato flakes are inexpensive, lightweight, and easy to prepare. When choosing which brand to buy, we examine the list of ingredients for chemical content. Nevertheless, they are not nearly as nutritious as fresh potatoes, so we do not eat them often.

A person can eat them cold by mixing the flakes in cold water. But mix them extra soupy and let them sit a few minutes to thicken. Otherwise they will thicken in the stomach, sapping the moisture from the gut and possibly causing discomfort. As with all dehydrated foods, drink plenty of water along with them. To serve powdered potatoes warm, heat the water first. They do not need to be cooked. Although they are palatable as is, adding powdered milk gives them more texture and taste; adding dried herbs, spices or seasonings makes them more interesting. A person could also add dry potato flakes to soups or stews.

Home-dehydrated foods

The process of dehydrating foods reduces their weight and gives them a much longer storage life. Unfortunately, it also destroys a high percentage of their food values. Jenny and I ate a considerable quantity of dehydrated foods during our earlier hikes, and found that they provided very little energy, certainly far less than their fresh food counterparts.

Nevertheless, food dehydrating is a simple matter of extracting most of the moisture. As described in the Spaghetti-Sauce Leather section, it requires a source of low heat to accelerate evaporation, and plenty of ventilation to carry the moisture away. The optimum temperature is around 100°F but this can vary considerably. As the food loses moisture, it also loses bulk. For example, a one-pound bag of frozen corn (3 cups) dehydrates to 4½ ounces (1 cup).

For meat eaters, beef jerky is another possibility. Pre-soaked jerky might make an interesting addition to the grain and legume meals. Store-bought jerky is expensive and usually loaded with nitrates, nitrites and MSG, but making one's own is easy. Buy lean steak, not necessarily an expensive cut, and slice it across the grain in strips a quarter-inch wide. Marinate the strips in the seasonings of your choice. When the strips of meat are well coated, spread them on the food dryer rack.

Fruit leathers are also easy to make. Place the fruit in a blender and pulverize to a thick paste. Pour the resulting mash onto a drying rack lined with plastic wrap, and

Dehydrating spaghetti-sauce leather beside a wood stove. The hanging bags contain previously dehydrated food.

place the rack in the food dryer. Use the same technique for sauces.

A person can also dehydrate cooked meats such as ground beef or turkey. And one can dehydrate fruits and vegetables that are fresh, canned, or frozen. In fact one can dehydrate entire meals. Chili works particularly well. Simply prepare the dish as you normally would, then spread it out on the plastic-coated drying rack. On the trail, rehydrate the dinner by adding water and allowing it to stand for three or four hours. Leave plenty of space for expansion; the re-hydrating food doubles in volume. While the food is re-hydrating, one can place it in the backpack, inside a resealable plastic bag or lidded plastic bowl, inside the cookpot. At dinnertime, cook the meal for a few minutes, or simply eat it cold.

Beverages substitutes

We drink pure water to stay hydrated, as opposed to sodas or flavored drink mixes, coffee and beer. Still, a hot beverage can be a satisfying addition, especially on a blustery day. And a hot "cuppa" at day's end can provide a welcome ambiance for the journal writing. Possibilities include hot cocoa, tea and herbal tea, and the caffeine-free coffee substitutes such as Cafix, a grain and fig beverage.

The task of preparing wholesome foods for a long backpacking trip is a major one, yet as with the trek itself, the easiest approach is to take things one step at a time. Having considered this chapter, a person might experiment with some of these ideas at home, well in advance of the outing. I recommend reading other books on nutrition, perusing cookbooks for ideas, preparing trial meals at home and testing various ingredients. Remember too, that your tastes and preferences may change once you have been on the trail a few weeks and as the need for metabolic fuel begins to spiral.

Also, with the exception of fresh fruits and vegetables, the dry foods mentioned above represent merely our compromises. That is, although they are not the perfect life-sustaining foods, they provide sufficient energy, pack well, and are long lived without refrigeration. At home we do not have to make these compromises so we do not eat most of these foods. However, we spend a lot of time in the wilds.

And once again, we think each person should draw his or her own conclusions about which foods are best, about what one likes and dislikes, and which foods are best avoided. We each have different preferences, but we also have a great many similarities in physical makeup and nutritional requirements. Fortunately the human body is remarkably adaptive when it comes to junk food and drinks, within limits. But even with this in mind, no one has all the answers, even concerning nutrition.

Jenny cooks corn spaghetti in the Three Sisters Wilderness during the filming for a BBC program.

Water

> "We'll never know the worth of water
> till the well goes dry."
>
> — *Scottish Proverb*

Seen from space, our blue planet reveals its surface to be mostly water, rather than the land on which we live. Water is the sustainer of life, and although we cannot live in it, this precious fluid most certainly lives in us. Our blood is 90% water, and is about the same salinity as seawater. Our brains are 75% water; and overall our bodies average 70% water.

These fluid percentages are vital to our health and well being. Yet we lose a great deal of water as we hike along the trail. With each exhalation we lose moisture, since our expelled breath is always 100% saturated. Moisture evaporates from our skin continually, in the form of insensible perspiration. We lose water through urination, of course. And we can exude tremendous amounts through sweat.

Eagle Creek gorge, PCT-1

In order to maintain adequate fluid levels, we have to drink a great deal of water. Or else we become dehydrated.

The effects of dehydration

Water lubricates the joints in our hips, knees and ankles – in much the same way that oil lubricates machinery. Dehydration reduces this lubricating effect, stiffening our joints and making them more susceptible to injury. Dehydration also stiffens our muscles, ligaments, and tendons, making them much more prone to hiking-related stress injuries. Moreover, as the body loses water, the blood thickens and decreases in volume, becoming more sluggish. This raises blood pressure and slows circulation. As such, it lowers the delivery rate of fuel and oxygen to the muscles. And it retards the extraction of by-products of metabolism from the muscles. This can make us feel sapped of energy. The thickened blood and restricted circulation also slows the brain's functions, impeding one's mental processes and destabilizing the emotions. These physiological changes can take the fun out of a backpacking trip.

H₂O is our rehydrator of choice

On any kind of backpacking trip, long or short, Jenny and I find the best fluid for keeping us hydrated is pure water.

Sports drinks supposedly replace lost electrolytes, but we feel that this is mainly a marketing ploy by the billon dollar industry. Humans existed on this planet for perhaps millions of years without sports drinks and so called "energy" drinks, and seemed to do just fine. In fact, I imagine that their lives were much more vigorous than ours. How did they get by? Most likely they drank pure water. And how did they replace lost electrolytes? By eating wild, natural foods.

I view sports/energy drinks in the much the same category as carbonated soft drinks. That is to say, they are loaded with highly processed sugars in various forms, and may contain all manner of added chemicals disguised as exotic or even so-called natural ingredients. Drinking too much of these in a short period would likely cause an insulin crash that might make the person ill.

> Read the label on a can or bottle of beverage (sports drink, soft drink, fruit drink, etc). It may give the number of servings per container, and amount of sugars per serving, in grams. Multiply these to get total grams of sugars per container. Divide this by 4 to get the equivalent number of teaspoons of sugar per container. A packet of sugar, such as found in a restaurant, contains one teaspoon of sugar (4 grams).
> Example: 12 fl oz. can of Coca Cola has 39 grams of sugar. (39 ÷ 4): 9.75 packets of sugar!
> Sobe 20 fl oz: (2.5x22g÷4): 13.75 packets of sugar.
> Knudsen 32 fl oz "Organic 100% juice, no sugar added" (4x28÷4): 28 packets of sugar (fructose).

In fact, the sugar rush is what these drinks are all about. Sugar type sweeteners are addictive, and this is why the industry makes so much money selling them. Sodas, coffee, and beer[8] are also money makers for the same reason. They are addictive to many people.

The best way to consume a sports drink is to water it down by pouring one or two inches of sports drink in a water bottle and filling the rest with water. And if the drink comes in a wide-mouthed plastic bottle with a screw on lid, you could recycle the bottle most beneficially for use as a water bottle.

Electrolytes mix

When hiking with vigor in hot weather, we may occasionally add some electrolytes to our water. We make our own by adding a small pinch of table salt (sodium chloride), a pinch of salt substitute (potassium chloride), and half a teaspoon of table sugar to one liter of water.[9] A person could instead mix a diluted powdered electrolyte drink.

The psychology of thirst

The sensation of thirst is a poor indicator of when to drink water. By the time a person feels thirsty, he or she is already dehydrated. And while a few sips of cold water will usually satisfy thirst, such a small amount is not nearly enough to rehydrate the body. So not only does thirst comes too late, it shuts off too soon. Also, when the water bottles are empty, thirst can be a tormentor, and the agony only worsens when one allows the mind to dwell on incessant thoughts of the cold drinks he or she does not have. All this is to suggest that thirst is mainly a psychological effect. It is a tool for helping one stay properly hydrated; but like any tool it has limitations. So rather than rely on thirst to tell us when to drink water, we tune in to our body's physical signals.

Signs of deepening dehydration

The surest way to know if we are staying hydrated is by remaining aware of our water consumption. For example, suppose that we have been hiking for five hours and have taken only a few small sips of water. Based on this information alone, we know that our bodies are dehydrated. Let's look at some of the effects of dehydration, in their general order of occurrence.

▶ After a half a day's hiking with only a minimum of water, one will notice (if one is paying attention) a marked

---

8 Not only is alcohol addictive and dehydrating, but just a single drop of alcohol kills 13,000 brain cells.

9 In contrast, a soft drink has up to 40 times the sugar content: 10 teaspoons in a 12-fl oz can. Store-bought fruit juice has just as much.

decrease in urinary output. This is a signal that something is amiss, but unfortunately—as far as the body is concerned—it is a signal that is easily ignored. Nevertheless, this stage of dehydration is common among hikers.

▶ The more hours spent hiking without drinking enough water, the deeper the dehydration. Higher altitudes and higher ambient temperatures accelerate the effect wildly. As the day wears on, and as the urinary output continues to decrease in volume, the urine also begins to darken in color. Although dark yellow is obvious, it is still easy to disregard. From here on, however, the body will start signaling in ways that are not so easily ignored.

▶ Namely, a headache, which is often referred to—incorrectly—as "altitude headache." Show me someone in the backcountry with a headache, and I will show you someone who is severely dehydrated. The dehydration may not be the only problem, but often it is. Unfortunately, most people fail to associate this signal with the dehydration. So rather than correct the problem by drinking volumes of water, they take a few pain-killing tablets. At least with these they drink a few gulps of water.

▶ Next comes queasiness, most often the result of introducing pain killing medication into a severely dehydrated body.

▶ And of course the constipation. Meaning that the digestive tract has slowed nearly to a stop. When this happens, the person may begin to feel seriously ill.

▶ As the dehydrated hiker continues disregarding these problems, his or her body becomes much more prone to stress injury. Initially this might be indicated by a budding hiking pain, for example in the Achilles tendon, or in the back, or joints. All too often, though, the hiker shrugs it off as "part of the hike," and takes more pain relief tablets, which dulls the aches and pains but only masks the real problem. If the person carries on, and allows the dehydration to continue its spiraling descent, he or she may

soon be courting a bona fide injury, perhaps in the knee or spinal disks – of course, calling it "accidental." The fact is, the severely dehydrated body is an "accident waiting to happen."

Any of these maladies make the trip less fun, and thoughts of returning home more tempting. And any subsequent outings, with equally negative results, only reinforce the notion that hiking and camping are not very enjoyable. All this for lack of sufficient water intake.

Chronic dehydration plays a key part in many more ailments. An excellent book on this subject is *Your Body's Many Cries For Water* by F. Batmanghelidj, M.D. The book's subtitle is *You are not sick, you are thirsty!; Don't treat thirst with medications*. In particular, if you know anyone who suffers back pain, neck pain, headache, migraine, anginal pain, high blood pressure, hypertension, high blood cholesterol, asthma, allergies, some types of diabetes, dyspeptic pain, colitis pain, false appendicitis pain, rheumatoid arthritis pain, stress and depression – hand them a copy of the "Batman" book.

Generous amounts

Once deep dehydration sets in, it takes two or three days—not just minutes or hours—of drinking water voluminously to recover. So the best tactic for avoiding dehydration is to consume generous amounts of water throughout the day.

When hiking longer distances between water sources, we do not let the extra weight of the water discourage us from carrying a decent supply. At the same time, it makes little sense to be a water hoarder – carrying it for purposes of security, or to simply ignore the need to stop and drink on a regular basis. Why arrive at a water source with a quart or more still in the bottles? At two pounds per quart, this is wasted effort. We think the best idea is to carry only enough to meet our needs, such that we arrive at the next source well hydrated, but with bottles nearly empty. With a good map or guide book in hand, this is generally not difficult to plan.

Water intoxication

Of course, a person can drink too much water, resulting in a condition known as hyponatremia. This would be extremely rare among hikers, but to counteract it a person could eat more salty foods, or mix up an electrolytes drink, described above.

Shortcomings of "purification"

According to conventional backpacking wisdom, giardia contaminates all wilderness water, and we hikers and campers need to purify every drop that we drink, as well as what we use for cooking and brushing teeth. You can read this in hundreds of magazine articles and books.

Hydration is important even in cold weather; PCT-3

Jenny and I followed this rule faithfully during our first four mega-hikes. And I was sick with giardia-type symptoms many times.

Obviously, something was wrong. If we were being meticulous about filtering our water, then why was I not staying healthy? Jenny remained healthy, and she was drinking the same treated water as I. Apparently my immunities were lower than hers in some manner. But the fact remains that somehow I seemed to be contracting parasites despite the assiduous use of the water filter. The filter cartridges we were using were common, brand-name varieties, and we had no reason to suspect they were not working properly.

Clearly, the conventional wisdom was not working. So we abandoned it and tried a different approach. While training for our fifth thru-hike we drank directly from clean, natural sources, a few sips at first, then gradually increasing in quantity over the weeks and months. In this way we helped condition our bodies to the water's natural flora. Then during the actual journey we drank all our water straight from the springs, creeks, and sometimes the lakes – after carefully appraising each source. And for the first time in years I remained symptom-free; and Jenny stayed healthy also.

I am not suggesting that hikers abandon their water filters. But I do think that our experiments yielded information that can be useful to anyone venturing into the wilds.

I doubt whether my illness had anything to do with the filtration or lack thereof. Rather, it had to do with the nature of the water sources we were using. During the initial thru-hikes we were collecting water from all but the worst sources, and treating it. In several cases that I can think of, I feel that this treatment—or any other available treatment—was incapable of making that water safe to drink. This is why, on that fifth trek, we collected water only from clean sources.

Based on these experiments and their successful outcome, the following are my recommendations: Learn to recognize pristine water, and **treat it** if you prefer. Learn to recognize water that could be contaminated with microbes, if only mildly, and **treat it thoroughly**. And most importantly, learn to recognize water that is beyond treatment, despite any reasonable degree of clarity. Such water can be extremely virulent, and no water treatment system available to hikers is capable of making that water safe to drink. **Do not filter, boil or add purification chemicals to this polluted water**. And do not use it for cooking or bathing. In the next section I explain how to recognize such highly contaminated water.

On the CDT

I also learned that our main sources of protozoa—such as giardia and cryptosporidia—are often our own bodies. Our intestines are breeding grounds for these protozoa, and when we fail to sterilize our hands after elimination, we re-introduce the microscopic pathogens in vast numbers, for example when we eat a handful of trail mix.

While **I am not recommending that anyone forgo the water filter**, Jenny and I did find that without it, we drank probably three times as much water as we would have had we been filtering. Such was the greater ease and convenience of drinking directly from good water sources. And we feel that this extra fluid intake was of tremendous benefit. With no filter to carry, we saved some pack weight. And being able to drink freely of the earth's life-force provided a refreshing connection with the natural world. But again this is not to suggest that we drank from any and all water sources. Each one we scrutinized carefully as to its safety. Those we considered unsafe—of which there were many—we bypassed.

Recognizing safe water

Judging the purity of water is a wilderness skill. The more knowledge one gains and the more experience one builds, the better the judgment will be. Later in the chapter I describe specific types of contaminants and methods for handling them, but I will start off with explaining how we judge a water source. Remember that the goal here is not to enable a person to drink "bush water" straight from the source. Rather, it is to show how we recognize water that is beyond treatment; water that might look all right, but that can make a person terribly sick regardless of how thoroughly it is treated.

The first step is to inspect the water visually.

159

Stagnation

If the water is stagnant, then processing it by normal means will probably do little to make it potable. This is because stagnant water collects anything and everything flowing into it, while allowing nothing to escape other than what can evaporate. So the concentrations build, year after year. Normally, a stagnant pool of water contains harmful chemicals, depending on what is leaching into it, and from where. It can also be laden with decaying plant matter and teeming with infective microorganisms. In times of dire need a person might be tempted to filter and boil it, and consume in moderation. This is rarely a good idea.

Foam

The presence of mats and balls of foam on the water's surface almost always indicates heavy pollution, usually in the form of agricultural or industrial runoff. Ag runoff can consist of fertilizers, pesticides, herbicides, and livestock and feedlot wastes, none of which can be treated effectively by normal means. Tannic acid (discussed below) does not create foam.

Algae

In addition to foam, agricultural and community wastes like sewage, detergents, and decomposing rubbish often encourage heavy algae growth, although sometimes the pollutants are so toxic that even the algae cannot subsist in it very well. Pure spring water also harbors algae, but of a completely different type; they feed on the organic minerals coming from deep within the earth. Normally, spring water is safe to drink.

If polluted water contains algae, and pure spring water does also, then what does the algae tell us about the water's quality? With experience we learned to recognize the types that grow in polluted water, and the types found only in pure sources. They are quite different in appearance. But more importantly, we consider where the water is coming from. Is it flowing directly out of a high mountain spring? Or does it flow from an area of industry, agriculture or human population? We look at the overall picture, and avoid making assumptions about the water in front of us based on our immediate surroundings. For example, that nice-looking creek flowing through a forest might have passed through a meadow upstream where livestock have been grazing. So we look at the overall lay of the land, and consult our map for clues as to what may lie above or around our location.

Root beer coloration

In some backcountry areas the water has a slightly brown hue, like diluted root beer. The coloring agent here is tannic acid, leached from organic growth, most often cedar. The tannic acid is not harmful in such weak concentrations, even when consumed in large amounts. But neither does it purify the water. The coloration tells us nothing about whether the water is potable or not.

Poison

In certain places, most notably in the arid Southwest, seeping springs can have poisonous, high alkali content, caused by the water dissolving certain mineral salts, namely those of carbonate or hydroxide of alkali metals. The first clue is the presence of brown or dark orange algae, microscopic in size and visible only as a bottom coloring. Sometimes a calcium-like encrustation forms around the water's margins. Alkali water has an immediate and long-lasting bitter taste. It is quite obviously unsafe to drink. Even in low concentrations it leaves a disturbing aftertaste.

In a very few areas of the Southwest, certain small springs contain arsenic. This water will usually be crystal clear, and there will be no algae or plant life growing in it whatsoever. And unlike the cartoons showing bones lying about, the animals and birds know not to drink it.

Good spring water almost always supports algae growth, normally green in color.

Mining operations are well known for polluting water sources in otherwise pristine areas. The on-site extraction of gold and other metals from ore is notorious for contaminating the area with cyanide. This type of pollution is often indicated by a telltale orange cast to the creek beds. It is called "acid rock drainage" and the color indicates the presence of iron sulfide. It is not actually cyanide, but could indicate mining contamination upstream.

Stock pollution

Stock pollution is the cause of most sickness in hikers. Cattle, sheep, horses, mules and llamas are egregious polluters, and will quickly contaminate springs, creeks of all sizes, and all but the larger lakes. After we have long been in the woods, our sense of smell becomes very acute, and we will be able to detect stock manure and urine in the water, even in minute amounts. In creeks with cattle grazing upstream, even far upstream, we may also find tell-tail clumps of long, stringy algae, dark green in color. But here again our map is our best ally. The combination of a road and a meadow upstream suggests cattle grazing in that meadow. Cattle-polluted water is extremely virulent, even in low concentrations.

Beaver Fever

The term "beaver fever" refers to the infection caused by giardia, and I suspect that the term was designed and widely publicized mainly with the intent of turning the hiker's attention from the main sources of pollution, which are human related. How convenient to make the beaver a scapegoat when cattle and sheep are grazing in the backcountry by the hundreds of thousands. We know that many other wild creatures live and/or forage in the water: muskrat, mink, otter, birds, fish and amphibians, to name just a few. In very low concentrations, this water can be safely treated.

Some of my most serious bouts with intestinal infection occurred in the alpine regions of Colorado, far above any beaver. Many times I would climb to the crest of some rugged range and find the ground littered profusely in sheep manure. When the livestock are allowed to graze that high, we find it difficult to avoid their pollution.

Examining the water source

The preceding visual clues help us identify contaminated water. Now for the various types of water sources:

Creeks

Mountain creeks, far removed from human activity, are usually suitable for treating. How do we know? We do not, for sure. But we can make an educated guess by examining where the creek is coming from. Looking at the map, do we find mines or human settlements nearby? Could there be cattle grazing upstream? Have we been seeing the tracks of horses or cattle and their manure? If the water is flowing from remote, alpine regions, with no sign of stock in the area, then the water is probably safe to treat by filtering or boiling.

The lower the elevation, the more contaminated the water, generally. So, before descending into a valley, we fill our bottles. But if we are in low country to begin with, and if we come to a creek wending along a valley bottom, we are very careful. Low drainages are well known for collecting all manner of pollutants, from farm and industrial runoff, to human effluent.

Lakes and ponds

When considering the potability of water in a lake or pond, we check its inlet or outlet for the rate of flow. Also we look at the lake bottom along the shoreline. Clean rocks and sand normally indicate good flow, while a thick, mucky bottom indicates stagnation. The less the flow, the greater the buildup of toxins and pathogens. And as with creeks, the quality of lake or pond water depends also on where that water is coming from.

Floating leaves, twigs and pollen are inevitable on lakes and ponds, and do not usually affect the water quality. When collecting water, we might wrap a bandana over our bottle or cookpot to filter out the floaties.

Sacred springs

Not all spring water is pure. The terrain above the spring could be boggy, and that bog water could be percolating into the earth and resurfacing as the spring. This type of water could be contaminated. Or there could be a mine uphill of the spring. Another possible source of spring contamination often found in lower terrain is the polluted aquifer, from which the water is upwelling, artesian-style. This is becoming more of a problem in the vicinity of toxic waste dumps and old landfills, which may leach all sorts of dreadful pollutants.

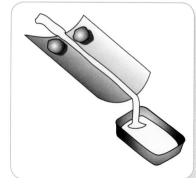

A spring along the PCT. For scale, the fir sapling was about a foot tall.

However, most springs in the higher regions are pristine, and these are our finest sources of water. In fact, since discovering how beneficial they are to good health, we have come to think of them as sacred – as did many Native American peoples. We did not perceive them as such when relying on water filters. But now when I drink from a pure, flowing spring, I feel like I am making a closer connection with the earth and its life-force. I see pure spring water not merely as another commodity, but as a priceless gift for the continuance of life. And I always give thanks, in appreciation of the water's true worth.

Seeps

A seep is a tiny spring that barely flows. And as with their more heartily flowing kin, we use the same criteria for judging whether its water is contaminated or not.

We tread carefully around a seep, since it is easily damaged and rendered unusable for the next person or wild animal. Collecting water from a seep can be a delicate process. The idea is to channel the water while leaving the dirt or debris behind. For a collection gutter we use a non-toxic leaf, or a piece of paper, plastic bag, or aluminum foil. Assuming the seep is flowing slightly, we place the gutter in the trickle, then weight it down with a pair of stones at its uphill end. Then we dig a small hole downstream, under the place where water is dribbling off the gutter. And we place a small container in the hole as a catchment. We once bought a single-serving of corn flakes in a café along the Appalachian Trail. The cereal came in a little plastic tub; and we have used that tub ever since as a miniature basin for collecting water from shallow sources.

Where the ground is only moist, we might try scraping a depression. We use a stout stick, and scrape deeply enough so that the hole fills with a reasonable volume of water, but not so deep that it would scar the landscape. We then scoop the precious liquid very gently so as not to stir

Using an empty wrapper to collect water from a seep.

the sediment; and afterwards we usually leave our small waterhole for the wildlife to use.

Water contaminants

The following is a list of possible contaminants in backcountry water.

▶ Chemical herbicides, pesticides, fertilizers, etc. These can enter the water through agricultural or industrial run-off. Many of these chemicals are in solution, and cannot be removed by boiling, adding purification chemicals, or filtration by ordinary devices.

▶ Coliform bacteria such as E. Coli. These bacteria are found naturally in the intestines, and are a necessary part of life. However, an outbreak of them can cause sickness. They stem from human and livestock waste, and can easily contaminate a water source.

▶ Viruses (ultra-microscopic infectious agents) and amoebas (parasitic protozoa). Rare in the U.S. wilderness, and easily disabled by boiling the water they inhabit.

▶ Cysts, including microscopic worms, parasites and protozoa. The biggest offenders are giardia and cryptosporidia, which can cause diarrhea and intestinal disorders (see below). Both are common in the wilds. When their environment becomes inhospitable, such as in the presence of iodine, or the absence of water, these parasites can transform into cystic form; like hard, round microscopic eggs. Once the cysts are ingested by a "host," the shells are discarded and the organisms infect the intestines.

Giardia

Giardia (pronounced gee-ARE-dee-uh), was named after the nineteenth century French zoologist, Alfred Mathieu Giard. Giardia is a protozoan, which is an animal-like, single cell organism. When ingested by animals, including humans, the organism metamorphoses into a trophozoite (tro-pho-ZO-ite) and attaches itself to the small intestine. The trophozoite is the protozoan in the active stage of its life cycle. Once attached in the intestines, it may begin interfering with the host's digestion. If the interference is pronounced, the result is the intestinal infection known as giardiasis (gee-are-DIE-uh-sis).

Later, the trophozoite multiplies, and the resulting cysts—millions of them—travel down the colon and are excreted. Thus, the host acts as a breeding reservoir. And if infected stools contaminate a water source, the disease can spread to those mammals later drinking it.

Giardia parasites have probably always been a natural part of the intestinal flora in mammals. However, giardiasis, the infection, is a different matter. Previously, when people and animals ingested the protozoa or cysts, they were not nearly as prone to illness. This is because they produced antibodies that fought off the microbes or at least staved off their effects. But within the past several decades, two factors have contributed to the increased risks of a person's contracting giardiasis.

▶ As a result of living in civil sterility, our bodies have essentially quit producing the antibodies necessary to maintain our natural immunities. This civil sterility comes from drinking municipally treated tap water or bottled water that is free of giardia (in most cases), and by taking medicinal antibiotics, eradicating any pre-existing giardia parasites in our bodies.

▶ Livestock including cattle, horses, mules and llamas are polluting the backcountry water in increasing numbers. This has almost certainly raised the giardia count. (Humans and wild animals do not defecate in the water sources.)

Regardless of the cause, when drinking from the natural water sources, a person risks becoming infected – irrespective of the methods of purification. This does not mean, however, that one will automatically become sick. Most of the time our bodies will be able to hold their own against the effects of the giardia, and we will remain healthy. Staying healthy is mainly a matter of ingesting a minimum of pathogens, while developing immunities to the unavoidable. But when the giardia overwhelms the body's defenses, sickness results.

This used to be a nice spring-fed creek before the horses and mules demolished it. This creek is located mid-way on a long, waterless stretch of PCT.

The typical symptoms are diarrhea and intestinal disorder. The infected person usually experiences a number of loose stools throughout the day. Those who choose to ride the symptoms out, as I have always done, would do well to increase their intake of treated water in order to reduce the malady's dehydrating effects. And they would be extremely fastidious about washing their hands after eliminating. Those who find themselves with increasing symptoms should visit a doctor, since the malady might not be what they think. Some doctors recommend carrying Diasorb in tablet form. This is one of the more potent non-prescription anti-diarrheal medications. Otherwise, you might plan ahead and carry a prescribed medication such as metronidazole (the generic name for Flagyl). But use it only as a last resort, since it will reduce your natural immunities even further.

Cryptosporidia

Cryptosporidia (KRIP-toe-spo-RID-ee-uh) is a one-celled protozoan that, like giardia, occurs widely in nature. The infection is called cryptosporidiosis, (KRIP-toe-spo-RID-ee-O-sis) or simply "crypto" and is a common cause of diarrhea worldwide. The symptoms are similar to those of giardia: watery diarrhea and intestinal disorders. Drugs are ineffective, but healthy individuals will normally recover on their own, although the symptoms may last a few weeks. Again, persons affected should drink plenty of treated water, and they may also wish to take anti-diarrheal medication.

Cryptosporidia is highly infectious, and can be transmitted in much the same way as giardia. Neither iodine nor chlorine will kill it, at least in the usual concentrations used in "purification." Boiling is the best method of treatment. Filtration is also effective, at least with units that remove particles smaller than two microns.

Giardia and crypto are found worldwide, so hikers might exercise the same precautions no matter where they are traveling. A malady similar in its symptoms to giardia and crypto but much more pernicious is protozoal amoeba diarrhea (as opposed to protozoal giardia diarrhea), more commonly known as amoebic dysentery. This disease kills millions of people annually. The initial symptoms are giardia-like except for one important difference. Giardiasis produces diarrhea day after day. Amoebic dysentery causes alternating diarrhea and constipation.

Water treatment options

Filtration is the hiker's most popular method of treating water. Other options include adding iodine or chlorine, and boiling. All these methods do nothing to remove or neutralize chemical contamination, and they are ineffective at treating sewage or effluent. As outlined above, one must know where the water is coming from.

Boiling

Boiling will destroy water-borne bacteria and other live organic pollutants, and it will deactivate viruses. Once the water reaches a roiling boil, the sterilization is complete, and you may remove the water from the heat and allow it to cool. Boiling can be used in addition to filtration, when you want the extra assurance. If short on stove fuel, a possible option might be to boil the water on a cook-fire (see the "Campfire and Cook-fire" chapter).

Iodine

As a water purification agent, iodine tablets are lightweight, compact and easy to use. The objectionable taste can be neutralized with ascorbic acid, 50 mg to a liter. The recommended two tablets of iodine for each quart of water, used in perhaps six quarts a day, would seem to be a considerable chemical accumulation. For occasional use I suppose it is acceptable, but surely not throughout an entire summer. To an extent, iodine is cumula-

tive in the body, which is why municipal water treatment facilities do not use it.

If the water collected from a certain source is cold, and most water in the natural environment is, then after dropping the iodine tablets into it, you must wait twenty minutes for the chemical to take full effect. Imagine hiking for hours between distant water sources, arriving at the next source and having to wait twenty minutes before taking a drink! What usually happens is that the hiker adds the tablets, then waits only a few minutes before drinking. Perhaps the hiker reasons that the iodine will continue working in the stomach. Unfortunately, this does not happen. The stomach lining quickly absorbs the water, along with the iodine in solution, and it leaves the microbes behind, where they then proceed into the digestive tract.

Filtration

Small, portable water filters are popular with hikers. These come in a wide variety of makes and models, take your pick. Filtration units with maximum porosity of about two microns will effectively screen out most protozoa. The finer the filtration, the greater the resistance to the water passing through it, meaning that the harder it is to pump, the slower it operates, and the less water it can treat before clogging.

"Hiker's Friend" water filtration system

Most water filters designed for hikers are operated by hand-pump. I find this method tedious, which is why I greatly prefer the gravity-feed method. I originated the idea, at least in this modern application, with the invention of the Hiker's Friend water filter system back in 1987 while preparing for our first thru-hike. Jenny and I have since used this system on hiking trips and sea-kayaking trips in Mexico and the Arctic. I recommend it highly. Although the system is not infallible, neither is any other type of filtration system. For a description of how it

On our 2nd PCT hike, we enjoy a dinner stop. Note our Hiker's Friend water filter hanging in the tree.

works, and how you can make one for yourself, see the "Sewing" chapter.

Other means of contracting pathogens

As I learned during my earlier thru-hikes, no water filter system or other treatment method can keep pathogens from entering our bodies. Assuming we use the filter correctly, and that the particular filter or its cartridge is not defective in some way, a few protozoa could still pass through the cartridge. However, a more likely scenario involves the microbes entering the body via other channels. One possibility is by washing the face in untreated water. Another is by washing the hands in untreated water, and then munching on a hand-held snack bar, for example. And while giardia is ordinarily a water-borne parasite, it does not need water to survive. Assuming you wash your cookpot, cup and spoon in untreated water, and towel them dry, many cysts could be left clinging to those items.

But there is a far more serious problem to consider here. We, ourselves, can be our own worst sources of protozoa. When we experience even a minor outbreak of giardia or cryptosporidia within the intestines, we become generators of these pathogens. As the protozoa reproduce inside the intestines, they do so by the millions, and the stools become extremely infective. So when returning from the privy or "bushes," we sterilize our hands, preferably with ethyl alcohol gel. If we are washing with an antibacterial soap, we use the dundo method.

Hiking between distant water sources

Nature does not always place water at intervals convenient to us. But she does give most of us legs to walk from one source to the next, and the brains to figure out how to overcome any inconveniences.

The 20 mile waterless stretch

Suppose that water sources "A" and "B" are twenty miles apart. Ideally, we would plan to arrive at source A in the mid-afternoon. There, we would cook dinner. But rather than eat it then and there, we stow it carefully into the backpack. After filling a quart-size water bottle with treated water, we pour two or three quarts of untreated water into a water bag. In very hot weather we would of course collect much more. After enjoying a dundo shower, we would "super-saturate" by drinking as much as our stomachs can hold.

We then set off, and hike a few hours, then sit down and eat dinner. Refreshed once again, we continue with a will another several miles into evening until leaving the trail and making a pleasant stealth camp (see the chapter on "Stealth Camping"). The next morning, we rise at dawn and resume hiking the remaining distance to water source B, arriving there mid-day, and not long after consuming the last of our water.

With this kind of timing, the twenty-mile distance between water sources is only a minor inconvenience, except for having to carry the extra water. At no time do we become dehydrated or tormented by thirst. Twenty-mile waterless stretches are fairly common along the Continental Divide Trail and Pacific Crest Trail, but are rare in the eastern states. But in any locale this kind of distance between pure sources, or at least easily treatable sources, might exist. Hikers using the above techniques should be able to traverse these long stretches without difficulty.

The 30 mile waterless stretch

Now suppose that water sources A and B are thirty miles apart. Reaching source A mid-morning, we fill our quart bottle and load our water bag with one gallon. After bathing and super-saturating, we press on. We hike until late afternoon, then stop to cook and eat dinner. We clean the cookpot by wiping it rather than washing it with our precious supply of drinking water. Then we carry on determinedly into the evening, and make a stealth camp away from the trail. Early the next morning, we set off once again, and hike to water source B, arriving there in the afternoon.

By splitting long waterless stretches into two days, we can manage the distance with less difficulty, thanks to the overnight rest provided midway. Of course, we cannot always time our departures from source A according to the above scenarios. In any event, the idea is to hike long into the evening, taking advantage of the cooler hours, and to start off again early the following morning.

We carry our treated water in bottles, and our untreated water in a larger water bag. We drink the treated water from the bottles, then as they become depleted, we stop and filter more water into them from the bag. We never carry all our water in a water bag, because should it develop a leak we could lose our entire supply.

While hiking long distances between water sources, and carrying a smaller, light-weight pack, we carry the extra water in soft water bags, or "bladders." These fit in the pack better than, say, gallon-size, rigid-plastic bottles. And when not in use, they take far less space.

The 60 mile waterless stretch

If the present trends of water pollution continue, we may find ourselves hiking ever farther between viable water sources. By reducing our baseline pack-weight, we can carry more water when needed. And by using the above methods, we can stretch our capabilities considerably.

During our third PCT trip, Jenny and I hiked through southern California in late summer. For about 800 miles we hiked in temperatures approaching 100° F. During this time we used our reflective-film covered umbrellas, which made a world of difference in terms of heat tolerability. Along the way we found most of the creeks dry, meaning that we often had to carry water for 40 and 50 miles between sources. At two gallons per person each day in those temperatures, including what we used for cooking, this meant that we each carried 25 to 30 pounds of water. This extra weight slowed progress, but the water kept us well hydrated and energetic. Our longest stretch of this section was about 60 miles, from Barrel Springs, over the scorching San Felipe Hills, bypassing trickling and probably polluted San Felipe Creek, and up the flanks of Mt. Laguna to the settlement at its summit. We arrived there – dying of thirst? No, actually with two quarts of water. A miscalculation, but at least we knew that we could have hiked a bit farther had we needed to.

Survival time

How long can a person survive without water? According

to contemporary medical knowledge, a person can walk without water in 90°F temperatures for five days. At 60°, survival is said to extend to eight days if the person is active, or ten if inactive.

Should we find ourselves without water for a few hours, or even a day or longer, as we have many times, this does not mean our lives are at stake. We do everything within our power to remain well hydrated; and when that doesn't work, due to unforeseen circumstances, we strengthen our wills, quiet our mind, and simply carry on as usual to the next water source.

———————

Oftentimes the ways of our society are more take than give, especially when it comes to the earth's natural resources. When Native Americans took something from the earth for purposes of sustenance or medicine, they usually left a

small offering of thanksgiving in return. It might have been a pinch of medicinal or spiritual herbs, a small feather or special pebble, or a carved twig. These objects were symbolic, representing something in the memory of the giver: a memory of a special place, an event, a lesson learned, or perhaps a meaningful vision or dream. The hiker who considers a natural water source, especially a spring, as sacred can do much the same, accepting the gift of water and leaving some small token of nature in return. And when others pass by, whether they choose to treat the water or drink it straight, these small tokens, set unobtrusively off to one side, may serve to remind them of the water's value, and of their need to protect and honor it too.

Collecting water in a Hiker's Friend, on the CDT

Part 4

WILDERNESS SKILLS

Trail Life

In the Sierras; PCT-3

Stealth Camping

"I made my bed in a nook of the pine thicket –
snug as a squirrel's nest, full of spicy odors
with plenty of wind-played needles to sing me asleep."
— *John Muir*

Forever wild and fresh

Picture a popular region of backcountry in the height of summer. It could be the Sierra Nevada, Yellowstone, or just about anywhere. Now imagine that one night, every camper shines a flashlight into the sky, and that a passing satellite photographs the scene with a powerful lens. The photo would show, not isolated pinpricks of light evenly distributed throughout the area, but concentrated clusters arranged in circles delineating the lakes, and in lines depicting the trail-side creeks. Otherwise, the picture would show vast areas of blackness. This blackness suggests that despite the crowded water-side campsites, the overwhelming majority of the wilderness is vacant.

Hikers who learn to camp away from water sources are at a wonderful advantage. For them, that expanse of blackness on the hypothetical satellite photo represents the potential for almost unlimited camping.

———

I coined the term "stealth camping" to denote camping in these vacant areas, away from the established campsites. The word stealth is a derivative of "steal," in the sense of moving or behaving inconspicuously. Most wild animals live by stealth. They move and act with quiet caution, in order to avoid being noticed. And they sleep in inconspicuous places, hidden from predators. No doubt early native peoples moved covertly in order to locate and approach their intended prey. And they probably camped in stealth to avoid attracting the attention of intruders, both human and animal.

The concept of stealth camping is aligned with these ways. Jenny and I might need to exercise at least some caution when near roads or populated areas. And we try to approach animals, not with spear and atlatl, but with camera and appreciative eyes. Stealth camping, like the ways of animals and early peoples, keeps us safer and more in tune with the natural world. And it offers a wealth of other advantages.

But before I describe the methods, let me first outline why I try to avoid the traditional, but opposite, approach: the established campsites.

The drawbacks of established campsites

Outdoor enthusiasts have long been attracted to the natural beauty of lakes and creeks. This attraction is so strong, in fact, that most people prefer to camp almost exclusively along the lakeshores and stream banks. And justifiably so, for these natural water sources provide a pleasing and contemplative ambiance found nowhere else. And of course they make the camping more convenient in terms of water availability. Unfortunately, in the past several decades these campsites have received a great deal of human impact through overuse. Campers have grown so accustomed to seeing this damage that they hardly notice it. They might think: "yeah, that's what a campsite looks like."

But let's take a closer look:

Compacted ground

Every summer, campers arrive at their lake and creek-side campsites and proceed to scrape away the freshly fallen leaves and pine needles, unaware that these materials are highly beneficial to the ecology, or perhaps simply ignoring the fact. Often they do not stop there, but continue to remove much of the beneficial duff and leaf decomposition. The intent is usually to remove the lumps and bumps, making the tent platform resemble the bed back home. In reality, they are making these campsites less comfortable, and ever more sterile.

All of this cleaning and scraping, along with decades of boot and hoof trampling, have compacted these established campsites into what can seem almost like pavement. Little wonder that these sites require inflatable mattresses or thick foam pads. And not only do humans find such compacted ground uncomfortable and cold, but the vegetation finds it nearly impossible as habitat. The loss of topsoil and the compacted subsoil represses regeneration enormously. The result is a long-lasting scarring of the landscape in the name of recreation.

Dished ground

As these overwhelmed and barren campsites continue to be scraped and trampled year after year, they become dished; meaning that they are lower than the terrain that surrounds them. So during a hearty rain, where does the groundwater flow? Into the lowest regions, namely the dished campsites. This calls for tents with "bathtub" floors.

Dust, soot and desiccated stock manure

If the days are warm and dry, the established campsites are often dusty. And this dust is often black with campfire ash. It lingers in the air and penetrates everything, including the tent, clothing, gear, food, and even a person's lungs.

If the ground were only dirt and ash, then the dust and soot would be fairly benign. But quite often, especially in the western states, this pulverized mess contains desiccated stock manure. Even though most of the manure

is dried, the pathogens and coliforms it contains can remain virulent for years.

Polluted surroundings

Adding to the filth are bits of rubbish, particularly in the deeply scarred campfire rings with their ubiquitous scraps of aluminum foil and their blackened rocks. One often finds wads of toilet paper stuffed in the crannies between nearby rocks and beneath fallen trees. The creeks and lakes next to these camps often harbor ugly food scraps from people's dishwashing. Contrary to what many campers expect, the fish do not normally eat this garbage. Equestrians lead their stock to drink at these water sources – downstream of *their* camps of course. And it is not unusual for the horses and mules to urinate and defecate while standing next to the water, or even while standing in it.

Marauding animals in the night

One of the greatest worries of many backcountry campers is bears. And where do campers most often encounter bears? In the established campsites at night. (See the "Bears" chapter.)

Bears are not the only animals that frequent these campsites. Camp rodents are also human habituated, and during the night they will chew on gear, gnaw into food bags, and nibble on any food they can get their little paws on. In so doing, the rodents may contaminate the food with urine, feces, mites, fleas, and possibly infective microorganisms, including hantavirus.

Insects

As if pilfering animals were not enough, mosquitoes, no-see-ums, blackflies, horse flies, yellow jackets, and wasps prefer wet areas, especially those near standing water. But the water is not the only thing attracting these insects; the rubbish and waste that campers leave behind, and the piles of stock manure attract them also.

Noisy campers

Jenny and I enjoy meeting other backpackers along the trail. But in the evening when we stop to make camp, and at night when trying to sleep, we do not care to be near a group of noisy campers. Most campers are not noisy, but it only takes two or three loud talkers, or even only one person playing loud music to detract from an otherwise quiet and pleasant night.

On our first PCT hike (PCT-1) we saw this beautiful cloud-filled valley. It reminded me of the way that katabatic air collects between mountains.

Katabatic (cold) air

Established campsites are typically situated in regions of katabatic[10] air. This air is much colder than that of the surrounding regions. Here is why:

Warm air is lighter than cold air, so it rises. This is what lifts hot air balloons into the sky. During the day, the sun heats the ground, which in turn heats the air immediately above it. The warming air rises in columns known as "thermals," and these are what keep sailplanes, hang gliders, and paragliders aloft.

As the sun begins to set, the process reverses. The mountain slopes begin to cool, chilling the air next to them. This cooler air is heavier, so it sinks into the valleys. The sinking, colder air is called "katabatic air," and in a way it behaves like water, because it flows down the drainages like invisible rivers.

In the evenings, then, the mountain drainages have two rivers; one of water (the river itself), and the other an invisible "river" of cold, katabatic air. Where the slopes above are steeply inclined, frigid katabatic air can flow down these drainages in veritable torrents.

When the river of katabatic air reaches the valleys, it tends to settle over the lakes and valley floors. And there we also find the established campsites – along the rivers and lakes, and in the valleys. All night long this colder, katabatic air hangs over these regions, and those who choose to camp there must endure its chill.

High mountains, deep valleys, calm nights and clear skies tend to accentuate the effect. In the western mountains, the layer of katabatic air over a valley at night tends to be, on average, about 20 or 30 feet deep. On rare occasions I have found it to be up to a hundred feet in depth. What this means is that during the night and early mornings, established campsites—indeed all campsites in the vicinity of drainages—can be as much as 15 or 20 degrees F colder than their surroundings. How do I know how thick the layer of katabatic air is? Very simply by hiking

---

10 Katabatic, from Greek Katabasis: descent.

out of the valley in the late evening or very early morning, topping out of the frigid katabatic air, and suddenly feeling a remarkable warming in the ambient air. The temperature difference can be that dramatic.

The Stealth Camp

When Jenny and I camp away from the water sources, and from the established campsites, then the many wonderful advantages of stealth camping are ours. We find stealth camping a cleaner, warmer and quieter way to camp. And it offers a deeper kinship with nature.

In all likelihood no one has camped at our impromptu stealth-site, at least in modern times, so the ground will be pristine. Its thick, natural cushioning of forest materials will still be in place, making for comfortable bedding without use of a heavy inflatable mattress. There will be no desiccated stock manure to rise as dust and infiltrate the lungs, nor any scatter of unsightly litter and stench of human waste. Our stealth-site will not be trampled and dished; so any rainwater will soak into the ground or run off it, rather than collect and flood our shelter. Bears scrounging for human food will be busy at the water-side campsites, and will likely ignore the far-removed and unproductive woods. Far from the water sources, we will encounter fewer flying insects, particularly on the more breezy slopes and open fields. Out of the katabatic zones, the night air will be markedly warmer. And when camped far off the trail, we can rest assured that our chances of being bothered by other people will be slim.

Hikers and campers normally cause most of their environmental damage at the established campsites. We have no impact on those campsites when we do not use them. Nor do the wilderness managers have to worry about us impacting our far-removed stealth-sites. We cherish the natural environment and are very conscious to care for it and protect it. As such, we practice no-trace methods exclusively. For after all, our love and respect of nature, and our quest for a better understanding and

appreciation of natural world is why we enjoy stealth camping to begin with.

In certain wilderness areas, the authorities require all visitors to camp in established campsites, exclusively. Part of the rationale behind this is that not all wilderness visitors are conscientious about their camping practices, and for the benefit of the ecology these people are best corralled into known and therefore more easily regulated campsites where most of the impact has already occurred. I tend to agree. And **I recommend against stealth camping for anyone who lacks a full awareness of the responsibilities this approach requires, nor where camping restrictions are in effect.**

In northern Idaho on the IUA

Cooking and stealth camping

At a stealth-site miles from the nearest water supply, how would we cook the evening meal, and wash up afterward?

We rarely cook at our stealth-sites, not just because of a lack of water availably. We dare not risk starting a wildfire, and we wish to avoid attracting park bears when we are in a national park. But mainly our appetites usually urge us to stop and cook dinner long before we are ready to retire to bed.

Instead, we stop at a water source in late afternoon or

early evening, and cook, eat and wash there. And we fill our bottles with enough water to meet our needs for that evening and part of the following morning. Refreshed and energized, we pack up and resume hiking. Miles farther, we leave the trail and head well into the woods to make our impromptu stealth camp. With the evening meal behind us, we may use the extra time for exploring, journal writing, or perhaps simply for quiet observation and contemplation.

Benefits of sleeping on a gentle slope

While searching for a stealth-site, we look for ground that is somewhat elevated above its surroundings, so that it does not pool rainwater in a heavy storm. If we cannot find such ground, we look for ground that is mildly sloped. Rain is unlikely to pool on sloped ground, and only the heaviest rain will actually run downhill. Usually the rain is absorbed.

On a mildly sloping stealth-site, we are careful about which way we situate our shelter.

The tendency when camping on a slope is to sleep with the feet downhill. However, this allows gravity to pool the blood into one's lower extremities. This restricts circulation and greatly reduces the restorative benefits of an otherwise good night's rest – at least for the high-mileage hiker. Or one might try sleeping laterally on the slope, only to spend the night clutching the bedding while trying to keep from rolling sideways downhill. Instead, on sloped ground Jenny and I sleep with our feet uphill. This obviates blood pooling, and it draws the day's swelling from the lower extremities. We find it excellent therapy for tired legs and feet.

Which way is down?

Judging which way is downhill is a simple matter when the ground is moderately sloped, but can be more problematic when the ground is barely sloped. Especially after a long day on the trail when fatigue begins to interfere

with one's sense of equilibrium. In such a case we might pitch our shelter in what seems the proper orientation, only to discover, when actually laying down, that we misjudged the slope.

Our solution is twofold. First, we walk around the potential site and examine it from all angles. While looking at the ground from one vantage, it might appear sloped toward us. But we are not fooled by this; for when we walk around and view the ground from the opposite direction, it may appear tilted toward us again. Nevertheless, this walk-around is our first method of determining which way is *probably* down. That done, we spread our groundsheet and lay down on it, with feet pointed in the direction that seems uphill. If the slope *feels* uphill toward the feet, it most likely is; and we may then pitch the shelter with confidence.

This inability to judge slope manifests itself on the trail as well. When fatigued, we often gauge downward slope as being far more gradual than it is. For example, we hiked the PCT northbound twice, so had become familiar with certain switchbacks where the trail's downward gradient seemed far too gradual. We were surprised, during our subsequent southbound journey, to find those same switchbacks amply graded while hiking them the other way.

How steep a slope can we sleep on? We have found it best not to rule out a more steeply sloped site until we have checked it by feel, lying on our groundsheet. We joke that if we awaken the following morning and find that we have slid out of the shelter, then the terrain was a little too steep.

If the area is hardly sloped, we look for a site on a slight rise that would provide runoff in the event of rain.

Warmer, softer bedding

The surface layer of a typical forest floor is called litter. It usually consists of needles, leaves, cones, twigs and other natural materials. Beneath the litter is a layer of decomposed and compressed litter called duff. In some areas this duff can be several feet thick. If you have never stretched out on a pine needle or leaf carpeted forest floor, you are missing one of nature's softest beds. It can be more comfortable than a foam pad; and it provides excellent insulation from the cold soil and rocky substrate. And as a bonus, those thick layers of litter and duff will tend to absorb any rain, wicking it down and away from the groundsheet. Of course, while this natural insulation is of considerable benefit to the hiker traveling lightly, it also negates the option of building a campfire or a cook-fire.

Minimizing impact

When establishing a stealth-site, we avoid altering the landscape and its flora. We might hand-preen any loose rocks, twigs, pine cones and sharp-pointed cone scales that would poke into the bedding, but we do not brush away the beneficial layers of forest materials: the long-fallen leaves and pine needles. We also avoid breaking away green limbs and yanking out plants or saplings that might occupy the prospective site. If we find such obstructions, we search elsewhere for a place naturally free of them.

Another kind of impact is noise. When stealth camping we remain reasonably quiet to avoid degrading someone else's wilderness experience while pursuing our own. And this way we are more likely to see and hear wildlife at closer range, and less likely to attract any unwanted human attention. In short, we respect the quietude of the wilderness as though in a house of worship; for in many ways we consider the wilderness a sacred temple.

Climb high, camp low

High, exposed areas tend to take the brunt of any blustery weather. With this in mind, we can greatly reduce any weather-related problems by avoiding the storm-whipped heights. Instead, we descend to the lower regions at night—but not all the way into the katabatic valleys—and there we look for small stealth-sites that offer protection from the elements.

During our Continental Divide Trail thru-hike, Jenny and I met only one other distance hiker; this was in the remote mountains of western Montana. He was traveling north, and we were headed south. The day was late, and after an enjoyable chat we went our separate ways. The

Climb high, camp low. PCT-2

fellow resumed his ascent of the mountain we had just come down, and we continued our descent. A short ways down from the trail we made a comfortable camp nestled in the pines. Our evening was very pleasant, and high-lighted by a pair of owls flying round the tent and landing on a branch within a few yards of our open doorway. In the morning we awoke to see the mountain enveloped in heavy cloud, and we felt concern for our friend, since he had planned to camp up there. Months later he sent us a few pages photocopied from his journal, describing how he had endured that harrowing night on top of the peak, hanging on to his tent in a "savage storm." Our camp and his were only half a mile apart, but ours was protected snugly in a vale while his was fully exposed to the ele-ments. This was another example of the wisdom in the adage "climb high, and camp low" – to which I would add: but not so low that you are in the katabatic zone.

Avoiding bear visits

Most animals are opportunists. If they happen upon one's food bags unattended, they might help themselves. And when it comes to marauding animals, bears can be the most formidable. So let's discuss bears first.

Here in the U.S., bears come in three types: wild black bears, park black bears, and grizzly bears. The personali-ties of these three are quite different from each-other. I describe these differences more fully in the "Bears" chap-ter, further along in this book. But in general, the follow-ing considerations might apply to stealth camping:

The "wild black bear" is a black bear found *outside* a National Park. It is subject to hunting and therefore wary of humans, including hikers. When a person is stealth camping outside a National Park, the wild black bears will likely keep their distance, regardless of any signal odors the camper creates such as cooking food, wear-ing deodorant, and so forth. The wild black bears are normally not a problem to hikers who treat them with respect.

The "park black bear" is a black bear found *inside* a National Park. It is protected from hunting and therefore tends to become human-habituated. This means that it will come into any campsite looking for food, regard-less of the presence of humans. Unlike the grizzly, the park black bear does not normally consider the campers themselves as part of the menu. The park bear only wants the campers' food.

Within a National Park, the park black bears may focus their perpetual quest for food in the more productive regions: usually the established campsites. Picture those overused lake-side campsites and how attractive they must be to bruin. Night after night these campsites fairly bristle with campfire smoke, irresistible odors of cooking food, the sight of food bags and trash. A hiker might find it difficult to elude park bears at many of these locations. The Park Service's answer to the problem is bear-poof food canisters. I think this is good idea, although can-isters do not necessarily keep the park bears away from these camps.

When Jenny and I want to stealth-camp within a National Park, we first check with the Park's regulations. If permitted in that particular region, we know that we can greatly reduce any bear-related disturbances by simply avoiding their nightly haunts, and camping well away from any established campsites.

A question that has come our way is: "Granted, at a stealth-site you are not camping in an area that bears visit regularly, but if a bear happens to travel by, how close must it get to smell food or any other smell which might entice it to roam into your camp?"

Bears have mediocre eyesight but an extraordinary sense of smell. This of course helps them locate food in areas of poor visibility, for example in thick timber and heavy brush.

In the right conditions, a bear can smell campfire smoke at a distance of about four miles. Same with a day-old campsite where the fire was put out with water. But most animals are accustomed to the odor of smoke, usually from wildfires, so it normally means very little to them. And once again, virtually all "wild black bears" here in the Lower 48 are generally wary of people.

However, the smell of someone cooking food is a very powerful signal odor, and it lingers at a campsite and is detectable by bears for many miles, and even for several days after the camper has move on. So if the park bears can smell it, they can probably find it.

This suggests the folly of imagining that by not cooking at an established campsite, the park bears will not be attracted to it. And it suggests the benefits of stealth camping far from where anyone has cooked. Lacking that one signal odor, our sites are already about 90% free of park bear visits.

Next on the list of undesirables are attractants like fishing gear and scented toiletries such as cologne, perfume, deodorants, scented soaps, highly-scented repellents, and so forth. For after all, these are designed to emit powerful odors. They might not smell powerful to humans with their senses subdued by living in society. But they certainly smell powerful to a park bear. And they also smell powerful to hikers who have been out in the wilds for many weeks and recovered their senses of smell. Yet even though a park black bear may smell a person's bug repellent or scented foot powder over a mile away, this does not mean that the bear will automatically make a beeline for this person's camp.

So here is my run-down on the odds:

1) If you cook food at your stealth-site within a National Park, and wear smelly things like deodorant or if you have fishing gear, your chances of attracting a park bear are very great.

2) If you do not cook food and have no fishing gear, but wear smelly things, your chances drop to about 10%.

3) And if you avoid the established campsites; do not cook food at your stealth-sites; have no fishing gear; do not wear smelly things; and bathe often, your chances drop to almost zero.

As mentioned in the "Bears" chapter, if a park black bear should wander into one of our stealth camps and show a reluctance to leave, despite our mild provocations, we would pack up and move on. This has occurred to me many times over the years, but only in the established campgrounds in Yosemite Valley. So far it has not yet happened while stealth camping anywhere else.

Other animal visits to our stealth-sites

At the other end of the size spectrum are the mice and their rodent cousins. In established campsites these creatures are well versed in associating humans with food bags, and are bound to invade the campers' domain. This does not mean that they are being pests; it means only that they are responding to the temptation of the food that a person places at their disposal. At the stealth-sites, these creatures will rarely associate us with food. Squirrels and chipmunks may be our neighbors, but usually they will be practicing stealth themselves, trying to avoid detection. So they will rarely venture close enough to investigate.

Not all nocturnal creatures are out to plunder hikers' camps. We are often amazed by how much animal activity takes place at night. Depending on the geographic locale, there might be deer, raccoons, boar, porcupines, skunks, owls, fox, coyotes and a wide variety of rodents. These animals will normally avoid human presence. Still, they may amble past our stealth-site in the night, which can be disconcerting if we hear their shuffling but cannot see what is making the noise.

One night a few bucks wandered into our camp, and began to rut close by. We should have chased them away, especially as the excited does were adding to the ruckus and tripping over our tarp's guys. One deer even nibbled at the edge of our tarp. This odd scenario was not singular; it happened to us a few more times on different trips.

Forever new and fresh

I think it makes good sense to practice a more respectful and sensible approach to wilderness camping. The natural world out there is forever fresh and new, so why not spread out, delight in it, and take care of it?

———

Jenny and I once enjoyed a wee visitor at one of our storm-bound camps during our kayak journey down the Yukon River. A redback vole skittered out of the brush and made a hasty inspection of our front porch area. Not too surprisingly it found a hearty snack in the form of a few crumbs of spilled cereal. And with that, we became fast friends. The little vole proved itself very well behaved. Not once did it nibble at a plastic bag or nylon gear bag. It did, however, have the temerity to crawl into one of our cups, from which we had just eaten, and proceed to lick the cup clean. Within a few hours our friend became almost tame, paying us little heed as we watched at face-close range. It reminded us of a miniature brown bear, little more than a wispy ball of cinnamon fur with a rusty brown stripe down its back. It had a short, fuzzy tail and two beady, coal-black eyes. We often name our camps for their more salient features, and this was our "vole camp."

Beautiful and remote country along the Idaho-Montana border of the IUA

Campfire and Cook-Fire

An evening campfire creates a comforting, outdoorsy atmosphere. Nevertheless, it also impacts its surroundings enormously. It greedily incinerates the natural supply of firewood, and sends dangerous sparks into the night – sparks that could start an uncontrolled burn. It scorches the subsoil deeply, sterilizing its microbiology while greatly suppressing regeneration. Many backcountry campsites and shelters feature large fire pits, and these only engender the old mindset by inviting campers to construct large fires. Even in less visited areas we often find visible evidence of the impact: the tell-tale ring of blackened rocks, the mound of ashes mixed with bits of aluminum foil and half-burned rubbish, and the charred and sooty ground. These are unsightly reminders that our numbers and carelessness may be threatening our wild lands more than we might imagine.

During our five thru-hikes, totaling more than eighteen months in the wilds, Jenny and I built a total of eight campfires. These we built mostly in established campsites, or in a few cases on bare dirt. Each campfire was small and utilitarian, solely for the purpose of drying clothing and sometimes the sleeping bag after a particularly wet day on the trail. We enjoy evening campfires as much as anyone, but during these treks we were trying to limit our effects on the land.

Any kind of fire, large or small, will have some degree of impact, and our utilitarian fires were no exception. But in times of genuine need, I think a small campfire is appropriate. For instance, should the hiker find himself or herself deeply chilled, and with clothing and sleeping bag hopelessly wet. At those times, a small, warming and drying campfire is well justified.

Fire safety

As discussed in the previous chapter, the rich layer of needles, leaves, twigs and other natural materials that make up the surface layer of the typical forest floor is called litter. Beneath this is a layer of decomposed litter called duff. Duff vaguely resembles dirt, and campers commonly mistake it for dirt and build fires on it. Even if they recognize it as duff, they might incorrectly assume that it is non-flammable because of its high moisture content. What they may not realize is how quickly their campfire will dry it.

On a winter mountaineering trip in the Colorado Rockies back in the late 1960's, my partner and I trudged into "base camp" and pitched our tents. Digging through a few feet of snow to the ground, we built a modest fire and cooked dinner. Afterwards we buried the fire under what seemed like a ton of snow, and packed it down with our boots. The next morning we left camp and climbed our intended mountain. Returning in the late afternoon, we were aghast to find a small hole in the snow bellowing smoke. For an hour we dug into the smolder, following a few spreading arms, one of which was heading for a nearby tree. This was an unforgettable lesson on the flammability of "wet" duff.

Wildfires are not always detrimental. Nature has used them to maintain her ecology for eons. Lightning triggers most wildfires, and these are both beneficial and necessary. They burn away the downed trees and branches, along with the forest's accumulation of undergrowth. This keeps the flammable materials to a minimum, and prevents a future fire from burning so hotly that it kills all the trees and scorches the subsoil. Regular, small fires merely expose the forest floor to sunlight, giving saplings and new plants the chance to flourish.

All was in balance until the early 1900's when the Forest Service okayed the hacking down of old growth timber almost to the last tree. These trees were highly resistant to fire due to their thick bark and not-too-close to the ground branches. With these old growth trees gone, new trees took advantage of the lack of shade, and sprung up in much greater numbers, spaced much closer together. So the forests started accumulating downed trees and underbrush in unnatural quantities, to the point that our second and third growth "tree farms" have become immense tinder boxes. Now when they burn, they sweep the land in an inferno of destruction. This has called for veritable armies of forest fire fighters to protect the logging interests and their timber "harvesting."

Policies are beginning to change, but meanwhile our National Parks, forests and wild lands are extremely vulnerable to devastating fire. This is why we hikers must be very careful to keep our campfires few, to give them much forethought and constant tending, and to extinguish them dead out.

The utilitarian campfire

Obviously our stealth-sites are not safe places for campfires. When Jenny and I need to build a drying fire we default to the established campsites and their fire pits, as stated. Or we find an area of bare dirt. Only in an emergency would a person build a campfire in dense, undisturbed forest. And then, only after scraping all ground litter and duff away to expose a wide circle of dirt.

To make a small, drying and warming campfire, we begin with dry tinder. For this, we might use pine needles, dry leaves, seed heads, birch bark, certain types of dry moss, and so forth. The problem is, we would need this small campfire only when the woods are wet. And in such a case, these materials are difficult to find dry. So we would collect a modest supply ahead of time, and keep it for emergencies in a resealable plastic bag, carried in the backpack. This tinder weighs almost nothing, yet could be a lifesaver.

If a person is not carrying such a supply, he or she would look for dry tinder under fallen trees, under large pieces of bark, in the hollows beneath rocks or boulders, and at the base of trees. Some trees, such as spruce, protect their lower branches from rain, so the thin, dead branches still attached are quite flammable. If dry tinder is unavailable, one could use a knife to cut into a wet stick. The larger the stick, the drier it will be inside. A small pile of extremely thin shavings will usually ignite readily.

Next, we collect pencil-size twigs called kindling. On wet days, we look for this wood on the lower branches of trees, and possibly under blowdowns and at the base of large rocks. Once a fire is burning well, it will accept damp or wet kindling collected from the ground. But to get the fire started, we use only dry twigs. After amassing a small pile of dry kindling, we collect larger pieces of wood, but nothing larger than perhaps ¾" in diameter.

Then we lay down two short platform sticks about ½" in diameter, 8" long and 8" apart. These will hold the tinder off the wet ground, and provide it with ventilation. We lay a few pieces of kindling across these to make a platform, then onto that we add the dry tinder. Atop this, we place more kindling, one piece at a time.

Now, we remove a single match from its container, and replace the lid. Then we strike the match with a thumbnail edge, or across the dry bottom of a rock. The instant the match ignites, we place it under the materials. But rather than laying the match down on the ground, which might snuff it out, we hold it carefully off the ground but directly under the tinder until the match is nearly spent. At that point, we withdraw the match from under the materials and insert it head down into them, where it will assist the wee flames and act as dry kindling itself. We now blow gently into the fire to feed it oxygen, adding more kindling between breaths.

If the fire dies, we set aside all partially burned materials, and build a new setup of tinder and kindling as before. But this time when we strike a second match, we use it to ignite a small candle. Short birthday candles work well for this. This we hold over the materials, dripping hot wax onto them. The damper the materials, the more wax needed. Then we place the burning candle under the wax-coated materials, which themselves will then act as candles.

The cook-fire

In addition to the eight small campfires Jenny and I built during our thru-hikes, we also crafted dozens of cook-fires on our fifth trek. The cook-fire is an open flame, but that is about the extent of its similarities to a campfire. It does not qualify as a drying and warming fire because it is not large enough. Rather, it uses only pencil-size kindling. Fed into the tiny fire at regular intervals, this kindling heats the bottom of a single pot.

The cook-fire is an art form, and a low-impact means of cooking a meal. We craft it to cook the meal quickly, and then to consume itself. Its tiny pile of ashes is then easily eradicated. The cook-fire leaves no scar, and no blackened rocks.

The cook-fire technique might be a good backup should one's stove break down or run out of fuel. It is also a method of cooking that affords the greatest connection.

The cook-fire requires proper technique and finesse. In fact, it demands it. Those who do not care to learn the correct methods should not attempt them in the wilds. The cook-fire is also illegal anywhere open fires are banned. And it is unsafe at the stealth camps where pine needles and duff have accumulated, or where dry leaves and grasses might be present – regardless of whether the

woods are dry or wet. It is unsafe in high wind, and it may be entirely inappropriate in areas of heavy use such as the John Muir Trail and Appalachian Trail.

Building a cook-fire

A good place to build a cook-fire, here again, is within an established campfire ring. If we are stopping to cook dinner in the late afternoon, we might find such rings near water, which we will need anyway. The previous campers will have likely incinerated all the wood, but they were looking for big wood, and we are looking for small, so we will likely find all we need a short ways from the area.

When searching for a suitable place to build a cook-fire, we take into consideration the direction and strength of any wind. We select an area that is free of vegetation, and wide enough to prevent shooting sparks from reaching any flammable brush or forest litter nearby. We sometimes build a cook-fire (as opposed to much larger warming fire) in an area lightly covered with litter and duff no deeper than ½". Any deeper and we look elsewhere. By scraping with the heel of a shoe, we know how deep the duff is. That test done, we carefully scrape away all flammable cover, so that the cook-fire will sit on dirt or sand. Nothing else will do. Safety necessitates a circle of dirt at least 3½ feet in diameter; the cook-fire will lie in its center. (A bigger warming and drying fire will require a much larger ground clearing.) But rather than scattering the materials scraped off the cook-fire site, we save them in small piles off to the side. These we will spread back over the area once the cook-fire has burned itself out, and the ground has cooled.

Tinder for igniting a cook-fire could be any of the small, dry materials like those found in our emergency fire starter kit. However, we save our kit for an emergency, and instead we look for dry tinder nearby. As for kindling, the only wood suitable for a cook-fire is again about a pencil's diameter. Anything larger will not incinerate completely, and will prevent us from restoring the site back to its original condition. To prepare the "fire sticks," we break dry sticks and twigs into 6-inch lengths, and pile these neatly and conveniently to one side. By amassing all our fire sticks ahead of time, we will avoid having to leave the fire to collect more sticks, thus interrupting the cooking process. Instead, we will be able to constantly tend the fire, keeping the flames licking at the

PCT-3

bottom of the pot without letup. Small and continuous: that is the secret to being able to cook quickly yet still zero-impacting the site.

Using a cook-fire

Since antiquity, humans have been devising all manner of methods to support pots over cooking fires. I think I have tried most of them, and have settled on the one that works best for me. This is the tripod, made of three sticks lashed together at their tops, suspending the pot over the fire.

Suitable tripod sticks are about four feet in length, and perhaps about 1½" in diameter. If we start looking for them while hiking along the trail, well before stopping to cook dinner, we will arrive at the dinner stop prepared.

With all three tripod sticks in hand, we begin looking for our cook-fire site. Once we have located it, and determined it to be safe for a small fire, we lash the three tripod sticks together at one end, using a short length of cord. Then we stand the tripod upright, not over the fire site just yet, but off to one side.

In order to suspend the pot from the tripod, the pot will need a bail. This is a wire, or a strip of metal, fitted to the pot near its top. If your cookpot lacks a bail, you can easily make one. Using a drill or hammer and nail, bore or punch two small holes, one on either side of the pot, just below the rim. Stainless steel pots are more resistant to drilling, while aluminum and titanium pots are easily drilled. Into these holes, thread a length of wire. Optimally, the wire would be about half the thickness of an ordinary wire coat hanger. Finally, crimp or twist the ends of the wire so that they will not slip out of the holes.

After filling the cookpot with enough water for the meal, we fit its lid in place. The lid will keep the water clean, and help retain the heat. To suspend the cookpot from the tripod, we use a length of cord or a notched stick. Either works well, but the cord is easier to adjust, raising or lowering the pot as needed with a taut-line hitch. The flame is quite small so does not reach the cord, which is why the cord does not melt or burn through. Beginners might use a hanging wire in case their fire grows too large. Nevertheless, we tie the suspension cord to the tripod, and hang the pot from this cord.

We have not started the fire quite yet; but the pot of water is now suspended from the tripod, which is standing off to one side of the fire site.

So now we start the cook-fire, and begin feeding it with fire sticks. As the cook-fire comes to life, which happens fast, we quickly place the tripod over it, and press the base of the tripod sticks gently into the ground to prevent them from shifting. Now we adjust the length of the suspension cord, if needed, so that the pot hangs about an inch off the kindling. This distance is important. We want the pot in the fire, not so closely that it suffocates the fire, and not so high above the fire that the flames dissipate before reaching the pot. Ideally, the cook-fire should engulf the entire bottom of the pot, without reaching high enough to burn the suspension cord, nor wide enough to ignite the tripod sticks. We keep the fire small, yet focused. Done correctly, this little cook-fire will boil water as fast as any stove. And with experience, the entire procedure can be done quickly.

If a draft is sweeping the heat away from the cookpot, we can block it by situating ourselves upwind, or by placing a few rocks upwind of the fire. However, we avoid placing the rocks so close to the fire that they would blacken with soot. If they do blacken, we leave them in dirt, blackened side down. The soil will transform the carbon faster than would the atmosphere.

Once the water reaches a boil, we remove the lid and stir in the dinner. Stirring with a spoon would place the hands and fingers too close to the fire, so instead we use a longer stick. After cooking the meal, we lift the tripod carefully away, then lean it over to bring the pot to rest on the ground. Then we untie the suspension cord and set the tripod aside.

Baking bread or dessert

As soon as the cook-fire has generated a few small coals, we might use them for baking a dessert. Jenny and I use the term "scones" to refer to any kind of baked dessert. We usually mix and package our own scone ingredients at home. An alternative for those who do not object to the white flour and chemicals would be the store-bought "just add water" muffin-type mixes. Even the type that requires egg and oil will bake nicely without these ingredients. Jenny mixes the batter inside a resealable plastic bag, or inside the commercial packaging, adding water a few dollops at a time while stirring with a small stick. The idea is to use as little water as possible. The drier the batter, the faster and more thoroughly it will bake.

For a baking sheet, Jenny uses a piece of aluminum foil about 12 inches square. She scoops the batter onto the middle of the foil, and shapes it to about 2" wide and 6" long, then brings the sides up to where they meet in the middle, and rolls them down, onto the batter. Then she rolls each end to create an air-tight package that will hold in the steam.

Next we scoop a small bed of coals out of the cook-fire, and place the foil-packaged batter on them. Then we scoop a few more coals over the top of the foil. Coals that are quite hot will tend to burn rather than bake. So we cool them by spreading them out. Mid-way through the baking process we turn the packet over, for better heat distribution, and continue adding a few glowing coals on top of the packet as the old ones cool. Properly baked, the scones will be nicely browned on the outside, and cooked all the way through.

We eat the scones piping hot from the foil, then fold

Jenny showing how to bake scones at one of our classes

Now it is time to do the Monster Mash. This erases the cook-fire and leaves absolutely no indication that it was there.

To proceed, I simply step on the cooled ashes with my shoe, keeping my weight on the ball of my foot, then twist the foot. This twisting action, combined with my weight, grinds the ashes into powder. I kick in a bit of dirt, and continue stepping and twisting, one foot after the other, as though dancing some sort of ritual. In jest, I call it the cook-fire-monster-mash-leave-no-trace ceremony. A few minutes of this will work the last traces of carbon into the earth, and completely erase any trace of unsightly ash or charcoal.

The real beauty of this method is that the ash and tiny bits of charcoal now spread out and buried, enrich the soil beneficially.

If planning to camp within range of the cook-fire area, we would return to the site the following morning and restore it to its original condition. For example, the cook-fire site could be in a dry creek bed, and the stealth-site a few hundred feet away in a glen. However, in bear country we would put several miles between our dinner site and our stealth-site. So if we will be moving on after cooking, we "zero-impact" our fire site before heading out.

To do this, we place our hands flat on the ground at the cook-fire site, and make sure the ground has cooled. The possibility is slight, but if the ground is too hot to hold a hand on, then an unseen ember under the ground could possibly ignite the surface debris long after we have gone.

the foil up for another use the next day. Handled carefully, the foil will bake three separate rounds of scones.

Even simpler than scones baked in aluminum foil is a type of bread called "ash cakes." For this we mix a stiff bread or scone dough, press it flat, and place it directly on a bed of fine coals, no foil required. We simply turn the ash cakes occasionally to ensure even baking. Once they have cooked, we brush away any small bits of ash that remain on the crust.

The monster mash

As we are eating the hot meal, we rebuild the cook-fire just a little, and place all the unburned ends of the sticks into the tiny fire, as well as any paper trash. We tend the little fire very carefully, encouraging the flames to consume the last of its embers. When the flames die out, and only ashes remain, we use a stout stick to stir in water, dirt, or both. This cools both the ashes and the ground.

If we detect any heat, we pour more water on the area if we have extra, mix and mash some more, and wait until the site has cooled. That done, we restore the original debris back over the site. Thoughtfully done, this *light* scattering of debris will erase any hint of the cook-fire's presence.

The cookpot will be coated in soot from the fire, and this actually hastens the cooking process. So we do not need to clean the exterior. Instead, we stow the pot in its own stowbag, so that the soot does not blacken everything it touches.

Lastly, we disassemble the tripod sticks and place them where they cannot possibly start a fire. By now, these sticks will no longer be hot to the touch, nor should they be charred if we constructed our cook-fire properly. If the tripod sticks are hot, rather than simply disperse them into the forest, we carry them a ways until they have cooled.

Fire starter kit

The fire starter kit is one of those items best kept tucked away in the backpack for the proverbial rainy day. It is not for igniting the stove or cook-fire on a daily basis; for that we keep a separate container of matches or a small butane lighter in with the stove or cookpot where it will be handy. The fire starter kit is strictly for emergencies. Whether the journey is 5 miles or 2,000, adverse weather always has the potential to thrust a person into hypothermia, regardless of the time of year. It is always a good idea to carry a fire starting kit. Keep it small and lightweight, and keep it absolutely dry. My kit contains:

▶ Kitchen "strike-anywhere" stick matches in a plastic bottle. The bottle has a screw-on lid with a serviceable gasket, for example a vitamin or spice bottle.

▶ A few birthday candles, in the same bottle.

▶ A small handful of dry tinder in a waterproof plastic bag.

▶ And a small, sharp knife.

The kitchen "strike-anywhere" stick match burns hotter and longer than a cardboard book-match, and the stick of the match adds to the kindling. It is also more wind-resistant, much more so than the common butane lighter. While packing for the trip, I strike one match from the batch to make sure that the supply is dry and functional. Also, I check the gasket of the bottle's lid for leakage. To do this, I empty the bottle, screw on the lid, submerge it in water, and squeeze. Any bubbles indicate a defective seal.

An excellent alternative to matches is the zirconium rod. When scraped with a piece of steel, for example a knife blade or a broken hack-saw blade, the rod emits an abundance of extremely hot sparks, capable of igniting all but the most reluctant tinder. These rods are commonly termed "flint strikers," but this is a misnomer since they

In a National Park, we use the cook-fire method in established campfire rings. PCT-3

are not made of flint. Zirconium is a lustrous gray, metallic element resembling titanium. Unlike matches, the rod is not put out of action by water, but it will deteriorate in time if left soaking wet. A small zirconium striker saved Jenny and me a lot of trouble one summer when we set out on a 6-week canoe trip and forgot to buy matches or lighters in the town where we put in. Fortunately we had a striker in our emergency fire starter kit, and we used the striker every evening to light our stove. It also saved me trouble twice at high altitude in Antarctica and the Andes when my team's supply of lighters and matches failed.

If you have tried starting a campfire when the woods are drenched, then you understand the importance of carrying dry tinder. For best results, collect the tinder when the woods are dry, and keep it that way inside your pack. The possibilities for tinder include dry grasses, seed heads, pine needles, and inner bark from downed trees. A small resealable bag of tinder weighs only a fraction of an ounce, but it can make a ton of difference when needed.

The beauty of the bow drill

The cook-fire offers a more natural means of cooking our meals, and with a much closer sense of connection. But the depth of that connection will also depend on how we ignite the fire. If we use a match or butane lighter, then the fire will be utilitarian and useful. However if we start the fire with a bow drill or hand drill, then that fire will be far more meaningful to us.

When we carve the bow drill parts—the fireboard, spindle and socket—from pieces of wood, we are investing our energy into them. And when we place the spindle to the fireboard, and use the bow to spin it with enough vigor to generate sufficient heat, we produce a glowing ember. That ember is an extension of ourselves, by virtue of the muscular energy we used to generate it. We place

the ember on the tinder bundle and feed it oxygen with our life breath, and if our technique is correct, the tinder will burst into flame. When not on journey, this is how we ignite all our cook-fires and campfires.

The techniques for using the bow drill and hand drill are beyond the scope of this text. Many books on wilderness survival describe the methods.

PCT-3

Knots for the Hiker

This chapter details the knots Jenny and I use while hiking and camping. They are the most simple yet functional, and easy to learn.

Overhand

The overhand is the first knot most people learn. When we tie our shoelaces, we start by tying an overhand.

Overhand on a bight

The working end in a cord is called its "bitter end." When you fold it back on itself to create a loop, you make what is called a "bight." If you then tie an overhand in that doubled line, you make an "overhand on a bight."

I use this knot to secure the ends of the guy-lines to the tarp. Run one end of the line through the webbing loop, bring it back alongside itself several inches, and then tie the overhand on the doubled line.

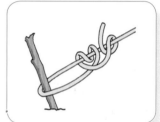

I also use the overhand on a bight to attach lanyards to items such as the ice axe and pocket knife. For the ice axe I use a piece of parachute cord. One end of the cord feeds through a hole in the head of the axe and attaches with the overhand on a bight. At the other end of the cord I tie another overhand on a bight, making the bight just large enough to slip my hand through. This will keep the ice axe secured to the wrist when in use.

On smaller items such as the pocket knife I simply loop a ten-inch length of parachute cord through the small ring at the end of the knife, bring the cord back so that both ends are even, then tie the overhand on a bight right near the two ends.

Taut line hitch

The taut line hitch is an adjustable knot, and quite secure when properly tightened. We use it for tensioning a tarp guy-line around a tree or bush.

The taut line hitch is also useful at one end of a clothesline running under a tarp or inside a tent. In this case one would cinch it only tight enough to take up the slack, without distorting the shelter.

We use a taut line hitch also to suspend the cookpot over a cook-fire. Thin nylon cord (1/8") works best for the suspension cord. Tie one end of the cord to the tripod with a couple of overhand knots (see below), then feed the lower end under the pot bail and secure the cord back onto itself with a taut line hitch. The taut line hitch enables us to adjust the height of the pot over the flames.

Two half hitches

When pitching a tarp, I use the taut line hitch to secure and tension the two ridge guys. And I use the two half hitches to secure the tarp's other guy-lines to rocks, logs, bushes, or trees, if I am not using stakes.

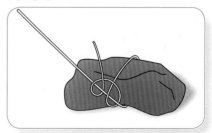

To tie this knot, I

tie the first overhand right against the object. Then I tie the second overhand against the first. This prevents the object from sliding out of the loop. I also add a quick release to the second half hitch. Tied correctly, a two half hitches looks like a clove hitch tied around its own line.

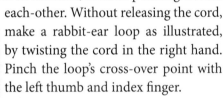

Pull

Sheet bend

Use the sheet bend to secure a line to the corner of a sheet of fabric or plastic. It makes an extremely strong attachment.

Clove hitch

We use a clove hitch whenever we want to secure some-thing part-way along a length of cord. For example attaching a tarp guy-line to a stake. The clove hitch is strong, yet it is quickly untied by slipping it off the end of the stake.

Hold the cord in both hands, thumbs pointing toward each-other. Without releasing the cord, make a rabbit-ear loop as illustrated, by twisting the cord in the right hand. Pinch the loop's cross-over point with the left thumb and index finger.

Slide the right hand along the cord to the right. Twist and make a second loop. Pinch its cross-over point with the right thumb and index finger.

Pass the right loop behind the left loop. The clove hitch is complete, and ready for a stake.

Run the tent stake through the loops, tighten the line, then press the stake into the ground.

If using extremely thin cord on a tent stake, the clove hitch can sometimes

bind so hard that it is difficult to slide off the stake. In this case we tie the clove hitch with a quick release. When you pull the free end, the knot unties itself. See the following descriptions.

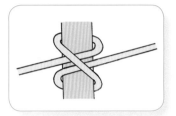 

The butterfly clove hitch with a quick release

Hold a length of cord in front of you, directly in line with the photo. The line leading to the left is attached to the tarp. The line leading right is the short, free end.

Twist the cord in your right hand by rolling your thumb toward you. This forms a loop. Note that the cord coming from the right hand goes over the cord from the left hand.

Grasp the base of the loop between finger and thumb of the left hand.

Roll the right thumb toward you to create a second loop.

Place the right loop under the left loop.

Grasp the base of both loops between left finger and thumb. The two loops are the "wings" of the butterfly.

Extend the left pinky and place it under the line.

Wrap the line under the finger and bring it up.

Lay the cord between the wings and grasp the cord between finger and thumb, along with the others.

Insert the stake between the two loops. Withdraw the left pinky, and insert the right one.

Pull the left line to tighten the knot around the stake.

Photography

"A man must carry knowledge with him
if he would bring home knowledge."
— *Samuel Johnson*

Camera, contrast and the art of seeing

Photographs can capture the magic of the moments, and are a great way to foster enthusiasm for the outdoors and to encourage wilderness preservation. The photographs taking during one's hiking and camping adventures can help show what it was like "out there" to family and friends. Some hikers may want to give more formal presentations to groups; others will need pictures for articles, books and the web. And almost everyone who takes photographs enjoys reminiscing over his or her pictures, refreshing the memories and reliving the experiences.

Regardless of the individual motivations for taking photographs or the type of camera used, one can greatly improve the photos' quality with an understanding of the basics of photography. Excellent books, articles, and websites on the subject abound, and the more one reads and studies a few of them, the better one's pictures will be.

The hiker's camera

If a person is interested in high quality, professional images, then he or she will need to carry more expensive camera gear, and this can add considerable weight

PCT-2

and bulk to the backpacking load. But one should not assume that these cameras, lenses, tripods, flash attachments and reflectors would automatically guarantee masterful photos. This equipment is truly useful only in the hands of someone well versed in the art and science of photography.

Those of us who are not accomplished photographers might be better off selecting a quality point-and-shoot digital camera, also called a compact. These have the features that most amateur photographers will ever need, and are capable of producing very satisfactory photos both for the novice and experienced photographer alike.

Of course, these compact digital cameras have smaller lenses that capture much less light, and smaller image sensors that convert the light to electrical signals. The result is less photo definition. But their main advantage is their small size and weight, compared to the more sophisticated single lens reflex (SLR) camera and lenses. They also allow more spontaneity, due to their accessibly and ease of use.

To learn more about these cameras, check the information online. Among the features that I look for are lens quality, self timer, built-in flash, optical zoom, image stabilization, movie mode with sound, auto and manual focus, auto and manual exposure, selectable ISO, the size and brightness of the display, type of memory storage, and the battery type.

The lens quality has a tremendous effect on the quality of images the camera can produce. I choose a camera with a very sharp lens. How to tell? By checking the comparisons between different types and models online.

I am not interested too much in the camera's resolution capability (how many mega pixels). Too much is over-kill, at least for my purposes. I am more concerned with storage space, speed of operation, and battery life. So I find that an image size of about 2.5 MB about right, at least with the current state of technology.

Several of today's point-and-shoot cameras are 'weatherproof' or weather resistant. These features can extend the life of the camera in harsh conditions, and permit taking pictures during inclement weather, allowing the hiker to capture a more realistic impression of the excursion. Still, one must be careful not to introduce moisture and grit inside the camera when changing a battery or chip. Water can damage the electronic and mechanical components. Regardless of our camera's type, we stow it in a waterproof bag when not needed.

For best results, we study a new camera's many functions as described in the product guide. Then we practice by shooting a variety of pictures. This gives us a better working knowledge of the camera, so that once on the trail we will not need to figure out how to use it.

Shadows: the photographer's nemesis

As we gaze at a scene to be photographed, the eyes constantly adjust focus as we look from one part of the scene to another. Our pupils constrict and dilate, adjusting to the varying intensities of light coming from objects in sunlight and shade. And most importantly, our brain interprets the image by automatically compensating for harsh contrast and filtering out extraneous detail. The result is a pleasing rendition, perceived via an unimaginably complex battery of human faculties.

Even the most technologically advanced cameras, lenses and sensors are severely limited when registering the same image. Therefore, the photographer must select scenes that lie within the capabilities of the photo equipment.

Today's cameras are generally not capable of accommodating scenes of high contrast. The term "high contrast" denotes the harsh differences in light, for example between objects in direct sunlight and those in deep shade. So it is up to the photographer to avoid situations of high contrast when composing the photos.

When I look through the viewfinder, I examine the scene carefully for shadows. In direct sunlight, even mild shadow will render as darkness or even blackness on the final image. The shadow does not appear nearly so dark to the human eye because the brain smoothes the contrast. The camera cannot do this, which is why photos taken mid-day in bright sunshine are not likely to turn out well. Depending on how the camera adjusts its settings, the areas in sunlight might be properly exposed, but those in shade will probably turn out much too dark. For best results when taking pictures in a forest setting, I try to shoot at times of lower contrast, meaning early or late in the day, or on a cloudy day when the light is diffused and the shadows are subdued. Or when a patch of sunlight fully illuminates the subject.

The same holds true of a photo taken of someone wearing a shading brim hat. In direct sunlight, the hat might turn out great, but the face shaded by it will be lost in darkness. Portraits and close-ups often produce better results, with or without the hats, when illuminated by a fill-in flash. The flash helps even out the contrast. However, if the subject is wearing eyeglasses, these can reflect the flash. Ask the subject to turn his or her head slightly, or to remove the glasses. And while the flash on a small camera seems extremely bright to our eyes, keep in mind that it is not capable of properly exposing the image beyond six or eight feet. We use the flash feature only within that range, day or night.

Most point-and-shoot cameras offer control over the f-stop (size of the aperture) and shutter speed settings. But an easier method is to center the viewfinder on darker or lighter areas, depress the shutter release half way to lock the settings (in cameras that have this feature) and then to frame the photo the way we like and snap the picture. The display will show if we got it about right, and if not we try again.

The self timer

I have seen many hikers' slide shows, and by far the best pictures were the ones in which the photographer took the trouble to set up the camera, activate the self timer, then move into the picture. Scenery shots can be beautiful and pleasing, but to capture the essence of the journey you need to impart a sense of presence. It might be a hiker walking along the trail with an interesting view in the background, for example, or a hiker at camp. Any shots that have people activity in them are effective at drawing the audience into the experience.

A tripod enables a wider variety of shots, but is too heavy and bulky for most hikers. In lieu of a tripod, you can set the camera on rocks, a tree stump, or on the occasional fence post. You can even tie it to a tree with a length of cord. For an interesting angle, try placing the camera directly on the ground.

Memory chips

On average, Jenny and I shoot about 2,000 photos and a few dozen video clips during each multi-month trip. The memory chips have no difficulty storing all this data, but because a chip can fail, we do not trust all our

On the IUA

data to a single chip. Instead, we carry several, and swap them out on occasion. And we also try to back up the data on another device.

Spare battery

How many photos a camera can take depends on the type of camera and its use. It also depends on the battery and its quality. On a long trip, we carry several spare batteries, and sometimes even a battery charger if we will be going out to civilization on occasion. In Antarctica we carried a solar charger.

To minimize the electrical drain of each battery when necessary, we try to limit the use of the flash and zoom, and the amount of time we use the LCD to review the photos. We may even turn off the LCD.

A touch of humor

Photography can be a great medium for exercising creativity. And while thinking of the possibilities, remember that hiking is not all serious. Be sure to include some humor. Some of the funniest hiking pictures I have seen were taken by Jeff Robbins, who has a penchant for making his slide-show audiences laugh uproariously. One of his shots, shown here, has a hiker ambling along a logging road with a massive sign lashed to his backpack. The sign had apparently fallen from the back of a truck. Another of Jeff's pictures showed a group of hikers imitating a rock band, but in a snowy, alpine setting. They carried toy instruments and strange costumes for the occasion. Another time he had placed a plastic golf club in the hands of the Walt Whitman statue along the Appalachian Trail. "Look for humorous situations," Jeff advises, "and you'll find them just about everywhere."

Artistic rendering

The hiker wishing to avoid higher technology while still

capturing images from the journey could carry a small sketchpad and pencils or pens. For those so inclined, sketching various scenes would be an excellent way to enjoy some of those trail-side breaks.

Whether you choose to capture your scenes on paper, film, or memory chips, your images will be a unique combination of sights and emotions from those moments in the journey. Photography can sharpen one's powers of observation, and bring a deeper appreciation of the natural world.

Part 5

HIKER'S WELL-BEING

On our PCT-2 trip, we happened to be hiking past this beautiful lake at sunrise.

Trail Life

Hiking Enjoyment

"We cannot control the wind,
But we can adjust the sails."
— *Unknown*

While planning our outings, Jenny and I have much to consider: Training, nutrition, pack-weight reduction and efficient footwear, matters of logistics and itinerary – along with the many other subjects detailed in this book. It all leads to the ultimate goal of spending more time in the wilds, learning what we can from nature, and finding our paths to a closer wilderness connection. And of course we hope that our outings will be fun. To that end, I would like to pass along a few ideas garnered from our experience.

The concept of hiking enjoyment would seem, at first glance, to be rather straightforward. We are either having a good time, or we are not; depending on the weather, the scenery, the other hikers and townspeople, and a multitude of other externals.

This is the usual reasoning. But it might not be the best. This is because we are letting these external influences dictate our mood. In other words, these influences are controlling us, for better or worse.

We cannot control most of these influences, but we can adjust the way we internalize them.

Happiness requires nourishment

Our tandem bicycle, which we peddled twice across the U.S. in 2004, had to be in excellent working order. Before setting off each day, we had to check the tires for proper inflation, lubricate the chain, and so forth. If these conditions were not met, then we would not likely be riding far. And so it is with a person's brain. If it is not in good working order, due to poor nutritional and fluid intake, then the mind may be far less able to interpret events or situations in positive ways.

Once the brain is properly nourished, it becomes much more capable of generating happiness and feelings of well-being. But only that: capable. Positive emotions will not flow automatically, but at least we can help them along.

Learning a skill

Hiking enjoyment is a skill. Not a physical motor skill, but a cerebral one. And as with any skill, it does not come naturally; it has to be learned then developed through practice.

Imagine that I am driving in busy traffic and suddenly someone cuts me off. One possible reaction is to get angry, shake a fist perhaps, and start driving more aggressively myself. In so doing I would send the whole incident cascading along. Or, I could shrug the matter off, like water off a duck's back. With no effort at all I could ignore the negative impulse and hang on to my good mood.

The same principle can be useful in the wilds. The natural world is full of situations and circumstances that could strike me as negative, if that is how I decide to interpret them.

Consider the rain. Most people know that rain is essential for the well being of the planet. Indeed, the more a person ponders the miracle of water—sustainer of people and their crops, the animals and plants, birds and fish—the more one might appreciate every drop of rain. Yet what is the usual reaction when rain begins to fall? Annoyance: "the rain is ruining my day." Unhappiness: "hunker down, plod on miserably, and hope the rain will soon stop." Do such attitudes banish the rain? Or do they merely frustrate and weaken the hiker? Does the rain take away the beauties of the natural world, or do our reactions take away our enjoyment?

With the appropriate gear (umbrella for rain, shell clothing for bugs, etc) and particularly with a focus on the positive aspects of whatever circumstances or obstacles we might encounter, Jenny and I have learned not to impose our will on them, or feel let down when they exhibit a will of their own. I might take this concept a step further. The umbrella and protective garments are merely tools to help us shift our mental gears.

Positive by choice

One stumbling block to happiness is a person's methods of processing negative externals.

We once met a fellow who had quit his thru-hike because, he said, of brush growing on the trail. It peeved him that much. By my way of thinking, brush growing on a trail is a simple fact of trail life in many regions, on par with mosquitoes and rain. I do not view brush as a genuine barricade to progress, or even as an annoyance or inconvenience; but rather as an external circumstance. For after all, that brush might be growing there for a good reason. It might help prevent soil erosion, provide cover, food, and habitat for animals, and so on. I appreciate a trail that is well groomed, but when I find one that is not, I relinquish my unrealistic expectations and shift my thinking to align more with nature.

Until a person learns to shrug off such externals, they have a way of returning, time and again. Only after one has taken away their power—water-off-a-duck's-back style—will they leave a person alone. Every time that hiker encountered brush growing on the trail, it tested him; and he reacted by wrestling with his torment. A person can never win such battles. This fellow's anger and hatred of the brush had no effect on that brush. But it did overpower his mind, and it sent him home.

Changing the station

We humans can tune our minds into various thoughts just like we can tune a radio to different stations. I enjoy listening to good music, but when my internal radio starts playing the same old drivel, I can simply change the station. Assuming a person's brain is well nourished and hydrated, one does not have to let any negative thoughts—such as anger, regret, or bitterness—keep gnawing at his or her mind.

Becoming aware of what station the mind is tuned to, and being able to change it, is a skill. This skill does not come naturally for most people, but it can be developed through practice. And a good time for practice is on a backpacking trip, or the training hikes, because they give a person lots of time to practice becoming aware of what stations one is tuned in to, and practice changing the stations to more pleasing and uplifting thoughts.

PCT-2

A duck oils its feathers so that water will simply run off them. Pour water on a duck, and the duck will stay dry. Pour water on a chicken, and the chicken will get wet – and very upset. This is because the chicken does not have the ability to oil its feathers.

So a person can behave like a duck, and swim in the waters of annoyance with equanimity. Or, he or she can behave like a chicken and let everything bother them.

Imagine a person writing this idiom on the hand where it will serve as a reminder: "Water off a duck's back." Each time this person looks at this, he or she is oiling their feathers.

Quicksand

Everyone experiences negative thoughts at various times and to various degrees. How do I free myself of wasteful negativity while tapping into the positive energy all around?

We were hiking cross-country through Yellowstone National Park, when we came upon a beautiful meadow. This meadow was lush and green, and far off the beaten track. Nearby flowed a small creek, but as we approached, the ground beneath our feet began to quiver ominously, as though the grass was growing on quicksand. And sure enough, the moment we stopped walking, our feet began to sink in. As the ground oozed and sucked at our shoes, we struggled to pull them free. Then as we retreated, we found that as long as we kept moving, all went well; but every time we paused, down into the bog our feet would start to sink.

Pulling one's thoughts free of the bogs of negativity can sometimes be a struggle. And just because I have extracted a foot, that does not mean I have solved the problem. The process has to be conscious and continuous, until eventually reaching firm ground.

Vis medicatrix naturae

(wes med-i-KA-trix na-TU-ri: the healing power of nature)

One way to avoid the bogs is to keep one's mind on the present moment. When a person does that, he or she will usually find that nature is the cure to the common negative mindset. Even the smallest stimuli such as the singing of a bird, or the babbling of a brook, can open positive mental channel-ways and allow life's simple but often profound pleasures to come streaming in.

As Thoreau expressed so simply: "nature is our medicine."

A mind that does not travel with the body can easily wander off course and fall into the bogs. I try to keep my senses open to the surroundings, and tuned in to the enlivening sights, sounds and lessons. In short, I try to live in the moment.

In his book *Flow, The Psychology of Optimal Experience*, Mihaly Csikszentmihalyi (chick-sent-me-highly) details his "principles to transform boring and meaningless lives into ones full of enjoyment." Happiness, he says, does not just happen, nor is it the result of money, power, good fortune or chance. Instead, happiness must be cultivated from within. And he continues with the idea that "the best moments usually occur when the body or mind is stretched to its limits in a voluntary effort to accomplish something difficult or worthwhile."

The dangers of self-absorption

Jenny and I have enjoyed a great many trips and adventures, and without exception these have been without fanfare. We do not elicit sponsorship, and we are not trying to impress anyone or prove anything to other people or even to ourselves. Simply stated, our trips are a way for us to experience life at its fullest.

We have seen countless people having a hard time with their trips for the simple reason that their trips were all about themselves – in whatever shades of lightness or darkness.

For example, we have seen people focused on their suffering. They went into the trips with that in mind, and that is what they experienced. With a focus on suffering, that suffering will manifest and snowball.

We have seen people focused on their desire to prove something. Their trips have usually defaulted to suffering as well. Or if nothing else, these people have soon stopped doing more trips, because the past trips did not satisfy the inner needs. And when a person is trying to prove something, he or she usually does not remain in the game for long. This is because on a grander scale, it is impossible to prove anything. So the person trying to prove something will be like a shooting star: the burst of glory will be short lived.

We have seen countless people living inside their own heads. It is all about the importance of "me," or the importance of "my suffering." With such attitudes, the adversities of nature will likely test him or her, and other people might join in the fray.

If you ask someone about their trips, you will soon learn what is inside them. Were their trips all about hardships and glory, or were they more about the enjoyment of the adventure, the beauties of nature, friendly people met, good food and the wildlife seen?

Many of our trips have been challenging – to say the least. But keeping them free of these self-absorbed elements has been our key to enjoyment.

Happiness in the wilderness experience does not happen automatically. Nor is it the result of high-tech equipment, stylish clothes, stunning scenery, or favorable weather. Yes, nature has the capacity to enrich our lives, but only the capacity. We must create any meaningful experiences and enjoyment from within.

Jenny having fun sliding down a creek in the Sierra, during our JMT hike.

Hiking Pace

"When I was on the Yukon trail,
The boys would warn, when things were bleakest,
The weakest link's the one to fail –
Said I: 'By Gosh! I won't be weakest.'
So I would strain with might and main,
Striving to prove I was the stronger,
Till sourdough Sam would snap: 'Goldurn!
Go easy, son; you'll last the longer.'"
— *Robert Service, Take It Easy*

Walking with lightness and economy of motion

To optimize comfort, wellbeing, and enjoyment on the trail, Jenny and I ensure that we hike with the minimum of energy expenditure. We accomplish this by maintaining a moderate and efficient pace. This conserves our energy and allows us to hike with less fatigue. And if our plans call for an extended mileage day, or for a climb to higher elevations, we know that with our carefully controlled pace we can accomplish it comfortably and enjoyably.

Power-hiking: Hurry up and stop!

When we hiked the Appalachian Trail in 1993, we shared the trail with more than a thousand other thru-hikers. Of course, everyone was spread out over many hundreds of miles, so we saw only a small percentage of them. I do not remember catching up to anyone who was actually moving along the trail; but a great many hikers passed us.

As we ambled along, someone would occasionally shoot by and disappear around the next bend. Then at the next trail junction to a shelter we would often see where their tracks left the trail. Or sometimes we would find them a mile or two later resting alongside the trail. As we strolled by, we knew that they would soon overtake us once again. And sure enough…vroom! They would race ahead.

These "power-hikers" (as we started calling them)[11] were not all athletic types; they were fit and not-so-fit men and women, young and old. To us, they seemed to be practicing a hurry-up-and-stop approach, like a series of sprints. And once the inevitable exhaustion caught up with them, it was time for a long rest.

Why were these people trying to hike so fast? Was it simply for show? Or perhaps like driving a car on a turnpike, they were only trying to get there sooner; a reflection of our fast-paced, competitive society. Jenny wondered whether there might have been an ice cream truck parked up ahead. If there was, we never found it – maybe because we were so slow. But in the late afternoons when the power-hikers were spreading their sleeping bags in the shelters, Jenny and I were still moseying comfortably along the trail. Thanks to our moderate pace, we felt neither deep fatigue nor any urge to stop early and make camp.

Pace and fatigue

The differences in style illustrated to us the relationship between pace and degree of fatigue.

Years earlier I had begun to wonder what was the optimum hiking pace that will gain me the best mileage for the least fatigue and discomfort?

Of course the answer depends on many factors: the goal, the terrain, the load on the feet, the weight in the backpack, one's level of fitness, etc. But mainly for Jenny

---

11 We coined the term in the book's 5th printing, Feb 1996.

and me, it is a matter of listening to our bodies, and finding the optimum cardiovascular rate.

Cardio-awareness

Basically, power-hiking is striving for maximum leg rate while disregarding the heart rate. My approach is quite the opposite. I ignore the urge for speed, and concentrate instead on my pulse. I keep the heart beating at a moderate but efficient rate, slowing or speeding my walking speed according to the trail's gradient. This is a conscious exercise in whole-body control, not merely leg control.

PCT-2

Physiologists describe aerobic exercise levels in terms of percentage of maximum heart rate, but I find this too mechanical. Jenny and I are not on laboratory treadmills monitoring our electronic pulse meters and varying our pace accordingly. But we have achieved much the same results by developing our natural sense of whole-body awareness.

I started at home with a simple meditation that taught me how to listen to the beating of my heart. To start practicing, I would find a quiet place to sit undisturbed, then block out the distractions and concentrate mainly on my breathing. Then with more concentration I learned to feel the blood pulsing through the arteries in the neck and upper arms, and to feel my heart beating. Once I developed cardio-awareness, I began using this skill on the trail.

Developing a controlled pace

Because of these exercises, I stay tuned in to my pulse. If I start hiking too fast, my heart will start laboring, and will let me know. I could hike like this for a few hours. But if instead I am careful to avoid over-revving the heart, even for a moment, I know my energy expenditure is at its most efficient level. Finding the most efficient level required a bit of experimentation. But once I found the heart rate that was the most efficient for me, I started feeling stronger and more energetic.

A controlled pace is not about speed or distance. Instead, it is about an absence of fatigue. To Jenny and me, that is what hiking and backpacking are all about: comfort, well-being and enjoyment. And a carefully controlled pace is our key to having fun, whatever the trip.

Taking it easy on the leg muscles

The steepness of the slope, the ruggedness of the terrain, and the weight on our feet and in our packs all affect our degree of leg fatigue and muscle tightness, particularly in the calves. Our gait—the actual sequence of individual foot and leg movements—can also influence muscle tightness. If we pull the heels off the ground prematurely with each step, and shove off too hard with the ball of the foot and toes, we are overworking the calves. These exaggerated motions waste effort. They also tend to stiffen the muscles, and increase their susceptibility to injury. And they can accelerate the formation of blisters.

We sometimes take a few moments to critique our

shoe tracks in soft ground. Craters at the ball of the foot and toes indicate an overly energetic push-off. When walking on firm ground, a certain amount of toe push is beneficial. How much is a matter of terrain and personal style. Too much is counterproductive. The over-energetic push-off is easily moderated, if consciously done.

Conversely, when walking on soft sand or crusty snow, the push-off can retard progress. In that case we practice lifting the toes somewhat at the end of the stride, rather than shoving ahead with them.

Sometimes when walking on soft ground, we turn around and look at our line of tracks. Are the toes turned out? This is "duck walking," and for most people it can be hard on the knees. For the most efficient stride, we keep our feet tracking straight ahead.

Hiking with the brakes on

Learning to properly coordinate the leg muscles used for walking is another technique for reducing fatigue.

On the front side of the upper legs are the quadriceps. On the back side are the gluteals and hamstrings. These are the primary muscles used for walking. But with each step they are not used at the same time. And if the gluteals and hamstrings do not relax fast enough, they resist the quadriceps; and vise versa.

This inadvertent braking action holds true with a multitude of opposing muscle groups throughout the body. To relax and help coordinate the muscles, we sometimes practice what I call the "robo meltdown." Without breaking stride, we tense all muscles like a robot, then slowly decrease the tension until achieving the bare minimum of stiffness required to carry on.

Interludes

The motions of hiking are repetitious, but this is not to suggest that we march along like soldiers. To break a monotonous walking rhythm, we sometimes shift into cruising mode for a short distance (see below). Or we may turn around and walk several steps sideways, or turn completely around and take a few steps backward. This may sound nonsensical, but for high-mileage hiking it takes the pressure off of the forward walking muscles. When we vary our step, we use different muscles in different ways. We find that our bodies, and particularly our feet and legs, benefit from these brief interludes. So we try to be creative with our hiking style. We strive for efficiency, but season it with a little variety.

Cruising

In his book *Maximum Performance*, Laurence E. Morehouse describes a technique he calls "walking in cruising mode." This is strikingly similar to the smooth and flowing rapid-walk slow-run mode of travel used by aboriginal peoples of South and Central America for no doubt thousands of years. The method is to walk crouched a few inches lower than normal, knees slightly flexed and the head held steady with minimal bobbing up and down. Lean back slightly and imagine balancing a jug of water on the head. Start slowly, then build a little speed. Cruising requires a light backpack and sufficient conditioning of the muscles involved with these specific motions.

Jenny and I normally walk at a very moderate pace. But at those times when we need to cover a few quick miles, we sometimes switch into cruising mode. We might use this technique when needing to descend quickly to more protected ground in the face of a threatening storm, or to reach a resupply station before it closes for the weekend.

Hiking uphill and downhill

Although the gangbuster's pace is typically counterproductive, sometimes the circumstances might prompt us to hike at a slightly higher pulse rate.

Suppose we hike 10 miles on level ground at 3 miles per hour. Excluding any periods of rest, we would cover the distance in 3.3 hours. Now instead of hiking level ground, let's say that we have a hill to climb. We hike slower uphill for 5 miles, and reaching the top we hike faster 5 miles down the other side. Will we still travel the 10 miles in 3.3 hours? For an answer, I devised the following table. In each case, I subtracted a certain speed from the 3 mph hiking uphill, then added it back double on the descent.

Steepness of hill	Speed while hiking 5 miles uphill	Speed while hiking 5 miles downhill	Time required to hike the 10 miles
flat	3 mph	3 mph	3.3 hours
moderate	2 mph	4 mph	3.8 hours
steep	1 mph	5 mph	6.0 hours
very steep	0.5 mph	5.5 mph	10.9 hours

So we see that scurrying downhill at a fast clip does not even begin to recover the time required to hike slowly uphill. This is because while hiking uphill we are traveling slower for a longer period of time, and the two effects multiply against each other. These numbers illustrate the advantages of hiking uphill at a *slightly* elevated heart rate, and the futility of trying to make up for lost time by surging downhill.

The rest step

I learned the rest step at a Sierra Club mountaineering class back in 1964, and have used it ever since for climbing steep slopes, particularly snow-packed slopes. The technique uses a different set of leg muscles than the typical uphill walk, and is an excellent method to moderate one's pace and control the heart rate while climbing a steep slope. One can practice the rest step on a flight of stairs.

Start with both feet together at the foot of the stairs. Transfer the bodyweight to the left leg, then lean forward and lift the right foot onto the first stair tread. At this point, one's body weight is still on the left leg.

Shift the weight to the right leg while straightening and locking the right knee. Leave the left foot touching the lower step for balance.

Rest for a moment, keeping the weight on the right leg; then repeat the motions with the left leg on the next stair step.

As you practice on the stairs, remember that the rest step is supposed to be slow and methodical. Picture yourself ascending a steep slope, perhaps at altitude where the air is thin, where each step (and even each breath) is labored.

Power resting

Frequent rest stops throughout the day will help defer weariness. And while resting, we keep in mind that the restorative effects are critically dependent on ample circulation. As the blood flows through the body it carries nutrients and oxygen to the tired muscles, and carries away the waste products of metabolism. As we hike along the trail, the muscles in our legs actually help pump blood back up to our hearts. When we stop and rest, our leg muscles relax. And if they are very tired, then

The proper power resting position during one of our training hikes

they actually hyper-relax and allow their blood vessels to enlarge. This is known as "vaso-dilation." If we are resting on a log or rock as though sitting on a bench, then gravity will pull the blood down into our lower legs and feet, and pool it there. This is an extremely inefficient way to rest, because the pooling hampers circulation in the legs and feet, and therefore it hampers their ability to recover from exertion. A much better resting position is to sit on the ground with the legs extended.

The best resting position, however, is to lie down and elevate the legs and feet to heart level or slightly above. We may prop up our legs on a log, rock, or backpack. As a resting pad, we could use our foam pad, groundsheet, or an open jacket. In jest, I call this "power resting."

A restorative night's rest

Optimum circulation is equally vital for a restorative night's sleep. The more the foot and leg muscles have exerted during the day, the more the blood will tend to pool in them during the night if they are even slightly below heart level. The blood pooling in the legs at night will also reduce the body's warmth, since this blood is not being circulated throughout the body. It is the proper circulation of blood, warmed by the heat of metabolism that, in turn, warms the entire body. This is true even while at rest. So for the warmest and most restful night's sleep, we sleep with legs somewhat elevated. In order to facilitate this, we look for a stealth-site on a slight grade.

The casual approach

Jenny and I appreciate how our lighter loads and moderate pace allow us longer days on the trail. This is important because we enjoy hiking.

And to us, hiking means more than passively walking along, blocking out what is happening all around while the mind is a thousand miles away, dwelling on some problem or memory that has nothing to do with the present moment.

Rather, we try to travel in a more active, tuned-in mode. That is, inwardly tuned in to our heart-rates and breathing, and our degree of cold or sweat; and outwardly tuned into nature, to the constant stream of messages emanating from the landscape and its creatures: a bird's chattering, a tree's whisper of an approaching cloudburst, the distant "huff" of an elk, the tinkling of a hidden trickle of water along a dry stretch of trail. And when our ears are tuned into the natural environment, the other senses tend to follow suit. Our seeing becomes more vivid and perceptive: out of the corner of our eye we catch a glimpse of a pine martin on a branch, we notice a deer laying in the brush over there, we find a piece of broken arrowhead protruding from the forest floor. Our sense of smell also becomes more acute, telling of imminent rain, a distant campfire, or a patch of ramps. It is a matter of integrating with the setting, rather than simply passing through it, en route to somewhere else.

With our moderate pace, frequent rest stops throughout the day, and a rejuvenating late afternoon dinner break, we can look forward to the evening hours. We hike on, watching the sky fade into night, absorbing the cooling night air and listening to the nocturnal sounds of nature. When finally we stop, it is with a feeling of satisfaction with the day's experiences. And yes, it is also with a good aura of tiredness that makes for a sound sleep.

Even though the day might have been long, it was not hard, since we did not overexert. So we can rise early the next morning to greet the dawn, without feeling the need to sleep late. We enjoy the early morning hiking, soaking in the stillness and the freshness of the new day.

All this is made possible by a moderate, well-controlled pace.

Physical Conditioning

"Success to the strongest,
who are always, at last,
the wisest and best."
— *Emerson*

Training is fun

When considering the hunting and gathering lifestyle of early humans, we can assume that most of these people were accustomed to running, walking, and carrying loads. They would have depended on their vigorous "exercise" for their sustenance, shelter and defense.

Since that time, the human physiology has changed very little. Yet in the past few hundred years people have become ever more sedate and unhealthy.

But not all is lost. To set out on a backpacking trip is to begin a restorative journey back in time; a journey that will strengthen, invigorate, and impart new life into a body atrophied by idleness. However, embarking on that adventure without strengthening the muscles, tendons and ligaments beforehand could lead to problems.

True, a person's body would likely be capable of adapting to prolonged and strenuous exertion. But one can acquire the necessary strengths only gradually, over many months. So this strengthening is best accomplished prior to the trek's beginning – during the conditioning, or training phase.

Why train?

Jenny and I find the pre-hike physical conditioning

extremely beneficial. By strengthening our bodies before each journey, we become more capable of handling the exertions during the actual adventure. And with stronger muscles, tendons and ligaments, we are less susceptible to injury, especially to the knees, ankles and feet. Thus, the training reduces the hardships and discomforts, both physical and mental. Training also increases our chances of an enjoyable and successful outing. In effect, the pre-hike conditioning shortens every mile and shrinks every hill.

Keep the training fun

We enjoy our training hikes. They prompt us to set aside our work, and to spend considerably more time outside than we otherwise would. At home, we usually have many pressing items on our agendas, but once we have temporarily left them behind, our priorities invariably shift as we focus on the training hike. And as a bonus, the exercise, fresh air and increased circulation stimulate our vitality and productiveness once we have returned home.

In order to keep the training routine fun, we avoid making it difficult. Otherwise, we might abandon it. Motivation is fueled by positive feedback. So we build the miles and packweight gradually, without ever overstraining.

Our simple training plan

Our method of training for a long hike is to shoulder our backpacks every-other day, step out of the house, and start walking.

People who live in a city surrounded by miles of civilization might imagine they lack a suitable training area. But this is not necessarily so. Wherever a person can walk, he or she can also train. The route might encompass several blocks to a city park, or perhaps a simple loop around the neighborhood.

When we lived in Oregon, we walked for 15 minutes

through the neighborhood to the edge of the forest, and that forest extended for hundreds of miles. So in those 12 years we racked up many thousands of enjoyable training miles.

After moving to Arizona, we trained for our journeys by walking or running around our neighborhood, augmented by driving to the nearest mountains and climbing those.

Start early

The idea is to begin the conditioning far in advance of the summer's outing, giving one's body a chance to adjust to the heightened activity, and strengthen to the task.

When planning to cover more than 2,000 miles in a single season's journey, we start our training at least five months prior to the start of the actual trip. If our adventure will be extra strenuous, we start our conditioning much earlier. We trained for 18 rigorous months before our ski trip to the South Pole.

Start easy

Whatever our hiking or adventuring goals, we begin conditioning by walking a comparatively short distance over gentle but irregular terrain. If a person were starting from scratch, fitness-wise, they might begin by simply walking around the block. Or, if they could handle a twenty-minute walk, then they might start with that.

Regardless of our fitness level, we walk only until we become a little tired, then we turn around and walk back. We resist the temptation to set geographic goals. Instead, we stay tuned to our bodies, and regulate our outings according to our present abilities.

Every other day

We limit our training forays to every other day. This allows a rest day between every hiking day. This plan we find the most beneficial.

Increase weekly

When training for a thru-hike, our target load is thirty-five pounds with a distance of twelve miles or more. However, we build up to this gradually.

In fact, we begin the training without packs. At the beginning of each new week we add more mileage. We continue with this until we can walk five miles without tiring significantly. When we can manage this comfortably, we start carrying small, light packs.

We are not trying to condition ourselves to the standard elephantine load. So we start by carrying only the things we need, like water, snacks and extra clothing.

Depending on a person's familiarity with the training region, one may eventually need a map and compass, as he or she builds mileage. We also carry a few survival items like a small knife, matches and tinder, flashlight and first aid kit. In cold weather we could carry an insulating pad to sit on, and warm jackets and hats to wear during the rest stops.

Week by week we increase our packweight by adding a bottle or two of water. Water works well because if we begin to tire midway through our training hike we can pour some of it out, perhaps on needy plants. In our present locale, that would be a few infant saguaro cacti.

A common myth

One might think that the training becomes progressively tougher from day one, as we add miles and pack weight. However, this is not the case. As we build strength and stamina, we become more capable. With the passing weeks, we find that we can walk farther without fatigue. So although we carry heavier loads for longer distances, we do not feel those differences.

Patience and persistence

Of course, the pre-hike conditioning has nothing to do with instant gratification; hence its lack of appeal with most people. Indeed, it commands a considerable amount of one's time. And unlike the actual hike, the training hikes generally lack adventure. But with the vision of our upcoming trip in the forefront of our minds, we know that the "start date" will come, and we also know that we need to be ready for it.

Water, snacks, and stretching

If we find ourselves tiring during the conditioning forays, we know we are either going at it too vigorously, or we need to drink more water and eat more snacks.

To avoid problems, we drink plenty of water to offset dehydration. Back pain or headaches—during or after the conditioning hikes—are almost always a sign of dehydration. The exercise tends to be dehydrating and calls for an increase in water intake.

We also snack often in order to boost our energy levels and enliven our day.

Additionally, the further we progress with our training program the greater is our need for quality nutrition at home. As much as possible, we eat wholesome and fresh foods. These help build our reserves.

And too, we pay careful attention to stretching out the muscles, especially the calves. We do this before, during, and after each training hike. See the "Stretching" chapter.

Developing a personal discipline

The traits that a person cultivates and nourishes during the conditioning hikes will tend to manifest during the actual journey. So during the training hikes we are not

If you are planning a hike with a partner, the training forays are the ideal proving grounds. Planning to share gear? Wondering about compatibility? Worried about blisters, or the partner not being in shape or vice-versa? The training hikes will tell all.

only conditioning our bodies, we are further developing our personal hiking style. In the previous chapter I discussed the advantages of learning how to tune the mind to positive thoughts. With practice, this ability becomes a part of one's hiking presence, along with patience, persistence, focus, ambition and all the other needed qualities.

So if we practice gentle and enjoyable conditioning with a positive attitude, the actual journey will tend to follow suit.

Log the mileage

We keep a log of our conditioning mileage. The amount of mileage logged depends on the nature and extent of our summer's hiking goals. For a two-week trek we might try for one hundred training miles. For a summer's thru-hike, we have found five hundred training miles about right. This might seem like a lot, but the training miles add up quickly when regularly done.

Train on uneven ground

On his second walk across the U.S., Robert Sweetgall traveled 11,208 miles of roads through all fifty states in 364 consecutive days. George Meegan spent seven years on a continuous trek from the tip of South America to the top of North America, walking mostly roads. Both of these walkers have written books about their accomplishments. Peter Jenkins and numerous others have journeyed long and far on roads. And as any pavement-pounder will tell you, roads are tough on the feet and legs.

Paved roads are not the best surfaces for conditioning a person for trail hiking. Walking on city-flat surfaces strengthens the fore and aft muscles, tendons, and ligaments of the ankles and feet, but it does little for the lateral ones. So we train on uneven, irregular surfaces: hiking cross-country through the forest, or following deer trails, or walking old rutted, bumpy, and rough jeep tracks. The idea is to gently work the ankles – make them rock and roll.

Train in inclement weather

The training hikes are good opportunities to practice dealing with the occasional lethargic mood. Especially in adverse weather.

We like nice days and clear skies as much as anyone; but on our training days we head out the door no matter what the weather's mood. On a sunny day we enjoy the

The training hikes: snow, rain, or shine

sunshine. On a rainy day we enjoy the rain for how it scents the air with its promise of life—as we hike beneath our umbrellas. If snow is falling, we enjoy the beauty of the crystals and their whitening of the landscape— again beneath the umbrellas. To compensate for a cold

and windy day we wear warmer and more protective clothing.

So too, the more time we spend hiking in various weather conditions, the more confidence we gain, and the more we tend to shed any weather-related anxieties. In fact, during our training hikes we use inclement weather to advantage by testing our clothing and equipment to see what works best.

Train for steep grades

Some trails have reputations for steep climbs and rough tread. The Appalachian Trail certainly comes to mind here; but although this trail does climb and descend a great deal, it is reasonably graded along most of its length. When Jenny and I were preparing for our AT thru-hike, only a portion of our training involved climbing and descending the local buttes. We concentrated mainly on mileage. And just as importantly, we spent a lot of time developing lightweight gear and our abilities to use it effectively in all sorts of conditions. We knew that the "lightness" would benefit us immeasurably in terms of surmounting those hundreds of hills along the AT. And this certainly proved to be the case.

Still, we find conditioning for the hills can be quite beneficial. If a person does not have access to a steep hill, he or she could incorporate some stair climbing and barbell squats (described below) into the training routine.

Supplementary exercises

Most gyms are equipped with stair climbers, stationary bicycles, Nordic tracks and so forth. But these might not be the best way to train for hiking. These machines isolate certain muscle groups, and exert them in very singular ways. So these exercises are completely unlike the motions of hiking, which works all the major muscle groups in a wide variety of ways.

Strengthening the quadriceps

Because our training hikes focus mostly on mileage, the thigh muscles (quadriceps) can still be somewhat under-developed, even with the other parts of our legs well-conditioned. So we use two supplemental leg-strengthening exercises that help us climb out of snowpack postholes and moats, surmount steep terrain, and climb over wind-felled timber blocking the trail.

Barbell squat

When performed correctly, the barbell squat is generally considered a safe and effective thigh strengthening exercise. The technique is to stand upright, hold a barbell

PCT-2

behind the head and across the shoulders, squat down, then rise back up. If new at this, you might use a broom handle with no added weight. Or simply hold a bottle of water in each hand. As you squat, keep the chin up and the spine upright. Most importantly, avoid squatting below the comfort level. Any knee pain indicates that you are squatting too low.

Leg extension

The second exercise we practice is the leg extension. This helps strengthen the muscles supporting the knees. Sit in a chair and place the leg to be exercised over the chair's armrest, letting the foot hang free. Loop a small weight, suspended by a short length of cord, over the foot. Slowly raise the foot by unbending the knee and straightening the leg; then ease the foot back down. Exercise gently, and use very little weight (one or two pounds) to begin with. If the knee makes grating noises, reduce the weight and merely hold the leg out horizontally, rather than raising and lowering it.

Developing a sense of balance

A well-developed sense of balance helps us walk across logs spanning small creeks, step from rock to rock, and scramble over rough terrain. And it helps us stand one-legged, for example while dumping gravel out of a shoe. No person was born with good balance; he or she must learn it, and practice it. To improve our sense of balance, we simply stand on one leg while looking ahead and upward for one to two minutes. Then we switch legs and repeat.

Excuses

Despite the obvious benefits of physical conditioning, hikers still find excuses not to train. "No time" is probably the most common. It is also the most unlikely, considering all the wasted hours expended browsing the internet or watching tv. There are other more imaginative excuses:

Magic-trail mistake

One of the greatest hiking-related myths of all times has to do with some magical quality of a mega-trail that supposedly buoys the hiker along. In reality, when backpackers head into the wilds, they are in for some real exercise. And the more ambitious their trail objectives, the better conditioned they need to be. At the far end of the scale is the long-distance hike, which entails walking day after day, climbing and descending interminably, and forging ahead in all types of weather for months on end. This is an intense physical challenge. We have learned not to underestimate the demands and difficulties, or overestimate our abilities. With the proper training beforehand, the journey will likely proceed as a matter of course. Without the training, it can be grueling.

Experience is strength mistake

Another mistake is to confuse experience with strength, and vice-versa. Even though Jenny and I usually embark on some type of adventure almost every year, we never assume we are still in shape for the next one. We start training again from scratch. And if we are perhaps accustomed to carrying heavy loads—for example carrying supplies in to a base camp, or portaging during a canoe trip—we do not assume that we have retained that strength and stamina for the next year.

Overconfidence syndrome

A hiker might feel that he or she is in pretty good shape to begin with, and does not need to train. Granted, a person might get away with this on a short trip. And even if carrying a heavy load, an ill-conditioned hiker will often manage to trudge along for a few days without major problems. But beyond that, the difficulties associated with being out-of-shape can manifest.

The hike will be the training

A *common* mistake is to assume the hike itself will be the training. The usual intent is to start out slowly and take things easy for the initial few days or weeks, while gradually building strength and endurance.

This plan would work if the person hiked only a few hours a day, carried a light pack, and enjoyed a rest day every other day. But with a long backpacking trip in mind, hikers must be on the move six or eight hours a day while carrying their clothing, gear, food, and water. The overall trail distance is great, and because the season is comparatively short, they usually try to keep this up day after day. This strategy places tremendous strains on their bodies, and is quite likely to cause a stress injury. Faced with these realties, few backpackers would call this kind of plan fun.

The all-important rest day

One of the most important features of the pre-hike training program, besides the gradual start and the slow buildup of pack-weight over many months, is the rest day it affords between each training day. We find this rest day vitally important for renewing energy and building strength. Moreover, we find this schedule so effective that at the end of the five-month training period, we no longer need many rest days. We are now fully capable of hiking vigorously every day.

Here is a typical comparison: Setting off from the trail's beginning, the poorly-conditioned hiker might manage six or eight miles the first day, while the well-trained hiker might cover twice that. In theory, both feel they have exerted themselves equally. After eight miles the one hiker feels tired; after sixteen miles, the other hiker, because he is more capable, feels the same degree of tiredness. However, training's main benefit comes not at the end of the first day, but at the beginning of the second. The out-of-shape hiker might struggle out of the sleeping bag stiff, muscle sore, and feeling inclined to take a rest day. The well-conditioned hiker is apt to arise feeling in excellent condition, despite the previous day's exertions, and anxious to resume the trek.

Training time reduces trekking time

For those back packers with their sights set on thru-hiking a long trail, every hour spent conditioning can shorten the journey's duration. Spend five months train-

ing beforehand, hiking maybe five hundred miles in the process, and rid the pack of every needless ounce, and a person should be able to cut a couple of months off the overall time. This reduction might be an attractive option for those with limited time off from work or classes, or for those who want to avoid harsh weather at the start and end of the summer hiking season.

Of course, hikers-in-planning often want to make their journeys last as long as possible. For them the journey is what matters, rather than the destination. But the fact remains that any backpacking trip will be that much

more enjoyable and injury free when the hiker starts in good physical condition.

"Weston the Pedestrian"

In 1909, Edward Weston walked 4,500 miles across the U.S. in 105 days. The following year, at age 72, he repeated the journey in the opposite direction in 76 days, for a remarkable average of 59 miles a day. One of the most accomplished walkers of his time, Weston believed that walking was as healthful and natural as sleeping. Throughout most of his life he walked 12 to 15 miles every day of the week except Sunday. He disdained the notion of "training" and considered his daily walks as merely a part of his lifestyle.

Our training hikes are a part of our lifestyle too. In fact, we consider the training as part of the journey. That is, the first day of our training program is also the first day of the actual journey. That gives us more to be excited about well in advance.

Backpacking trips can be fun and enjoyable, and free of stress and pain. One of the best ways to insure that they actually turn out that way is to devote some time to getting in shape—conditioning the body and strengthening the muscles—beforehand. Whether it is a thru-hike, a week-long hike, or anything in between, we make sure we have trained for it sufficiently.

Stretching

Supple muscles for safer hiking

The more we use our muscles, the stronger they become. But during *vigorous* exercise our muscle fibers tend to develop microscopic tears. These tears are what produce the typical "muscle soreness" the following day. In an attempt to guard against this micro-damage, the muscles stiffen. And if the vigorous exercise continues, this stiffening can lead to more tears.

The hiker's leg muscles are the primary areas for these stress tears, especially when long-distance hiking. Regular, gentle stretching encourages the muscles to relax, and can do much to prevent the micro-tears from growing larger and leading to bona-fide stress injuries.

In his book: *Yoga 28 Day Exercise Book*, Richard Hittleman writes, "Stretching requires a minimum of effort to attain maximum results." In other words, the proper stretch is pressed only until a slight pull is felt, and no more. If over-stressed, the muscles will contract and shrink in an attempt to guard themselves from injury.

I have completed Hittleman's 28-day program many times. However, for backpackers I would caution against working the joints away from the axes of normal hiking motions. Out-of-axis *exercising* strengthens the ligaments; but out-of-axis *stretching* tends to weaken them. An example of out-of-axis *exercising* is walking on uneven ground, making the feet, ankles and legs rock and roll. An example of out-of-axis *stretching* would be practicing the lotus position (seated on the ground, legs crossed, each foot atop the opposite leg). This particular stretch can weaken the knees laterally, something that Jenny and I prefer to avoid.

Keeping these two principles in mind, I would like to describe and explain a couple of hiking-related stretching exercises that we use to keep our legs limber and to reduce the chances of an injury.

The hiker's calf stretch

Before we can stretch a muscle, we must first relax it. Otherwise, the stretching could injure that muscle. Also, we must insure that our muscles are properly hydrated, by drinking plenty of water. Dehydrated muscles tend to be far less capable, and also quite stiff. When dehydrated, one must stretch only with extreme gentleness.

The leg stretching exercise we use most is what I call the "hiker's calf stretch." This is a modification of the classic runner's calf stretch. We practice this in the morning before setting off, then several times during the day's hiking, as well as in the evening before retiring.

Imagine I am standing facing a sturdy object, such as a tree, rock, or an embankment. Let's use a tree for this example. I position my feet a yard or more out from its base, then lean forward and brace my hands against the trunk, elbows straight, as though I am about to do a vertical push up.

I stretch one leg at a time; say, starting with the right leg. I straighten the right knee, and let the heel rest on the ground. I cross the left leg in front of the right one, and place its left toe on the ground with the left heel slightly elevated. Now I press the back of the left knee against the front of the right knee, locking the right knee into position. This helps the right leg relax by preventing its knee from buckling, and it shunts most of the balancing mechanisms that would interfere with muscular relaxation. At the same time, I am careful not to let the right ankle pronate, or roll inward, because this would place great strain on the ligaments. If one's ankle naturally pronates, which most do to some extent, included mine, I place the inner edge of my right foot on a small rock or stick for additional support.

Once in position, I slowly bend the elbows, bringing my body closer to the tree. Then I relax, feel the stretch in the right calf, push away slightly, and hold for twenty heartbeats.

Now I lift the right leg and let the foot hang limp. If I have been hiking vigorously, I may feel a throbbing sensation in the calf muscles. This is caused by the muscle relaxing and dilating its blood vessels, allowing the blood to pool. And it is a sure indication that I need to pay more attention to the stretching exercises, and to keep them gentle. When the dangling calf has relaxed as much as it will, in ten or fifteen seconds, and the throbbing has eased, I place the foot back down gently, and repeat the stretching procedure with the other leg.

Note: I do not practice this stretching exercise while standing totally upright. In this position the many muscles in the legs are constantly flexing, first on one side of the legs then the other, keeping the body in balance. Before a muscle can stretch safely, I must relax it. This is why I lean against a fixed object: to shut off the balancing mechanisms and allow the calf muscles to relax.

The hiker's ankle, foot, and toes stretch

Another exercise of particular benefit to us while hiking is the ankle, foot, and toes stretch. I can use the same tree as before, but in addition I must have a small platform, such as a rock, log, or a sloped embankment; something no more than six-inches high. So before starting the first exercise, I look for a sturdy object that happens to have this six-inches high platform located about 18" out from its base.

Now, leaning forward against the tree, I position the right foot as before, a yard or more out from its base, heel flat on the ground, but without locking the knee.

I bring the left foot forward and place it on the platform, with the heel hanging off the edge.

Without placing body weight on the forward foot, I pitch it up onto the ball, flexing the toes back gently. At the same time, I am careful not to pivot the ankle sideways, or in a circular motion, because this would stretch the ankle's ligaments out-of-axis.

I hold for five heartbeats, then without removing the foot from the platform, I relax the forward leg completely. This pitches the foot back down, and stretches out the calf muscle. I hold this relaxed position for twenty heartbeats. Then I repeat this stretch with the other foot.

————————

Regular stretching does much to keep the muscles injury free. We make these exercises a part of our everyday routine, and pay particular attention to the calves. We also drink plenty of water throughout the day. If muscles become dehydrated, they tend to lose their suppleness; in which case we stretch only with uttermost gentleness.

Stress Injuries

"Keep walking and keep smiling."
— *Tiny Tim*

Prevention and treatment

The natural world beckons Jenny and me to explore its wonders, and our favored mode of travel is on foot. Walking allows greater freedom and more time to savor the beauties of nature. And we find it extremely beneficial to health.

Most people today rarely walk for any real distance. Instead they rely mainly on vehicles and other labor saving devices. As a result, they are generally less fit. So when heading into the wilds, their tendency is to compensate for their lack of physical conditioning by turning to modern equipment that supposedly makes up for the difference. They buy "advanced" backpacks that are purported to carry heavy loads in comfort. They carry trekking poles that are supposed to relieve the stress of walking. And they wear stout boots, often advertised to take a person virtually anywhere on earth in perfect comfort.

To each his or her own. But our plan is to ignore misleading advertising, and concentrate instead on our months of pre-hike fitness training. Once we have achieved that, we have no need for any so-called advanced equipment.

Causes of injury

Regardless of the type of equipment carried, (or in many cases because of it) the rigors of wilderness trekking can sometimes overtax the hiker's body. The result is discomfort at best, and pain at the worst. Pain is a natural warning signal, telling of an impending injury. It is the body's method of saying, "Please stop this, because you are over-stressing something." If the hiker ignores the pain and continues ahead, the overexertion may indeed lead to a full-blown injury.

Let's take a look at a few of the more common hiking pains, their causes, prevention and treatment.

Carrying too heavy a load

Those backpacks advertised to carry heavy loads in comfort only encourage a person to carry larger loads, while doing nothing to assist the knees, ankles and feet in sustaining those loads.

Imagine a normally sedentary person driving to a trailhead, then reaching down and picking up a heavy backpack. Crack! The back lets loose, and this person is now suffering a "slipped disk."

Or imagine that the person manages to shoulder the pack without incident, and proceeds to follow the trail leading steeply uphill. The hiker reaches the top, sweating and breathing hard, and all is apparently well – until descending the far side, which is also steep. Grind! The knees give out, and that person now has "blown out" knees.

Let's say that, fortunately, neither accident happens, and our heavily burdened, ill-conditioned hiker manages the steep climb and descent, and proceeds along the trail without incident – until accidentally stepping on a protruding rock with the edge of his boot. Snap! The ankle twists sideways, a ligament is stretched beyond its range of capability, and some of the fibers are torn. The person has sprained an ankle.

These accidents happen almost every day of the summer. But does this mean that the wilderness is inherently risky or that hiking is dangerous? Or might it suggest that these people are carrying loads far too heavy for them?

Inadequate physical conditioning

As described in the "Physical Conditioning" chapter, pre-hike training will be important to success on trips lasting weeks or months. But even for the occasional day-hike, Jenny and I benefit by conditioning our bodies ahead of time with regular exercise. Short but regular "training" walks with a small pack would suffice for a weekend outing, at least if that outing will be done with lightweight gear. A multi-month trek would require a more definitive training program. In addition to the training walks, certain exercises can benefit specific areas of the body. The Leg extension exercise, also described in "Physical Conditioning" chapter, will help mitigate knee problems. Certain other exercises can raise fallen arches and help straighten pronating ankles. Even old injuries to bones, tendons and cartilage can be strengthened with gentle and regular exercise.

Wearing boots that are too heavy

Heavy footwear increases the exertion and reduces the hiker's overall progress. It also subjects the hiker to greater risk, since it makes the walking awkward and clumsy.

Wearing footwear with soles that are as stiff as boards

Boots or shoes with steel shanks or other sole-stiffeners restrict the legs, ankles and feet from flexing naturally. These devices can lead to soreness, pain and possibly to injury.

Wearing footwear that is ill-fitting or broken down internally

Based on my own experiences and the feedback from many other hikers, I estimate that the chances are about 70% that any pair of shoes or boots will eventually cause pain. The person who tries to ignore this pain is heading for a debilitating injury. The two most common shoe problems are improper fit, and worn-out internal materials – even though the shoes or boots may appear fine on the outside. Either of these problems can create unbalanced forces with every step, and can lead to pain and injury. Proper fitting and non-restricting footwear in serviceable condition can reduce this type of injury.

Dehydration

Adequate water intake is essential for health, particularly while hiking. Our joints need water for lubrication and cushioning; our muscles, tendons, and cartilage need water as well. Deprived of adequate moisture, these members lose their elasticity and become increasingly brittle. This can happen to our bones also, making them more susceptible to stress fracture. In any pain-injury situation, acute dehydration almost always plays a key role.

Neglecting hourly calf-stretching exercises, while training and on journey

Strenuous hiking places great demands on the calf muscles. In an attempt to "guard" themselves, these muscles tighten and become less elastic. Gentle but regular calf stretching encourages these muscles to relax, and helps restore their suppleness. This is described in the "Stretching" chapter.

On longer journeys, tight calves can be more of a problem. The stiffness and pain can be accompanied by swelling, discoloration, and sensitivity of the skin of the lower leg and ankle. I have experienced these symptoms while wearing certain shoes and not while wearing others. The usual causes are dehydration, lack of regular calf-stretching exercises, a stride that places undue strain on the calves—such as an overly aggressive toe push-off—and faulty footwear. If I stop for a few times each hour, drink water, and stretch out the calf muscles, the swelling reduces and the symptoms subside. And with new shoes, the symptoms vanish.

The pain that stabs with every step

Another foot condition specific to hikers, particularly long-distance hikers, is the stress of repetition. This is caused not by the hiking itself, but by the repetition of taking step after thousands of steps in poorly fitting or broken down footwear. The shoes or boots may not fit properly. They may have some small manufacturing defect, unnoticed at first but worsening with wear. Or they may have broken down internally over the course of many miles. I have hiked a great many miles in scores of different shoes and boots, and nearly every one of them has ultimately broken down; and many have started causing problems. Footwear of any type is artificial, and the technology is still a long ways from perfection. This is why virtually any shoe or boot has the potential to cause a stress injury if walked in for too many miles.

In Washington; PCT-2

Footwear-related stress problems are characterized by a pain that stabs with every step. While the budding injury itself may be in the foot, the pain can be elsewhere: either in the ankle, leg or knee, or even in the hip or lower back. Regardless of the location of the sharp pain, it almost always signals a dire problem calling for prompt attention. This is one instance where determination will work against a person. I know runners who have tried to "run through" various stress pains, only to undergo multiple surgeries in the lower extremities that left them permanently injured. But the good news is that normally we hikers do not have to endure these pains for long. A few minutes is about my limit. How do we stop these pains? By realizing that our footwear is causing them, and by taking the appropriate corrective measures.

A pain that stabs with every step may be gradual in its onset, or it may be sudden. Either way, the alarms are sounding and the red lights are flashing. First and foremost, I take off the shoes or boots I am wearing. It does not matter how many miles I have hiked in them, or how few; or how expensive and widely advertised. Nor does it matter how terribly fond of them I might have become. If I am walking with a sharp pain, then those shoes or boots are threatening my health and the continuance of my journey. Many hikers have not recognized this simple truth, and have left the trail and returned home. Yet the solution is straightforward. I remove the offending footwear, place them in my pack, and carry them out to civilization. There I would send the broken-down shoes or boots home, or if well worn, deposit them in a rubbish bin. Either way, the key is to recognize the footwear as the source of the problem.

After removing the offending shoes or boots, my next step is to begin rehydrating in earnest. The more water I can drink, the speedier will be the recovery. So I chug down as much water as possible, then I change into my spare pair of shoes or sandals and hike to the next water source. There, I start drinking water by the liter.

Rest and rehydration can be extremely beneficial, especially if I elevate the painful foot or leg. But no amount of rest will remedy faulty footwear. If I put those shoes (or boots) back on and continue on my way, they will probably disable me once again.

If I am not carrying spare shoes or sandals when the stress pains strikes, then I will have to experiment. After resting, I try walking barefoot a ways, assuming that the terrain is accommodating. If the pain continues to stab while walking barefoot, then I know that I need a longer rest and lots more water. So I haul off the trail and make camp, and try again in the morning, but not before stretching the calves ever so gently. Since the cells of the body take two or three days to rehydrate completely, I concentrate on my hydration efforts for that period of time.

If the pain is less severe, and if I have no spare footwear, then I will experiment with ways of modifying the offending footwear to at least enable me to reach the next town. I might jam a bandana or handful of grass or moss into the shoe (or boot) of the affected leg, placing a sizable wad under the arch. I walk a ways and see if this helps. If not, I move the wad under the heel, and try that. If I cannot find a way to continue in the footwear, then I might try walking in several pairs of socks. Or a person might fabricate a makeshift shoe by wrapping the hurtful foot in a shirt and lashing it in place with cord.

While experimenting with any of these remedies, I place the painful foot down gently with each step. No more tromping. Also, I rest often, and with the feet uphill. Then at the next town, I buy a new pair of shoes.

Better yet, to save all this trouble I carry spare shoes in my backpack.

As Jenny and I pursue our wilderness goals, we know we can greatly reduce our vulnerability to hiking-related injuries by conditioning our bodies ahead of time, by drinking plenty of water, and by paring down our pack-weight to a reasonable minimum. And when long-distance hiking, the best way to prevent stress injuries is to avoid ill-fitting or internally broken down shoes or boots.

PCT-3

Foot Care

*"And forget not that the earth delights
to feel your bare feet, and the winds
long to play with your hair."*
— *Kahlil Gibran*

Why is it that we tend to neglect our feet during regular personal hygiene? Perhaps because they are so far away – out of sight, out of mind, as it were. Yet these distant members deserve our very best care and attention, since we depend on them every step of the way, on every journey. After all, if our feet are suffering pain or injury, then we may not be hiking far.

Imagine the complexity: each of our feet has some 250,000 sweat glands, which altogether exude about a pint of sweat per day. And this is when at rest; the sweating is much more profuse while hiking, especially in hot weather. This perspiration serves to keep the skin moist and supple, but mainly helps cool the hard-working feet. This cooling is meant to be evaporative.

Even "highly breathable" running shoes and lightweight socks restrict evaporation. Heavy boots and thick, cushioning socks effectively block it altogether. Breathability in our footwear is important, not only during our hikes, but in the months preceding them.

The ravages of athlete's foot

Athlete's foot fungus is always present on everyone's skin. This fungus consumes callus, to one's benefit. Without the fungus, the calluses would grow thick and crusty, especially on the soles of the feet. Yet when we wear heavy footwear that restricts ventilation, we only encourage the fungus to multiply unchecked; and this can lead to the removal of nearly all foot callus. This is bad news for the hiker who needs a certain thickness of callus on the feet to protect them from abrasion. Stripped of all callus, the feet are much more likely to blister.

The surest indication of a moderate athlete's foot infection, then, is a notable lack of foot and toe callus, where the skin on the bottom of the feet and toes is paper-thin. A more serious infection will cause itching, blistered surface layers, and in more severe cases, oozing pustules. In such a condition, the fungus has consumed the callus and is now feeding on live skin.

Whether Jenny and I think our feet are infected or not, we begin treating them for athlete's foot infection long before we head into the wilds. If planning a long hike, we start the foot treatment at the beginning of the pre-hike training program.

We are careful not to step barefoot on any possibly infective surfaces, such as bathtubs or showers, not only in motels or gyms, but in the case of a person who shares a bathroom with other household members, even on the bathroom floor at home. These are places where other people with possibly infected feet have stepped, and where the warmth and moisture encourages microbial growth.

To protect our feet from suspect floors and surfaces, we wear beach thongs or the like, and disinfect them occasionally. When on journey, we wear home-made shower booties when showering in public campgrounds or motels. These are like inverted shower caps for the feet, with elastic around their tops. Lacking these, one could use plastic bags, or perhaps lay spare towels down on the shower and bathroom floor.

After showering, we dry our feet, then if needed we apply antifungal medicine, carried in a small vial.

These precautions might seem excessive, but they come from years of hiking with the difficulties of blisters.

Another hazard associated with showering barefoot in public stalls is that of contracting a plantar wart. This type of wart feels like a sharp pebble on the bottom of the foot, and it can make walking painful. It is viral in nature, and is normally transmitted on floors that someone else with such a wart had walked barefoot on.

On-trail foot care

An important part of our on-journey foot care involves resting, ventilating and cooling our feet during the trail-side rest breaks. At each stop, we remove our shoes and socks, shake out any gravel, and pull the insoles out of the shoes for better drying. We try to rest with our feet and legs elevated to encourage good circulation and reduce swelling. If the day is hot, then we might be able to cool our bare feet by placing them flat against a shaded rock, or wiggling them down through the top layers of dirt to the cooler soil underneath.

The ultraviolet component of sunlight kills athlete's foot fungus. A friend suggested simply spreading the toes apart to the drying and healing sunshine, to quickly kill the fungus.

Before setting off from the rest stop, we tie our recently removed socks to the outside of our packs, where they can air dry. Then we brush the dust and debris from our feet and between the toes, massage them encouragingly, tape any sensitive areas, and put on fresh socks. Next we stretch the toe areas of the socks lengthwise and widthwise to give the toes more room. Before putting on the shoes, we check for wrinkles in the socks. Wrinkles can induce blisters

PCT-1

in short order. But in hot weather we put our shoes away in our backpacks, and put on our second pair of shoes or sandals, if equipped with them. These will be drier and cooler than the shoes we had been wearing, and a genuine pleasure to change into.

We carry at least three pairs of thin socks at a time, and for maximum comfort we wear a pair of socks for no more than a third of the day, before swapping them for fresh ones. This means that we need to wash our socks often. With thin nylon socks, this is easily done, using the "dundo" method described in the "Hygiene" chapter. To do this, we collect water from a natural source, then move away so as not to pollute that source. Then we pour water on the socks and wash them by hand. Also, we wash our feet often, dry them thoroughly, and if needed we apply antifungal solution to the bottoms of the feet and between the toes.

Moreover, where possible we often toughen our feet by walking a short ways along the trail barefoot each day, being careful where we step of course. This allows the feet access to the fresh air and gives them chance to toughen as nature intended. We also may walk barefoot around our stealth-camps.

Hot-spots

While hiking, we pay particular attention to our feet as to whether our shoes and socks are chafing them. An increasing pain warns of a blister in the making. The minute one of us feels a "hot-spot," we stop and remove the footwear, and try to figure out what is causing it.

Most hot-spots stem from lack of callus, in combination with shoes or boots that fit too tightly.

As mentioned, we prevent paper-thin skin by treating our feet for athlete's foot infection well in advance of the hike. And we make certain that our running shoes do not fit too tightly, by buying them larger than what we normally wear around home.

That takes care of most of the blister problems, but sometimes we develop hot-spots anyway. So after sitting down and removing the shoes and socks, we apply rubbing alcohol to the area.

Rubbing alcohol

As an antiseptic, rubbing alcohol cleans and disinfects the skin. Also it dries the skin and dissolves the skin oils, making the dressings stick to the skin better without any peel-ups. It also seems to toughen the skin. We carry the rubbing alcohol in a small vial. Or if we have more serious blister problems after starting the hike, we may carry an entire bottle of it. It works that well. A person could also use gel alcohol, or liquid isopropyl or ethyl alcohol stove fuel.

Padded adhesive strips or athletic tape

For dressing the hot-spots, we use either padded adhesive strips or athletic tape.

For padded adhesive strips we use Band-Aids® or the like. But we choose the type that are highly breathable. Many kinds are non-breathable and do not work as well for our purposes. We usually carry about a dozen of these for each person; most size large, 1" wide, and some size medium.

The athletic adhesive tape is white in color and 1.5" wide. We carry a partial roll of this. It is also breathable, and it works well for covering hot-spots. We do not apply it directly to blisters because it could tear the damaged skin while being removed.

The point is, we sit down and treat the hot-spots, rather than merely carrying on and enduring the pain of blisters in the making. If we stop and treat the hot-spots

appropriately, they will usually get better. If we do not treat them, they will likely get much worse.

If we are carrying a spare pair of sandals, we change into those. This reduces the heat and the friction causing the hot spots. Another option is to revert to our thinnest pair of socks inside the shoes. This gives the swollen feet a little more space. Or we might be able to wear no socks in the shoes. I have wide feet, and usually have to widen my shoes by slitting the upper forefoot with a knife. And as mentioned, we often toughen our feet by walking a short ways along the trail barefoot.

Blister first aid

If a blister has formed, we remove the shoes, socks, and any dressings, then apply rubbing alcohol to the area. After that has dried, we apply a piece of Spenco 2nd Skin™ gel, or the equivalent.

2nd Skin

The product 2nd Skin is the closest thing to heaven for a blister. It consists of a sheet of moist, aloe-vera-like gel, along with a thin sheet of breathable adhesive knit. To apply this to the blister, we cut out a piece of gel only as large as the blister itself, with some overlap. The gel comes sandwiched between two layers of plastic-like cellophane. We remove the plastic on one side, apply the raw gel to the blister, then remove the plastic from the outside. Finally, we secure the gel in place with the adhesive knit cut to a wide overlap. Or if we are running short of adhesive knit, we cover the gel with white athletic tape. The tape works about as well if we also are using the alcohol.

The gel is good for about half a day of hiking. After that, it begins to dry out and disintegrate, so it must be replaced. To do that we remove the dressings and the old gel, and dispose of them in our litterbag. Then we apply more rubbing alcohol to the area, allow this to dry, then cut and apply a new piece of gel and cover it with fresh dressings.

At day's end, we remove everything, wash the feet again if we have enough water, apply more rubbing alcohol, and put on clean, light-weight socks if the weather is too cold to remain barefoot all night. This gives the blister a chance to air-dry during the night, and greatly accelerates the healing. If we find that the blister needs protection again the following morning, we apply fresh gel and dressings.

Draining a blister

A blister is the skin's response to damage caused by heat and chafe. By filling with fluid, the blister lifts the injured top layer of skin (epidermis) away from the underlying healthy skin, (dermis) cushioning and protecting the healthy skin.

We find, however, that the fluid actually slows healing. If we have to walk many days on a blister, we drain the fluid. This eases the pain and speeds healing, provided we do it properly. The procedure is to apply rubbing alcohol to the area as an antiseptic, then to lance the blister with a flame-sterilized needle. We then blot the oozing fluid with a square of clean toilet paper, and apply more antiseptic.

The main risk with the lancing procedure is that of introducing infection. This is why we keep the area clean and sterile.

Applying rubbing alcohol to an open blister is painful, but well worth it in terms of its healing effects.

Two or three days after lancing, we usually have to cut away the blister's dead skin, to prevent infective bacteria from growing under it.

Other blister treatments

We rarely use moleskin. It tends to stick so tenaciously, at least to clean, dry skin, that it can tear a blister as it is being peeled off, and actually pull away small chunks of healthy skin also.

Tincture of benzoin supposedly acts as a skin toughener. I used this as a taping base for many years while climbing. It makes the protective adhesive tape stick better to the fingers and hands, but it did not toughen my skin.

Duct tape is supposed to be a good blister bandage, since it is more friction-free. But because it does not breathe, it greatly inhibits healing. The best way we have found to reduce the friction is by reducing the crowding inside our footwear; again by buying shoes larger than what we normally wear at home.

In years past we used to powder our feet with foot powder, but found that after so many miles it tended to create more friction, and more blister pain.

To prevent hot spots or blisters, some hikers have reported success by rubbing petroleum jelly (such as Vaseline®) or other lubricating compounds (such as Bag Balm) onto the feet and toes before starting a walk.

Over-taping

A hiker would gain little benefit by over-taping in an attempt to protect especially troubling blisters. Too much tape can actually worsen the predicament by increasing the crowding inside the footwear. Jenny and I discovered this during our first thru-hike.

On our third day we found ourselves hobbling along blister-footed, and needing a layover day. We took the layover day, and it did wonders for our feet, and got us hiking again. In the next few weeks of hiking my feet gradually improved, but Jenny's worsened due to an athlete's foot infection combined with lightweight boots that fit her too tightly. So there she was, bravely mincing along with some 27 blisters festooning every toe and the heels of both feet. Every morning she treated the athlete's foot infection and applied fresh bandaging, yet every day her progress diminished, despite her best efforts. Finally it became clear that we needed to leave the trail for a few days of foot healing. We stopped for a rest by a cold brook, and there she removed the several layers of bandages, and washed her feet. As an experiment, she put her shoes back on without the bandages or socks. We plodded on, and much to our surprise her pace began to improve. By mid-day her gait was back to normal. What we discovered was that all that bandaging, intended to protect the blisters, had actually been aggravating them.

I remember a time on our fifth thru-hike when a sizeable blister formed on the side of my heel. This was unusual in that it persisted for days on end. Finally, I cut a large hole in the shoe, removing the part that was causing the irritation. That solved the problem.

A large hole cut into a shoe to relieve a persistent blister.

Blisters are caused by footwear. The moment a hiker removes the shoes and socks, and any tape applied, the blisters will begin to heal. Three days of such airing, while staying off one's feet, will in many cases make the feet feel nearly as good as new. Even a single day of bare-footed resting can work wonders. A person might keep this in mind should the blisters become so painful that they threaten to send the hiker home. During the rest days, keep the feet clean and well aired, and apply antifungal liquid twice daily. And remember that when starting out again, the feet will likely re-blister if one fails to rectify what caused the blisters to begin with; namely, cramped footwear.

Cracks in dry skin

Adequate ventilation in the footwear is essential, but too much ventilation can lead to other problems. As mentioned in the "Footwear" chapter, a person hiking in sandals all summer without socks, or someone who walks barefoot all summer, is likely to develop calluses that are so thick they become deeply cracked, at least in drier climates. These cracks cannot heal because callus is dead skin. However, they can still be painful because the cracks pull the live skin apart and keep it that way.

Cracks on the fingertips are a similar malady, and are fairly common with active people.

Superglue can close the cracks on feet and fingers, and provide relief from the pain. To apply, we clean both the crack and the surrounding skin with rubbing alcohol. Once dry, we lay a bead of this adhesive over the crack, pinch the cracked skin together, and hold the crack closed until the glue has set. Interestingly, superglue was invented during the Vietnam War era specifically to close lacerations; yet the packaging now warns against applying it to the skin.

However, superglue is a temporary fix. Used on the skin, it is not long lasting; and once the glue begins deteriorating in a day or so, it causes even more irritation until a person has peeled it painfully away. Also, it does not address the real problem, which is ultra dry skin. So it will not prevent new cracks from forming.

My long-term solution when distance-hiking in a dry climate while wearing sandals is to also wear three pairs of thin socks. These hold just enough beneficial moisture to prevent the skin from cracking. Jenny uses superglue to close a new crack on a finger, then applies an adhesive strip or a piece of adhesive tape to increase the skin's moisture. Sometimes instead of the superglue, she applies a dab of lanolin to the crack before covering it with the adhesive strip.

Foot care kit

When hiking, we carry a small foot care kit. The contents are specified in our Sample Gear Lists near the end of the book. We carry these materials in a resealable plastic bag, usually kept handy in our pack's outside pocket.

Our feet deserve all the attention and meticulous care that we can give them, both before and during the hike. With a good balance of fresh air and sunshine, ventilation and protection, comfort and roominess, cleanliness and care, our feet will likely carry us happily along virtually any trail.

Heading for the pass; southbound PCT-3

Hygiene

"If you don't have comfort,
you give up the trip for lack of enjoyment,
before you give out for loss of energy."
— *Verlen Kruger*

Backcountry practices for good health

When backpacking in the wilds, most hikers seldom concern themselves with society's typical grooming requirements: using deodorants, hairstyling gels, moisturizers and following other styling rituals. These tend to lose importance on the trail. Of course on the trail there is no access to running hot water, toilets, showers, and washing machines, except when visiting trail towns. Nevertheless, most hikers like to keep themselves and their clothing reasonably clean. Cleanliness fosters a more positive attitude, and shows respect for oneself and for others met along the trail and in the towns. Good hygiene also discourages bacterial skin infections and intestinal disorders. Personally, I am much more comfortable when I am clean, and I have a better sense of well-being.

Bathing in the wilds

The human skin is an excretory organ. That is, the pores of the skin eliminate toxins and waste products, including various salts and urea. This suggests the need for regular bathing. Keeping the skin clean also reduces clogged pores and the buildup of dead skin cells.

Jenny and I enjoy the occasional swim or dip. But we also consider that the next hiker coming along might not care to collect drinking water from that in which we just swam. So we limit our swimming and dipping to the larger lakes and rivers.

In the wilds, the smaller water sources are more susceptible to contamination from bathing.

Imagine plugging the shower-drain at home and taking a quick shower using soap and shampoo. That water would become a murky soup of dirt, grime, body oils, dead skin, hair, salts and acids from the sweat, and residues from whatever we had previously applied to the skin or hair: moisturizer, ointment, perfume, deodorant, bug repellent, sunscreen, and of course the soap and shampoo used in the shower. Living on a sailboat, where our small shower pan accumulated all this muck, we learned that taking a simple bath or shower could be far more polluting than most people might imagine.

To keep from contaminating the smaller backcountry water sources—the ponds, brooks, and springs—we collect water from them, and then carry that water to somewhere else for bathing.

The dundo method

As we hike along a trail, our skin becomes coated with "trail patina," (dirt and grime) and we feel better when we remove it. The "dundo" bathing method makes this easy. With this approach we do not bathe with water only. We can also use soap.[12] The dundo with soap is more effective than a swim or a dip, and almost as convenient and refreshing. And correctly done, it has no adverse effects on the water sources.

Jenny coined the term "dundo" (DUN-dough) during our AT hike. An excerpt from our trail journal describes how this came to be: "After a day of crossing the Skyline Drive, climbing the next hill, thrashing through

---

12 Many primitive humans used natural soaps such as tannic acid and saponin-rich plants.

brush, and descending to the road again, ad infinitum, we passed the turnoff to the Blackrock Shelter and continued a few miles to the Dundo Picnic Area. The place was deserted, so at a drinking fountain we stripped and, ignoring a light rain, filled our water bottles and poured the contents over ourselves while hastily rubbing on a bit of soap. We had not been long re-dressed when a car drove slowly past, its three women passengers gawking at us. Never mind the publicity; one cannot describe the wonderful feeling of the chilly splashes embellished with a small bar of soap after a long, hot and sweaty day." Jenny started referring to this type of bath as the "dundo," and the name stuck.

Regardless of the type of container used, one simply dips it into the water source and carries it to the showering area. Similar to a stealth area, this dundo shower area is used only once by one person to keep the overall impact to a minimum. And we locate it far enough away from the water source such that heavy rains would not carry any soap back to the source. For best results, we scrub vigorously with a wet hand towel and a small amount of soap. Next we collect more water, move well away from the water source again, rinse off, and repeat as necessary. Then we wring out the hand towel and use it to dry off with, wringing the towel of excess water now and then. We wash our hair in the same manner.

For hand towels, we use a cotton washcloth for each of us, about eight inches square. For soap we use a small chunk of home-made bar soap. This works better in cold water, we find, and is also biodegradable and free of chemicals and perfumes. The chemicals of store-bought soap can be partially absorbed by the skin, and the perfumes can attract bears. But of course our soap works even better if we heat the water first, which we sometimes do on our longer trips.

The water-bag shower method

Another method of bathing is with a water bag or a Hiker's Friend bag hung from a branch and fitted with a showerhead. This uses more water so it allows for a full soap shower, shampoo, and a good rinse – away from the lakes and creeks. And yes, the water is usually cold, but also invigorating.

Sponge bath method

A shortage of water or a blustery day is hardly an obstacle to bathing. I can sponge bathe while wearing clothing by reaching under it and scrubbing with a wet or damp hand towel. I can also sponge bathe at camp while under the tarp, or inside a tent, again using a wet hand towel. If I have not been able to bathe during the day's hiking, this is my preferred method of freshening up before retiring to bed. Either way, I sleep much more comfortably when my skin is clean.

Oral hygiene

The extra exercise of the hiking lifestyle, in combination with good nutrition, promotes better circulation, and consequently better vitality throughout the whole of the body. This includes teeth and gums; nevertheless, I brush my teeth often, and use dental floss and soft-picks™.

Some dentists think that toothpaste actually complicates various gum problems. Toothpaste is an abrasive, and it is loaded with chemicals and so-called natural ingredients, most having nothing to do with oral hygiene. I brush without toothpaste in the wilds. After all, who appreciates the typical splats of toothpaste around camping areas and water sources? The best way to dispose of toothpaste is to dilute it with a mouthful of water, and disperse it in a vigorous spray, well off the trail.

I make a habit of brushing my teeth while hiking, and often carry a cut-off toothbrush in the pocket of my shirt for this purpose. When brushing while hiking I breathe through my nose rather than the mouth. Brushing creates a fine mist that is not beneficial to inhale. And of course, I am careful not to stumble with a toothbrush in my mouth.

I first learned of what I call "adventure brushing" during a climb of the North Face of the Grand Teton, in Wyoming. Peter Lev and I were bivouacked on a tiny ledge that we had chopped out of the head of a steep glacier. Sitting there, strapped to the ledge to prevent ourselves from sliding into the abyss, I looked over at Peter, and saw him blissfully brushing his teeth. I asked why in the world he bothered, and he replied, "It's refreshing."

Rinsing a toothbrush in suspect water could introduce giardia or other pathogens into a person's system the next time the brush is used. Instead, I rinse my toothbrush in treated water. And at some of the resupply stations, or at home after a short trip, I disinfect the toothbrush by soaking it in hydrogen peroxide, or by plunging it in boiling water.

At home Jenny and I brush our teeth, not using toothpaste, but with our home-made soap which we also use for showering and shampooing. The soap cleans our teeth and gums better. To apply the soap, we simply stroke the wet toothbrush bristles lightly across the bar.

The primitive privy

When the wagon trains headed west across the U.S. in the mid and late nineteenth century, cholera killed more emigrants than anything else. In a bad year, some wagon trains lost two-thirds of their travelers. Cholera is caused by a certain bacterium, and virtually the only means of contracting it is by eating food or drinking or washing with water contaminated by the stools of other cholera sufferers. Prevention of the disease is a matter of strict sanitation.

Hepatitis A virus (HAV) is another disease spread when infected individuals do not wash their hands after using the toilet, and then handling food. People who eat this contaminated food run a high risk of becoming infected. The virus also spreads in drinking water that is contaminated, even minutely, with excrement.

Traveler's Diarrhea is another malady resulting from poor sanitation and hygiene. It is caused by infection with one of a number of bacteria, protozoa or viruses that are ingested when eating food or drinking water again contaminated by stool. Dysentery is a particularly severe form of diarrheal disease.

All this suggests the importance of maintaining good sanitation, especially when it comes to the primitive privy.

Along developed and often busy paths such as the Appalachian Trail, a person is obliged to use the installed privies. But plenty of hikers do not. Instead, they dig cat holes behind trees and bushes, often in the vicinity of the shelters and established campsites. Obviously, we avoid pitching our shelter in these areas.

While hiking less frequented trails, we are generally free to head for the proverbial "bushes," as long as we move well away from the trail and any water sources. On the way, I collect a handful of natural toilet paper such as smooth stones, leaves, small clumps of dry moss (going easy on the live ecology), small twigs, or Douglas fir cones. Flattened snowballs work particularly well. If well chosen, any of these materials work just as well as toilet paper.

At the selected site, I dig a "cat hole" about six inches deep. If the hole is much deeper than that, the earth's microbes will not be able to decompose the stools. To make the hole, I normally dig with the heel of the shoe, or in firmer ground, a stick, or the adze of an ice axe. If a person finds squatting low awkward or uncomfortable, he or she might try sitting on the edge of a log or rock.

In his book *Chips from a Wilderness Log*, Calvin Rutstrum writes: "You also need to train your evacuation organs. Once trained they will respond by reflex. Don't sit on the seat for long periods straining. Watch an animal. He does it as you should, in one fell swoop. Forget what you can't readily evacuate with the first generous effort, and proceed with the cleaning process. In time you will have trained the bowel to give forth a stool in one single release."

After using the natural "toilet paper," a person can finish the job with a few sheets of toilet paper. The idea is to minimize the use of TP, since it can remain intact for a long time, particularly in drier climates and at higher elevations. Rather than leave it lie, or bury it, a better idea might be to bag it, and either carry it out or burn it at the next opportunity. One should never burn TP at the cat-hole site in the woods; a number of devastating forest fires have resulted from this practice.

After burying the cat hole, I place a small marker on top of it, to warn someone else not to dig there also. For a marker I use a pair of sticks lying flat on the ground in a small and unobtrusive "X".

I keep a small vial of ethyl alcohol gel (recommended in the "First Aid" chapter) in the same small resealable bag with the toilet paper. And I follow the rule practiced by many cultures around the globe: wiping with the left; eating and shaking hands with the right. That way I can pick up the bag of toilet paper in the right hand, unwrap a few squares, and also squeeze some alcohol gel from its vial without contaminating any of these items. After using the alcohol gel, I can then wash my hands dundo style using soap and water from a water bottle, knowing that I am not contaminating these items also.

The stools of an infected individual contain *millions* of protozoa. So sterilizing one's hands after eliminating greatly reduces the chances of reintroducing giardia and cryptosporidia protozoa and other bacteria and microorganisms, the next time one eats from one's hands.

Lamentably, not all hikers wash their hands after voiding. So one should not eat food that other hikers have touched; for example by reaching into their bag of trail mix. Refer to the "Water" chapter for more information about infective pathogens.

Women might be interested in Jenny's chapter regarding women's sanitary concerns on the trail and in public restrooms.

Washing dishes

Washing dishes with soap and hot water is a carry-over from home, and that is where we leave this practice when venturing into the backcountry. This is not to suggest that we ignore the job altogether. But dishwashing soap has serious drawbacks. It will cut some of the grease and food residue, but certainly not all. And the residues left on the pots and dishes will begin to harbor harmful bacteria. Dishwashing soap does not sterilize the dishes against these microorganisms. Soap residue left on dishes can cause diarrhea (and soap left in camp-laundered clothing can irritate the skin). Moreover, the entire process is wasteful of treated water, and it introduces unnecessary chemicals into the environment, due to the large amounts some people use.

Scouring dishes with a nylon scrub pad is particularly unhygienic. The pad collects bacteria and provides an ideal breeding ground for it. In effect, the scrub pad actually contaminates the dishware it is supposed to be cleaning, to say nothing of the water sources when being rinsed out.

If one's camp dishes are greasy or oily, water by itself will clean them very little, particularly if the water is cold. And unless a person first purifies that water, it could expose one to giardia and other undesirable protozoa. Even long after the dishes have dried, a percentage of the microorganisms can remain active.

Jenny and I use a different approach. First, we eat from our cookpot. Leaving the plates and bowls at home obviates the incessant chore of washing them, and then having to sterilize them. After eating from the cookpot, we clean it. Depending on what we have cooked, we might pour water into the pot, then after scraping and stirring with a spoon, we might drink the resulting gruel if we are low on water. Or if not, we simply disperse it far away from any water sources. We then wipe any remaining grease or residue with a handful of weeds, dried fern, leaves, or pine needles. Any persistent spots, we scrape with a stick. Afterwards, we disperse these materials, leaving no indication that we had cooked, eaten, and cleaned our pot there. The next time we boil water in the pot, we are automatically sterilizing it. And we can dip our spoons into the boiling water also.

We do not normally carry drinking cups. But when we do, we would be effectively sterilizing them every time we pour boiling water into them, when making hot drinks.

Sterilizing water bottles

We also sterilize—or replace—our water bottles at regular intervals. This is especially important if we are using the bottles for mixing flavoring or electrolyte powders. To sterilize a water bottle, one method is to boil some water for a hot cuppa, and pour it first into the empty water bottle, and swishing it around a bit before pouring it into the cup. Another possibility at our next town stop is to zap the water bottles in a microwave oven, as long as the bottles have no metal parts. And while we are at it, we could zap our lexan spoons as well. Or we could soak the water bottles overnight in a strong solution of water purification chemicals or household bleach. But the option that we use most is to dispense with commercial water bottles, and use recyclable beverage containers as water bottles. By replacing them every two weeks, we obviate the need to sterilize them.

Speaking of water bottles, if a person were to mix powdered milk in a plastic water bottle, the pores in the plastic will absorb some of the milk, and the milk residue will be impossible to remove. Such a bottle will never again keep water fresh.

Incinerating trash

When finding bits of litter along the trail, candy wrappers and so forth, we often pick them up. This small deed helps keep our wild lands litter free. Our own accumulating trash (mainly empty food wrappers and plastic packaging) can become bulky and somewhat heavy, especially when hiking for many days between way-posts of civilization. Along some of the more developed trails we might find trash receptacles at trailheads and road crossings. But when these are not available, we carry out our litter and dispose of it properly, even if that means carrying it for several days.

In remote regions, incinerating the trash might be an option, if carefully done. Burning plastic is never a good idea, since most types emit toxic fumes when burned, and breathing those fumes can make a person ill. On a windless day we might be able to burn paper, toilet paper, and cellulose (a wood product) but only if we can manage it in a low-impact way; since hastily burned trash leaves an unsightly mess.

If we decide to incinerate our burnable trash, here is how we do it. We select a place on bare dirt or sand, making absolutely certain the ground is not humus or duff. And we stay away from tree roots, since a smolder could work its way underground, consuming the sap-rich root until eventually reaching the tree. We build a tiny fire, no bigger than 4 inches in diameter and 4 inches tall, using matchstick-size twigs. Into this fire we feed the paper and cardboard, small bits at a time, adding more kindling as required. Without the kindling, the fire will not burn hot enough to consume the trash. As the ritual is winding down, we place the unburned shards of wood back into the little fire. When the flame self-extinguishes for want of fuel, we do not simply bury the ashes. Instead, we stir them into the earth. The more we stir them, the more we grind them into powder, and the more the admixture of dirt will cool the particles and distance them, rendering them incapable of rekindling. Sufficient stirring will erase the little fire site altogether. Lastly, we "monster mash" what remains, as described in the "Campfire and Cook-fire" chapter.

Restaurant sanitary measures

Restaurant meals are sometimes few and far between, but when available they are highly desired in terms of nutrition and the way they bring more enthusiasm into the day.[13]

But visiting the restaurants calls for certain precautions in terms of hygiene. They are potential sources of colds, flu and other ailments, the results of germs left behind by infected customers. When long-distance hiking, our bodies are particularly vulnerable because we tend to lose some of our immunities while living in the wilds, which are relatively free of these types of germs. And once we become infected, our trek can lose much of its luster while the ailments run their course.

Our best defense is to keep from touching the usual infectious objects: doorknobs, tabletops, etc., and to eat with our own spoons rather than the house silverware. In fact, we view all house tableware with suspicion, particularly the forks because the spaces between the tines are well known for harboring microbes; and the laws pertaining to sterilizing dishware are loosely interpreted and rarely followed. To keep our health intact, we drink water from our own water bottles, or ask for a straw. Also, the tabletop is almost never sterilized, which is why we refrain from eating bits of food that we might have dropped on it.

These precautions might seem a bit extreme, but most hikers who have become sick would no doubt endorse this advice heartily. They, like myself, have learned the hard way that when hauling into a town, the hiker would do well to avoid handling things that other people have touched. This holds true not only at the restaurant table, but in the restrooms.

———

By following these guidelines we have a much better chance of staying healthy. And as anyone who has ever been sick will affirm, remaining healthy is the more desired option.

PCT-2, Mt Adams.

13 Incidentally, at a restaurant we sometimes order a second "take-out" meal, and carry it to our next camp. It makes a great dinner.

Personal Security

Awareness

In this book we examine some of the vicissitudes of trail life: the obstacles and challenges both expected and unexpected. The more time Jenny and I have spent in the wilds, the more we have honed our skills and built competence and confidence in meeting those challenges. Snow travel has become something to look forward to rather than something to dread. Wild creatures are more fascinating and less offensive. Shifts in weather are less troublesome as we have changed our attitudes and adjusted our clothing and equipment to suit. In short, the so-called hazards of the natural world have taken on more manageable proportions, although they will never lose their potential to develop into dangerous situations.

And so it is with our personal security. Both on the trail and off, the potential for theft and personal threats from other people will occasionally exist. But rather than carry on down the trail with the careless attitude of "it won't happen," a safer approach is to maintain awareness of what could happen, and then to take the appropriate measures to prevent it from happening. This allows us to enjoy our outings with more confidence.

Vehicles encountered on the trail

Bicycles, Motorbikes, Horses

Many of the popular hiking trails are open to bicycles. And even the trails that are not open are still subject to renegade cyclists who pride themselves in tackling such challenges. Actually, I find it quite amazing to see what these hardy souls will sometimes attempt. We once followed a pair of bicycle tracks many miles through the deeply snowbound Sierra. So even though we may be hiking a trail closed to bicycles, we are not surprised if we suddenly see a cyclist hurtling toward us.

Whenever we hear or see a bicycle coming, we stand aside, nod a friendly greeting as they wheel past, then continue on our way. In true speed-junkie fashion, trail cyclists are forever crashing into things; such is the price of their rapid technology and need for adrenaline. But in terms of our own safety, our ears are our best allies and any ear-phones are handicaps. We listen for sounds of a fast-approaching bike: the telltale whir of freewheel and the squeaking of brakes. And we keep in mind that when one bicycle flashes past, others could soon follow.

Off road vehicles (ORV's), all terrain vehicles (ATV's), dirt-bikes, and the rest of their motorized ilk present similar problems to hikers. Luckily, we can hear the internal combustion machines long before their arrival, giving us ample time to stand well aside. Still, when in known ATV country, we refrain from resting on the trail, let alone camping on it.

Speaking of camping on the trail, remember that in some areas, particularly on trails leading to popular mountain summits, hikers such as myself can come bumbling along at night without flashlights. I have stepped on people sleeping on the trail, unseen. I remember one such incident when as a teenager I suddenly tripped on someone and went down onto this hapless person full-body, face-to-face. This shocked me half senseless, as undoubtedly it did the other person. But as I stumbled away I began to see the humor in it.

Jenny and I have, in turn, been nearly run over by motorbikes traveling a trail at ultra-high speeds, so we know the dangers posed to hikers by these vehicles. But in our experience these pale in comparison with the dangers of horses and mules. Having to suddenly scramble off the trail to prevent being trampled is not the usual image of enjoying the wilderness. One problem is that *many* equestrians expect hikers to scurry out of their way – or else. I have been knocked off the trail twice. But our most desperate moment came one afternoon when Jenny and I heard a pack train coming around the bend. We had no idea that the lead horseman would try to run us down. Eight heavily-loaded horses and big mules came charging down on us, at a place where the trail was narrow and the hillside steeply sloped. We barely made it out of their way. The horseman turned and looked at us with a malicious glare, and I shudder to think what might have happened on that blind corner had we been, instead, a group of hikers with children.

Most of the time we hikers can move off the trail well in advance of approaching equestrians. If the terrain is friable and exposed, then logically it would be up to the equestrians to stop and wait until we can decide what to do; but the equestrians do not always stop. When stepping aside, hikers should always leave the trail by climbing the slope, rather than descending it. The animals will probably be nervous, particularly the closer we are to them. If one should suddenly bolt, and we are down slope of it, then it could fall on us, or buck its rider or panniers onto us, or dislodge rocks onto us. Or the horse could kick out and knock us down the slope. So the highest position is by far the safer, so long as we take care to ensure that we, ourselves do not fall. And once again, hikers should never get close to these animals; they are well known for kicking and inflicting serious injuries.

Miscreants

Fortunately for hikers, the criminal element in society rarely braves the natural world. Isolated incidents have occurred, but compared with the cities, our wild areas are quite safe. Even so, a certain amount of caution is always in order.

In general, troublemakers travel by vehicle, and they tend to remain near the roads. So it is usually not the best idea for us to linger at the road crossings, or to camp near roads – especially four wheel drive roads in more remote areas. If Jenny and I want to camp near a resupply station or trailhead, we move well away and make a stealth camp, and remain inconspicuous. While moving away, we are extremely alert to any onlookers. If we look back and notice someone watching, we change our plans.

To increase safety, one could hike with friends, or at least camp with them. If traveling alone, one could act as though part of a group whenever meeting strangers. If questioned, speak collectively, using "we," rather than "I." Say something to effect that the rest of your group is right behind you, and will be along shortly. When speaking with strangers, never give details about your hiking and camping plans. Trust your instincts; if they urge you to move along, even though the person is persuading you to talk awhile, then follow your instincts and leave. If you feel vulnerable when by yourself, consider carrying mace or pepper spray. In all likelihood you will never have to use it, but if it gives you added peace of mind, then it is worth its weight.

Hitchhiking

In the right company, hitchhiking can be an expedient means of travel and a great way to meet friendly and interesting people. In the wrong company it can be disastrous. Hitchhikers are vulnerable, and the lone woman hitchhiker is even more so. One of the most sobering incidents in my experience came after a wilderness course in the 1970's, when one of the students was hitchhiking home from her month in the mountains. She never made it.

When planning our hikes, Jenny and I try to minimize our need for hitchhiking. On longer treks involving resupplying, we can avoid many of the longer hitchhikes out to towns by carrying more food and skipping those towns altogether. When this is not practical, we might figure in an extra block of time for walking out to the distant towns. This takes longer, but also helps preserve our journey's continuity.

One cannot plan for every contingency, and occasionally a person might find the need to leave the trail and travel to a distant town. The safest way to hitchhike is to choose your drivers. One method is to head for a parking area, and ask any likely looking motorists for a ride. This can be particularly effective at popular trailheads, where other backpackers may be loading their vehicles and preparing to drive out of the hills. If they appear to have room, introduce yourself and tell them of your need for a ride.

Various other strategies might improve one's chances of getting a ride, such as combing the hair and removing sunglasses, and perhaps making a large sign stating your destination. But these will not increase your chances of getting a safe ride. In holding out the hitchhiking thumb you are relinquishing much of your control. Be wary and don't be afraid to make quick decisions. Even though you may have been trying to hitch a ride for hours, if someone pulls to a stop and appears, or acts, in any way suspicious, pick up your backpack and move away.

Road walking

Hikers have been hit by cars while road walking and some have been killed. I remember one heart-stopping incident that occurred to Jenny and me along the PCT. We were walking along the busy paved road below the Hat

Creek Rim in Northern California, back in 1987 before the trail along the rim had been developed. We were on the left shoulder of the road, facing the oncoming traffic. And since we were not on the pavement and could see what was coming at quite a distance, we felt safe. Unfortunately we were not thinking about cars coming from behind. And we had not imagined that if one of those cars were passing another, then the overtaking vehicle would come close to us. Which is what happened. As the two cars flashed past together, peddles to the metal, the overtaking vehicle missed me by inches.

From that we learned to stay well off the roads in the presence of any vehicle, regardless of which direction that vehicle is traveling. Especially because every now and then, a motorist will use a pedestrian as sport, steering straight at him or her, then jerking away at the last possible moment.

That same year, Jenny and I were road walking along Whitewater Creek in Southern California, before that section of trail had been built. We stopped for a rest beside the creek, hidden from the road in an area of thick brush. A vehicle passed by, and a beer bottle whizzed past our heads. I doubt whether the person who tossed the bottle knew we were there. But it does illustrate the risks of being even close to a road.

Hang onto those valuables

Trailside towns and resorts normally offer the usual assortment of amenities, including stores, restaurants, laundromats and lodging. The ambience in these places is often welcoming and relaxing, and may encourage hikers to let down their guards. But these are hardly the best places to become negligent about leaving backpacks and various items of gear strewn about unattended.

First and foremost, we carry our valuables—money, credit card, identification, journal and camera memory chips—in a small bag, and we keep this bag with us at all times. In town, one could place such a bag inside a ratty-looking sack that looks like it might hold a half-eaten sandwich from the deli, or something equally non-tempting. Or a person could sew a small nylon bag with a zipper closure and an attached strap, and wear it under the shirt. Either way, you should carry this bag with you whenever you must leave your backpack, for example when going into a post office to pick up a resupply box, or into a store to buy groceries.

However, by "leaving your pack," I am not suggesting that you leave it unattended. Several hikers who have done so have returned to find their packs missing. At a post office, leave your backpack inside the building where you can keep an eye on it, and even then, carry your bag of valuables with you.

When entering a grocery store, you might set your pack inside the doorway, and keep an eye on it. And yes, carry your bag of valuables with you. It helps if you greet the cashier with a smile and ask permission to leave your pack there. Some stores have a "no backpacks or bags inside" policy. If you are with hiking companions, then one of you might have to wait outside with the packs. The lone hiker who leaves a backpack outside a store, unattended, is tempting someone to grab it and speed away.

When entering a restaurant, ask if you may bring your backpack with you. If the answer is "yes," then you might request seating near the door, so that you will not have to lug your pack through the dining area and risk bumping tables and customers. If the answer is "no," ask to be seated by a window, then place your backpack outside that window where you can watch it. And once again, keep your bag of valuables with you. If all else fails, simply place a take-out order.

Take caution, also, in public facilities like restrooms and showers. When showering in a public stall, leave your backpack very close by, and part the curtain just enough so that you can watch it. Keep your bag of valuables

inside the stall but out of the spray; and out of sight of anyone standing on a bench in an adjacent stall, and out of their reach.

Leaving a vehicle at a trailhead

A person must not assume that because a trailhead parking area exists, it is safe to park a car there. Vehicles at these places are easy targets for any vandals. And in some areas, these vandals do not just happen along; the trailhead-parking areas are on their routes.

The basic scenarios include theft of possessions left inside the vehicle, vandalism of the vehicle and/or its contents, and outright theft of the entire vehicle. These scenarios happen all too often, and unfortunately the concern for their vehicle is what keeps many hikers out of the wilderness, at least for any length of time. Cars are supposed to provide us with freedom; but they can actually reduce our freedom by increasing both our dependence on them and our reluctance to leave them. And they can affect the quality of the outing when worrying about the vehicle parked at the trailhead.

A much better idea might be to leave the car at home, and to figure out a method to reach the trailhead without it, even if that means more walking. When Jenny and I lived in Salt Lake City, we often rode the city bus to the edge of town. From there we hiked far into the Wasatch Mountains. When we lived in central Oregon we would take the Greyhound bus to our chosen area, and then hire someone to shuttle us to the edge of the wilderness. At journey's end we would spend the final day walking back out to the bus station for the ride home.

To locate a shuttle driver for your chosen area, you might telephone the Chamber of Commerce nearest to that area, or any guide services for backpacking or river rafting. Or phone someone locally, for example at a convenience store, and ask whether they know of anyone who might be willing to drive you to such and such a place for a specified payment. With a little effort this almost always works.

Jenny and I sometimes paid someone locally to drive us to the nearby mountains, since our small town lacked any kind of public transportation. One time we hired a friendly chap who, on reaching the trailhead, was so taken by the natural beauty of the area, that he said he was going home for his fishing pole, and was coming right back. So the arrangement worked very well for all of us.

Dogs

Opinions vary widely on the dogs-in-the-wilderness issue. Most hikers do not mind seeing the occasional dog on the trail, provided its owner is acting responsibly. By this I mean keeping the animal on a leash so that it cannot chase wildlife, jump on other hikers, or snoop around their camps. And cleaning up the dog waste and burying it a safe distance from the trail and any water sources, or bagging and carrying it out.

This is not to suggest that all owners act so responsibly, nor that all dogs encountered in the wilds are friendly. While I certainly would not wish harm on anyone's pet, I feel that the hiker's safety comes first. My advice is: whenever you see a dog at a distance—any dog off its leash—pick up a few hefty rocks. Ninety-nine dogs out of a hundred are well-intentioned, and you will know by the way they charge at you. The bark and tail wagging mean only that the dog is excited. The ears are the best indicator of intent. If the ears are upright, then the dog is probably friendly. If the ears are pinned back and the teeth are bared, then that animal could be dangerous.

Most ferocious dogs will veer away at the sight of someone picking up a few rocks. And those rocks can be quite effective if you have practiced your aim ahead of time. Another defense option is oleoresin capsicum pepper spray.

On the John Muir Trail

First Aid Supplies

The subject of wilderness first aid is beyond the scope of this book, so I can only refer you to a first aid manual or two. By studying some of the more prevalent ones, you will know how to handle most first aid situations.

PCT-1

The hiker's first aid kit is somewhat more specific than the ones described in the manuals. A kit containing enough first aid items to meet every contingency would be impracticably heavy, bulky and expensive. So Jenny and I compromise by including only the basic items intended to handle some of the more possible situations.

A few items carefully chosen

The contents of each hiker's first aid kit will vary. Our kit is quite small and very basic. We carry some of the foot care related items in a separate resealable plastic bag, and keep this "foot care kit" handy in one of the mesh pockets of a backpack. The remainder makes up our first aid kit and, except where noted, we stow this kit inside a water-proof clothes bag, inside the pack.

▶ Small bar of home-made soap for washing hands and bathing dundo style, and for washing any scrapes or scratches. We usually carry the small sliver of soap in the same resealable plastic bag as our toilet paper and the gelled ethyl alcohol, mentioned below. Note: Any soap, even the "biodegradable" kinds, should not be used directly in a natural water source.

▶ Gelled ethyl alcohol, characterized by the stationary bubbles, and sold as a waterless hand sanitizer. Contains about 60% ethyl alcohol in a glycerin-like base. We avoid the strongly scented types. Comes in small vials (0.5-oz or more) and is used mainly as an antibiotic scrub for the reduction of giardia and other protozoa on the hands after eliminating. We also use it for sterilizing blisters and superficial cuts and abrasions, and decontaminating the skin after contact with poison ivy and oak. For longer journeys we include more of these in our resupply parcels.

As noted in the "Foot Care" chapter, we also carry a small amount of rubbing alcohol (or liquid ethyl or isopropyl alcohol stove fuel) in our foot care kit. We use the alcohol as an antiseptic on blisters and minor abrasions. It stings but speeds the healing. Used when we want the wound to breathe, same as the Betadine®.

▶ Small vial of Betadine for more serious cuts and

punctures. Does not sting like liquid alcohol or hydrogen peroxide. Leaves a protective film.

▶ Small tube of triple antibiotic ointment, for treating minor cuts, burns and abrasions against infection. Non-breathable.

▶ Small, partial roll of white adhesive tape, also known as athletic tape. Useful for bandaging hot spots and blisters, and wrapping a sprained ankle (although a properly tied bandana would also suffice).

▶ Small tube of super glue for closing cracks on fingertips or foot callous.

▶ A dozen adhesive strips, such as Band Aids®, and a couple of small, sterile gauze pads.

▶ One or two sheets of Spenco 2nd Skin™ or the equivalent, for blisters and burns. Because our foot care bag is so handy, we carry our small pocket knife with the scissors in that bag also, so that we can cut the tape and 2nd Skin.

▶ A small needle for lancing blisters.

▶ Small vial of antifungal solution for the treatment of athlete's foot infection.

▶ A small pair of tweezers for the removal of ticks, thorns, stickers, cactus spines and wood slivers.

▶ Aspirin or other mild pain reliever. Note: like most drugs, these do not actually cure a malady, they only mask the symptoms.

In addition, some hikers might consider carrying the following:

▶ In venomous snake country, a suction device such as the Sawyer Extractor™.

▶ Poison ivy and poison oak preventatives and/or medications.

▶ Epinephrine kit for those who might be allergic to bees or wasp stings. Both Jenny and I have been stung when hiking past a trail-side bee or wasp's ground burrow.

Your doctor would no doubt recommend a physical exam prior to embarking on a longer hike. In addition to alerting you to any potential problems, the physician can prescribe medication you might need for your first aid kit, such as that for giardiasis, poison oak / ivy, and so forth; and can caution you in their use. During the visit, explain that you will be hiking in the wilds. Some types of medication can affect a person's capacity for strenuous exertion. And some types can cause photo-sensitivity of the skin.

———————

A simple first aid kit containing a few well-chosen items will suffice for most hiking endeavors. Of course there is no substitute for knowledge, and a person would be wise to review a first aid manual every now and then. Remember, too, that any serious accidents requiring major first aid treatment are often the result of carelessness. Safety in the wilds depends mainly on common sense, alertness while hiking and camping, and watching out for potentially dangerous situations.

Part 6

OVERCOMING OBSTACLES

PCT-3

Trail Life

Avalanche of Adversity

"Obstacles are those frightful things you see
when you take your mind off your goals."
— *H. Ford*

Projecting one's consciousness beyond obstacles

One of the more powerful forces of nature is the climax avalanche. When one comes crashing down a mountain slope, it snaps even the largest and strongest trees like matchsticks, hurls them into the air, and drives them far down into the valley. And there, the avalanche piles these trees in acres of tangled heaps.

As we try to pick our way across one of these tangles, Jenny and I are humbled by the awesome natural power that placed them here. Yet gazing up the slopes, we see that the avalanche did not strip the mountainside bare. When the mass of snow smashed into the young willow and aspen, and other types of supple vegetation, it could not exert its power on them. They simply bent over to its incredible pressures until the avalanche had passed, and sprang back upright.

When Jenny and I venture into the wilderness, we are bound to meet with various obstacles and adversities: brush on the trail, wet vegetation, incessant rain or driving thirst, trails too steep or too gradual, tread too muddy or dusty, deep snow or sweltering heat, bridgeless torrents or dry, thirsty creek beds, slippery roots and rocks, mosquitoes, blackflies and bears, resupply stations too far from the trail or towns too close to it – and other hikers complaining about same.

We cannot avoid most of these obstacles, but we can temper our reactions to them. Like stalwart trees we could let the avalanches of adversity mow us down; or like the supple vegetation we could bend and spring back, unaffected.

Accept and adapt

Nature has perfected her ways throughout the eons, and in most cases we humans can benefit by accepting those ways. When we enter the woods with unrealistic ideals born and bred in Urbania, we may instead expect nature to cater to us. Haven't we all heard someone say, "I'm going hiking today … I hope it doesn't rain." Well, what if it does rain? Our sodden hiker returns home, expectations unfulfilled: rebuffed by the Avalanche of Adversity. When we expect things of nature, we weaken ourselves with our own inflexibility. Our hiker could have said, "I'm going hiking today, and in case it rains I'll carry my umbrella." It is one's rigid expectations that make the wilderness seem so hostile; and is what keeps many people at home.

237

Focused on the goal; PCT-2

When it comes to obstacles, the way in which we react to them stresses us far more than the obstacles themselves. Those adversities listed above are not nearly as hostile or life-threatening as they might seem. But we build them up in our minds as such, based on imagined possibilities. Our minds then treat the imagined possibilities as real because our central nervous systems have no way to distinguish the differences. This is mainly why adversities can stress us so. Only after hundreds of miles on the trail did I finally learn that I could surmount these obstacles simply by projecting my consciousness through them. In other words, I accept the obstacle, adapt if necessary, and focus my attention beyond the current difficulties.

Citified thinking

In order to focus beyond the difficulties confronting us, we need to set aside certain parts of our citified thinking. As an example, when people enter a restaurant, they expect the service to be punctual and polite; they expect the food to be fresh and hot; and if they are non-smokers, then they expect their dining experience to be free of second-hand smoke. If each of these conditions is not met, then they might become upset. They might even complain to the management or at least they might not

return to this particular establishment. Granted, the customers are paying for these services, and for the most part these expectations are justified. But this same attitude of demanding that any and all situations meet one's expectations can make a person unhappy in the wilderness. Why? Because this mentality is rigid, like the trees in the avalanche.

So Jenny and I have learned to soften our thinking when venturing into the wilds.

More examples of this might be in sports or the military. The football coach hammers his team into delivering absolute maximum performance. The Marines teaches its recruits to "do-or-die-trying." This approach might be effective in defeating an opposing team or hostile troops, but in all our experience we have not seen it succeed against the vastly superior powers of nature.

We once met a hiker resting alongside the trail, wearing camouflage-type clothing and clasping a cigar stub in one corner of his mouth. Nearby was his backpack, a gargantuan affair loaded with all manner of what appeared to be Army surplus gear. It was not surplus we soon learned. "One hundred and twenty five pound's worth," the soldier informed us, adding that he could carry it only fifteen minutes between rests. I asked why he didn't lighten his load by sending a few things home. "I started with it," he replied, "and by god I'm gonna finish with it. I come from the military and that's how we operate." This fellow was quite personable once we got to know him. And while his inflexible approach may have increased the labors of his journey, he was obviously proud of what he was doing.

One of the great benefits of backpacking is how it allows us to pursue our goals however we like. Each individual has idiosyncrasies, personal ambitions, hiking parameters and philosophies. But when it comes to dealing with natural obstacles along the way, known or unknown, real or imagined, Jenny and I try to change our methods when we find them not working well.

The positive aspects

When encountering brush overgrowing the trail, we do not take it personally, but simply accept it as is, and proceed confidently ahead. Rarely will it physically stop us, or even slow us down. In fact, in the absence of rattlesnakes I sometimes imagine that I am skiing through ultra-deep power instead of hiking through thick brush. Frustrations with brush on the trail are actually struggles with one's own unrealistic demands. When I remove the thought of the brush from my consciousness, it no longer has any grip on me.

Wet bushes on the trail? We proceed ahead wearing nylon shell pants and running shoes; knowing they will dry soon enough. Rain? We anticipate it by carrying umbrellas. Driving thirst? We carry more water. Trails too steep or too gradual? We accept these as the reality of the moment, and focus instead on the pleasant things all around. Deep, residual snow? We might have neglected nature's timetables and ventured into the high country too early in the season. In which case we might haul off the trail for a couple of weeks and allow the snow to consolidate. Searing heat? We carry plenty of water and hike beneath our reflective-film covered umbrellas wearing the minimum of lightweight and loose-fitting clothing. Bridgeless torrents? We might try heading upstream in search of a fallen tree bridging the creek. That, or we might turn around; the do-or-die-trying creek-crossing mentality has killed many hikers. Dry creek beds? Again,

we carry more water. Mosquitoes? We wear mosquito-proof clothing. Bears? We enjoy seeing them by day, and at night practice stealth camping away from their nightly haunts. Resupply stations too far from the trail? We minimize off-trail hiking by choosing resupply stations carefully ahead of time. Towns too close to the trail? We accept the trail routing as is, and value its diversity of both landscape and culture. Other hikers complaining about all the above? We might change the subject to the positive aspects of the day. Otherwise, we leave these people to interpret their journeys in their own ways.

Of course, these solutions are not the only ones, but the point is that we try to deal with adversity in ways that do not weaken us. Also, we have found that fatigue can make an obstacle seem far more foreboding. A good night's rest may well reduce what seems like a monumental obstruction to an easily manageable one. And too, a positive mind-set can replace fears and anxieties with tolerance and patience, which will then increase the chances of a successful and rewarding backpacking trip.

Nature can easily rebuff the rigid minded hiker. And she may begin prodding from Day One of any wilderness outing. Those who proceed ahead with unrealistic ideals and rigid expectations are likely to meet with obstacles. But those who recognize the need to bend and flex are far more capable of hiking and camping safely and enjoyably.

So rather than fight the inevitable obstacles, we project our consciousness through them. We do this by remaining flexible, like the willows.

Rain

The rain is heaven-sent.
They must not like up there.

– r.j.

Picture yourself plodding up a long hill while carrying a heavy backpack. A cold rain is falling, but you have come prepared with the latest and most sophisticated technology. You are wearing a $230 thermal wicking shirt beneath a $450 rain jacket. The farther you progress, the more heat your muscles generate, and the more your body sweats. You unzip the jacket's front opening, but still you sweat. You open the pit zips, but with no improvement; since heat rises, and the zips are under your arms. The sweat is soaking your shirt, and the rain jacket is dripping with condensation on the inside. So there you are, slogging along in the rain, nearly as wet inside as out, and feeling like a $5.25 poached Wienerwurst.

Surely there must be a drier and more comfortable way to hike in the rain.

In more than twenty five thousand miles of hiking together, Jenny and I have backpacked in a lot of rain. Rain that is hardly more than a falling mist, to rain that pummels down in torrents. Rain that lasts only a few minutes, to rain that continues for days, and even weeks. Through most if it, we have hiked comfortably beneath our sheltering umbrellas.

The umbrella

The umbrella shields us from rain, but its most salient feature is the ventilation it provides. This ventilation eliminates the poached wienerwurst syndrome – the typical clamminess of a waterproof-"breathable" or vapor-permeable rain jacket and the associated sweat-soaked clothing. Even in heavy rain, our umbrellas allow us to dress for the temperature, rather than for the rain. This means that we can wear our normal hiking clothing. And because our umbrellas keep the rain off our faces and eyeglasses, and from running down the inside of our breathable shell jackets and shirts, they make rainy-weather hiking a lot more pleasant.

As mentioned in the "Umbrella" chapter, in moderately strong wind we hold our umbrellas at an angle to the wind. In semi-strong wind we can hold them at angle and also partially collapse them to reduce their windage. But of course in extreme wind we stow the umbrellas in our backpacks, and resort to our rainwear.

The rain jacket

We usually carry lightweight rain jackets for use in extreme cold or strong wind with or without rain. We make these jackets ourselves of waterproof-breathable fabric. They weigh about six ounces each, and occupy but little space in our backpacks when not in use.

Uninsulated and unlined

Our rain jackets are not insulated. Otherwise, we would likely sweat-soak the insulation, adding to the jackets' weight and reducing their usefulness when at rest.

Nor do our jackets have sewn-in liners. A liner's main function is to protect the inner membrane from wear, supposedly. But in truth, it only hides that wear. A liner also is meant to keep a person's skin oils off the membrane; but one's clothing worn at the time serves the same purpose. And the liner is supposed to wick away one's sweat. But unless the day is frigid, a liner would actually increase the sweat by acting as extra insulation. A mesh-hung liner is said to offer better ventilation for breathability and comfort. Yes, without the jacket. But a mesh liner inside a jacket is not exposed to the outside air, so the liner's breathability serves no benefit. Comfort, yes, because the liner keeps the hiker from feeling the sweat. Never mind the trapped moisture building up inside hiker's clothing.

We have found the liner serves no useful purpose, and again it only adds to the weight and complexity of the jacket, and increases the sweat factor and moisture build-up inside the jacket.

Zippers

Our jackets have full-length, front opening zippers that allow them to open wide for improved ventilation when possible. We have tried pullovers, but found that they restrict the all-important ventilation when needed most. The full-length zipper also permits us to wear the jackets backwards for even greater ventilation where applicable. The advantages of this are described in the "Cold" chapter.

We use water-resistant zippers, and make the full-length front opening without a storm flap and hook and loop clasps. In our experience, these storm flaps interfere with the zipper, making the jacket difficult to zip and unzip.

Sizing

We make our rain jackets oversize so that on a cold day we can wear one or more layers of insulating garments under them. The jacket sleeves extend several inches beyond the wrists, permitting us to withdraw our mittened hands into the sleeves. This keeps the mittens out of the cold rain. The jackets themselves extend well below the waist, providing ample coverage of our lower torsos. The hoods are basic in design, but roomy enough to wear an insulating hat inside.

On the AT

Nothing superfluous

To keep the weight of my rain jacket in the six-ounce zone, there is nothing superfluous on it. No pit zips; side, chest or cargo pockets with their extra zippers and storm flaps, fleece comfort collar liners, multiple-panel sleeves with shaped elbows, multi-piece hoods with adjustment straps and buckles; and built in brims, ventilating flaps, adjustable elastic sleeve cuffs with cord-locks; and hook and loop tabs, mesh liner, inside pockets, adjustable elastic waist, and designer seams crisscrossing the fabric.

And I have yet to see a corporate logo that increases a jacket's rain protection. But I have seen logos that greatly increase the jacket's sales price.

Fanciful advertisements

Speaking of consumerism, here are a few fanciful advertisements:

Ad: "Our fabric will fight off any moisture that Mother Nature throws your way."

Reality: While fighting off moisture, would this fabric thrust the hard working hiker into the poached wiener-wurst syndrome? Probably.

Ad: "You will laugh in the face of oncoming rain clouds when you have our jacket."
Reality: Someone who laughs in the face of oncoming rain clouds should be avoided.

Ad: "Our lightweight hood keeps your head dry when you're battling through brutally wet weather."
Reality: Jenny and I do not battle wet weather, and certainly do not consider it brutal, thanks mainly to our umbrellas.

To extend the life of the jacket

We have found that a summer of long-distance hiking wears out even the most expensive rain jacket in a single season. The pack straps pressing against the jacket, over time, abrade the inner membrane. This is another benefit of the umbrellas in all types of rain except those driven by strong winds. An umbrella used instead of a rain jacket where possible will extend the life of the jacket considerably.

Waterproof-NON-breathable

Some rain gear is made from waterproof-NON-breathable materials, for example urethane-coated nylon. Rain jackets and pants made from this type of material will quickly soak the inner layers of one's clothes in perspiration. While the waterproof-breathable materials are not highly breathable by any means, they do allow a small degree of moisture to pass through; at least enough to keep the inner layers reasonably dry while resting or walking leisurely.

Leg wear

My preference in rainy weather is to hike beneath an umbrella whenever possible, and wear highly breathable pants. My legs do not mind being wet, as long as they are warm. And when I am hiking at a steady pace, the leg muscles generate this warmth.

Breathable layers

In rain where temperatures are mild, I usually wear spandex shorts, while Jenny prefers nylon. If we are hiking in a cold rain, we wear shell pants over the shorts.

These shell pants are not waterproof or even water resistant. We make them of lightweight, highly-breathable nylon. But even so, they offer considerable warmth and wind protection. And when wet, I find them far more comfortable to hike in than waterproof-breathable rain pants.

When the rain eases, the shell pants will start to dry immediately, along with any damp layers underneath. That is a huge advantage over waterproof-breathable pants; because it means that during intermittent rain, the shell pants will be dry most of the time.

In continuous rain, our shell pants and any layers worn underneath will get wet, but normally only from the thighs down, thanks to our umbrellas. Then at camp, we wring out the wet pants and hang them on the clothesline under the tarp. Without delay we put on dry clothing and slide comfortably beneath the quilt, knowing that by morning the pants will be at least reasonably dry and ready for another day of hiking.

In very cold and wet conditions we hike in an additional layer of thermal pants under the shell pants.

In any kind of wet conditions, our focus is on staying warm and comfortable. As such, the combination of umbrella, rain jacket and shell pants, has worked exceptionally well for us. And should we ever become chilled (which has never happened yet) we would stop and make camp.

Sweating

As Jenny and I hike at an average clip, our legs perspire much more than do our torsos and arms. This requires a higher level of breathability in our pants. The more breathability, the less sweat-soaking.

Waterproof-breathable rain pants offer far less breathability, and once the pants become wet on the inside, they tend to bind at the knees with every step. Even the multi-panel articulated knees do not seem to help much. This binding can retard forward progress and sap a lot of energy and enthusiasm. We find it most uncomfortable.

Also, once the rain pants become wet on the inside, they would be unsuitable for wearing at the rest stops and at camp. Sitting around in wet clothing of any kind in cold weather can lead to hypothermia.

Emergency item

There are times, however, when a pair of rain pants might be needed. As such, I consider rain pants an emergency item, to be kept in the pack for use when needed; for example in an unexpected rainstorm that brings gale-force winds and lower temperatures. And the rain pants might also be appropriate if one is ambling along at a slow pace or sitting around camp on a rainy day.

Simple WP/B pants

Normally we do not use rain pants ourselves. But if we did, we would make them of the same waterproof-breathable fabric as our jackets. And they would be equally simple in design; no liner, pockets, fly, belt, or Velcro flaps. No leg zippers, storm flaps, or gusseted zipper expanders at the base of pant legs to fit over the boots. Instead, we would simply and quickly slip out of our loose-fitting running shoes before putting the rain pants on, or taking them off.

On the AT

Mittens for rainy weather

When hiking in a pouring rain while wearing a rain jacket, (no umbrella) we cannot raise our hands, for example to hook our thumbs in the pack straps or thumb loops as Jenny often does. Otherwise, the rain would funnel into the sleeves. So we hold our arms down, and withdraw our hands up into the jacket's sleeves, as described earlier. In such case, our mittens do not need to be waterproof. Simple fleece mittens will usually suffice, and they work also if we are carrying umbrellas. And should our fleece mittens become wet, we take them off, wring them out, and put them back on. In extra rainy weather, a person might wear a pair of W/B shell mittens over the fleece ones.

Footwear appropriate for wet conditions

In the "Footwear" chapter I describe our unsuccessful attempts at keeping our feet dry while hiking in the rain. After a few hours, even the most expensive boots could not stop the pervading wetness, both from the rain outside and the perspiration inside. So we wear lightweight, highly-breathable shoes and nylon socks or wool-synthetic blend socks. These work well for us, even in cold, wet weather. Yes, the shoes and socks will become wet. But the exertion of hiking keeps our feet surprisingly warm. And once the rain has stopped, our shoes and socks will soon dry.

Pack covers

The standard method of keeping a backpack dry is to put a rain cover over it.

We have tried wrapping a plastic garbage bag around the pack, but this leaked dreadfully and was not long lasting.

We have also tried commercial rain covers made of coated nylon. The store-bought ones were heavy, and so baggy that they tended to flog in strong wind. And after a time they leaked, soaking the backpacks and their contents.

Nor could they be adjusted to fit a pack that starts out fully loaded with supplies, and then gradually becomes smaller as the food is consumed day-by-day. When the pack was at its smallest, the pack covers were excessively baggy. A baggy cover acts like a catch-basin, as it channels the rain from its leaky perimeter and pools it in the sagging bottom. We dumped a lot of water out of our store-bought pack covers, and even punched drain holes in them.

Tired of this, we began making our own pack covers. We custom fit them and went through several design improvements. And we hiked thousands of miles with these. But still we found them less than ideal.

For one thing, they leaked around the perimeter. So in wet weather we had to also line our packs internally with a plastic trash bag each. To use this method, we emptied the backpack, lined it with the trash bag, filled it with our gear, pushed some of the air out the bag, twisted the top closed, then folded the top over before closing the backpack. We sometimes used "trash compactor bags" made from a heavier and more durable plastic and available at most large department stores.

When we switched from heavy-duty backpacks to light and simple packs for our AT hike of 1993, we still used home-made external backpack covers and internal plastic bag liners. But during that hike we discovered that these simple backpacks did not need to be kept dry. And after we eventually switched from the small, cramped tent to the roomy tarp, we found that we could keep our packs under our spacious shelter at night, out of the rain. This meant that we no longer needed the backpack covers.

Waterproof stowbags

During a rainy day on the trail, our packs will get wet. But we now protect our clothing and gear from the wet with home-made waterproof stowbags. These are much more durable and easier to use than plastic trash bag pack liners, and they are a bit lighter in weight.

We use two of these for each person: one stowbag for each half of our two-person quilt, and one for each person's spare clothing and other items. For more information about waterproof stowbags, see the "Quilt" chapter and the "Sewing" chapter.

In severely wet conditions, we might augment the two stowbags with an internal pack liner. This could be an extra-long stowbag made of the same waterproof nylon, or just a plastic trash compactor bag.

Camping in rain

With the right gear, techniques and attitude, we have found camping in the rain hardly more problematic than camping in dry weather. A common mistake among hikers and campers is to choose an unsuitable site. This can put the wetness into one's wilderness experience in a big way, should the rain intensify during the night. So rather than look for a level clearing without paying attention to surrounding terrain, we look for a protected location that slopes gently away on all sides. In other words, one that is slightly elevated above its surroundings. As the rain runs off our shelter, we want it to course away from us, rather than pool next to us.

Using a tarp in wet weather

The tarp is particularly well suited to wet weather camping, since it affords much more living space with far better ventilation than tents. In the "Tarp and Tent" chapter I describe how and where to pitch a tarp in different weather conditions, but I will review the specific rainy weather considerations here.

As we search for a site, we first look for natural protection from wind such as behind trees, rocks, logs or tall bushes. Next we look for good drainage. If we cannot find a site that is a little higher than its surroundings, we look for one on a slight slope. And if rain starts falling so hard that water courses down that slope, we could use a stick to dig a shallow V-shaped groove uphill of the tarp to divert the flow; however, we would do this only in times of genuine need.

The harder the wind is slanting with rain, the lower we pitch the tarp, streamlining it aerodynamically. In any kind of wind, we pitch the tarp with the ridgeline perpendicular to the wind, and its windward side flush to the ground. Keeping in mind the possibility of the storm intensifying in the night, we make certain that we have secured the guy-lines to sturdy anchor points and tensioned them well – before crawling under the tarp. We exercise that extra bit of care while still in our wet clothing, so that we will not have to emerge from our cozy shelter in our dry clothes to make adjustments.

Wet ground does not automatically necessitate a tent with a "bathtub floor." Where the ground is pooled in water, we would not pitch either a tent or a tarp there, regardless of the shelter's floor construction. But if the ground is merely wet, then a tarp should work better. Once we have pitched a tarp over wet ground, that ground will begin to dry. And our groundsheet, along with our body heat will start to drive the moisture into the earth. If this seems unlikely, think about the times you have pitched a tent on wet ground, and the next morning packed up to find that ground dry.

If rain is still falling by morning, a person might be reluctant to break camp. But the ability to pack everything but the tarp while still under the tarp, makes the prospects of setting out a lot more appealing. All we then have to do is deploy the umbrellas, step outside, take the tarp down and give it a few shakes to remove some of the wetness, and stow it in an outside mesh pocket. And we are ready to set off.

Should the rain subside temporarily during the day, we can pull out the wet tarp and spread it to dry. Rocks can make good drying racks, and so can bare ground. If the ground is covered with wet vegetation, we might spread the tarp on it anyway. While the side facing the vegetation will remain wet, the skyward surface will start to dry. Furthermore, once that surface has dried, it can provide a convenient place to spread out any damp clothes.

Even when the sun is not shining directly, the tarp will normally dry fairly quickly on ground that slopes generally toward the sun. But if the rain continues and I cannot dry the tarp, I know that it will perform just as well. The reason I try to dry it is to reduce its carrying weight.

The tent in rain

The key to pitching a tent in the rain is to plan ahead. The quicker one can get the job done, the less rain the tent will absorb.

First, locate a suitable site that affords good drainage and hopefully protection from wind. Preen the site of any sticks and pinecones, etc. Pull out the tent fly and spread it on the ground to one side of the site, right-side up. Remove the tent poles from their bag, section them together and place them under the fly. Try to keep them dry, since the shock cord inside them can absorb moisture and would be slow to dry. And be extremely careful not to step on a pole. Breaking one could put the tent out of service. Walk around the poles, rather than step over them.

Pitch the tent and quickly throw the fly over it. If the tent is free-standing, move it to one side, spread the groundsheet onto the site then position the tent quickly back over it. This minimizes exposure of the rain-catching groundsheet to the elements.

Place your backpack under the tent's vestibule or rain

Trail Life

awning. If your tent lacks either, you may have to leave your pack outside, preferably under some kind of a cover. Inside the tent, a small hand towel will be quite handy for mopping the wetness acquired during the pitching process, and from one's wet clothing. For a description of our tent awning, see the "Tarp and Tent" chapter.

The tarp-tent combo

Using a tarp over the tent might be an option when camping in persistently wet conditions, and when one is not hiking far and thus is not overly concerned about the extra weight. A tarp pitched over a tent will keep the tent dry, and will allow one to keep the tent door wide open for the best ventilation and enjoyment of the surroundings – even in pouring rain. An awning allows this also, but the full tarp gives all the more coverage. A simple and inexpensive option is a sheet of 3-mil plastic, cut about three feet larger than the tent all around. For more information about how to use these "poly-tarps" please refer to my *Tarp Book*.

Care of the sleeping gear

No matter what kind of quilt or sleeping bag, it will need to be kept dry. For this, I use the waterproof stowbag described earlier, carried inside the backpack. If necessary I also use the pack liner.

In periods of heavy rain, a wet synthetic fill quilt or sleeping bag will still keep a person fairly warm. And if drenched, it can be wrung out. However, a sodden down-filled bag may not keep a person warm at all, and wringing it out will not likely

restore any of its loft. This is one reason why I use synthetic insulation.

If a sleeping bag becomes wet, one might be able to dry it next to a campfire. See the "Quilt and Sleeping Bag" chapter for details.

Care of the clothing

The more garments we bring on a hike, the more time and effort we will spend in rainy weather trying to keep them all dry. In wet weather, Jenny and I carry only what clothing we need.

We keep our spare clothes in waterproof stowbags for use once we reach camp. When we stop hiking for the day, our wet trail clothes can quickly begin to chill us, because we are no longer generating so much metabolic warmth. So we promptly set up camp, and keeping the camp chores to a minimum we change into dry clothes and crawl into the sack. If a hiker has no dry clothes to change into, he or she should still remove the wet ones, quickly hang them to dry, then cover up with the quilt or slip into the sleeping bag to preserve body heat. Assuming the quilt or bag is reasonably dry, it will hold in that body heat and continue to provide warmth.

Our hiking clothing must be fast drying, and this is particularly important in wet weather. Except for wool-blend socks, this means 100% synthetics. We do not use clothes made of cotton, not even a very small percentage of it. Cotton is much slower drying, since its individual fibers themselves absorb moisture.

Cloudy sky, bare rocks, drying the gear; PCT-2

246

Resting in the rain

During our first thru-hike we carried fairly heavy loads, so most days we had to rest often – typically hourly. But while resting on the cold and wet days we found that the inactivity would invite a penetrating chill. So we tended to hike longer between stops, and to keep the breaks short.

A few thru-hikes later, we had more confidence in our abilities and we carried less weight, so naturally we were more comfortable taking fewer rest stops. Especially in cold and rainy weather. In fact, in very cold and rainy conditions, we might not take any rest breaks at all, but to hike from camp to camp.

But make no mistake: on a frigid and wet day, the wilderness hiker is courting hypothermia. So whatever one's level of fitness, it is important to eat wholesome snacks and drink water at least hourly, to maintain energy and warmth. For the relatively fit, that does not necessarily mean hourly stops. One can carry the snacks in one's pocket, and munch on the move. In fact, this eating and sipping while hiking is very important to just about anyone in those conditions, to keep the metabolic warmth flowing.

Jenny and I do not set waypoints for ourselves, trying to hike from point A to B regardless of the conditions. In extended periods of very wet and cold weather, we might shorten the hiking days and make camp early. If absolutely necessary, we could even build a small campfire to help dry our clothes and gear.

The importance of ample hydration

On an extremely rainy day, a hiker might not drink much water, imagining that with all that water falling from the sky, he or she would not become dehydrated. But the fact is, the exertions of hiking can be very dehydrating in any kind of weather. And the more dehydrated a person becomes, the worse one will feel, and the colder one will become. Good hydration improves blood circulation, and this brings energy, warmth and vitality.

Cooking in the rain

Ordinarily, we tend to cook in the late afternoon, then hike for another few hours before making camp. But on a rainy day, we might keep hiking until we make camp, and cook under the shelter of our tarp – at least when not in park-bear country, as opposed to wild-bear country (see the forthcoming "Bears" chapter). Beneath our tarp we can safely use a stove, as long as we take precautions to ensure that the stove does not flare up. That means extending the stove at arm's reach, outside the cover of the tarp, in order to light the stove; then once the flames have settled we bring it back in to start the cooking.

In light rain, however, we may decide to cook a reviving meal mid-afternoon, before stopping to make camp. But rather than stopping just anywhere to cook, we look for a naturally sheltered area or objects that will deflect some of the rain and wind – perhaps in the lee of a hill or a cove behind a cluster of boulders. Even trees will offer some protection, as long as their branches are not dripping heavily. After stopping we put on a few extra clothes, a warm hat, and our rain jackets. And we position ourselves so that the rain and wind are at our backs. The umbrellas can also provide shelter for both the stove and us. We can tuck the umbrella shaft under one arm so that both hands remain free, or we can set one umbrella on the ground such that it protects the stove.

Because it is raining lightly, we keep our cook breaks short. Only 30 minutes at the most. A quick and efficient cook break requires that we plan the cooking routine ahead of time, to help smooth the process. We think about what we want to cook and where that meal is in our packs. We consider also the whereabouts of our pot, lighter or matches, fuel and stove. Such forethought helps us eliminate the inevitable digging through everything looking for this and that. Also, we fill our water bottles ahead of time, so that we will not have to interrupt the cooking process to collect more water. In rainy weather, the less time we spend at the open meal stop, the better. So we also keep the meal simple, and save the more elaborate dishes, if any, for a drier day. A familiarity with the idiosyncrasies of one's stove will also greatly expedite the process.

———

One rainy afternoon on the Appalachian Trail, Jenny and I stepped into a shelter for a short break. There, we greeted a lone hiker reclining in his sleeping bag, brewing tea and listening to a weather forecast on his radio. "My trail name is Fairweather," he said. "I got it because I never hike in bad weather. Been here for two days."

After a pleasant chat we wished the fellow good luck, deployed our umbrellas and stepped back outside into the "bad" weather. And while rambling cheerfully along I recalled my own reactions to rain years ago, when I, too, had been intimidated by prolonged wet weather, and had endured most of it inside my tent. The contrast made me appreciate our lightweight, more functional gear, in terms of how it had freed us of those weather-related concerns. And I began to appreciate anew that day, how with the appropriate choice of clothing, gear and attitude, we were experiencing yet another example of the beauty and rhythm of nature in all her moods, including the cleansing, purifying and life-giving aspect to the miracle we call rain.

In northern California. PCT-2

Lightning

The white-hot sledgehammer

Lightning plays a fascinating and important role in the ecology of our planet. As a bolt rips through the sky it releases nitrogen. Twenty million lightning storms annually deposit some 100 million tons of nitrogen on the soil and plants, carried to the earth by rainfall. Nitrogen is sustenance to the world's flora. Have you ever stood at the base of an immense tree and wondered where all that mass came from? Not from the earth, otherwise the tree would have made an equal-sized hole in the ground. Rather, the mass came mainly from the nitrogen (and carbon dioxide) in the air, created in lightning storms and brought to the earth by the rain. Thus through the miracle of photosynthesis comes the profuse plant life.

Lightning is also beneficial to old-growth forest ecology. It starts fires that clear away dead undergrowth and make way for new plants and seedlings. But sometimes it also injures and even kills animals and people.

A thunderstorm builds intense electrical charges, and lightning is the sudden relieving of the electrical potential. The most common type of bolt travels from the cloud's upper part to its lower part. The other type, and the one we hikers are most concerned with, travels almost instantly from the ground up to the cloud's lower regions.

To the human eye, the bolt seems to travel from cloud to ground. And indeed, microseconds before a ground-to-cloud bolt, the cloud sends down an electrical structure resembling the roots of a tree. The electrical root nearest the ground becomes the chosen path; and in the immediate vicinity the highest grounded object will tend to attract the root and close the circuit. Boom!

With this in mind, we hikers can take a few precautions that will greatly reduce our chances of being struck by lightning.

Avoidance - Western U.S.

In the summer months in many of the western states, lightning tends to be most active on the higher mountain ranges during the afternoon thunderstorms. These thunderstorms come in fairly predictable cycles. Let's look at how this works:

The cycle can vary from five to ten days. It begins with a day or two of cloudless skies. Then, little puffy cumulus clouds will develop in the late mornings, and clear off in the evenings. Each day these clouds will generally grow more extensive. They do not produce rain, but they start to form sooner in the morning, grow more extensive, and break up later in the evenings. Then one day the clouds "over-develop" and fill the sky. Still, they dissipate at night. The next day the clouds re-form, but more quickly, and may grow dark and start spitting lightning. Rain usually follows. After a few days of this, the front will pass through and fill even the morning sky with clouds. Rain may or may not fall, but the lightning will have ceased. Then, after the front has passed, the weather cycle will begin anew, initially with clear skies throughout the day.

Observing these cycles can help us foretell the weather.

For example, if the previous afternoon brought thunderstorms, then we know that the present afternoon may also. And should another afternoon thunderstorm appear to be building, Jenny and I would be extremely cautious about following a trail up into the rocky heights. Instead, we might pitch our shelter and enjoy an early camp. There we may indeed begin to hear the clapping of thunder echoing from the ridges above.

Avoidance - Eastern U.S.

Eastern weather patterns do not give such specific clues as to where and when lightning may strike. A stronger, more active jet stream combined with an abundant source of moisture in the Gulf of Mexico provides the necessary ingredients for thunderstorm activity, but it also complicates matters of prediction.

Eastern summers are frequently humid, even in the mountains. The more humidity in the air, the greater the chances of thunderstorms during the day. If the air feels humid at dawn, and if the sky is at all clouded, or even hazy, then we know that thunderstorms could develop any time from late morning through late afternoon, with or without rain. In any event, one day a front will pass through, bringing less humid air behind it. As it passes over the area, short-lived but sometimes violent thunderstorms can erupt. At places along the trail where we can see the horizon, we look generally west and north for an approaching line of black clouds. If they are progressing steadily toward us, and if the sound of thunder is growing louder, then we would make a hasty descent from an exposed high point.

Lying in a ditch

During our CDT thru-hike, residents of the Wyoming flatlands cautioned Jenny and me about the lightning, saying that it could be deadly. We were hiking across the Red Desert when tremendous thunderstorms began developing in the afternoons. The terrain out there is featureless and flat, offering nowhere to descend. The storms treated us to some spectacular shows of nature's raw power, with great bolts of lightning and even a few tornado funnels. Then one time the sky blackened directly overhead. We were following a seldom-used dirt road at the time, and we had no choice but to lie down in the roadside ditch. Rain started hammering down, so we covered ourselves with the tent fly. Mighty explosions all around kept us pinned down for an hour, while our ditch gradually collected cold rainwater. By the time the storm had passed, we were drenched and muddy, but thankfully no worse for the wear.

Wet and muddy but safe in the ditch; Wyoming CDT

Descending for safety

Thunder is the supersonic shock

wave caused by a lightning bolt ramming air away from it. Thunder travels at the speed of sound, approximately one mile in five seconds. To estimate the bolt's distance away, watch the flashes and count the seconds until hearing their thunder; then divide that number by five.

But a person should not wait for a lightning storm to develop before taking action. If you find yourself in a high, exposed region with black clouds approaching, begin an immediate descent. Below tree-line, take refuge in the trees but do not sit beneath a tree as shelter from the rain, due to the danger of lightning striking that tree. For some reason, lightning seems to know which tree has a person or an animal crouched against it. Or at least that is how it sometimes seems, judging by the many accounts. So as a general rule: be among the trees, but not too near any one of them.

If you cannot descend, perhaps because of cliffs, and if the lightning storm overtakes you, remember that lightning tends to strike the highest grounded object in the vicinity. Make yourself as low as possible by descending as far as you can. Remove your pack, then assume the lightning defensive position: crouch low on both feet, taking advantage of the shoe or boot sole's dielectric insulation. Keep your knees together to lessen the spark gap between them, and keep your mouth open slightly to reduce the pressure differential in the ear canals. Crouching on a foam pad might provide additional protection from ground currents. Members of a group should spread out; if lightning strikes one person, the others might not sustain injuries from the "splash" and would be available to administer CPR (cardiopulmonary resuscitation) to the strike victim. Also, set aside any metal or carbon-fiber objects, including backpacks with stays, umbrellas and ice axes.

Jenny and I were thru-hiking our first long trail, and had just surmounted snowbound Forester Pass in the Sierra, at 13,000 feet. The snowfall was accumulating heavily on our jackets and packs, and obscuring the descent ahead. Trudging in deep snow and grappling in the fog, we descended to a long, rocky buttress and finally came to a cliff. Obviously, the trail had switch-backed somewhere behind us. At that point lightning started hammering all around. We needed to descend to safer ground, but could not because of the cliffs dropping away on all three sides. So we climbed down only to the brink. We removed our packs and were just sitting down when our clothing started making loud, ripping sounds – the effects of electrostatic discharge. As long as we remained seated, all was well; but each time we began to stand up, our parkas again made those ominous ripping sounds. The storm gradually moved on, so we clambered back along the ridge, and after a great deal of searching found the switchback and followed the hint of the trail down to safer ground.

Whether on flat lands or in the rugged mountains, the lesson is simple: If caught in a dangerous thunderstorm on exposed terrain, we do not simply "hike on through" hoping for good luck. Instead, we take whatever precautions are possible to minimize the chances of being hit.

First aid

Being struck by lightning has been described as sustaining a total-body blow from a white-hot sledgehammer. The results usually include unconsciousness, a shut down of the heartbeat and breathing, rupture of the eardrums, and possible burns. The strike victim will appear dead. In most instances, however, the heart is only in a quivering state known as ventricular fibrillation. Usually CPR will restore the heart to its regular beat, though this can take an hour or sometimes much longer. And even after the heart does restart, those giving the CPR must maintain ventilations (artificial respiration) until the breathing restarts also.

Oregon PCT-2

St. Elmo's Fire

One pre-dawn morning in the Colorado Rockies, my students and I set out for higher regions near the Continental Divide. Unfortunately, in the darkness we had not noticed an approaching thunderstorm. Caught short, we spread out and sat huddled beneath our ponchos, experiencing the usual electrostatic discharge: the buzzing and crackling in our ponchos, and the hair standing on end. Some experts suspect that the slow discharge means that lightning is dissipating and is therefore not likely to strike. Nevertheless, in such a situation it is best to stay crouched low until the buzzing ceases.

A fellow instructor and I shared a tarp in that storm, in which we watched a glowing ball of energy slowly climb his arm, moil about his beard, and descend the other arm. This eerie phenomenon is known as Saint Elmo's Fire, and although it is normally harmless, it is rather unsettling, and serves to remind us of nature's mysteries and power.

Umbrella hazard

An umbrella having metal or carbon fiber parts (not all do) would be highly conductive. Obviously, carrying one of these overhead when the air is electrically charged is courting trouble. If you are holding the umbrella in your hand, it would be best to avoid touching the shaft. I credit the plastic handles for saving Jenny and me once.

While hiking through New Mexico during our CDT trek, we were splattered by a nearby strike. One minute we were hiking under our umbrellas in a pouring rain—with no evidence of lightning anywhere—and the next minute an explosion knocked us momentarily senseless. The next thing we knew we were both chasing after our umbrellas, without any recollection of having dropped them.

On another occasion we were hiking in the California desert, holding our umbrellas overhead for shade from the blazing sun. As we walked beneath a set of high-tension power lines, the umbrellas started making those ominous sizzling and crackling sounds. Imagine the irony of being struck by lightning on a clear and hot day. Since then we have always doused the metal-handled brollies when walking beneath power lines.

Creek Fording

Exercising sound judgment

Imagine a stretch of mountain trail, climbing the flanks, dipping into valleys and crossing streams and creeks, and leading ever onward. Suppose what that terrain would be like without its waterways coursing through it, providing water to animals and vegetation, shaping the land, and carrying rain water, snowmelt, and sediment to the lakes and valleys below. Where our trails cross these creeks we can observe firsthand the dynamic processes of the watershed in action, and can better appreciate the equilibrium of the mountain ecosystems. And of course where these rivers are bridgeless, they sometimes confront us with dangerous crossings.

In my years of adventuring I have gained considerable experience in fording creeks and rivers. As a result, I have gained an enormous respect for the power of moving water. I have come to realize that nearly every fast-flowing and unbridged creek of size poses risks to those who attempt to ford it. This chapter is about assessing those risks and "reading" a river, to better know where and how to cross safely – and most importantly, when not to attempt a crossing at all.

Trial and error

Working as wilderness instructors years ago, my colleagues and I experimented with every technique we could think of for using ropes to safeguard creek and river crossings. Then, as now, there was no fail-safe method, and certainly none that were widely agreed upon.

Initially, we waded our 10-person groups across the rivers in "human chains," in lines parallel to the water's flow, elbows locked together and without carrying backpacks. The idea was that the person upstream took the brunt of the current, while the second in line offered support to the first, and so on down the line. With enough people in the chain, the technique worked fairly well, except when someone became frightened and released

Looking for a safe crossing; PCT-2

their elbow grip. At that point the group broke apart, and a few people would be swept downriver at great peril.

So the next time we instructors rigged a safety line angling obliquely across the river, on the surface and downstream a short distance. The next student to lose his grip on the gang jettisoned predictably downstream onto our rope. But to our dismay the rope only entangled him and threatened to drown him. The program director swam to the student's rescue and pried him free of the rope. That was our first and last experiment with such floating "safety" ropes, and our last use of the human chain method.

In ensuing years we experimented further. We tried wading individually while holding onto a rope fed from a belayer controlling the rope on shore. But the drag caused by the water's flow pressing hard against the rope made the crossing extremely difficult, and compromised the wader's concentration and balance, threatening to pull him into the water.

Realizing that the rope could not be in the water, we installed "sky-lines" over creeks, tree-to-tree, and experimented with rigging them at various heights and tensions. Initially, the students waded across secured by their climbing harnesses to the sky-line with long lanyards and carabiners (metal snap-links). But this, too, proved dangerous. The sky-line stretched with the person's weight, so offered little balance; but its tension tended to upset the wader and drag him face-first into the river. Then we tried using the sky-line as a hands-on support only; but with much the same results.

In an attempt to avoid the water altogether, we set Tyrolean traverses—pairs of taut ropes—across which students hauled themselves bodily, suspended in mid-air by harness and carabiners. Setting up those took a great deal of time, and the weight of even one person hanging on the ropes stretched the ropes beyond their elastic limits. We also constructed complicated rope lattice-

works in the form of Burma bridges. Both these techniques required that someone first swim across the river while towing a pilot line, and this was very dangerous.

I mention these "trial and error" experiments to illustrate how firmly we believed the myth that ropes are a viable means of safeguarding river crossings.

A roped drowning

A friend of mine and his climbing partner had completed a technically difficult, multi-day ascent of the Leaning Tower in Yosemite. Descending the Tower's back side, these two decided to return to the valley via a shortcut that led across Bridalveil Creek. The precipitous falls lay immediately downstream, so my friend waded in with his climbing rope attached to his harness and leading back to his partner seated on the riverbank in the standard belay position. In an instant the wader became not just a swimmer, but a submarine. The torrent's force, countered by the strain on the rope, submerged the victim and pinned him to the riverbed. His belayer could not pay slack because of the nearby waterfall. So the belay rope, intended as a safety device, now became a drowning device. The belayer told me later that the force on the rope was unimaginable. After struggling to secure the rope to his anchors, he rigged a haul system commonly used to hoist haul-bags up rock walls. And after a protracted struggle he finally managed to winch the body out of the water.

Every year, dozens of hikers across the country drown in their misguided attempts to ford creeks and rivers, sometimes while using "safety" ropes. These accidents happen, in part, because the water is usually deeper than it appears (due to light refraction), more swift, and far more powerful. And, too, because no matter how strong the current, or how cold and clear the water, algae will usually be growing on the riverbed. This algae is often invisible, and can be extremely slippery.

Lack of bridges

Jenny and I encountered unsafe creek or river crossings on five of our six mega-hikes. The late-season southbound PCT was the only exception, because by that time of the year the creeks were low. On the AT we waded the Kennebec rather than ride the canoe ferry, because we wanted to walk the entire way. Our most hazardous crossings, by far, were on our first PCT hike when taking alternate routes through the high Sierras in very early season. Next in difficulty were the creek crossings on our second PCT hike, again in early season. And in those years, most Sierra creeks north of Tuolumne Meadows were bridgeless.

Someone planning to hike the John Muir Trail in mid to late-summer, as we did in 1989, might find no difficult crossings. The same might hold true with most other popular summer trails in the contiguous 48 states.

Nevertheless, in early season, say from May through July, many western trails are replete with chancy crossings. And actually, Jenny and I have enjoyed our early season trips and the extra challenges they presented. So here is how we have handled the creek and river fordings:

Trails leading across bridgeless creeks

In the high mountains, the creeks and rivers of mid to late-summer are oftentimes benign, with stepping-stones leading across them. This is the condition that the trail builders normally worked with, when planning their routes and constructing and maintaining the trails. But earlier in the year, the snowmelt runoff can turn those waterways into raging torrents. The same can happen in summer following a downpour. Therefore, when hiking a trail that leads into a creek, only to emerge from the far side, a person should not assume that this is a standard, safe crossing.

Obviously, the easiest and safest crossing of a sizeable creek is on a man-made bridge. Unfortunately, back-country bridges have a way of disappearing; victims of floods, avalanches or simply time and decay. So where a map indicates footbridges, this does not guarantee that we will find them in place and still usable.

Or they might not have been built to begin with. The agencies that manage our public lands are woefully strapped for funds, so bridge construction and repair is typically low on their agenda. Sadly, maintaining trails

If a trail leads into a creek and emerges at the far side, a person should not assume that this is a standard, safe crossing. PCT-2.

255

On the PCT-1 in the High Sierra, we found this bridge apparently demolished by an avalanche.

running through them. But the ones that do, I feel should also have safe bridges where necessary.

The natural bridge

Where no bridge exists, Jenny and I look for big rocks or fallen timbers spanning the watercourse. Searching upstream is usually best, because the main creek and its feeder creeks become

for equestrians takes higher priority, because the vast majority of trail damage in the West is caused by pack and saddle stock. Without horses and mules on the trails, the government funds might be better used to construct and repair more bridges. This would undoubtedly keep the trails and existing bridges safer for human use.

The main reason many of the highly constructed trails do not have bridges is because many regions of our public lands are regrettably controlled by the outfitters, who do not need so many bridges. A horse or mule with its long, thin legs can easily ford many creeks too dangerous for a hiker.

Some people might view the construction of anything man-made as not belonging in the pristine wilderness – including bridges. Some bridges can be eye-sores in an otherwise unbroken landscape, to be sure. But most hiking trails are also man-made. The John Muir Trail, for example, required tons of dynamite and thousands of person-hours with pick and shovel. I am glad that every wild valley does not have such highly constructed trails

PCT-1

smaller, the closer to the rivers source. If we hike downstream along the banks, we will find feeder creeks enlarging the main creek. Also we are more likely to come to an un-fordable feeder creek barring further progress.

Fallen logs often provide the only safe crossings, and walking across one requires good balance. The chapter on "Physical Conditioning" describes an exercise that can greatly improve one's balance.

However, before walking across a log spanning a creek, we always consider the consequences of falling off. If the water is shallow and easily waded, and the log is not too high over it, then falling off might not be serious. Otherwise, we do not cross the log by walking across. Instead, we might crawl on hands and knees. This lowers one's center of gravity and greatly improves stability. Or if the log is not sufficiently wide, we might remove our backpacks and balance them in front of us on the log, and sit down on the log and straddle it. The feet dangling on both sides contribute greatly to balance, and if necessary one can squeeze the log between the legs for added security at times. In this position we scoot across, one person at a time, a few inches at a time, shoving our backpacks ahead. One caution with this technique, gained from experience: make sure the log cannot roll.

The fording staff

Where a map shows the trail crossing a creek, and where we assume wading might be necessary, perhaps half a mile from the creek each of us will start looking for a stout stick to assist with our balance. If creek-side campers would cease from burning these fording staffs in their campfires, hikers would no doubt find a number of staffs on both sides of the creeks. So after wading the creek, each with the aid of a staff, we carry them well beyond the campsites and deposit them along the trail for the benefit of hikers traveling in the other direction.

In shallow water, trekking poles or hiking staffs may suffice; but in deeper water one needs a single, stronger and longer staff that can be grasped with both hands for better stability. This fording staff should be chest high, and at least two inches in diameter. It must be strong enough to withstand one's weight and the force of the water without buckling.

Unlatch the hip belt

Before stepping into any creek, large or small, we unlatch the buckles of our backpack's hip belts, if any. Some

The high country snowmelt has sent this cascading creek overflowing onto the trail. PCT-2

PCT-2

shrugged off in one quick motion. For an even quicker release, a person might carry the pack on one shoulder only. One should also unclip any sternum strap.

These precautions are not based on theory, but again on the tragic experience of losing a climbing friend who slipped on algae while crossing Bubbs Creek in the Sierra, in water less than knee deep. Unable to shrug off his backpack because of the hip belt and sternum strap, he was swept over a waterfall.

I make a habit of unlatching the hip belt when tackling any situation where a heavy, bulky backpack might increase the dangers: wading a creek, crossing a creek on a log, stepping from rock to rock across a creek, and also when traversing precipitous terrain and steep snowfields.

Where to ford

As a general rule, if the river is swift and knee deep or deeper, we do not attempt a wade. Rather, we scout the bank for a natural bridge. We have hiked as much as five miles along a creek in search of a safe crossing.

If we find a place that appears safe to wade, but where whitewater lurks immediately downstream, we do not risk it. One slip, and the current could sweep a person quickly into the rapids.

Also, if the creek is swift and its bed is solid rock, as with many places in the High Sierra, we look elsewhere. In all likelihood that riverbed has been polished by grit and coated with a translucent layer of algae that can be unimaginably slippery. I have experienced this. I started out with confidence, but two steps later I was suddenly struggling to return to shore. Fortunately I was able to grasp the riverbank with my hands.

We never cross at the outside bend of a river, where the water's centrifugal force drives it into the far bank. The water there is usually much deeper and more powerful.

hikers may be reluctant to do this, concerned that the pack could shift and throw them off balance. Or that if they slip into the water, they might lose their backpacks. But the hikers' safety comes first. And remember that one cannot swim very well, if at all, encumbered with a heavy backpack, particularly in rough water.

As one treads carefully across a creek, the pack will remain on the shoulders without a hip belt. And should one plunge into the water, the shoulder straps can be

For the safest ford, we choose an area where the creek is reasonably straight.

Also, we look for an area where the creek is wide and shallow, rather than narrow and deep. In the shallows, the water may be faster moving, but less powerful due to the reduced depth. And once again, from the vantage of shore the water will appear much less deep than it actually is.

We are cautious, too, about mid-channel boulders. Some offer safe resting partway across, but others create turbulence that can form holes in the creek-bed and deep water around them.

Finally, we eye the opposite bank and judge whether the water there is much deeper, or if the bank itself may be too steep to climb.

Fording techniques

If all looks well, I proceed slowly while clutching a stout fording staff in both hands. If the stream becomes precarious, rather than shuffle ahead facing the opposite bank, I might turn sideways and face upstream. "Streamlining" my feet reduces the water's force on them, and gives more control and stability. I lean forward, upstream, using the staff for balance; and I sidestep, keeping the feet about a shoulder width apart. This creates a more stable tripod with feet and staff.

If the riverbed proves too slippery, or the water proves much deeper than it appeared from shore, or if I find the flow more swifter

than I had expected, exerting more strain than I can safely manage, I reverse direction. Still facing upstream, I shuffle carefully back to shore, to look for a safer crossing elsewhere.

And too, I have attempted crossings that, when half way across, I thought the conditions might be too dangerous for Jenny with her somewhat shorter legs. If so, I will turn back.

However, if all is well, then I proceed ahead, step by cautious step. With each step, I avoid placing my weight on a foot until it has explored the bottom by feel and found secure footing. If I step too quickly, a rock could roll out from underfoot.

During a precarious ford, I rivet my eyes on the far shore to prevent the water's motion from upsetting my equilibrium. But I do not lock onto the far shore as my goal, at the expense of judgment. I gaze ahead, but anchor my mind on the present situation. I feel the current

In the Sierra; PCT-2

pressing powerfully against my legs, trying to wrench each foot as I lift it free of the bottom while taking the next step.

Always, I try to keep a cool head and maintain control, never allowing brain lock to take hold. Should I begin to feel insecure, I slowly reverse course and carefully work

Crossing this creek on cables; the CDT in Glacier Park.

my way back. Returning is generally easier, because I am now more familiar with that part of the riverbed already covered.

Before reaching the halfway point, I assess my strength. If I find myself tiring, I consider turning back. Fatigue can greatly undermine composure. At the same time, I do not let the biting coldness of the water dissuade me. The cold may be excruciating but it is only temporary. I know that my feet and legs will begin to re-warm after stepping ashore.

Drawing closer to the far shore, I may find the water becoming deeper and swifter than expected. In such a case, I do not let the nearness of shore tempt me into a careless bolt for the bank. If prudence suggests turning back, I do.

Of all the safety precautions for creek crossings, the most important is to remain on one's feet. One must not assume that one can swim in a torrent. If the water is too swift and deep to wade, and the bottom too slippery, then it is extremely dangerous to presume that, in a last ditch effort, one will be able to swim across. Strong turbulence can make swimming even a few feet impossible, due to the difficulty of remaining on the surface.

Jenny and I make the crossing one at a time. Usually I go first. This allows Jenny to watch my moves carefully, and to gather information about the easiest route across by studying my actions. Once I am safely on the opposite bank I watch her progress just as carefully as she then crosses.

Foot protection

Most often we ford a creek in our running shoes. But because we wear the shoes with their laces tied very loosely while hiking, giving our feet more breathing room, we tighten the laces before wading into the water. Otherwise the currant might rip a shoe off and send it floating downriver.

Sometimes we ford in sandals with the straps cinched tight.

If the water is deep, then one must not try to ford

wearing heavy boots. Boots create a great deal of drag, but more importantly, should a person slip and fall into the water, the boots will make swimming far more difficult and dangerous.

Wet shoes are acceptable for hiking, but dry ones are even better. In situations where the wade will be minor, we might ford barefoot, after tying our shoes to the packs and stuffing the socks into an outside pack pocket. A sandy bottom can make for a relatively easy barefoot crossing.

In some other situations we might protect our feet with a few pairs of dirty socks, without the shoes. Once at the creek's far side, we remove the wet socks, wring them out and hang them on the backpacks to dry. Then we slip back into dry socks and shoes, and continue on our way.

Jumping small creeks

Sometimes a trail may cross a streamlet too wide to step over, yet too small to justify taking off the shoes and wading. In such cases, we think twice before attempting a leap. The rocks or logs on the other side might be coated in slippery algae. Or in early morning, the diffused light may not reveal the glimmer of verglas (frozen dew). Either way, a person could land off-kilter and pull a muscle or sprain an ankle. In such circumstances, wading is usually safest.

PCT-3

Safety in creek crossings is mostly a matter of exercising sound judgment. And a big part of that judgment comes from within, from some part of a person's mind that has nothing to do with logic and reasoning. It is like a sixth sense, innate in us all. So when standing at the bank of a swift creek, Jenny and I assess the situation while paying attention to those inner feelings. If things do not feel right somehow, we honor that intuition and look for a safer crossing elsewhere.

Hot

"I walked in a desert.
And I cried:
'Ah, God, take me from this place!'
A voice said: 'It is no desert.'
I cried: 'Well, but –
The sand, the heat, the vacant horizon.'
A voice said: 'It is no desert.'"

— *Stephen Crane*

Crisp mountain heights, shaded forests, lakes and cascading streams: these are the usual mountain idylls drawing us into the high country for relief from the sultry, dog days of summer. Yet as we explore a closer connection with all wild places, Jenny and I have found ourselves also in the arid foothills, dense lower woodlands, and deserts – places where the temperatures can soar. We consider ourselves fortunate to have access to so many climatically diverse regions. And by learning to adapt to each of them, we are much less limited in the scope of our ramblings.

Desert dwellers thrive in their torrid environments, traditionally by wearing heavy clothing to shield them from the strong ultraviolet radiation, and to insulate them from the parching heat. But we hikers cannot emulate them in hot weather. The metabolic heat we generate while hiking would grow intolerable inside the heavy, insulating garments. So instead, we need sun protection that offers the best possible ventilation.

The reflective-film covered umbrella

First and foremost, Jenny and I need shade. If hiking beneath natural shade, such as cloud cover or trees, then all is well. But if we are out in the open, we will need to provide our own shade. The best way that we have found is to carry a shading umbrella. This provides ventilation nearly on par with the clouds and trees. If the day is positively scorching and the sunshine intense, then we can also cover the umbrella with reflective film. This is extremely effective at reducing the sun's thermal radiation.

During our fifth mega-trek, Jenny and I traversed the desert-like regions of southern California in late August and early September. These regions see very few hikers at that time of year, due to the intense heat. Yet our reflective-film covered umbrellas allowed us to hike those eight hundred miles without difficulty. Beneath the umbrellas we dressed as lightly as possible, and of course we drank plenty of water. This combination facilitated the greatest cooling effect through evaporation of perspiration.

Overall, we consider the umbrella an indispensable piece of gear for hot weather hiking. For details see the "Umbrella" chapter.

Clothing and footwear considerations

In the "Clothing" chapter, I detail our clothing suggestions for hiking in hot weather, so I will mention them only briefly here.

Whether the humidity is very high or low, we choose clothing that is loose-fitting, light in weight, and fast-drying. Most importantly, it must provide maximum ventilation, allowing sweat to evaporate. In very hot weather, my usual hiking attire is simply the spandex shorts and the short-sleeve, button up shirt when necessary. Jenny wears nylon shorts and a light polyester shirt, or in extreme heat, shorts and a tank top.

In warm to hot weather we wear lightweight socks with shoes that provide good ventilation. We sometimes also carry sandals as spare footwear, and wear them for several hours each day, usually with thin socks. And when not using umbrellas we wear wide-brimmed sun hats to help keep the sun off our scalp, face, ears and neck.

Under a hot sun with no shade, the ground can become extremely hot. When hiking on this type of terrain, we wear running shoes with thicker soles that provide more insulation.

Cotton for hot weather?

Wearing cotton clothing can be unsafe in cold and rainy weather, but what about lightweight cotton shirts and shorts on a hot day? Unfortunately, the same shortcomings apply. The individual fibers of cotton absorb the moisture and salts of one's perspiration, making the garments slow to dry. Wearing wet clothing is rather unpleasant for most people, and can lead to chafing where the fabric rubs against the skin.

What about wearing wet cotton clothing in the desert to help cool the skin? We have tried this, and found that—here again—cotton fails to perform. The warmer the conditions, the more we need the cooling effects of evaporation. Cotton clothing wicks the sweat from our skin, granted, but it also tends to hold onto it. As the moisture in the fabric slowly evaporates, the fabric cools. But it is not cooling our skin. It is cooling only the fabric. Our clothing may be slightly cooler, but what good is that if we are fairly broiling inside it? Wet cotton is also more restrictive of ventilation, and the reader can demonstrate this for himself. On a hot day, hike in a cotton shirt until it is quite soaked. Remove the shirt, deploy a shading umbrella unless you are hiking beneath shading trees, and continue on your way bare-skinned.

The cooling effect you will experience will be immediate and dramatic. This is as nature intended. So we need the evaporative cooling to take place on our skin, not on our clothing.

Minimize clothing

When sweat evaporates from the skin, it cools the skin in an effect known as the "latent heat of vaporization." Each gram of water evaporating from the skin reduces the skin's temperature by about 540 calories. Therefore, the evaporation is all-important. And any breeze moving across the skin accelerates the evaporation, thereby improving the cooling. Clothing of any type—thick or thin, cotton or synthetic, light or dark—hampers evaporation.

When Jenny and I thru-hiked the Appalachian Trail in mid summer, along the southern half of the trail we often encountered both temperatures and humidity in the 90's. At such times our pace on the uphill grinds was often limited less by our heart rates than by our inability to dissipate metabolic heat. Many were the times we had to slow down in order to keep heat exhaustion at bay. A week into the journey we discovered that by minimizing our clothing we stayed much cooler and could hike closer to our normal pace. After that, I went shirtless most of the way, except in towns. I found that the bare skin made an enormous difference in comfort. Especially because the AT is generally well shaded beneath a magnificent forest canopy.

Sunburn and SPF

In intense sunshine we stay much cooler and have less exposure to harmful rays if we keep the sun off of us. A dense tree canopy is ideal, but where there are no trees we use the shading umbrellas.

Another option to shield against sunburn is lightweight clothing. Although the clothing we wear is heated by the sun, and therefore it can be quite warm to hike in, at least it keeps the intense ultraviolet radiation from damaging our skin. Or mostly so; for according to some dermatologists, the Sun Protection Factor (SPF) rating for most lightweight fabrics is 8 to 10. And when that clothing is wet, for example with sweat, its SPF is theoretically much less.

SPF ratings indicate how much longer than normal a person can remain in the sun without getting burned. So for example, lightweight clothing boosts our bare-skin exposure tolerance 8 or 10 times.

One can buy clothing with much higher SPF ratings, but I find these too restrictive of the all-important ventilation. Still, they might be helpful for someone who sunburns easily.

Another option is of course sunscreen with a high SPF. So for example, if one normally tolerates only 15 minutes of sun before starting to burn, then an SPF 45 sunscreen would boost the sun tolerance to 15 x 45 = 675 minutes, or 11¼ hours. If hiking all day, a person might apply the sunscreen in the morning as soon as the sun emerges, and reapply a small amount two or three times a day as needed. Areas that typically need special attention are the backs of the fingers and hands, the nose, forehead, ears and the back of the neck.

When Jenny and I are exposed to the sun for extended periods, we prefer covering ourselves with clothing rather than applying sunscreens. I have even used adhesive tape on my ears, which are especially sensitive to the sun. The reasons we tend to avoid sunscreens is because they can clog the pores, and most importantly by our way of thinking, the chemicals in these lotions and creams can affect the skin, and actually soak into it, possibly reaching the underlying tissue.[14] Which is why, for example, PABA and benzophenone, the two active ingredients used in most sunscreens, can produce allergic reactions, one of which is photodermatitis.

---

14 For which type to choose, search online the "Cosmetic Safety Database."

Photodermatitis

When hiking in intense sunshine, many times we have experienced the unpleasant effects of photoallergenic and phototoxic contact dermatitis. Unlike sunburn, this type of skin damage is characterized by raised, pus-filled blisters that usually itch like poison ivy or oak. Dermatologists have attributed the malady to the application or ingestion of chemicals that increase the skin's sensitivity to solar radiation. The responsible agents might be something in a food or drink, soap, shampoo, hand lotion, insect repellent, or ironically, even in the sunscreen.

The backs of our fingers and hands are particularly susceptible to photodermatitis. To treat the affected areas, we rinse repeatedly and gently in cold water without soap, then dab the areas liberally with antiseptic. If we happen to have hydrocortisone cream, we might use that also. The rash can rapidly worsen if left exposed to the sun, so it is important to cover the affected area. For this we use home-made, lightweight and breathable "sun mitts," or bandanas wrapped around the hands, or even an old pair of socks. For improved ventilation, we cut off the fingertips of the mitts, or the toe sections of the socks. One could also use thin gardening gloves. However, at night we leave the affected areas uncovered for the best ventilation.

Another type of sun-related reaction is the itchy rash that sometimes develops on bare arms and legs, even under the socks. This is "heat rash," and is also known as prickly heat. It looks like tiny clear or red bumps on the skin. These are actually sweat glands plugged with accumulated dead skin cells which have trapped the sweat. The remedy is to scrub the area gently with soap and water. Hydrocortisone cream may help ease the discomfort.

Water is life

In late April during our first PCT trek, Jenny and I experienced the hottest temperatures of our hiking career. The nearby town of Palm Springs was recording 120 degrees Fahrenheit. This was a dry, desert heat that sapped body moisture. The available water sources along our route were from five to twenty miles apart, and initially we each carried only two or three quarts of water between sources. With our packs already overloaded with excessive clothing and gear, we were disinclined to load up on more water. So our method was to hike with determination from one water source to the next. Unfortunately, this did not work well; and typically we would reach the next source only through sheer will. After one particularly demanding jaunt we arrived at a distant source and drank five quarts of water each, on the spot.

In the ensuing days we tried other strategies, but finally decided that the weight of water is inconsequential compared with its value in sustaining life. With this realization we resumed hiking in reasonable comfort and health, despite the extreme temperatures and the extra weight of water. By the time the heat had eased to 110 degrees we were each consuming three gallons of water a day, including what we used for cooking. On our most recent PCT journey, we hiked that same stretch of trail in late summer in 100 degree temperatures, and averaged two gallons per person per day, which again included water used for cooking the evening meals.

In humid heat, such as that of the eastern states, water consumption is equally important, although the quantities may not be quite as great. During our AT thru-hike, Jenny and I found water amply available along most of the trail, or at least within easy reach of it. So even in the hottest weather we could usually set off from a source carrying no more than a quart or two each.

Heat exhaustion

Heat exhaustion is a comparatively minor disorder, but if not treated it can lead to heat stroke, which can be fatal. The symptoms of heat exhaustion include gradual weakness, dizziness, nausea, anxiety, or faintness.

During our 2003 IUA Hike-&-Bike, we were cycling along a highway in Arizona in oven-like temperatures, when Jenny started to complain of feeling sick and needing to get out of the sun. The creosote bushes offered no shade to speak of, but we could see civilization looming ahead, so I felt it best to press ahead. I felt fine, and thought her symptoms were only psychological. Later in the day I would learn how wrong I was.

In a few miles we reached a convenience store, and consumed a few cold drinks. We pedaled on. However, in another five miles I began having trouble staying on my bike. And once again Jenny was saying she needed shade. Yet there was no shade to be found.

I dismounted and laid my bike down by the side of the road, and at Jenny's suggestion I sat down. But the ground was like a frying pan, so I stood back up. Then I felt like I was drowning, going under despite my best efforts to

Emerging from the culvert during the IUA.

remain afloat (conscious). This frightened me, because I knew that if I fainted onto the searing hot ground, it would burn me, or at least worsen my condition enormously. But looking around, I could find nowhere to lie down out of the killing sun.

Never mind the traffic whizzing past ignoring our plight; we gathered our resolve, mounted the bikes, and peddled a short ways back until seeing a culvert beneath the road that we had not noticed before. Gratefully we crawled inside and lay on its shady, sandy bottom. We were carrying a bottle of ice water in a bike bag, so this was a big help. The culvert's interior was far from cool, but at least it was not deathly hot like outside. So we lay there for over an hour, as our body temperatures slowly returned to the operating range. Meanwhile it took thirty minutes before I regained my ability to focus my eyes.

Lying there, I realized that Jenny's earlier plight had not been psychological. She must have been in the initial throws of heat exhaustion.

We have hiked many hundreds of miles in very hot conditions, but it wasn't until that day that we came close to the edge. In so doing, I learned a valuable lesson:

One should not underestimate the heat. If a hiker starts feeling a desperate need for shade, perhaps with anxiety and weakness, this could be psychological, or it could be genuine heat exhaustion. The transition from heat exhaustion to heat stroke can happen fairly quickly. So it is not worth the gamble. Many people have collapsed into unconsciousness and died in this manner.

If someone in your party begins to fade in the heat, get them to lie down in the shade. Where shade is lacking, have them lie down on a couple of foam pads as insulation from the hot ground, and shade them with your body. Have them drink large quantities of water along with an electrolyte drink. Suggest that they remove extraneous clothing to promote evaporative cooling. Where water is abundant, have them pour it on themselves and their clothing.

Far better is to prevent heat exhaustion in the first place. Do this by hiking only at a moderate pace, wearing lightweight and minimal clothing, and of course drinking plenty of water all along the way and mixing in some dilute form of electrolytes. Rest often, and in intense sunshine carry an umbrella. And where available, eat fresh, uncooked fruits and vegetables for their minerals and electrolytes.

Hiking at night

In very hot weather, we sometimes hike in the cool of the night, depending on the location. In order to maintain a decent pace, we normally use flashlights to avoid stepping in holes, tripping on rocks or roots, and possibly treading on a snake. With the bright LED flashlights, the problems of batteries are greatly reduced.

In desert-like regions, we use reflective-film covered umbrellas to obviate the need to hike at night, since they allow us to carry on in reasonable comfort throughout the day. But sometimes night hiking is just plain fun, and well worth the effort. Where snakes are absent, we might even hike without flashlights. Naturally our pace is slow, as we step more cautiously to remain on the trail while avoiding obstacles. Yet when we slow down and allow a simple shift in consciousness, lessening our reliance on our day vision, the night becomes a fascinating realm. I find that occasional night hiking is of great benefit to the outward journey—to beat the heat, and the inward journey—to broaden my perspectives.

Cold

"In the heating and air conditioning trade,
the point on the thermostat in which
neither heating nor cooling must operate
—around 72 degrees—is called
'The Comfort Zone.'
It is also known as
'The Dead Zone.'"

— *Russell Bishop*

When Jenny and I remain indoors in winter-time, we know we are missing a great deal of what nature has to offer. When we venture outside, with the thermometer dipping well below 72 degrees, we can still maintain our comfort zone by generating our own warmth, metabolically, and retaining (and regulating) that warmth with our clothing.

———

"Bundle up! It's cold outside." As children most of us heard this well-intentioned advice often. And granted, during our outings we must not ignore the cold, as children often do, and dress so lightly that we become deeply chilled. At that stage, re-warming can be difficult. But at the same time, Jenny and I have learned to be extremely careful not to over-bundle while hiking. Otherwise we might be hiking toward an encounter with hypothermia.

In 2006 we skied for 57 days across Antarctica, from near the edge of the continent to the South Pole. The temperature was always low, and the wind usually strong. Yet we skied all day, every day, with no place to rest and get out of the wind except at day's end when finally pitching our tent. For those 10 hours a day, we were exposed to a wind-chill factor that was off the charts. So what did we wear? Not nearly as much as one might expect for those circumstances.

The body's microclimate

In cold weather, a person creates a microclimate next to the skin that is much warmer than the external ambient conditions. This warmth is produced metabolically, and retained with clothing of the appropriate kinds. So while the eyes see the chilly, external environment, the body "sees" the warm microclimate next to the skin.

This microclimate is quite effective at keeping a person warm. But he or she must regulate it throughout the day with the type and amount of clothing worn. What makes this problematic for most people is that they tend to be sight oriented rather than skin oriented. So they see their needs for clothing, rather than feel them as they should. As such, in cold weather they tend to overprotect themselves by piling on too much clothing.

All is well while at rest, or moving only slowly. But when hiking with any amount of liveliness, a person may generate a surplus of metabolic warmth. And if he or she is bundled up, the extra clothing will cause the person to sweat.

Sweat is the body's reaction to overheating. It is very effective at cooling the body in hot weather, as long as the sweat is allowed to evaporate. But if a person is wearing heavy clothing, that clothing will absorb the sweat. And when the sweat fails to cool the body, the body produces even more sweat.

I liken this to wrapping a blanket around a car's engine and radiator. Even on a cold day, the radiator of an internal combustion engine must do its job of cooling the engine. Otherwise, the engine might soon overheat. The combustion generates power, but also heat. Metabolism does the same.

So no matter how cold the day, a hardworking engine

does not need a blanket wrapped around it. Neither does a hardworking hiker need to wear extra-thick pants and jackets.

On a cold day, sweat is the enemy

Heavily bundled and hiking hard, a person might have a tendency to ignore the sweating, no matter how profuse. But this can lead to trouble. Not only are the sweat-soaked garments uncomfortable, but they will have lost a great deal of their ability to insulate. So they will be much less serviceable at the rest stops and at camp when needed most: when the person is no longer producing as much metabolic warmth.

This is why, in very cold weather, wearing too many clothes can be just as hazardous as not wearing enough. In fact, I consider this one of the most fundamental skills of cold-weather hiking: body awareness in terms of the microclimate.

PCT-3

During our South Pole trip, we had to be extremely careful to avoid sweating. The days were so cold and windy that any sweat would have quickly frozen inside our clothing and rendered them practically useless.

From the edge of the continent to the South Pole is quite a distance: about 750 miles along our chosen route. And in Antarctica, 750 miles is a very long way. Especially while skiing gradually uphill on rough ice and pulling heavy sleds containing our food and gear. So we

needed to ski hard in order to cover those miles in the comparatively short season. This meant we were always working hard and generating a great deal of metabolic warmth. But any sweat would have been a showstopper. So we had to dress as lightly as possible.

In temperatures of minus 30-degrees centigrade and winds of 30-mph, we each wore breathable shell jackets and pants over one or two layers of thermal underwear. That was all we wore on our bodies, legs and arms.[15] We dressed this lightly, not by choice but by necessity: to keep from freezing.

Although this is an extreme example, the same principles apply to most hikers in chilly to cold weather out for an afternoon jaunt, a weekend peak climb, or a multi-

---

15 The extremities generate much less metabolic warmth, so on our feet we wore thick boots; on our hands we wore extremely thick mittens; and we covered our faces and heads with face masks, hats, neck gaiters, scarves, goggles and hoods.

day trek into the high country. When the temperature starts to drop, one must pay close attention to the micro-climate, and regulate it by adjusting the clothing layers to prevent sweating.

Wearing clothes dynamically

When hiking in cold weather, I actively regulate my temperature by donning a layer or two the moment I begin to feel a chill, and by removing layers—and possibly slowing the pace—at the first hint of a sweat.

Better yet, I have learned to anticipate the condition and make the appropriate adjustments ahead of time.

For example, suppose I am hiking the Colorado Trail in the early or late season. I know that when hiking in cold weather, a moderate pace produces the best flow of long-term energy. But say that I come to a long and steep climb. I do not wait until mid-way up the hill to stop and remove some of my now sweat-soaked garments. Instead, before actually commencing the ascent I remove a layer of clothing. And while climbing, I keep the pace slower specifically to minimize sweating.

In a certain sense, anticipating the need to increase or decrease warmth is like balancing a yardstick on one's finger. Until a person learns to anticipate the stick's leaning, the corrections will always come too late; so they will have to be more drastic.

Say that I am hiking in cold weather while a little too lightly dressed. My body is losing heat, but I am ignoring the fact. However, when it comes time to take a rest break, I will need to put on far more clothing in order to regain my comfort.

So if my clothing adjustments come too late, I will need to carry thicker clothing and more of it in order to warm back up. This is a very common scenario with many people while backpacking in cold weather.

But if my corrections are made in advance, my adjustments will need to be only slight.

So for the greatest comfort in my hiking, and for the greatest performance in my clothing, I put on or shed layers before I actually need to.

Clothing for hiking in cold weather

Depending on your hiking style, level of conditioning, pace, and the ambient conditions, you will need to experiment with various clothing layers to determine what works best. While experimenting, carry several different layering options, of course being careful not to sweat-soak anything.

As described in the "Clothing" chapter, when hiking in cold weather Jenny and I typically start with an inner layer of lightweight clothing. For example a polyester shirt and spandex or nylon shorts. These are our warm-weather clothes, but in cold weather we think of them as underwear. We are carrying them anyway, so why not put them to good use?

Torso

With my polyester shirt as the base layer, I would then pull on a long-sleeve thermal shirt. These two layers are my initial cold-weather torso cladding.

For added warmth and wind protection when needed, I would put on my next layer: the breathable shell jacket.

Provided I keep moving at a reasonable pace, this combination keeps me comfortably warm without sweat-soaking these garments.

However, if I were merely ambling at a slow pace, or if the adventure takes me into frigid climates, I would need to dress more warmly. So I might wear two thermal shirts under the shell jacket, with an insulated jacket handy for the rest stops.

When needed, my outermost layer is the waterproof-breathable rain jacket. This adds insulation and blocks cold wind. To prevent over-sweating while wearing this jacket, I sometimes wear it backwards, see below.

Legs

While hiking, my leg muscles generate a great deal of heat, even on a cold day. So my selection of pant layers is slightly different than for the torso layers. As mentioned above, the lycra shorts are my base layer worn next to the skin. Next are the breathable shell pants. In colder conditions still, I wear the thermal pants sandwiched between the shorts and shell pants.

I do not normally wear waterproof-breathable pants while hiking, as I find them insufficiently breathable to handle the moisture given off by my legs. I much prefer breathable shell pants. I find these warmer, more comfortable and less restrictive in the legs; that is, my legs can move more freely in them.

Still, a pair of waterproof-breathable or vapor-permeable pants might be nice for someone not generating much metabolic warmth, or for someone hiking slowly through a cold and blustery storm.

Head

The head loses a higher percentage of warmth than the rest of the body. So if I begin to feel a chill, I first put on a warming hat. Later, if I begin to feel too warm, I know I need to increase heat radiation so I remove the hat. Thus, I don and doff the hat as needed to regulate warmth. These adjustments are small, but quick and effective.

As described in the "Clothing" chapter, for warm hats I have a thin skull-cap and an insulated bomber hat. During a cold day of hiking I usually wear the skull-cap, saving the bomber hat for the rest stops and camp.

Hands

The hands are especially susceptible to cold, so in cold conditions I wear fleece mittens. And I pull up my hands into my jacket sleeves to protect the hands from wind and wet.

Like a person's head, the hands do more than their

share of radiating heat. This is due mainly to the relatively large surface area of the fingers, and the close proximity of blood vessels to the skin.

If my hands begin to feel sweaty, I remove the mittens temporarily, knowing that my hands will cool quickly. But because the blood circulation in the hands and fingers is not as great, I am careful not to let them become cold. Otherwise they will be very slow in warming; especially as they do not produce much metabolic warmth on

PCT-3

their own. This may call for at least a thin pair of mittens even on moderately chilly days.

Feet

I also keep close tabs on my feet and toes to insure that they are not becoming cold or even numb. For hiking briskly, I usually start with one or two layers of thin socks. If my toes begin to feel cold, I remove the thin socks and put on one pair of medium-weight wool-blend socks. If the temperature continues to drop, I may double up on the wool socks.

Shell fabric

Before each trip Jenny and I make our shell jackets and pants from breathable material. But we choose the material carefully. We like a looser, more breathable weave for hiking on western or eastern trails, and a tighter weave for colder, windier regions.

Clothing for hiking in cold wind

In cold wind, I hold my umbrella so that it shields my upper torso from the icy blasts. I also wear the appropriate layers, as described above. As long as I am producing enough metabolic heat, I am in no danger of hypothermia.

If the wind becomes boisterous, I stow the umbrella and put on my waterproof-breathable jacket over the shirt and shell. The rain jacket helps keep me warm by blocking the wind and by adding a bit of insulation.

Wearing the jacket backwards

Back in the days when I carried a heavy pack, I often found the back of my shirt soaked in sweat. This was also true with that part of the backpack pressed against the shirt. Even on a very cold or windy day, the backpack was over-insulating my back. And yet the front of my torso was sometimes cold, especially in any kind of wind. If I tried wearing the rain jacket to block that wind, my back would sweat all the more.

It did not take me long to come up with a solution: to wear the jacket backwards. I put the jacket in front of me, and ran my arms through the jacket's sleeves, letting the jacket drape in front of my torso and covering my arms and shoulders. This shielded the front of me where I needed the protection, but left the backside open where I did not. My back muscles were already over-insulated by the backpack.

To keep the jacket in place, I could have put it on before shouldering the backpack. The shoulder straps would then have kept the jacket in position. But instead, I shouldered my backpack and then put the jacket on backwards. This provided easier on or off options as the conditions changed. For example, should the day begin to warm, I could remove the backwards-worn parka without having to stop and unharness the backpack. I simply slid the jacket off my arms. For stowage, I folded and draped it over the lower portion of a shoulder-strap, beneath my arm. This easy-on, easy-off feature was particularly useful while hiking in highly viable wind, where the trail weaved in and out of the protection of hills or stands of trees.

In stronger wind, I could pull one arm out of the jacket's sleeve and also out of the pack strap; then put the sleeve back on, and then run the arm back through the pack strap. This would pin this sleeve in place. In strong wind coming from one side, I could do this on the windward side only, leaving the other side of my torso free. Or if the wind was blowing straight at me, I could pin both shoulders in this manner.

The wearing-the-jacket-backwards method has many advantages for better regulating one's body temperature while hiking in cold wind. It works extremely well, and I still use this method when carrying a heavy pack. But while hiking with a typically lighter load, which I carry usually on one shoulder only, I can wear the jacket "frontward." This is because the pack is not pressing against my back, so my back does not sweat nearly as much.

Clothing for resting in cold weather

When a person stops hiking and sits down for a rest in the cold, the body slows down its production of metabolic heat, and the temperature associated with one's microclimate will begin to drop off. Very soon he or she will need to do something about it …

Well before stopping, Jenny and I look for a resting place that is naturally sheltered from the wind. Once we have found a bit of protection, only then do we stop. If the rest break will be more than a few minutes, and if our hiking clothes are damp, we remove them and hang them to air. Then quickly we put on dry garments, such as the thermal shirt and pants, a warm hat, and maybe even an insulated jacket with its hood. In blustery conditions we might also don our waterproof-breathable jackets. If the clouds are without rain or snowfall, and we intend to rest for a while, for example to cook an afternoon meal, we might also remove our shoes and socks and change into dry wool-blend socks. And we could even pull out the quilt for use as a comforter.

The point is, at the rest stops we do not ignore the cold. That is one way people become hypothermic. Should we begin to feel a chill, we either put on more clothing, or we cut short our rest break and resume hiking. Once we get moving again, the exercise will soon re-warm us. And when comfortably re-warmed, we will stop for a moment and change back into our hiking garb, and put our more insulating, rest-stop garments back into their waterproof stowbags.

However, if we have become deeply chilled and cannot re-warm by hiking, we would stop and make camp, and re-warm ourselves under the tarp and quilt.

Dressed for stress

In 2007 we enjoyed two months of climbing in the Andes of Argentina. The weather was usually frigid and windy, and we dressed in much the same type of clothing as we had worn on our South Pole expedition: Lycra shorts, two pairs of thermal underwear, and full-length tight-weave wind shells for each of us. This clothing system had proven fabulously successful in Antarctica, so we were confident that it would work at the high altitudes also. After all, the conditions were much the same – extraordinarily cold and windy.

But what we had not figured into the equation was how much a lack of oxygen at high altitude would decrease our ability to generate metabolic warmth, on which our clothing system depended. At elevations over 18,000 feet we had to climb extremely slowly, as nearly all climbers at those altitudes must, in order to catch our breath. And while moving at such a slow rate, our bodies generated very little metabolic warmth. So at those altitudes, our clothing was insufficient.

What we learned in the Andes actually applies anywhere: the slower you move, the more clothing you will need to wear in order to maintain body warmth.

When we hiked the PCT the third time in thin, lightweight clothing, we were relying on our metabolic warmth to keep us comfortable in the cold. And this system depended on our ability to keep moving at a moderate pace. Same with our hike of the IUA, our sledging on the Greenland ice cap, and so forth. We were not hiking or skiing particularly fast, but certainly not slow either. We were moving at our regular in-shape, comfortable pace, and wearing only lightweight clothing to prevent sweating.

We are not athletes by any means, but for someone less fit and therefore less able to generate metabolic warmth, he or she might be more comfortable wearing more clothing layers.

Eating for warmth

While a person is hiking, his or her muscles "burn" fuel and oxygen. In cold weather, this "combustion" greatly increases one's ability to remain in the comfort zone. But the effect depends on a constant supply of fuel. So the food intake—the fuel—must be ample, nutritious, and high in energy-producing potential. This is especially so in cold weather.

A hiker's high-octane fuel is that which yields the most useable energy and warmth. What kind of food is that? This seems to be matter of conjecture, especially as the science of nutrition appears to suffer from a few antiquated concepts and a great deal of pressure from outside interests. The nutritionists tell us that the energy-producing potential of food is the "calorie." And the way they measure calories in food is simply to burn that food – in a device called a "bomb calorimeter," and measure the heat output. They could do the same with a piece of wood. Wood is loaded with calories (energy potential) but that does not mean we can eat a chunk of wood to boost energy and warmth.

By the same token, just because we can eat high-calorie, sugar-laden junk food does not mean it will provide the most useable energy and warmth.

Of course, most hikers will have their personal meal and snack favorites; and these usually differ greatly among individuals. Bottom line: to each his or her own.

We have found better luck with foods and snacks containing the fewest artificial ingredients and refined sugars, especially in cold weather when we must eat more food.

A hot meal on a cold day is usually most welcome, but we may not want to stop and cook a meal along the way, especially when hiking exposed terrain. When the temperature is frigid and the weather boisterous, we might prefer to cook and eat a hot breakfast at camp before starting out in the morning, and then to snack regularly throughout the day; and finally when arriving at our next camp, to heat water for a hot drink and to cook a well-deserved dinner.

During a cold day's travel, we try to bolt down a snack at least every hour. This might consist of a home-made snack bar, small candies (as opposed to candy bars, which are too much sugar for us), trail mix in varied forms, or other ready-to-eat foods kept handy in our packs.

In very cold conditions we might keep the day's travel relatively short. This ensures maximum hiking energy and therefore the greatest margins of safety.

Another cold weather option is to cook a double-sized breakfast. After eating our fill, we would stow the remainder inside a backpack, still in the cookpot with its lid secured. Insulated with spare clothing, the meal would still be at least somewhat warm by mid-day, at which time it served as the afternoon's supply of energy and metabolic warmth.

Early evening chill on the John Muir Trail

Hydrating for warmth

As discussed in the "Water" chapter, dehydration thickens the blood and reduces its volume. This hampers circulation, which in turn affects the body's ability to transfer the warmth generated by the working muscles to the extremities, and to the body's core where that warmth is vital. Dehydration also slows metabolism, which causes a decrease in energy. And it robs the brain of rational thinking and the ability to make wise decisions.

Cold weather does not reduce one's need for water, yet on a cold day one may not feel like drinking much water. At such times, just the thought of drinking cold water can make one shiver. And what small amounts of cold

A frosty morning in northern Washington, PCT-3

water a person does manage to gulp down, can indeed physically chill the stomach. Fortunately there is a way around this. Unlike in warm weather when the best plan is usually to chug the water in order to ensure an adequate intake, in cold weather we find it best to take frequent but small sips. This allows the body to warm the water gradually, which it will. To facilitate frequent sipping, we each carry a water bottle in a mittened hand, and while hiking we take a sip every few minutes. On a

cold day, this method is particularly effective when we have collected water from an icy cold spring.

Hot drinks such as home-dried soups, hot cocoa, herbal teas and reconstituted milk might be warming, but we do not rely on them for re-hydrating. We sometimes drink them in addition to pure water, but not instead of it. This is because hot drinks are satisfying to the mind more than they are to body. In other words, a hot drink tends to extinguish a person's desire for drinking more water urgently needed by the body.

Camping in cold conditions

On a western trail in cold weather, we try to avoid camping in areas where the trees are stunted or entirely absent. This is often a sign of katabatic pockets – places where frigid air from the mountain heights settles in the evenings. If these environments are too cold to suit the trees, we know they will be less than suitable for our comfortable camping.

If the wind is strong and cold, we try to situate our camps behind natural wind barriers such as rocks, logs, tall brush or trees. However, in such cases we usually avoid camping too close to a tree, due to the danger of it crashing down, or a large branch snapping off.

Once we have chosen a protected site and set up our shelter, we do not squander precious body warmth by fussing with unnecessary camp chores. We will have collected a generous supply of drinking water ahead of time, and we now have it handy for filtering, so that we will not have to leave our warm bed. If the temperature is subfreezing, we place our water bottles under the edge of our foam pads such that in the morning we will find water in those bottles, rather than ice.

Of course we situate our packs next to us, under the

tarp, (or inside a tent) so that we have access to whatever we might need.

For more information about selecting the warmest and most secure campsites, see the "Stealth Camping" chapter.

The Rubicon

Sometimes if the weather is particularly cold and stormy, Jenny and I may decide to remain in camp. But if we choose to set off hiking in such boisterous conditions, we will continually assess our situation, whether we can safely continue ahead, or whether it would be more prudent to leave the trail and descend in order to make a sheltered camp. To minimize any risks, we carefully study our maps ahead of time, so that we know—throughout the day—whether the trail ahead climbs to a more exposed position.

If I had only one rule of wilderness travel, it would be this: Stay alert to the situation and never cross a Rubicon – the point of no return. That rule has saved me a few times on different types of adventures.

When riding thermals high above the earth in a motorless hang glider, I often flew for hours – usually far out of sight of my take-off point. During each flight I had to find and recognize possible landing sites: small fields or clearings of some sort, where I could land without crashing into trees, a fence or power lines. But usually those places were few and far in-between; so I had to be careful not to fly out of range of the last possible clearing without finding the next one. Flying beyond the point of no return would have been extremely dangerous. I started referring to these decision points as "Rubicons."

While hiking on a frigid day, if the cold should begin to stiffen our fingers and hands, we know that we may soon lose our ability to make camp. That point of realization is a Rubicon, beyond which we would be hiking on borrowed time. So if our attempts at warming our extremities are not working, then we know not to continue ahead while merely hoping for the best, but to quickly descend to more sheltered terrain and set up camp.

Every year people develop advanced hypothermia by crossing their Rubicons. They unwisely, and in most cases unknowingly, continue hiking past the point of no return, until losing their ability to make camp.

Hypothermia

The term "hypothermia" comes from "hypo" meaning low, and "therm" meaning heat; and refers to a dangerous reduction in the body's vital core temperature. In his book *Medicine for Mountaineering*, author Dr. James Wilkerson[16] describes the progression of deepening hypothermia in stages, from mild – with shivering, chilliness and loss of dexterity in the fingers, to severe – resulting in unconsciousness and death. And he points out that what makes hypothermia so dangerous is that it impairs a person's ability to detect the condition as it progresses through the stages.

The threat of hypothermia is ever-present in cold weather, yet we hikers can take definitive measures to ensure the upper hand. We do this by staying aware of our microclimate versus the ambient temperature, by wearing sufficient clothing while being careful to not overdress, and by eating nutritious foods and drinking plenty of water – all of which we have discussed.

Also, while hiking in cold weather a person must be careful not to over-exert by carrying too heavy a load, or trying to hike too fast relative to one's level of fitness. These can deplete one's energy, and thus curtail heat production.

Depending on how a person is dressed, over-exerting can also lead to sweating; and I have already described how sweat-soaked clothing becomes far less serviceable.

16 Dr. Wilkerson and I were on the same expedition to climb Peru's Nevado Huascarán in 1969.

In cold weather, the judicious hiker will take all possible measures to minimize sweat. In a frozen landscape, sweat can lead to hypothermia.

And too, a person's physical conditioning governs how much—or how little—metabolic warmth he or she can generate. The out-of-shape hiker will be rather less comfortable in the cold, whether hiking, resting, or sleeping; and more prone to hypothermia. In the "Physical Conditioning" chapter I describe methods of gaining fitness prior to a trek.

The ingestion of certain substances can accelerate the onset of hypothermia. Alcohol or chili peppers (capsi-

Another blustery day, early June in Washington; PCT-3

cums) for example might give the sensation of warmth. And indeed they can warm the extremities slightly, although certainly not enough to prevent frostbite. But rather than create heat, they merely borrow it from the body's core.

Recognizing hypothermia

Hypothermia is such a subtle malady that unless a person knows what to watch for, he or she might not notice its initial effects. So most importantly when hiking with a partner, one should watch him or her for signs of physical or mental sluggishness. These signs might include slow and incoherent speech, uncharacteristic clumsiness, or apathy. You can also test yourself by monitoring the dexterity of your fingers. The method is to extend the fingers straight, then touch each finger tip, one at a time, to the thumb of that hand; and repeat quickly. You can perform this test without removing your mittens.

If your partner is behaving oddly, or if your own fingers are stiffening, this might be a good time to descend to lower, more protected terrain and make a sheltered camp. If your partner is becoming less coherent, or you find that you can no longer touch your index finger to your thumb, then you should stop immediately and build a warming fire, where possible. For this, use your emergency fire-building kit, so that you don't waste precious time and body heat searching for dry kindling. Where you cannot build a fire, you would make camp on the spot. In such a case, you should not be reluctant to pitch your shelter on the trail, or next to it, as long as the place is naturally protected from the wind, and with adequate drainage in the event of rain.

Even if your hiking clothes feel dry, they are probably

at least somewhat damp from hiking, and therefore they can sap warmth if left on. So once inside your shelter, remove the damp garments and change into dry ones. Then crawl into the quilt or sleeping bag and start eating snacks and sipping more water. You might then ignite your stove for a hot beverage and a reviving meal.

If using a tarp in strong wind, remember to pitch it low-lying, with its windward edge flush to the ground, and with its ridgeline perpendicular to the wind. But avoid pitching it so low that it would contact the quilt, because the tarp's condensation could dampen it. Under a tarp, cooking will be easy and convenient. Inside a tent, you will have to reach outside in order to use your stove safely.

———

We were kayaking along the coast of British Columbia in a heavy, penetrating rain. The day was numbingly cold, the wind boisterous, and the seas were rough. We had not rested well the previous night while camped on a pile of logs. And while loading the boat early that morning, a rogue wave had half-filled Jenny's wading boots. She quickly dumped out the cold brine, and put her wet boots back on over her wet socks.

Pressing ahead, I began to notice a lack of enthusiasm in my partner. I asked how she was doing. With a weak voice she admitted to feeling a bit ill. She is not one to complain, but as we paddled for another hour or so, with me frequently asking her how she felt, the fact became increasingly apparent that she was not finding life on the high seas particularly suitable this morning. Cold, wet feet had apparently led to a general decline in her body temperature, and with nausea and a headache she was not paddling hard enough to stay warm. I found a small bight and steered in.

When Jenny climbed ashore, I could see that she was in the initial throes of hypothermia: she stumbled clumsily, and was uncharacteristically slow and listless. So with a quick search I found a cramped cave beneath a tree. Its rock floor

A warming fire thwarts hypothermia; BC coast

was reasonably dry, so we climbed into it, bringing in the stove and the bag of hot drink mixes. I scrounged a bit of dry tinder and struck a small but warming fire. Jenny attempted to ignite the stove, but her hands were too cold to flick the Bic. I leaned over, and with a flaming shard from the fire, lit the stove.

A medium sized cedar had fallen and crashed onto the rocks nearby, splintering into small pieces perfectly suited to our fire. The heat of the growing blaze began to warm Jenny's frigid feet and hands, and soon dried her socks and boots. Within an hour she had regained her warmth, energy and enthusiasm. We restocked our bag of dry tinder and resumed our northward journey.

Snow

> Calvin: Wow, it really snowed last night!
> Isn't it wonderful!
> Hobbes: Everything familiar has disappeared!
> The world looks brand new!
> Calvin: A new year…a fresh clean start!
> Hobbes: It's like a big white sheet of paper to draw on!
> Calvin: A day full of possibilities!
> It's a magical world Hobbes ol' buddy…
> …let's go exploring!
> — *Bill Watterson*

New Worlds of Adventure and Excitement

For many, the thought of hiking in snow brings to mind bitterly cold winds and interminable knee-deep snow trudging with no trail to be found anywhere. In short, something to be avoided.

Yet snow is a part of the Grand Scheme; another facet of nature's many wonders. Hiking across a snow-covered landscape requires appropriate clothing and gear, good route-finding abilities in the absence of trails, and an awareness of when and where the risks lie. It also calls for more pre-hike conditioning, and a determination to face the extra challenges. But with the skills for safe, three-season travel, the snow hiker can experience new worlds of pristine beauty, solitude and unbounded adventure.

———

This chapter does not pertain to wintertime snow travel. Yet snowpack is not a wintertime phenomenon exclusively. In fact, the higher regions of the western states are often snow-laden nine months of the year, while the lower regions of alpine terrain usually harbor snow into late spring and early summer. And as this photograph shows, winter-like storms can happen any time. I took this picture on August 25th at nearly 13,000 feet in Colorado, during our thru-hike of the Continental Divide Trail.

The amount of snowpack at any given place will depend on the region's elevation and latitude, the amount of snow deposited the previous winter, and the springtime melt rate. Hikers have no control over these variables, but they can choose the time of year they plan to visit a region. This choice alone usually determines whether they hike in snow, or on bare trail.

Obviously, to avoid most of the snow, one would

CDT in Colorado, a winter-like storm on the actual continental divide.

Left: A section of the PCT in early season, during our PCT-1. Note the lack of ice axes. I have chopped steps and handholds with a rock, and have carried Jenny's backpack across. Above: That same section in mid summer during our hike of the JMT.

venture into the high mountains only during the summer months: usually from late June to mid September; although with the current climate trends we may see the bare-trail summer hiking season expanding.

A matter of timing

Jenny and I enjoy early-season travel across the whitened landscapes. But we have noted an important difference between the snowpack in early spring and late spring. In early spring, the snow is usually soft, such that one's boots sink in. But as the season progresses, the snowpack begins to consolidate. Before then we will flounder deeply in soft snow. After the snow has compacted, we will walk mostly on its hard surface.

One of our most important snow travel techniques, then, is to wait until the snowpack has coalesced.

We learned this during our first PCT thru-hike, while trudging for 30 days through the soft snow of the High Sierra in the month of May. Then a few years later we traversed the range a second time, but because we were there a month later in the season, we walked on the snow's surface nearly the entire way; and covered the distance in ten days. So our timing determined whether we wallowed or walked.

We have also seen the late-springtime snowpack melt very quickly once the summer sun starts bearing down. In regions where we encountered a great deal of deep snow, other hikers following a few weeks later reported finding the same terrain largely snow-free.

In retrospect, while preparing for that first thru-hike, we felt the need for more time in order to complete our trip, and therefore that an earlier start was justified. But we learned—through a great deal of toil—that a later start date could greatly reduce the effort and shorten the journey's overall time; and thereby improve our chances of success.

No need to camp on snow

Camping on snow requires a thick foam pad—or two of them—as insulation from the cold. However, just because we are hiking in snow does not mean that we have to camp on it.

During our long hiking trips Jenny and I have spent weeks at a time walking on snow or wallowing through it. But not once did we camp on snow. We always managed to find at least a small patch of bare ground on which to pitch our tarp or tent. This has allowed us to carry only a thin foam pad each, saving weight and bulk in our backpacks.

The photo at the beginning of this chapter would seem to contradict this, since it shows our tent in snow. But this was not an example of camping on snow. We pitched the tent on bare ground, and the wintry wonderland developed in the next 24 hours, as deposited by a sudden mid-summer storm. Had we been hiking during that storm, we would have descended out of the snowfall and into the rain, and made camp on snow-free but wet, ground.

In our experience, ground that is covered in snow is far colder to sleep upon than ground that is merely wet. The reason is this: Some of one's body heat leaks down through a thin foam pad. If the underlying ground is merely wet and cold, then the body heat will encourage that ground to absorb the moisture; and

Camped on a small patch of bare ground in the High Sierra; PCT-2.

the ground will then begin to warm. From that point, the ground serves as extra insulation. That is why we can get by with a thin foam pad. However, if the ground is covered with snow, our body heat leaking through the thin foam pad is absorbed by the snow. But rather than melting, the snow stays cold as it attempts to change phase from solid to liquid. So even with only a thin layer of snow beneath us, our beds will stay cold.

In early spring while trekking across the alpine regions, we camped in the intervening lower terrain which was usually snow-free. Or if the weather looked good, we might decide to camp in the high country. And up there we looked for small stands of trees, tall brush, or rocky outcrops that might offer snow-free ground along their south-facing edges. These objects collect the sun, and in turn, radiate heat that often melts the snow around them.

During our training hikes, we sometimes camped on snow. Of course for this we each carried thicker, full-length foam pads. To prepare the campsite we cleared away the bulk of the snow by scraping with our boots or stout sticks.

If the snow was too deep for scraping, we tromped it down as much as possible before spreading our groundsheet. If the snow continued to fall during the night, we used the palms of our hands to softly bang the ceiling of our tarp or tent, to occasionally knock off the accumulating snow. This prevented the weight of the snow from over-stressing the shelter.

High winds and fresh-fallen snow in Colorado on the Continental Divide, during our CDT hike.

Footwear for snow travel

Wintertime snow travel requires specialized footwear, clothing and gear – all beyond the scope of this book. Even so, I have worn many different types of boots and gaiters in winter mountaineering conditions, and I do not recall an instance when I removed them at day's end and found my socks dry.

In late spring or summer the conditions in the contiguous U.S. are fairly mild compared with, say, the Alaska Range, the European Alps, the Andes or Himalayas. As such, Jenny and I do not need to worry about keeping our socks and feet dry. Freezing our feet during the hiking season in Colorado or New Hampshire is unlikely. So, for summertime hiking, rather than trying to keep our feet dry, we think a more important quality in our mountain footwear is mobility. The more easily we can cover the miles in them, the happier we are. And even lightweight boots keep our well-exercised feet at a comfortable temperature.

But while running shoes are well suited for making miles on bare ground, they are wholly out of place on steep, hard snowpack. Lightweight boots with hard edges allow us to kick much better steps for greater security. See the "Footwear" chapter for more details.

Gaiters need only keep the snow out of the tops of the boots. This means they can be short, light-weight, and simple in construction.

For walking on snowpack, our lightweight boots must not fit too tightly. Otherwise they will restrict circulation which might cause the feet to lose their warmth. So for hiking in snow, we buy our footwear slightly oversized. This will also allow for extra socks, and if we find the boots are fitting too loosely, we snug up the laces. However, we know from experience that our feet will not swell in the cold nearly as much as they will in hot climates. So we do not buy the lightweight snow boots too large.

Existing snowpack in fine weather

On a sunny day when Jenny and I are crunching our way across a snowy late-spring landscape, we must protect our skin from the sun's ultraviolet radiation. In fact, this is true whether the skies are blue or cloudy because much of the UV penetrates the clouds. And the snowbound alpine terrain—in all its white, featureless splendor—acts as a giant mirror, reflecting the UV powerfully. With radiation coming at us from all angles and directions, it can be very burning, particularly in the mountains of the western U.S. where the higher elevations and dry air offer less atmospheric protection from solar energy. At eleven thousand feet, for example, the sun is four times as intense than at sea level.

Protected from the glaring sun at high altitude. PCT-2

When tromping across the unbroken landscape of whiteness, we need to cover virtually every square inch of our skin. Using an umbrella or a hat is not enough, because of the powerful reflection coming from below. So we each cover our faces with a bandana, and wear dark glasses to shield the eyes. As a further precaution,

we apply a high-SPF sunscreen to the lips, ears, nose, and to any other exposed skin. While we are at it, we apply the sunscreen to the insides of the nostrils a ways. And whenever possible we keep our mouths closed to prevent a painful sunburn to the roof of the mouth.

In fine weather we usually hike in cool and airy short-sleeve shirts. But for snowpack we sometimes carry a pair of long sleeves each, cut from old button-up shirts. We simply attach these to our short sleeve shirts with small safety pins. Then after descending out of the snow, off come the long sleeves. These sleeves work well for desert travel also.

Protective clothing for snow travel

In snow flurries we use our umbrellas as portable shelters. These keep the snow off our heads and upper body, and shield our faces and eyeglasses. And they cover most of our small backpacks as well. The umbrellas are also useful at rest stops and meal breaks. But if a strong wind begins driving the snow sideways, then we might need to stow the umbrellas in favor of waterproof-breathable jackets.

Our bomber hats keep our heads nicely warm, and if they have a waterproof-breathable outer covering they will tend to shed the snowfall. We find this type of hat much less restrictive than the hood of a rain jacket or insulated jacket.

See the preceding "Cold" chapter for a description of our cold weather hiking attire.

Special equipment

Winter mountaineers typically carry skis, crampons, climbing rope and other technical gear intended to facilitate and safeguard their adventures. And generally they know how to use that gear to best advantage. In terms of three-season trekking, hikers rarely, if ever, need any of these items. For details, refer back to the related information in the "Remaining Equipment" chapter.

Even so, I consider an ice axe essential for everyone who ventures into snowy terrain.

The essential ice axe

One might imagine that since a trail is mostly free of snow, it can be traveled safely without an ice axe. The fact is, whether the previous winter's snowfall was massive or minimal, the snow hazards of early season highland travel (in spring and early summer) are about the same. The main concerns are not the expansive, deep snowfields, but the lingering patches and ribbons of sometimes hard and slippery snow lying across a trail – in places where the trail traverses steep slopes. Owing to the steepness of these slopes, these patches can be difficult and even dangerous to circumvent by climbing or descending around. And due to the often compact and slippery nature of the icy patches, especially in the early mornings before the sun has softened them, they can be extremely risky to set foot upon without a safeguarding ice axe.

Granted, many hikers of various levels of experience have crossed snowy terrain without ice axes. And most of these people have met with good luck. But some have slipped and sustained serious injuries.

Learning the technique

Should a hiker accidentally slip on steep and frozen snow, he or she would dig the pick of the ice axe into the snow to stop from sliding down into any rocks or trees below. This procedure is known as the "self-arrest." It is not difficult to learn, particularly under the guidance of a qualified

In early season, the trail harbors lingering, steep snow; PCT-3

instructor. And once learned, this skill will stay with the person for life.

To locate various schools, search the internet or check with your local mountaineering shops. Those who live in mountainous regions might check with any nearby colleges to see if they offer winter mountaineering classes.

Anatomy of an ice axe

Pick
Adze
Shaft
Point

The pointed end of the shaft is called the point, or spike. The top end is called the head. At one end of the head is the long and narrow blade called the pick, used for self-arrest. To help remember, think of a gold miner's pick and pan. Also on the head but opposite the pick is the spoon-shaped, step-chopping blade called the adze (pronounced "adds"). The adze need not be razor sharp; using it for digging daily cat holes in soft earth does not degrade its ability to chop steps in hard, steep snowpack. In fact, the sharper it is, the more it will tend to get stuck in hard-frozen snow while chopping steps.

The self-arrest described

The photo shows Jenny in the self-arrest position. She demonstrates on a concrete slab so that the pick of the axe is not buried in the snow, obscuring the important

nuances of the position. Note that the body does not lie on the surface, nor do the knees. Rather, these are held up off the surface in order to exert maximum plowing pressure on the pick of the axe and the toes. Note also that the feet are spread apart somewhat. These three points of contact—the two feet and the pick—form a triangle that provides the optimum stability. The strongest hand grips the head of the axe, with the fingers wrapping over the top. The other hand grasps the shaft near the spike, stabilizing the shaft while holding the spike off the snow.

The grip

The head of the axe is held close to the body for a secure grip, but safely away from the face. The greatest hazard when learning to self-arrest is that of dropping down onto the slope in the self-arrest position but allowing the adze to gouge one's face. So before dropping down onto

a slope, one must hold the axe firmly in the self-arrest position and focus on one thought: keeping the adze away from the face. On a steep slope, one grasps the head of the axe very tightly, to prevent it from being pulled out of one's grip as one slides down the slope. This means holding it fairly close to the shoulder and head.

One can practice the self-arrest position in the backyard. Not by dropping down onto the ground as though it were snow, but simply by lying in place. Think about bracing your body off the ground, about spreading the feet, and about holding the adze away from the face. Once you get the position right, commit it to memory. Then review it in your mind once in a while.

Actual practice

Lying in the backyard, face down in the self-arrest position, a person will learn a great deal about the proper stance and grip. But one must also practice on a snow slope in order to coordinate the aggressive movements of jamming the pick into the snow safely. However, one should be extremely careful to choose a soft and gentle practice slope that offers a safe and gradual run-out. The slope must be very forgiving of any mistakes.

Once again, remember to keep a tight grip on the axe, and to keep the adze away from the face. With each practice fall, concentrate mainly on the adze.

A person new to the game should hold the head of the axe always with the strongest arm. A right-handed person would grasp the head in the right hand, and vice versa if left-handed. Should a sudden slip occur, this person might not have time to think about which hand belongs where. The action must be reflexive. So a good plan for a beginner is to hold the axe the same way every time, resisting the tendency to switch hands when facing the other way on a slope. Then once this person has become well practiced, he or she can safely switch hands when changing directions; making for the most secure ascent.

Head-up

In the event of a slip, a person would likely land on the knees or stomach. This is also the most favorable position for a speedy self-arrest. Should you land on your backside, roll over onto the stomach – but only in the direction away from the spike, to prevent the spike from catching the snow. Thus, right-handed people would roll to the right. Practice the roll to become familiar with it.

Head-down

Should a person slip and land head downhill, he or she would need to know the appropriate maneuver. Practice on a very gentle slope by laying in the self-arrest position, face down as before, but with your head downhill and your feet uphill. Digging the pick in gently, but well off to one side, will swivel you around.

Also you might rehearse the head-downhill maneuver when lying on your back. Start by facing the slope; then stoop down and slowly fall backwards. Now you are head-down on your back. Start the slide, then quickly reach out to the side with the pick and grab the snow with it. This will swing you around, at which time you would then roll over onto the stomach.

As a precaution, do not let a friend or even an instructor send you head down on a steep slope without first practicing this on a gentle slope. For more information, refer to a book on winter mountaineering skills.

The hiker's ice axe

My hiking axe is curved along the head only moderately from adze to pick. It does not have a drop point head, such as the tools used for ice climbing. Self-arrest axes are usually available in steel, lightweight alloys, or some combination. I prefer a type with at least some steel in the pick, because the steel provides far greater stopping power on hard snow. My hiking axe has a straight shaft, not a curved one, and its shaft is about 21 inches in length, with a head of around 9 inches long. This is generally a good all-around size for most hikers, large or small. A smaller, shorter axe would save weight, but in my experience it would not be nearly as effective at stopping a slide.

Axe secured to the backpack

While hiking, I carry my ice axe on the outside of my backpack in such a way that the axe will not snag overhead branches, or inflict injury in the event of an accidental slip – for example while rock-hopping across a creek. I stow my axe vertically, and centered on the pack at the point farthest from my body. To secure the axe, I sew special straps to the backpack to hold each end of the shaft, top and bottom.

Axe in the hand

However, if there is any chance of slipping on snow, I carry my ice axe in my hand, with its pick pointing away from me to avoid injury in the event of an otherwise uneventful slip. When climbing a steeper slope, a beginner might be safer holding the axe in the self-arrest position, rather than plunging the shaft into the snow with each step.

Lanyard

I also fit my axe with a lanyard (cord or thin webbing) about three feet in finished length. One end is permanently secured to the head of the axe. The other end is tied in a loop just big enough to fit around my wrist. The lanyard prevents the loss of the axe should I accidentally drop it, or reflexively toss it away during a sudden slip. (When winter mountaineering, I use a longer lanyard attached to my harness so that I can easily switch hands.)

Climbing a snow slope

Walking on compact or frozen snow is not much more difficult than hiking on bare ground. At least on level or moderately sloped terrain. This type of snow contains irregularities and grit, so it is not ice-rink slippery, and can be negotiated without a great deal of slipping and sliding. Even so, footwear with a deeper waffle pattern tread will give better traction.

Edging

As the snowfield leads more steeply uphill, we reach a point where we must rely less on the waffle-tread of our boots for traction, and more on their edges. In this case, we climb the snow with the bottom of the soles horizontal, rather than parallel to the slope. This presents the edges of the boots to the snow where they can more effectively bite in.

Picture yourself on a pair of metal-edged skis. If you place the bottom of the skis flat against the slope, you will start sliding, and will quickly build up speed. That is not what we want in this case. But using the edges of the skis to bite in will provide the best grip and prevent you from sliding. This is called "setting the edges."

Stomping

The technique is much the same with boots. And for an even better bite, we would not just set the edges of our boots on the slope, but stomp the edges in aggressively, making small footholds. If the snow is so hard that it resists, we kick repeatedly until we can make an adequate step.

Chopping steps

As mentioned earlier, the adze of the ice axe can be used to chop steps. I can chop a series of steps straight across a slope, as in a traverse, or diagonally up it. However, I do not chop steps in snow that is frozen so hard that even the most vigorous kicking fails to produce a usable toe-hold. Snow this solid is often found in the early mornings of late spring. In such a case, I stay off of it, ice axe or no.

If a person slips on rock hard snow, he or she might find self-arresting difficult. But even if the person were to stop the slide with the ice axe, he or she might not be able to stand back up. This is because while lying in the self-arrest position, one might not be able to kick adequate steps into rock-hard frozen snow. And in such a position, one could not release the axe from the self-arrest position in order to chop steps, without risking a fall. Short

Ready for self-arrest. PCT-2

of a rescue from one's partner,[17] only the most violent kicking might save the person. Or, if he or she can see safety below, then the person might be able to descend in a slow, controlled slide, using the ice axe as a brake.

However, a far more prudent idea would be to avoid stepping on rock-hard snow to begin with. One might be able to traverse around it, where safe and practical, or wait until it softens, which it probably will as the day warms.

Only if I can kick at least barely adequate steps with the boots do I even consider chopping larger, more secure steps with the ice axe. Safety aside, chopping steps can also be extremely slow and laborious, due to the need to make the steps large enough to stand on with comfort and security.

Descending a snow slope

The snowpack's conditions on either side of a high mountain pass can be as different as day and night. Say I am climbing the south, sunny side in the early morning, have reached the crest, and at last am gazing down at the north slope. I know, by experience, that this shaded slope could be frozen rock-hard. Nor am I fooled by deeply imprinted boot tracks leading down. The hikers who made those tracks obviously descended in the late afternoon, when the snow was soft. So I test the slope by taking a few cautious steps, prodding ahead with the axe. If the snow is too hard to kick adequate steps, I am not tempted to chop steps with my ice axe. Trying to work below the level of one's feet is awkward, and could result in loss of balance. Instead, I would return to the ridge and enjoy a lengthy rest, allowing the snow to soften. Otherwise, if the slope is already sufficiently soft, then I proceed on down with caution, while assessing any avalanche hazard.

---

17 See the story "Early one morning" in the Climbing Rope section of Remaining Equipment.

Sledding

Wilderness snow slopes are not groomed ski resort bunny hills. Very often they are pockmarked with invisible soft spots or rocks that may not be visible from above. Do not be tempted to slide down such a slope.

Even more dangerous and foolhardy would be for a person to sit on a groundsheet and zip on down as though gleefully riding a sled. In a flash, this person could find himself or herself traveling at breakneck speed, while completely out of control. Any rocks or trees encountered along the way could be killers. And if the area is remote, a rescue party might be slow in coming.

Glissading

Sliding while seated on the snow, and using the spike of one's axe as a brake, is called "glissading." I consider this technique too risky, unless I have first climbed that slope and come to know its idiosyncrasies and condition. As with any other kind of slide, glissading affords very little directional control. And it soaks the seat of one's pants, a consideration in stormy weather.

Boot skiing

If the slope is not very hard or steep, rather than slide, Jenny and I like to "boot ski." The method here is to use one's boots like skis, and head on down while carving a few turns. This often works well because we can keep our speed to a safe minimum while steering clear of any holes or rocks. One should never try this on hard snow, or build up any real speed even on soft snow. Should a foot suddenly break through the crust, the leg could jam into a hole between underlying rocks, and the body's forward momentum could snap the leg like a matchstick. So keep the speed moderate.

The plunge step

The safest descent of a moderately steep but soft snow slope—again, one that is not frozen—is with the "plunge

287

step." As we take each step, we lock the knee and let the body weight pile-drive the heel down into the snow. This creates a solid and secure platform for the foot; one that will hold one's weight securely. Exercising caution, we proceed slowly and make each plunge step deliberate and forceful. And as with boot skiing, we hold our ice axes at the ready, so that if we lose balance we can quickly assume the self-arrest position.

Avalanche!

When the high peaks are deeply snowbound, avalanches can pose genuine dangers to the backcountry traveler. To increase our margins, we have learned to recognize the conditions of greatest peril, and avoid the danger zones. Unfortunately, our chosen trail may lead straight through avalanche-prone regions. For this reason we never follow a snowbound trail inattentively. When the route ahead appears unsafe, we turn back and find a safer line of travel. This may require descending to lower terrain and hiking many additional miles. But in our view, no journey is worth the risk of tangling with an avalanche.

After coalescence (see below) the avalanche hazards are greatly reduced. But earlier in the season when the snow is still soft, a person must be extremely careful.

Danger clues

If we are hiking above tree-line on snowbound terrain, we avoid cutting across any steep slopes, or even hiking beneath them.

Many times a trail will switchback up a steep slope, to gain a high ridge or pass. The trail that crosses Glen Pass in the Sierras is one example. Not only can such a trail be difficult to locate when buried deeply in snow, but the steep snowpack itself can present an avalanche hazard when the snow is soft. There is no safe way to climb or descend such a slope. Dozens of skiers and winter mountaineers perish each year in avalanches on steep slopes.

The European Alps alone claim more than 200 lives a year.

Check consistency

Snow slopes frequently offer clues as to their avalanche "disposition." The steeper a slope, the more gravity tugs at its snow, so the more likely it will cut loose. Also, a winter's snowpack is like a multi-layer cake, with each layer consisting of the snow deposited by a particular storm. And because each storm varies in moisture content, duration, and ambient temperature, so is the snow it deposits. The greatest avalanche danger occurs on a steeply inclined slope where a heavier layer of snow rests upon a lighter and less cohesive one.

Before starting any ascent, examine the slope carefully to determine the best route. You might climb along one edge, keeping away from the likely path of any avalanches. Then part way up, check the slope's consistency by carefully digging a slot a couple of feet deep with the ice axe, and examining the layers. If you find all layers compact, then the slope is less likely to slide. But if you find an icy layer, or a layer that lacks cohesion (called "corn snow" because the flakes have metamorphosed individually without bonding together) then however thick or thin that layer might be, do not proceed. Even your body weight could trigger the slope into motion.

Swim for the surface

The unfortunate hiker caught in an avalanche should quickly shrug off the backpack, roll over onto the back, and "swim" frantically and continually for the surface. When avalanche alluvium comes to a stop, it tends to set up like concrete. A friend of mine was once overtaken by a small avalanche that buried his head and one shoulder only; the rest of him remained above the surface. Yet he could not struggle free. After his buddies had dug him out, they had to administer artificial respiration.

Those hikers wishing to test their mettle in very early season would do well to study a few books on avalanche safety, and to carry transponders and probes. But of course the best way to avoid avalanche hazard is to plan the hike for summertime.

Brain lock

Another danger of snow travel is a phenomenon I call "brain lock." Remember the cartoons of the coyote forever chasing the road runner? Road Runner zooms off a cliff into space—for after all, Road Runner is a bird—and Wile E. Coyote unthinkingly pursues. Suddenly realizing that something is dreadfully amiss, the coyote stops. Suspended in mid-air, he ponders the enormity of the situation for a few moments before giving the audience that look of resignation. Then he plummets.

The coyote's reaction is not so far removed from our own tendencies. Despite the actual circumstances, the hiker on a steep snow slope will not drop until his brain tells him that he must.

I was leading a group of students across a snowfield in which our boots were barely imprinting. I was so accustomed to walking on steep snow that I could easily secure myself when needed by stomping the edges of my boots aggressively into the snow. The slope gradually steepened, but we were doing fine until one fellow piped up, "Hey, this is really steep!" Suddenly five of them went down like bowling pins, and slid a few dozen feet to the bottom of the snowbank. Fortunately none of them landed hard enough to sustain any injuries. The others held their mental timbers tight, and together we safely traversed off the slope.

This is an example of brain lock. I have witnessed it many times, and have noticed that once it happens, the effect is difficult to reverse. The situation must resolve itself for better or worse. Brain lock is the result of irrepressible fear leading to panic. It is a natural mechanism designed to relieve one of having to deal with a frightful situation. Yet the consequences of not dealing with it can be fatal.

A situation saved

I was cruising solo near the Continental Divide in the Colorado Rockies, planning to meet with students farther along. I came to a snow slope and found it in excellent condition, so I began to boot ski on down. As the slope steepened, I happened upon a most unexpected scene. Someone was lying in the middle of the slope, clinched in the self-arrest position. Three others were seated off to one side in the talus fifty feet away. These others were afraid to risk their own lives to help the person in desperate trouble, even though all of them had ice axes and

With the cliff dropping away for hundreds of feet, this would have been a good place for an ice axe, had I been carrying one; PCT-1.

wore stout mountaineering boots. I boot-skied down the slope to help, and found this person brain locked. Never mind that I did not have an ice axe myself. My point here is that her brain lock was caused by the possibility of her plummeting down the steep slope, not by any certainty of doing so. Had she given up the fight, her slide could have been fatal. But once I had her safely in my grasp, the possibility of her slipping disappeared, and the situation resolved itself. Her brain unlocked, and together we traversed across the slope to join her friends. Had she kept her cool from the beginning, she could have walked off the slope by herself.

Preventing brain lock

How do we anticipate brain lock, and how do we prevent it?

Early one mid-August morning during our second PCT hike, Jenny and I were descending Fire Creek Pass on the slopes of Glacier Peak, not too far from the Canadian border. A hundred miles earlier I had consigned my trail-ragged shoes to a trash bin, and to avoid a hitchhike out to buy a new pair, I had appropriated Jenny's spare shoes. These were three sizes too small for my feet, but since we had only a few hundred miles remaining, I had slit those shoes in all manner of ways, and managed to enlarge them just enough to walk in.

Part way down from the pass we came upon a steep, frozen slope that dropped away far below. This slope was inconvenient to circumvent, as often they are. So, exuding confidence despite our lack of ice axes, I led across and Jenny followed. But the farther we traversed, the harder became the snow's surface. Yet my shoes were so tight that the uppers bulged far over both sides of the soles, and rendered the soles practically useless for edging. To hack each minuscule step, I slashed repeatedly with the blunt shoes, and in retrospect I probably could have done better wearing roller skates. A few dozen feet from the

I'm wearing Jenny's spare shoes. To get my feet in them, I have split the shoes along both sides, the top of the forefoot, and the back of the heel. I am wearing the tops half of the socks to protect my ankles somewhat from mosquitoes.

far side, I judged the ever-steepening slope too dangerous to proceed. Feeling a brain lock hovering menacingly overhead, I clinched my resolve and very calmly, matter-of-factly, told Jenny that we were, ho hum, turning around. Unaware of how insecure my footing was, she easily walked back across our small footholds.

I prevented brain lock in myself by keeping a level head. And I prevented it in Jenny by projecting calmness and confidence. We circumvented the snow slope by climbing around it, and I went away with an increased distrust of those shoes, and a resolve to carry ice axes next time.

Should you find yourself in dire straits, realize that the dangers may lie primarily in your own mind. Use foresight to keep yourself out of trouble, and clear, prudent thinking to get yourself out of trouble when you do get into it. Remember too that where the mind leads, the body follows. Keep your mind off what could happen, and focus instead on a positive outcome.

Differing types of snow

To the casual observer, both soft snow and hard snow look about the same. Yet despite similarities in appearance, the differences in texture can be profound. And to mistake one for the other could be fatal. Stepping out onto a patch of steeply-inclined snow—thinking that it is soft—could be a serious miscalculation. That snow could be as hard as an ice-skating rink and very slippery.

I remember a ranger telling us a story of a family of five driving up into the mountains of southern California to beat the heat. At a lookout they all got out of their car and jumped with glee into the apparently soft snow. But in actual fact that snow was frozen; and they all slid to their deaths in the trees below. This happens frequently, the ranger said, never mind the warning signs.

I have been hiking and climbing on snow for decades, in all sorts of snow conditions, and still I cannot judge with accuracy whether a patch of snow is soft or hard just by looking at it. I have to physically test it in some manner. If we are hiking a bare trail that traverses a steep slope, and come to a patch of snow covering the trail, I do not test it by simply walking out on it. This could prove disastrous. Instead, I probe with my ice axe or by kicking at it, with one foot on solid ground. Also, I know that snowpack is softest around its margins; invariably it is more compact and slippery farther from the edges. So even though my initial few steps feel secure, that is no assurance of the snow's condition farther along. This would be a good place to have an ice axe in hand before starting across, held in the self-arrest position just in case.

The coalescing snowpack

Winter and early spring snowfall in the high mountains is usually soft and fluffy, depending on ambient temperatures. Traveling on powder snow requires the use of skis on steep terrain, or snowshoes where it is less steep.

Otherwise, the boots alone would sink in too deeply with each step. But with the passing of weeks, the snowpack will begin to coalesce – from the surface down. And as it does, it begins to support the hiker's weight better. Meaning that the feet do not sink in quite so deeply. As late spring approaches, the warmth of the daytime sun accelerates the melting of the upper layers. And when the nighttime temperature plummets, those upper layers freeze. Generally, the clearer the sky at night,

The snowpack has consolidated and we are making miles of barely indented tracks on the PCT-2.

A fine day in the high country, early summer on the IUA

on consolidated snow that is twenty five feet deep is no different than walking on consolidated snow that is five feet deep. What does matter is the snow's condition – and that, once again, is a matter of timing.

Plying the transition zones

Snowpack melts in three ways. On the surface it sublimates, meaning that it simply evaporates directly from the solid state. Sometimes on a crisp morning we see the snowfields steaming. This is the vapor of sublimation condensing into visible form. Snowpack also melts on the surface from the heat of the sun and the sun-warmed air. A person might not actually see puddles of water on the surface because the underlying snow absorbs them. And thirdly, snowpack melts from the heat of the underlying earth, rocks and vegetation. It is this latter type of melt that most concerns us here.

As a late spring snowfield is melting—with imperceptible slowness—it becomes less deep. Nevertheless it remains structurally intact, able to bear a person's weight. However, all around the snowfield's edges it typically becomes slushy, or "rotten" as it is commonly referred to. This slushy snow is not much different in appearance, but it will not bear a person's weight.

I refer to this rotten, fast-melting snow as "transition snow." It is soon to vanish, and for the hiker descending from the mountain heights it is the transition between relatively solid snow and bare ground. Transition snow occurs mainly near a snowfield's lower boundaries. Depending on the depth of snowpack and slope of the

the harder the freeze, since a clear sky allows the most heat loss through radiation. The problem for the early-season hiker is that this upper layer of coalescing snow might not yet be thick enough to support body weight. So when taking each step, most of the weight is applied, and then suddenly the foot will break through the crust and drop deeply into the soft underlying layers. This is called "postholing" and it can be exhausting. One is forever climbing out of holes, and immediately falling back into new ones.

As the weeks pass and the snowpack coalesces further, it will support more of a hiker's weight, until finally it is becomes so compact that it will barely indent. Yet even this compact snow will conceal soft spots. So while walking on its surface, one should be careful of each step, particularly while hiking steeply downhill.

In light of this coalescing process, it is obvious that the snow conditions we encounter are not a matter of chance, but of timing. Much too early in the season and we will flounder deeply. A few weeks later this snowfield will have a crusty surface and we will posthole laboriously. A few weeks later still, and we will walk easily on its surface. Moreover, the snow's depth is of little concern. Walking ground, the transition zones can be from one to several hundred feet in width, as measured from the margin toward the middle of the snowfield.

But not all of the snow in the transition zones is rotten. And once a hiker has learned to read the clues, he or she will travel across snowpack far more quickly and easily, simply by avoiding the soft spots.

How to read the snow

The following clues apply only to the coalescing snowpack typical of late June and early July, mainly in the highlands of the western states. It does not apply to winter and early spring conditions when the transition zones are minimal, or to blankets of fresh autumn snow when the transition zones are entirely absent.

▶ In meadows and open areas that are gradually sloped, the transition zones can be hundreds of yards wide. As I make my way through these areas, I pick a line that keeps the farthest from rocks and trees, and I try to pass uphill of them. These objects absorb more of the sun's heat, and conduct it beneath the snow's surface. This sub-surface heat slowly melts the surrounding snow. The resulting moisture flows imperceptibly downhill, not near the ground as one might expect, but as a horizontal effusion throughout. This horizontal effusion saturates and weakens the adjacent snowpack. To step onto this weakened snow is to posthole suddenly into it. I recognize it in two ways: by what objects are uphill of it, and by the subtle sagging or depression in the snow's surface, running downhill from the object causing it.

▶ In any type of snow, I avoid the margins around protruding, or noticeable underlying rocks. Not only do rocks absorb heat and melt the surrounding snow, as mentioned above, but they also radiate heat, even when deeply buried, and melt the snow surrounding them. The resulting void, often covered, is known as a moat. Generally, the larger the rock, the more cavernous its moat.

Those who have not inadvertently fallen waist deep into hidden moats at least ten times have not yet qualified for the cosmos-is-avenging-me merit badge. Those who have seen gaping moats as large as dump trucks might not care to try for this badge. Either way, it's usually best to stay away from underlying rocks.

▶ Finally, as I descend a snowfield and am about to reach its lower margin, I watch for subtle lines indicating the boundaries of the transition zone. The rotten snow is often a little more crystalline in appearance, and sometimes slightly more yellow. If I step only a few inches to one side of a crystalline margin, (and to one side of someone's posthole) I will probably avoid sinking in.

Into the clouds; PCT-3

No matter how assiduously I adhere to these recommendations, I might still find myself wallowing and postholing a fair amount. Faced with acres of unavoidable, rotten and thigh-deep snow, it is time to change gears. I disconnect from the urge for forward progress,

Searching for the trail on the PCT-3.

slow down, and concentrate on my heart rate. I think of this soft snowfield as a steep hill. If hikers feel that they are clawing ahead at a mere snail's pace, then they know that they are struggling with their own impatience. Using brute force will deplete a person. Instead, I proceed thoughtfully and in control, striving for the proper balance of heart rate, pace and mental serenity. Once I have found that balance, I will cruise ahead with far less effort.

Following a snowbound trail

When alpine trails are snowbound in early or late season, they can be difficult to follow. This is particularly true where they are not blazed at regular intervals. A GPS receiver coupled with a microchip containing the trail's coordinates can pinpoint a hiker's location and specify where to look for the trail. But I prefer to rely on a few trail-sleuthing techniques.

Map and time of day

At the start of each day I study our maps. By examining the topographical features I know what landmarks and features to look for. At each of these features, I note our location on the map, and check my wristwatch for the time of day. This is for the purposes of dead reckoning.[18] And most importantly, I study the map's line of the trail, noting the general location of any switchbacks. It is the switchbacks that cause the greatest route finding difficulties. At one of these, the trail suddenly changes direction, often without any indication above the snow's surface. And since we cannot see the trail buried beneath the snow, we certainly cannot see where it switchbacks. Beyond the switchback we will be heading one way and the trail the other.

Tree corridors

A trail does not lead directly through a tree. Therefore, where we see a tree, we know the trail is not there. Conversely, where we see no tree, the trail might be there. And developing this logic: where we see a line of no trees in an area of otherwise thick forest, the trail is probably there.

18 Described in the Compass section of the "Remaining Equipment" chapter.

The trail builders likely felled that line of trees. In areas of dense timber, these treeless corridors are common, and they are the best clues. However, in areas of large trees, the trail builders usually route the trail around each one, leaving no evident corridor.

Even where corridors are lacking, the trail crew might have left other clues.

Tree branch stubs

During our third PCT hike, we traveled a deeply snow-bound trail much of the way through Washington. I reckon we navigated about 60% by snipped tree branch stubs. One does not see these much while hiking a bare trail because one does not need to see them. On our south-bound hike we needed to see them, since often they were the only part of the trail there was to see. When hiking through the forest with no hint of a trail, and when finding a tree that had only a stub of a snipped branch with a clean edge that appeared to have been cut with a saw or nippers, we knew that we had almost certainly found the trail.

Sawn logs

A log protruding from the snow that has one end cleanly sawn off is sometimes an indication of the trail, and sometimes not. When the trail crews saw off an offending log, they discard the part blocking the trail possibly by giving it a shove that sends it rolling down the slope. Or they might carry it a ways into the forest, out of sight of the trail, nice and tidy like. And there we may find it, protruding above an ocean of snow. We have not necessarily found the trail, but we are probably somewhere near the trail.

Shovel cuts

In addition to snipped branch stubs, Jenny and I navigated about 20% of the way by shovel cuts. We look for these on steeper terrain, in the vicinity of large trees.

Each large tree normally has a snow-free moat around it, melted away by the tree's relative warmth. Very often where the trail comes close to a tree on steeper ground, the trail crew's shovel cut will lie close enough to the tree to be visible in the tree's moat. The shovel cut will not look like fresh-cut dirt. But it will look like dirt. Exposed dirt is rare in timbered country, especially near trees. If we find even a little, the chances are, it was shovel-cut.

South-facing slopes

Following a snowbound trail is much easier while hiking in a northerly direction. As we scan the terrain ahead, we are looking at south-facing slopes. These slopes are exposed to the sun's warmth, and are far less snowbound than their north-facing counterparts. By continually looking ahead, we can often locate at least a small line or piece of the trail on a patch of snow-free, south-facing ground. As we climb over a rise and start down the other (north-facing) side, the trail may again disappear beneath unending snow, but by looking far ahead we may see at least another piece of it leading up the next south-facing slope.

On the other hand, if we are traveling southbound, and looking ahead at north-facing slopes, as we were that year in Washington, we need to look for other clues.

Straight lines

One such clue is a faint but straight line, like a depression in the snow, leading across a snow slope. Jenny and I navigated about 10% of the time by studying the terrain far ahead for these faint lines. Straight lines leading across slopes are unnatural. Each time we saw one, we memorized where it started and where it went. Even though apparent from quite a distance, these lines are rarely visible at close range. So rather than search for the trail at our feet, we searched for it well ahead.

The remaining 10% of our navigating was a combination of map study and logical assessment, familiarity with

Large backpacks in the High Sierra on the PCT-2

Hidden lakes and creeks

Lakes, ponds and tarns can be dangerous to cross when covered with snow. A person has no way of accurately judging the solidity of the underlying ice. And should he or she break through an invisible soft spot in the snow, and plunge into the frigid water, and if that water is deep, then the person might not be able to extricate him or herself. Rather than shortcut across, it is usually much safer to circumvent any snow covered bodies of water.

Creeks are a different matter, at least the small and shallow ones. In the early season they are often bridged with compact snow that one can safely walk across. But again, it depends on the depth of the water. If one breaks through and lands in water only ankle deep, then what one gets is wet feet. But if the water is over-the-head deep and running swiftly, then the risks could be considerable. As a general rule when crossing snow bridges, we listen for the creek's muffled gurgling at our feet. If we hear it, we turn back immediately. The noise means that the snow bridge is thin at that spot. Otherwise, if it looks and sounds safe enough, we unbuckle our pack's hip belts, if any, so that we can shed our packs quickly if necessary.

Autumn snow travel

So far in this chapter we have considered snowpack that has spent the winter consolidating, and which we encounter in spring or early summer. Now let's say that the summer has passed, and that we find ourselves hiking the high country in late season. So late, in fact,

the trail and relying on memory, and a bit of guesswork thrown in for good measure.

Stay with the trail

Where the land is covered in tall but patchy snowdrifts, we find it best to resist the temptation to walk around those drifts. We might save energy, but we can easily become disoriented as to the trail's directional trend. Instead we follow the trail's general trend up and over every snowbank and drift. If they are five or ten feet tall, then so much the better to see that much farther ahead.

When trying to follow a snowbound trail through dense forest, we do not strike out cross-country unless we know exactly where we are, and where we are going. In an area of "where-is-the-trail" perplexity, we have only so much trail-searching time in one day, and this time is best spent near the trail rather than far from it. So if we lose the trail, we will search the area repeatedly, always returning to our last known point, until eventually finding the snowbound trail a short ways further on. In dense timber, the trail will lead us to our destination in the easiest and usually the most expedient manner. So we stay with it.

that pre-winter storms are starting to play over the landscape. These storms are well known for bringing sudden and severe conditions, with heavy snowfall, strong winds and freezing temperatures. As such, they call for extra clothing, including wool-blend socks, more layers of warm shirts and pants, an insulating jacket and of course a rain jacket. If the storms persist and the route ahead begins to look intimidating, a hiker might consider descending out of the high country. Remember that in late season, should a major snowstorm catch a person at a higher elevation, the situation could be extra challenging. This is because the new-fallen snow will not bear a person's weight, since it has not coalesced. And if it is

deeper than what a person can wallow through, then it can fairly immobilize the person, unless he or she is carrying snowshoes. So in the event of a major snowstorm, it is usually better to descend out of it, rather than make camp and wait it out.

On our third PCT hike, we made this comfortable camp on the flanks of Glacier Peak. This was on a small patch of bare ground amid miles of snowpack, in the small grove of trees shown at lower left.

Part 7

TRAIL BIOLOGY

PCT-2

Trail Life

Mosquitoes and Insects

"A man thinks he amounts to a great deal;
but to a mosquito,
he is merely something good to eat."
— *Don Marquis*

Guardians of the wilds

Venturing into the wilderness, we seek the richness of the landscape, the peace it affords, and the life it sustains. Well, maybe not all life, since hoards of mosquitoes, blackflies, or no-see-ums can be discouraging. But like the rain and snow, the wind and the heat, to say nothing of the glorious sunsets and endless views, the insect population certainly has its place in the grand web of life. This does not mean, however, that we have to remain beneath the bugs on the food chain. By taking a few simple precautions we can do much to thwart their feeding frenzies.

Blackflies

Blackflies are small, dark flies with humped backs. In the western states and north country, they are also known as gnats. Unlike mosquitos, which suck blood through a proboscis, black flies slash the skin and lap up the pooled blood. In very large numbers they can kill birds and animals both wild and domestic. More often, they are considered merely a nuisance, although in tropical regions they can transmit disease.

Unless they are truly swarming, blackflies tend to lose interest in a person when entering any kind of enclosure, such as a tent, even with its doorway wide open, or a tarp. Nor can they bite through even the thinnest clothing. However, they are adept at crawling under any gaps in a person's clothing to get at the bare skin. Once there, they inject a natural anesthetic that eliminates any sensation of their bites, making the person unaware of their presence – until he or she removes the clothing and discovers the bloody welts.

During our AT hike, and our canoeing and kayaking trips in the far north, we have found the blackflies at times to be more than just a nuisance. Even on the PCT we have experienced a few days when they were particularly bothersome. In such cases we wear head nets, and

Swarms of blackflies in the Barrenlands of Canada

shell jackets tucked into our shell pants, with the pant legs tucked into our socks.

One evening in the Barrenlands of Canada, after a day of wading the canoe in the rocky shallows, I crawled into the tent, removed my shell pants, and found hundreds of bloody welts on both legs. I was new to this game, and from then on I was more careful about keeping my pant legs tucked in. But interestingly, the welts healed quickly and never bothered me, mainly because I did not scratch them.

Deer flies, horse flies and no-see-ums

Deer flies and horse flies are fairly common across North America, and are most prevalent during the warm months. Their bites are instantly painful, but since these insects are large and rather noisy in flight, they give plenty of warning of their approach.

No-see-ums, on the other hand, are so small that a person can barely see-um, let alone hear-um. Also known as midges or punkies, they are common across most of North America. Chemical repellents are not as effective against these tiny insects, but adequate clothing easily rebuffs them, as does no-see-um netting, even if it lies against the skin. No-see-ums are so small they can crawl though regular mosquito netting, but they are unable to breach no-see-um netting, which has a much finer weave.

Mosquitoes

Most mosquitoes live for about two weeks in their adult form. But some live for as long as two or three months. At the time of this writing, the majority of mosquitoes here in the contiguous U.S. do not carry disease.

In other regions around the globe, mosquitoes are said to be the most dangerous animal on earth. They can carry parasites that kill an estimated 1 to 3 million people a year.

Even across the U.S. mosquitoes present some small risk. Witness the spread of West Nile virus and other types of encephalitis. With the changing climate, the Aedes mosquito, which transmits dengue fever virus, is starting to spread northward, as is the Anopheles mosquito infamous for carrying malaria. To say nothing of other emerging pathogens.

When swatting a mosquito, Jenny and I have sometimes found it contains old, darkened blood, not our own. From that we have surmised that mosquitoes and other bloodsucking insects, like ticks, might spread disease organisms picked up from feeding on the blood of birds or other animals. Disease organisms like West Nile, for example.

West Nile virus first appeared in the United States in 1999 and now is found in all 48 contiguous states. The risks of contracting the disease are low, and those who are infected usually have no symptoms. However, some will experience a headache or fever. Other symptoms might include skin rash, body aches, nausea, vomiting, or weakness. This is termed West Nile Fever, and it usually resolves itself without medication within 7-10 days, although, speaking from experience, the fatigue can last some weeks.

If West Nile virus enters the brain it can cause serious illness, although statistically this has happened in less than 1% of the cases.

Near the end of our round-the-world sailing voyage, I contracted malaria in the jungles of Panama. For the next 10 years I experienced almost yearly relapses. These came at the worst of times, invariably when we were on journey. They were also very sudden, meaning that we had to make hasty camps in some very unlikely places. From this I learned to take mosquito and other insect-borne diseases seriously.

Bug defense

Jenny and I defend ourselves using a number of options,

but have found clothing, and if necessary a bit of repellent, the most effective.

Chemical "repellents"

In mosquito season, most hikers out for a few hours, or even a few days, can use chemical repellents without discomfort or adverse reactions.

Of the many brands and types to choose from, many contain DEET (look on the label for N,N-diethyl-meta-toluamide). This was developed by the U.S. Department of Agriculture in 1946, and can be used on exposed skin, as well as on clothing, socks, and shoes; but should not be used near the eyes, under clothing, or on the hands of young children.

Picaridin (Icaridin) is an interesting alternative, and is said to work slightly better for repelling mosquitos, but may not be as effective against ticks, nor last as long –although it may be less irritating to the skin. Some brands of repellents containing Picaridin are laced with perfumes so strong that, personally, we would not use them, especially in bear country.

Repellents containing oil of lemon eucalyptus, a natural ingredient, are said to provide protection similar to low concentrations of DEET or picaridin.

Picaridin and oil of lemon eucalyptus repellents have been available elsewhere in the world since the 1980s. But it wasn't until 20 years later that they were approved by U.S. health officials.

DEET and Picaridin do not actually repel bugs, as the term "repellent" would imply. Instead, they seem to work by masking the essence of what parts of our skin we have treated. If we have not treated nearby skin, the mosquitoes will hone in on that. As an example, a few times I have found a mosquito squeezed under my watchband to get at the untreated skin there.

Regarding DEET, a 30% solution seems to work best for us. (Picaridin usually comes in a 7% to 20% mixture.)

We avoid the "long lasting" types because they can be uncomfortable on the skin.

For application we use a spray pump, which distributes a thinner and more even coat onto the skin. However, these chemicals can irritate the eyes, so we first spray the repellent onto our palms, then apply it carefully to the face.

Purportedly, six hours after application of DEET, about half of it will have absorbed into the skin, and most of that will have entered the bloodstream. So while DEET (and Picaridin) are said to be safe, we prefer to keep their use to a minimum, especially when we are out for longer periods. And when used, we always try to wash the repellent off at day's end, at least what remains. For this we use the dundo method away from the water sources, so as not to contaminate the streams and lakes.

Still, we find that after a few weeks of using repellents, we start to lose our tolerance of these chemicals. Even the very thought of them becomes nauseating. Many other long-distance hikers have reported the same. When we reach this point, the buzzing hordes begin to seem far more tormenting – such is the chemicals' effects on the brain. At least the symptoms might not be cumulative; for they appear to subside after we have not used the products for a few months. Even so, we do not consider chemical repellents our main protection, especially on our longer trips.

Spraying these repellents on clothing is not as effective, we find. But a person could spray clothing (not skin) with products containing permethrin, a poison that actually kills mosquitos, ticks, chiggers and other insects. The only appropriate use of permethrin we can think of is spraying one's shoes in an attempt to kill any nymphal (juvenile) ticks. Permethrin is extremely toxic to fish, so for example one must not wash one's permethrin-treated socks in a lake or stream. To each his or her own regarding this product, but personally we do not use it.

B vitamins as repellent

During one lengthy kayaking journey to the Arctic, we experimented with B-vitamins as repellent. (The story is recounted in our book: *Siku kayak*.) At the beginning of the trip we took one B-vitamin tablet a day. Even though we used no additional chemicals, the B-vitamins enabled us to stand out in the open, mosquitoes swarming everywhere but not landing on us. This was a great help, especially while bathing. Except that after bathing we were typically attacked. Apparently our skin was exuding a B-vitamin related chemical that acted as a repellent, and the bathing washed this chemical away. Nevertheless, with the passing of weeks, we found we needed to increase the dosage to achieve the same results. Eventually we were up to three pills a day, and even then the mosquitoes were starting to breech our defenses. And it was about at this point that our bodies and minds began rejecting the vitamin, with nausea and a tendency toward seasickness. Also, our bodies began to reek of the vitamin chemicals. So we stopped taking the vitamin, and instead resorted to our shell clothing and head nets, with a little DEET on our hands. In the wake of this experiment, we no longer use B-vitamins as a repellent.

A few people are naturally immune

We have met a few people who do not attract mosquitoes or black flies. One fellow in particular would have made a good subject for research. He was a Caucasian working as a postmaster in a remote village in Alaska. A group of us were out on the tundra, insects swarming around all of us except him. I asked what kind of repellent he was using. "None," he said. "Mosquitoes are not attracted to me, for some reason." He must have been exuding some kind of natural repellent, which made me ponder the possibility of researchers identifying and synthesizing whatever that substance is; and what a breakthrough that would be.

Protective clothing

Of all the options Jenny and I have used to guard against insects, we find bug-proof clothing the most effective.

After all, our clothing is our main source of protection from the "elements." In the same way that we wear insulating garments in cold weather; light and airy clothes for the hot deserts; rainwear for rain, and wind proofs for wind – in like manner we wear bug-proof clothing during those times when mosquitoes and biting insects are particularly numerous. In other words, we dress for the weather. And in a certain sense, the mosquitoes and black flies are like a weather phenomenon.

We have tried "bug-proof" shirts and pants made exclusively of mosquito or no-see-um netting, but have found them less than ideal. In places where the netting contacts the skin—for example at the shoulders, elbows and knees—mosquitos can insert their proboscises through the mesh, and easily reach the underlying flesh.

To that end we developed our shell garments, as described in the "Clothing" chapter. These are the same, ever-adaptable jacket and pants for use in wind and brush, rain and cold. And because the insects cannot pierce this material, we need not worry whether it lies pressed against our skin. At the same time, the material is very breathable, allowing us to wear these garments while hiking, even in warm weather if necessary.

For protecting hands and feet, we make shell mittens and booties of the same tightly-woven material. In their most simple form, the mittens could be little more than large, loose-fitting cylinders, closed at one end like a tube sock. Usually, though, we make loose fitting mittens that extend half way up the forearms for added converge. Elastic in the wrists hold them in place. When the bugs are bothersome, we use these mitts both while hiking and resting. The booties cover our feet and lower legs, and we wear them only while seated or lying down with the shoes off – for example at rest stops when we want to dry or air our feet. The booties are also useful at camp, and even while sleeping beneath a tarp on warm nights.

To keep the bugs away from the face, we use a loose-fitting head net made of no-see-um material. The netting extends below the shoulders with a pair of flaps. One flap extends about eighteen inches down the back, and the other down the chest. We tuck the flaps inside the shell jacket to secure them in place, and to seal out the bugs. The head net fits quite loosely; otherwise the mosquitoes would reach the skin. We also wear a wide brim hat or baseball-style cap underneath the head net to protect the scalp and keep the netting draped away from the face.

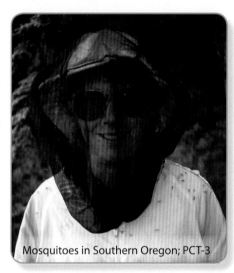

Mosquitoes in Southern Oregon; PCT-3

See also "Netting sewn to the quilt" in the "Quilt" chapter.

Color

Many times in buggy regions I have noticed that as Jenny and I sit together, one of us in light-colored clothing and the other in dark, the person wearing the darker garments is the one the mosquitoes and blackflies are most interested in.

That said, the head net should be dark in color, at least the part covering the eyes. Black netting absorbs more of the scattered light reflected by its fibers, and is therefore a little more transparent when close to the eyes.

Revenge

We usually carry small face towels, one for each of us, used for mopping the sweat off our faces on a warm day. But if we dampen the towels, they make good mosquito swatters. And we have found that if we dispatch these flying hypodermic needles, their replacements are often slow in coming.

We call this method "active defense," and sometimes it works so well that we can hike in comfort for hours without "passive defense" such as repellent or bug-proof clothing. It does require two people, as in: "cover my back, and I'll cover yours."

However, sometimes the insects are swarming. Then it is time for insect-proof clothing and head netting, possibly augmented with a little repellent. With these, we can hike and camp with equanimity, even during the height of bug season.

Ticks

"It is better to travel alone
than with a bad companion."
— *Senegalese proverb*

Ticks are parasites, relying on warm-blooded animals for their food. Adult ticks measure about ¼-inch across, about like the one wandering around on this page. As I watch one of these little bloodsuckers crawling through the hairy jungle of my arm, I am amazed at how tenaciously those stubby legs can propel the creature along. I have to admire its single-mindedness, that driving desire to find a meal. Not that I intend to provide that meal.

———

Ticks are fairly common in the temperate climes around the world, especially in spring and summer. Technically they are not insects, but arachnids – like mites, scorpions, and spiders. As such, they cannot fly or even jump. Instead, they simply wait on the ground or vegetation for an unwitting "host" to happen along. Then they reach out and grab a hold. But rather than biting right away, they usually wander around on the host sometimes for several hours as though searching for just the right spot.

However, the wandering delay does not always hold true. While hiking through Glacier National Park in mid June, Jenny and I passed through an area where the ticks were large and so voracious that we would stop on the far side of a large clump of brush, and inspecting ourselves we would find a few ticks that had already bitten in. That was quick!

In parts of southern California in late spring, the brush can be teeming with adult ticks. We have found fifty or more on our shoes, socks and legs after scraping through a single clump of brush. Even so, in late season these areas tend to be less infested. While hiking the PCT southbound, we passed through these same areas in early September, and found not a single tick.

Thwarting ticks

Not all ticks carry disease. But as with mosquitoes, ticks thrive better in warmer climates; so a warming climate could compound their numbers and expand them into new areas. And because some of the diseases they carry can be serious, certain precautions are in order.

Normally Jenny and I hike in shirts and shorts, but when in a dense tick environment our first defense is to wear protective clothing.

Most ticks are dark brown, so they are more visible when crawling upon light-colored clothing. In the "Clothing" and "Mosquitoes" chapters I discuss our light-colored shell jacket and pants. Ticks seem to find these garments slippery; in fact Jenny and I have never found a tick clinging to our shells.

When hiking through brush and other common tick environments during peak season, we also tuck our pants into our socks, to discourage ticks from crawling up our legs. We tend to hike in lightweight socks, but have found that ticks can force their mouth-parts through the thin weave of these socks and get at the underlying skin. So as a stop-gap measure we might use insect repellent sprayed on our socks from the shoes up. We might also apply repellent to our skin around the margins of the clothing where ticks could crawl under that clothing.

Despite these precautions, ticks can sometimes find their way under the clothing. At that point, the clothing only serves to conceal the ticks, essentially protecting (hiding) them instead of protecting us. Very important when in tick country, then, is to inspect one's bare skin every few hours, and particularly before retiring for the night.

If we are inspecting ourselves at least every few hours throughout the day, we will usually find any ticks crawling on us before they have bitten in. Someone who is not making these regular inspections is essentially giving the ticks carte blanche, since the ticks' bite causes no sensation that might give them away.

So we peel back our clothing momentary to visually inspect each other's torsos, underarms, and the back of the necks and ears. If hiking alone, self-inspection will be necessary, by sight where possible, and by feel otherwise.

Before falling asleep, I carefully inspect my body by running my fingers over every square inch of my skin. A tick feels like a little mole that I did not know that I had. Should one of us feel something crawling on us in the night, we do not simply scratch it and return to sleep. Rather, the person sits up and shines a flashlight on the area, to see whether it might be a tick. If it is, we do not kill it by crushing it, because that could expose any disease bacterium inside of it. Nor would we simply flick the tick a short distance away, since it might then follow our trail of carbon dioxide back to us. In my experience, the limit for the tick's sense range is about four or five feet. So instead we place the tick on a small rock or piece of bark, and give that a hearty toss.

A tick crawling on us during the night does not mean that we should have been camping in a tent or a net-tent for its protection against ticks, rather than under an open tarp. In every likelihood we acquired the tick elsewhere and brought it to our camp unnoticed.

Furthermore, at night we do not worry about armies of ticks roving about in search of prey. If an adult tick crawls three feet, that might be a long trip. But also, we do not camp in areas that might abound with ticks. Deer lays are one example.

The deer usually live in certain areas throughout the spring and summer. In these areas will be their food source, usually a meadow with foliage or grass; and off to one side, hidden in the brush, will be their lays where they spend their afternoons napping, and part of their nights sleeping. These lays are usually evident by the matted appearance of the grass, leaves or pine needles. To a stealth camper, such lays might look like inviting places to pitch a tarp or tent. However, they are often teeming with ticks and fleas.

We also avoid camping in areas that might harbor field mice. Here again, mice live by their food source, grass for example. Where one finds mice, there will likely be ticks.

Incidentally, we never camp in, or around old abandoned buildings, due to the danger of acquiring rodent-related hunta virus.

Larval ticks and nymphs

Ticks undergo a few stages of development: from eggs to larva, to nymphs, to adults. Like all aspects in nature, we find these life cycles interesting. And we also know that understanding the basics of the tick's life cycle can help us avoid their bites. The following is a very generalized synopsis:

Tick eggs hatch in summer into larvae. The larvae look like ticks, but are almost infinitesimal in size – about the size of a period at the end of a sentence. Because of this, they are most difficult to detect when crawling on one's skin, or embedded in it. But because they are usually free of disease, they are also not much of a concern to hikers and campers.

The larvae usually cannot climb very high, so they simply wait for small animals passing by at ground level. Mice are their usual quarry, but unfortunately the blood of mice is often infected with disease bacterium. So as the larvae feed on the mouse's blood, the larvae can become infected also. And this infection will stay with a tick for its entire life cycle. As one example, the white-footed mouse is the host primarily responsible for infecting larval ticks with the Lyme spirochete.

After a single blood meal lasting two to three days, the larvae drop from the host. Then in about a month's time they molt into the second, juvenile stage called "nymphs."

Nymphs spend a dormant winter in the forest litter, then late the next spring they become active. They have now grown to the size of a pin-head. But despite their small size, they are thought to cause most cases of Lyme disease in humans. That is because they are difficult to detect.

Tick nymphs are ground dwellers. The live in the leaf or forest litter, and do not climb onto vegetation. So we hikers should not expect to pick them up while traipsing through the brush.

So where do hikers and campers pick them up? Just about anywhere on the ground. But ironically, most people who have contracted a tick-borne disease have picked up nymphs unknowingly in their own back yards.

When hiking or camping in serious tick country, Jenny and I might spray our shoes with repellent. Also, we do not sit or lay directly on the ground in such environs. When resting, we might sit on a rock or log. Most times, however, we will sit on the ground, but not before spreading out our shell jackets. The jackets protect our backsides from picking up any ticks – whether larvae, nymphs, or adults. And even when not in tick season, the jackets keep the seat of our pants free of dirt and tree sap. After we have finished resting, we give the jackets a few hardy shakes, to encourage any arachnids or insects to fall off.

Our preferred camping shelter in tick country is the Net-Tent suspended beneath our tarp. The netting enclosure keeps the bugs at bay, and because the outside of our net-tent along the bottom is steep and slippery, any ticks would have difficulty climbing it. The underside of our net-tent is also slippery, so in the morning we simply give the whole net-tent a firm shake, fold it bottom-side-in, and put it in its stowbag.

We also refrain from laying our clothing, socks, or sleeping quilt directly on the ground in order to air-dry them. Instead, we hang them up on a line strung between two trees, or from a tree branch. This keeps the clothing or quilt from picking up bugs; and moisture and dirt also.

In the morning, before donning clothing and shoes and shouldering backpacks, we of course check these items for ticks.

Adult ticks

Ticks that are still in the nymph stage feed only once, usually on small animals. Their meal lasts from three to five days; then they drop off, and in about three months molt into the adult stage.

Adult ticks are more mobile, and typically climb as high as one meter on vegetation. There, they wait for a host to come walking along. Once attached to a host, adult females feed typically for four or five days, after which time they drop off and overwinter in an engorged state in the forest litter. The following spring they lay eggs in masses of several hundred to a few thousand. The eggs hatch a few weeks later into new larvae.

Tick removal

Ticks attach themselves to a host by inserting their mouthparts into the skin.

When removing a tick, I use the standard method: Using a pair of fine-tipped tweezers—like those found in my suggested pocket knife—I grasp the tick by the head or mouthparts where they enter the skin. I pull gently but steadily, without twisting, until the tick releases its grip.

Pulling too hard can break off the mouth-parts and leave them embedded.

One should not grasp the tick by the body. Doing so could easily break the tick and contaminate one's skin with its fluids. And worse, the tick might regurgitate its fluids and inject them beneath one's skin. After attempting to improvise with thin sticks used like chopsticks, in my early days, I learned to carry the tweezers.

After removing a tick, a person should wash the bite site thoroughly with soap and water, then disinfect the site with an antiseptic such as isopropyl alcohol. Also, one might scrub one's hands with an alcohol gel or antibacterial soap.

Remember that if you find a tick attached to your skin, there is no need to panic. You will not automatically contract a tick-borne disease. Not all ticks carry disease, by any means. And removal of an infected tick within 36 hours is said to reduce the risk of disease transmission to nearly zero. So if you remove the tick carefully, you should be fine.

However, the problem is not how to remove a tick, but how to become aware of it in the first place. The small size of a tick, especially in the nymph stage, may make detection difficult. In fact, in most cases of tick-borne disease, the person does not remember being bitten.

The tick-borne diseases in the United States include Lyme disease, ehrlichiosis (er-lick-ee-o-sis), Rocky Mountain spotted fever and tularemia (too-la-ree-me-a). Deer ticks spread Lyme disease in the Northeast and Midwest. Western black-legged ticks spread the disease along the Pacific coast, mostly in northern California and Oregon.

Initially these may cause flu-like symptoms, such as fever, headache, nausea, vomiting, and muscle aches. Symptoms may begin from 1-day to 3-weeks after the tick bite.

Tick or no, if a suspicious illness develops, a person would be smart to see a physician right away. The doctor will likely specify blood tests, and if necessary, prescribe a course of oral antibiotics.

Like mosquitoes, blackflies, and the rest of the insect and arthropod world, ticks are part of the intricate cycle of nature. With that in mind, Jenny and I do not let a fear of ticks keep us out of the backcountry. We take an active role by following the preventive measures outlined above. Then we carry on enjoying the wilds.

Poison Ivy and Oak

Itching for knowledge, or lack of it

Each plant species that we find in the wilds offers new insights about our wondrous ecology, and about some of the unique ways the plant has adapted for its survival. Some plants rely on chemicals that impart a foul taste to discourage browsing animals. Other plants defend themselves with spines or thorns. Fiddleheads, for instance, have hair-like needles. Holly has sharp leaf tips. The tiny needles of stinging nettle inject formic acid, a painful toxin. Despite their many forms of defense, these plants are nonetheless beautiful: cactus in bloom, wild roses scenting the air, succulent berries borne on thorny stems. In the fall, fiddleheads tint the hillsides in glorious shades of yellow and gold. The leaves of stinging nettle lose their sting after a light boiling in water, and are highly nutritious; and from their stem fibers we can make strong and supple cordage.

The more time we spend in the wilds, the more we come to understand the intrinsic value of each and every plant species found along the way, even the toxic varieties. And so it is with poison ivy, poison oak and poison sumac – poisonous to the touch, and known collectively as the toxicodendrons.

Distribution and identification

The U.S. is home to five different toxicodendrons. The poison oaks and poison ivies are closely related, and their leaves grow in distinctive clusters of three. Poison oak leaves are serrated or lobed, whereas poison ivy leaves have smooth edges – although the patterns fre-quently overlap. Poison sumac has a different leaf pattern altogether.

▶ Eastern poison ivy (Rhus radicans) is found in parts of New England, in certain areas of the mid-Atlantic states, and despite its name, throughout most of the Rocky Mountain states. It grows as a small plant or climbing vine, and is ubiquitous in temperate forests along creeks and on mountain slopes.

▶ Rydberg's poison ivy (Rhus rydbergii) grows in the Rocky Mountain states as a small shrub up to three feet high. It prefers moist, sunny areas. Watch for it in creek drainages below 6,000 feet.

▶ Eastern poison oak (Rhus toxicodendron) is found throughout the southeastern states, as well as portions of the Midwest. It grows in sandy soil, and also in areas devastated by fire.

▶ Western poison oak (Rhus diversiloba) grows as an isolated plant, a thick bush, or a climbing vine – from sea level to 5,000 feet. It is most prevalent in the lower elevations throughout much of California and some parts north. It prefers shaded slopes and creek banks, even where the creeks are dry.

▶ Poison sumac (Rhus vernix) grows in marshy areas east of the Mississippi River. It has toothless leaves and drooping clusters of small white berries. Non-poisonous sumac (Rhus spp.) has toothed leaves, and dense, upright clusters of red berries growing from the ends of its branches.

The poison content

Despite differences in appearance and habitat, all five species contain the same defense mechanism: a toxin called urushiol (oo-ROO-she-all). This causes the blistering, itchy rash one commonly experiences after inadvertently touching these plants. This toxin is present in all parts of the plants: the leaves, stems, berries and roots, regardless whether the plant is dead or alive, and even in the smoke of the burning plant. When someone touches the plant—or even brushes against it lightly—it deposits some of this toxic oil, or sap onto the skin, clothing or footwear.

The disguise of bare stems

During our first PCT trip, Jenny and I met a hiker who had recently hitchhiked out for medication. The doctor had treated him for a severe case of poison oak, yet this fellow was adamant about not having touched the plant. I explained how toxic even the leafless twigs can be, and pointed them out all around us, including some small ones he happened to be sitting on.

Avoiding contact with these plants is a person's most effective preventive measure. And to do this, one must learn to recognize them in all seasons and stages of growth – including when still leafless in early season.

Poison ivy and poison oak tend to grow in small, scattered communities. In the early season, look for bare, thornless stems standing one or two feet tall. The hallmark of these stems is their characteristic curve, and the small, pointed bud on top: the coming season's new growth. Bare vines pose the same risk; look for these growing on trees and rocks. To be on the safe side, avoid touching, sitting on, or placing clothing or equipment on *any* bare stems or vines found along the trail, especially in the drainages. Should you find bare stems draping unavoidably across the trail, shove them aside with a stick, or circumvent the area altogether. If you are searching for a stealth site, or moving around in the woods after dark, be cautious of the stems; they might be hard to spot.

In late spring, the bare stems of poison ivy and poison oak begin developing their foliage. Normally growing in clusters of three, the young leaves are beautifully colored in reds and greens, and are shiny or greasy-looking. By summer they turn dark and vibrant green. And in autumn they tend to bright reds and yellows.

Mistaken identity

Left: poison oak; Right: squaw bush

"Leaves of three, let them be" is a useful adage for poison oak and poison ivy, but in the plant world the trifoliate arrangement is common. Many berry plants (Rubus spp.)—for instance blackberry, raspberry and salmonberry—have leaves grouped in three, and even though the stems of blackberry and raspberry are thorny, hikers and campers will sometimes mistake them for poison oak or ivy. Squaw bush (Rhus trilobata) is fairly widespread across the West, and is almost universally mistaken for poison oak. But in fact

Bare twigs of poison oak

Poison ivy along the AT

squaw bush is harmless. The key to its identification lies in the center leaf of each three-leaf cluster. The center leaf of squaw bush has no stem, while that of poison oak and poison ivy does. My mnemonic: No central stem–No poison.

Symptoms

Early Native Americans were largely immune to the irritants in these poisonous plants. They even made baskets of the vines. I have read of a few brave individuals, here in modern times, who were trying to develop immunity to urushiol by actually eating tiny parts of the plants. This, they said, was how the Native Americans did it. And they also said that developing immunity takes many months,

if not years. However, I would not recommend this to anyone, by any means.

According to some, about two-thirds of the population would be affected to some extent by an "average" contact – for example a bare leg brushing against a few poison ivy twigs reaching across the trail. But nearly all of us would suffer severe skin irritations from a massive exposure to any of these plants.

One to several days after the contact, a small, itchy rash will manifest. This will resemble a mosquito bite. However, if touching it causes an intense, almost fiery sensation, then it is probably not a mosquito bite, but rather the onset of "contact dermatitis" from the urushiol. This itchy area may enlarge, and soon become reddened, raised, and often blistered.

Scratching will not spread the rash, but it certainly can aggravate it. Scratching can also lead to bacterial infection that in more serious cases can result in blood poisoning. Despite appearances, the rash spreads only by means of the toxic oil itself, not by the oozing fluid issuing from the blisters. The blister fluid is a product of one's own body, and contains no toxic oil. The reason the rash often continues to break out in new areas, is that people often re-expose themselves to more toxic sap, usually from their sleeping bag and unwashed clothes, especially socks, shoes and laces. Almost anything that comes in contact with the plant can carry and transmit the sap, including pets.

Another common skin condition that may resemble a contact dermatitis rash is phototoxic dermatitis. As discussed in the "Hot" chapter, this is caused by mild sunburn in combination with a skin allergy to a soap, lotion, or to some type of food or drink.

Treatment

If you happen to brush against one of the toxicodendrons, you should not ignore the fact and continue on your way. Instead, stop and try to remove some of the toxins. If successful, you could spare yourself some or all of the inflammation. Theoretically, a person has ten or fifteen minutes before the toxic oil begins to chemically combine with the skin.

The best way to remove the toxin is to pour a mild solvent over the exposed area, and then to rinse it copiously with cold water. One of the better solvents is alcohol, either the gelled type hand sanitizer mentioned in the "Hygiene" and "First Aid" chapters, or a liquid alcohol such as isopropyl or denatured ethyl alcohol. Dab it on, and rinse with large amounts of water. If you let the solvent evaporate without washing it off, it will leave the toxic oil in place. Water not only flushes the alcohol from the skin, but it also tends to slowly oxidize, or inactivate, the urushiol. Adding a small amount of hydrogen peroxide or bleach to the rinse water will enhance this oxidizing effect.

One problem with the solvent is that it will remove not only the toxic oil from your skin, but also the skin's natural, protective oils. Therefore, after washing with a solvent, be very careful not to touch any more poison ivy or oak, since a new exposure could then take a better hold.

Lacking a solvent of some kind, you should wash the affected skin liberally with soap and water. Soaps with active ingredients designed to break down the oil, might be a bonus. Still, any type of soap will do. Or simply rinse with cold water alone. Even if too late to prevent the rash, washing the skin to remove excess plant oil will keep the rash to a minimum, by removing much of the remaining transmissible toxins.

After detoxifying, you should change out of whatever clothing you were wearing and that might have brushed against the plants. Place the contaminated garments in a plastic bag and stow them in the backpack. Arriving back home, or in a town, empty the suspect clothes into a washing machine. Machine washing will effectively remove the toxins from clothing and shoes, without contaminating the machine for the next user, as long as you use plenty of laundry detergent.

Once the oil has bonded to your skin, some of the best possible treatments are the gifts of nature – aloe vera or Jewelweed (Impatiens spp.). The Jewelweed, found mostly in the east, is easily identified by its yellow or orange flowers, and seedpods that resemble miniature cucumbers. When mature, the pods pop open when you touch them. Jewelweed is fairly common in damp, shady areas, along roadsides and stream banks, and often grows in the vicinity of both poison ivy and poison oak. To use this remedial plant, pinch off a few leaves and stems, crush them, and rub them gently on the exposed area. Jewelweed also soothes the sting of nettles and insect bites.

Most pharmacies offer a number of commercial remedies for treating a toxicodendron rash. Drying agents like Calamine or other lotions can be soothing. Hydrocortisone creams or sprays will reduce the inflammation, swelling, and itching. However, the over-the-counter varieties are much too weak to be very effective. In my experience, the prescription concentrations work

Poison Oak overgrown on the PCT in northern California, PCT-1

extremely well, as long as they are not petroleum jelly-based. In severe cases, a physician can also prescribe antihistamine creams, tablets or injections. Grapefruit Seed Extract is also said to work well.

———————

Yosemite Valley, as many rock climbers know, is a wonderful environment – especially for poison oak. During the many years I spent in the Valley, I became all too familiar with this plant. I was forever thrashing through the brush and getting into poison oak, mainly while scouting for new routes. But in those days I had little money, so could not afford to visit a doctor for a prescription of the needed hydrocortisone ointment. I had to tough it out, by washing the effected areas with Fels Naptha laundry soap about ten times a day, applying thick layers of Calamine lotion, and so forth – none of which seemed to help. So my rashes of poison oak would fester for three to six months. I learned right from the start that scratching them with the fingernails would ease the horribly irritating itch, but only for a few moments, at which time the fiery itch would return with a vengeance. About the best I could do was to pour nearly scalding water on the blisters. That treatment eased the misery for a few hours, but I am sure that it also prolonged the malady.

One time in particular, a climbing partner and I were descending Elephant Rock, when our rappel ropes became jammed above us. We finally reached the ground in pitch dark; so while groping our way down to the river, we thrashed through a great deal of poison oak, unseen. My resulting rashes were so severe that they ended whatever tolerance I might have felt toward this plant.

Unfortunately, it was not until several years later that I could afford the prescription ointment. When applied, the blisters would somehow disappear within a week's time; almost magically it seemed to me. In my climbing years that followed, I used a great deal of this ointment, mainly because the poison oak in some places was difficult to avoid, at least while hiking off-trail.

On most maintained hiking trails the plant is not so ubiquitous, although I still keep a sharp eye out for it.

PCT-3

Snakes

"Travel teaches toleration."
— *Benjamin Disraeli*

Hiking with eyes and ears

Snakes are among nature's most fascinating creatures, and play an important role in the balance of their local ecology. They feed on rodents and other small animals, helping to keep these populations in check. And in so doing, they help reduce disease. In turn, snakes are food for birds of prey and larger animals.

Sometimes a snake will slither across our path when least expected. This does not mean it is being aggressive towards us; only that it is moving to a safer place for it. Sometimes a snake will remain perfectly still, relying on its camouflage to remain unnoticed. And sometimes a snake will quickly coil into a defensive posture, a move that warns us not to come close. Whatever the case, we can ensure our own safety by remaining alert and keeping a safe distance, as nature intended.

Snakes find their prey by sight and scent, and sometimes by sensing variations in temperature. They lack ears, but their bodies are ultra-sensitive to vibrations. Their vision is quite good, as is their sense of smell, thanks to a harmless, flicking forked tongue that carries scent to a sensory organ inside the mouth. Some species kill their prey with venomous bites, others with constriction, and yet others by overpowering and swallowing. Snakes have

A black snake in one of the huts along the AT

no chewing-type teeth, so they must swallow their meals whole.

While hiking, we rarely see snakes, mainly because they spend much of their time hidden in piles of rocks or leaf litter, in decaying logs, or in tree cavities or underground hollows such as those created by tree roots. Even when resting in the open, they usually conceal themselves under at least some vegetation. And depending on temperature, they tend to be less active during the day.

Common non-venomous snakes

Gopher snake

The gopher snake (Pituophis spp.) is common in drier regions—sandy woodlands, chaparral and prairies— from sea level to 9,000 feet. This snake and its various subspecies are found across the U.S. except in the northeast. In the mountain states it is called the bull snake, and in the eastern states, the pine snake. Some members of this group grow quite large, with recorded lengths in excess of eight feet.

Intimidating as they may appear, they are harmless to

hikers who leave them alone. The gopher snake normally behaves passively, but if confronted it may hiss and sometimes flatten its head and vibrate its tail. If threatened it may even lunge at an intruder. And of course if molested it is likely to bite.

Due to the gopher snake's behavior, and the patterns of brown or black blotches on its back, people regularly mistake it for a rattlesnake and often kill it. This is most unfortunate. The gopher snake is extremely beneficial to the ecology, and also to farmers troubled by rodents.

While hiking through the desert-like Tehachapi Mountains of southern California, Jenny and I came to a shading tree, and were about to sit down when we noticed a gopher snake nearby. Over the years we had seen many gopher snakes, often stretched across the trail looking like sticks from a distance. But we had not seen one quite as large as this six-footer. Leaving it ample room we sat down anyway, and soon it slipped behind us, only inches away, before continuing on its way.

Black rat snake

The black snake, or black rat snake (Elaphe obsoleta) is related to the water snake. It eats insects, rodents and other small mammals, frogs and lizards. It is normally harmless to humans, but when provoked it can bite. These snakes inhabit hardwood forests, old fields, farmlands, and wooded canyons from sea level to 4,400 feet. They range from Vermont south into Florida, and west into Minnesota, Michigan and Texas.

Species such as the black snake consume great numbers of rodents, and their presence around barns is of great benefit to farmers. Hikers reap

the same benefits in and around many of the Appalachian Trail lean-tos and shelters, where the black snake helps keep the mice population in check.

This snake can grow quite large also, up to eight feet. We remember one big fellow who had taken up residence in a shelter along the AT. As we were approaching, we saw the snake crawling through the rafters. Realizing that it meant us no harm, we took its picture, then sat inside, appreciating the creature while eating our lunch and signing the register.

King snake

Several types of king snakes have beautiful bands along the length of their bodies, in red or orange, black, and yellow or off-white. These color patterns are similar to those of the venomous coral snake. Such "mimicry" is thought to be nature's way of discouraging predators. And of course, these similarities often lead people to mistake the king snake for the coral snake. See the description under "Coral snake," on how to tell the difference.

The many subspecies of the king snake (Lampropeltis spp.) are distributed widely across the U.S. They range in size from two to six feet, and are adaptable to a variety of habitats, including woodlands, chaparral, brushy and rocky canyons and talus slopes, from sea level to 9,000 feet. This is generally the same elevation range as for the gopher snake, although the king snake is not nearly as common. King snakes are constrictors and they feed on rodents, birds, and even on other snakes, including venomous ones. Curiously, they are immune to rattlesnake venom.

A gopher snake, PCT-2

Venomous snakes

North America is home to only four types of venomous snakes: the rattlesnake, copperhead, cottonmouth (also known as the water moccasin), and the coral snake. These snakes rarely cause human fatalities, but are dangerous nonetheless.

Coral snake

Two species of coral snakes are found in the United States: the Eastern coral snake (Micrurus fulvius) of the southeastern states; and the smaller Western, or Arizona coral snake (Micruroides euryxanthus) found from the southern regions of New Mexico and Arizona to northwestern Mexico. The eastern coral snake lives in many habitats, including pine woods and hardwood forests. The western coral snake is found mainly in dry habitats. Both are timid and seldom seen by hikers. They spend much of their lives underground in cracks and crevices, feeding on small lizards, other snakes, reptiles and amphibians.

The coral snake tends to be small, averaging only twenty-four inches in length. It is not a pit viper like the rattlesnake, copperhead or cottonmouth (see below). Rather, it is an elapid, related to the Asian cobra and many Australian snake species. It has a small mouth, and tiny, fixed fangs. It is not normally aggressive, but like any snake it will bite if handled or accidentally stepped on. Coral snake bites are rare in the United States, only about twenty-five bites a year by some estimates.

Almost all subspecies of the coral snake are brightly colored, and have regular patterns of red, yellow and black bands. Many subspecies of king snake are marked in similar ways, but the arrangement of the colors differs between the two species. The king snake's red bands are bordered on both sides by black bands. The coral snake's red bands are bordered by yellow bands. This gave rise to the saying: "Red and black, friend of Jack. Red and yellow, kill a fellow." This is an easy way of remembering the distinction between the two.

Cottonmouth (water moccasin)

The cottonmouth (Agkistrodon piscivorous) lives in streams and swamps of the south and southeast United States and parts of Illinois, Kentucky, Missouri, Oklahoma and Texas. Like all pit vipers, it has hollow fangs that inject toxin. The bite is rarely fatal, although it can be painful and can cause local tissue damage. The snake is brown or olive, with broad black bands across its body. Growing to four feet or more in length, it feeds on fish, amphibians, reptiles, birds and small mammals. The term cottonmouth derives from the color of the snake's mouth lining, which is white, and from the snake's mannerism of holding its mouth agape when threatened.

Copperhead

Another venomous member of the pit viper family, the American copperhead (Agkistrodon contortrix) is identified by its regularly spaced bands along its length, and its flattish, triangular head. The adult snake is from two to three feet in length, and occasionally larger. It is copper in color, but this can vary from light brown to pinkish, helping camouflage it among leaves and forest debris. It prefers rocky, forested hillsides and wetlands, and ranges from Massachusetts to northern Florida and westward to Illinois and Texas. It is gregarious, and hibernates with other snake species.

Small mammals and frogs account for most of the copperhead's diet, as do birds and insects. This snake, in turn, serves as food for red-tailed hawks, possums and even bullfrogs.

When approached, the copperhead will either move away quietly, or lie motionless while relying on its camouflage for protection. Like all snakes, this one prefers to be left alone; but may exhibit a tenacious personality when approached. It can jump twice its length, and if aggravated it may strike with vigor. Bites usually occur when someone unknowingly steps or reaches too close, unaware of the snake's presence in the leaf litter, the hollow of a log, or a crevice in the rocks. Hikers therefore need to remain vigilant when in copperhead territory. At least the snake's venom is milder and less dangerous than that of other venomous snakes, and its bite is rarely fatal.

Rattlesnake

In our many miles of hiking, Jenny and I have encountered snakes of all kinds: rattlesnakes, copperheads, gopher, king, and many others. And no doubt we have walked past many without noticing them. But it is the rattlesnake that seems to be the most prevalent, especially on, or alongside a trail.

Both eastern and western rattlesnakes (Crotalus spp.) have many subspecies. The eastern diamondback (C. adamanteus) tends to be the largest, and is found in some of the southern states. The timber rattlesnake (C. horridus) can also grow quite large, up to six feet and more in length. It is found from southern Maine to northern Florida, and west to Minnesota and Texas.

Several species of rattlesnakes inhabit the mid-western and western states. Along the CDT they are common in Wyoming and New Mexico. Along the PCT they occur throughout much of California, but are almost unknown along the trail through Oregon and Washington, except in the Columbia River Gorge.

Rattlesnakes prey mostly on small rabbits and rodents such as ground squirrels, chipmunks, rats and mice – creatures that tend to reproduce prolifically in years of abundant food. So we are most likely to see rattlesnakes (as well as copperheads in the east) in areas where rodents feed, namely along streams, in rock piles and stands of grasses, and under brush and wood piles. But of course they can be found almost anywhere. In warm weather, rattlesnakes are active throughout the daylight hours; however, during the hottest months of the summer they limit most of their activity to the cooler hours, generally from twilight to dawn. Rattlesnakes hibernate in dens shared with other rattlesnakes and other snake species. They are also good swimmers.

How to recognize a rattlesnake

The rattlesnake, like all pit vipers including the copperhead and cottonmouth, has pits on each side of its head between the eye and nostril. These pits house its infrared sensors, which allow the snake to detect its prey at considerable distance. Once the rattlesnake finds the heat signature of a mouse, for example, it simply follows the heat trail leading to the creature's den or nest.

The pupils of the rattlesnake are vertical and thinly elliptical, rather than round like those of non-venomous snakes. But if you are close enough to see this, then you are much too close. Rather, what you will notice from hopefully a safe distance is the stout, heavy body with a flattish, triangular-shaped head, wide in the jowls and fashioned improbably onto a thin neck. This is the viper look.

And you will probably see and hear the jointed tail rattles, although in some cases these might have broken off. The rattlesnake is normally marked with brownish "diamonds" (actually hexagons or ovals) along the midline of the back. And hikers should remember that the harmless gopher snake has somewhat similar markings, but without the triangular head or tail rattles.

In desert regions of the Southwest lives a particularly venomous rattlesnake, known as the "Mojave Green." It is common, and the chances of a PCT hiker seeing one are good. Fortunately, the ground cover in these regions is sparse, so with even a modicum of attentiveness, the hiker's chances of being bitten by a Mojave Green are slim. This snake has much the same markings as other rattlesnakes, but is further identified by its pale green hue, similar to the dusty sage-green color of the surrounding scrub brush. The reason it is more dangerous is that its type of venom can affect the brain or spinal cord.

The snake's primary defense

Being exceptionally sensitive to ground vibrations, snakes can sense our approach from quite a distance. They may slither for cover, but only if this will increase their chances of remaining unnoticed. Otherwise, their primary defense is to remain motionless and inconspicuous. And this makes rattlesnakes (and copperheads) hazardous to hikers, especially as the snakes' camouflaging helps them blend into their surroundings. The hiker can unknowingly approach, and only after the rattlesnake's primary defense has failed will it buzz a warning.

When so threatened, the snake will rarely retreat. This is because it cannot turn from danger without increasing its vulnerability. Nor can it travel fast. So it usually holds its ground, mouth agape in an intimidating manner. This defensive mechanism is ineffective against people who can throw rocks or sticks, but it works well against birds of prey, the snake's usual predator.

I once stopped to drink from my water bottle when a rattlesnake buzzed me from behind. I turned and saw it coiled at the edge of the trail. I had just walked past without noticing. The snake had buzzed only when I stopped, undoubtedly interpreting my stopping as a threat.

Hiking in snake country

Before setting out on any backpacking trip, we find out what venomous snakes inhabit the area, if any, and learn to recognize them. Then during the hike itself we walk attentively, scanning the trail ten or twenty feet ahead. Where the trail is overgrown in brush or grass, we may probe ahead with a long stick. Trekking poles are much too short for this. As far as clothing is concerned, shorts and sandals obviously offer no protection from a snake bite. Long pants, socks and shoes are preferable but still leave the legs vulnerable. The more layers, the better the protection. Those hikers wishing to take every precaution could wear snake chaps, or pieces of cardboard or foam taped around the lower legs and ankles. If hiking at night, we use a small flashlight held low to illuminate the ground just ahead.

When I see a rattlesnake on or alongside the trail, blocking the way ahead, I step back several paces and pick up a few rocks. Then from a distance of about six feet I start lobbing rocks to prompt the creature to move off the trail. How big the rocks and how hard a person throws them is of course up to the individual. Some people would leave a venomous snake to endanger other hikers coming along behind, while other people would not.

Sometimes while hiking we will chance upon a rattlesnake lying fairly at our feet. This can be unnerving and dangerous.

Seen at an outpost along the PCT:
"BEWARE - BABY RATTLERS"

Jenny and I were ambling along the AT in Connecticut when we heard the characteristic buzzing of a rattlesnake. Jenny was in the lead, and the buzzing was coming from somewhere between us, off to one side. I stopped while she continued ahead, out of range. I scanned the brush-covered ground for a few long moments, then saw the source of the rattling – the tail of the snake. I was relieved to see that it was about six feet away. But imagine my chagrin to then discover the head of this large timber rattler very close!

A coiled rattlesnake can strike to about half its body length. If the snake is not coiled, which is how we usually find them as they are trying to remain undetected, then its range will be far less. I have inadvertently stepped within as little as a foot or two of a rattlesnake, fortunately without being bitten. This illustrates not only the difficulty of avoiding venomous snakes and keeping a safe distance from them, but also that they don't always strike when presented the opportunity. In my observation, it seems to depend on the timing, the distance, and the snake's posture—coiled or outstretched—and how great a threat the snake perceives in us.

One time Jenny was walking behind me when she stopped abruptly and called out that I had just stepped over a rattlesnake. I turned and saw a 24-inch rattler moving off into the surrounding brush. In the center of the trail we found a circular indentation in the dirt, apparently where the snake had been resting or possibly sleeping. A few years later this happened again, in a different area. One would think that a rattlesnake lying on the trail would be obvious. Most are, but some can be amazingly camouflaged.

The rattlesnake's warning is exactly that. And this suggests the risks of hiking with earphones. One fellow told me about an encounter with a timber rattlesnake. Apparently two other hikers in front of him had walked past the snake, and were watching it from a distance when this earphoned hiker happened along. "I noticed their stern faces and wild gestures apparently aimed at me, but I saw no need to stop, until my eyes finally registered on the snake a few feet ahead." And he went on to say that he never again hiked with earphones.

Before we stop to rest alongside a trail in an area known for venomous snakes, we might probe the nearby bushes with a long stick. If later a snake crawls out of the brush near where a person happens to be sitting, one's best course of action would be to sit still and wait for it to leave—if it appears inclined to do so, which it probably will—or if not, then to back very slowly away. One should never try to swat a rattlesnake with a book or short stick, as one hiker I know of did. These creatures can strike in one one-hundredth of a second – far faster than a person could ever swing at them.

Every time Jenny sees or hears a rattlesnake, she dashes away. And every time, I assure her that a couple of snake-lengths away from the creature's head is a perfectly adequate distance, as long as she remains on guard and leaves plenty of room for retreat. On the final stages of our fifth thru-hike a rattler buzzed her, and this time she merely moved aside and studied the area for the snake's whereabouts. I was coming along behind when I heard a shriek. Lesson learned: do not stand a couple of snake-lengths away from where you think the snake might be. It could be much closer.

Snakebite first-aid and protocol

Every state but Alaska and Hawaii has venomous snakes. According to the American Red Cross, about 8,000 people a year sustain venomous bites in the United States, and about ten of these bites are fatal, mostly to the very young or infirm. I asked Dr. Anthony Manoguerra, former director of the San Diego Regional Poison Center, about the incidence of rattlesnake bites to hikers. He said they are fairly common. How serious are they? He explained that the damage depends on the amount of venom injected, its potency (which varies considerably) and the amount of time elapsed en route to the hospital. In cases of heavy envenomation, the patient may spend a couple of days in the hospital, or a week at most.

According to Dr. Manoguerra, the most important thing to do if bitten by a venomous snake is to stay calm. In nearly half the cases of venomous bites, the snake injects little or no venom. So weakness, sweating, nausea and fainting are not signs of poisoning. Rather, they are simply the reflection of the mental trauma of being bitten. The person will usually know within five minutes whether or not venom was injected. The signs are swelling and increasingly severe pain. More serious bites will also cause a tingling sensation, accompanied by a gradual discoloration of the skin. With envenomation, it is important to get medical treatment as quickly as possible.

Envenomation by a Mojave Green rattlesnake does not produce these early symptoms. Only after six to twelve hours will the neurological symptoms become apparent, and by then treatment is long past due. The chances of receiving a bite from a Mojave Green are remote, but such a bite is considered a medical emergency, and requires administration of antivenin in a hospital.

If bitten by a snake of any kind, keep your wits about you. If you are carrying a snake suction device such as the Sawyer Extractor (recommended in the "First Aid"

chapter) then apply it. But do not cut slits in the skin and do not suck with your mouth; these out-dated practices can lead to a serious infection at the bite site, since the traumatized skin there is much less able to defend itself from bacteria. And do not apply a tourniquet. Some authorities recommend a lightly constricting band, and while this may reduce the danger to the body, it could increase the risk to the affected limb; so use your own judgment.

The California Poison Control System gives this advice for rattlesnake bites: "First immobilize the wounded area, especially for a hand or arm bite, then proceed slowly to a vehicle. (If bitten on the leg or foot, you will have to use that limb to get to the vehicle, unless someone can carry you. In that case, it is very important to move slowly. Running would increase the heart rate and thus the spread of toxin faster.) Drive to the nearest phone, call 911, and wait for assistance. If there is no phone nearby, proceed to the nearest hospital."

Camping in snake country

The chances of a snake coming into one's campsite are slim. On warm nights, snakes are busy looking for their meals, while being wary of becoming a meal for some larger creature, especially one as large as a person.

A tent with its netting doorway closed might seem to provide necessary protection, but Jenny and I have slept a great many nights beneath an open tarp, and also under the stars in the mountains and beautiful deserts, and have not been bothered by snakes.

Many backpackers carry fishing gear, and have no moral objections to eating a few nice trout for dinner. And with the exception of vegetarians, most people have no moral convictions against shopping for fish or steaks that someone else had killed for them. But for some reason, nearly all hikers consider rattlesnakes off the menu, as if these snakes are tabu, like the cows of India.

I do not normally eat meat; nor do I fish in the mountain lakes and streams. So **the following is for informational purposes only.** I am not recommending anything.

But, the fact is, rattlesnake meat makes a delicious meal when properly cooked, and its skin can make handsome leather goods.

One should never kill a gopher snake or any other harmless snake. Doing so will take away the tremendous benefits that they are providing – reducing and controlling the rodent populations and so forth. Rattlesnakes do the same, but they also occupy much the same ecological niche as gopher snakes, and serve the same basic function. So in culling a few rattlesnakes, one might be encouraging gopher snakes and other non-dangerous snakes to move in and take their place.

A rattlesnake can be safely and easily dispatched with a few well-aimed rocks thrown from a distance of not closer than twice the snake's length. Aim for the head. But one should never grab a rattlesnake that appears dead. Surprising as it might seem at the time, the snake can suddenly come around. Or even if genuinely dead, its reflexes can still be active for hours. And those reflexes are to bite. A great many careless people have sustained snakebites in this manner. Only after having removed the head is the body safe to handle.

Although a sharp pocket knife can be used for this, putting one's hand that close would be hazardous. A safer technique is to use a couple of stout sticks, at least four feet long. One of these should have a shallow fork or notch at one end to firmly clamp the snake to the ground, just behind the head. The other stick would be used to remove the head from the body. Be ready for reflex spasms and keep the snake's head firmly pinned to the ground.

A sharp knife can slit the belly along the full length, but when pulling out the guts one should be careful not to rupture them and make a mess. Think of cleaning a fish; the process is the same. The skin is removed by peeling it away from the flesh. To preserve the skin for shipping home, rub a half-pound of salt on it, then roll it up and place it in a plastic bag.

The flesh can be cooked over a campfire, using the same methods for cooking fish. Or cut the flesh into 2-inch lengths and skewer them on roasting sticks, like shish kebabs. If the meat does not taste a bit like chicken, it is not quite finished cooking.

Ridge "running" on the CDT

Bears

"When a man wants to murder a tiger he calls it sport;
when a tiger wants to murder him he calls it ferocity."
— *George Bernard Shaw*

Wild Blackie
Park Blackie
Grizzly

Some native peoples of North America hunted the bear for its meat as food, its fat as lamp oil, and its hide as clothing, blankets and rugs. Others considered the bear a reincarnated relative, or sacred in other ways, and left it strictly alone. As settlers moved west and started clearing land for towns and agriculture, the wolf, cougar and wolverine lost habitat. So the populations of these carnivorous predators dwindled. But the bear is omnivorous—its molars are flat-topped, allowing it to eat plants as well—and this has helped it adapt and flourish.

The black bear is far less aggressive and more predictable than the grizzly, and therefore not as greatly feared (and obliterated). Today, hikers are likely to encounter "Blackie" as far afield as the thick woods of northern Maine to the mountains and arid lowlands of southern California.

So let's get to know our backcountry neighbor.

———

The black bear (Ursus americanus) is not always black. It can be brown, reddish, cinnamon, blond, or cream-colored. It is powerfully muscled, equipped with claws and incisors, and forever in search of a meal. However, it does not view humans as food. Most of its diet consists of vegetation, grubs, fish, and small mammals. So black bear attacks on humans are quite rare, especially in light of the many thousands of black bears that humans come across each summer.

In the early 1960's I worked in Yellowstone National Park, and part of my summer's job entailed picking up rubbish that the bears had dug out of the trash-cans, usually in plain sight. (We did not have bear-proof litter bins back then.) As such, I was often in close proximity with these awesome creatures; and so began my close relationship with them.

These were black bears, not grizzlies. And the first thing I learned from them was that just because you see one, that does not mean that it will attack you – far from it.

While making my rounds, I sometimes had to chase a bear away, in order to perform my duties. But one time my self-invented tactics proved less than effective. The bear stood its ground, and no amount of bluffing would change its mind. By bluffing, I mean stabbing at it with my rake, without making contact of course. However, with one particularly emphatic jab the rake head flew off the handle and hit the bear smack in the face. Woops! Fortunately it only backed away; so I proceeded to pick up the trash. Then I noticed them: Five big, beautiful trout that a fisherman had discarded into the bin. I could not believe it! "Ok, bear," I said, "you win this time" and walked away, leaving it to its feast.

In the 1970s I coexisted with black bears in Yosemite National Park. Jenny and I have also observed a great many bears while hiking those untold miles through the varied backcountry of North America, both east and west. From these experiences I have come to recognize the black bears in two general types: the "wild" bear and what I call the "park" bear.

Wild Blackie

The "wild" variety of black bear lives outside the National Parks, so every hunting season it becomes prey to big-game hunters and their hound dogs. For the wild black bear, these encounters reinforce the notion that humans are to be feared and avoided. And the bear's behavior usually reflects that.

The "wild" black bears that Jenny and I have encountered on our hikes, almost without exception have fled into the woods when approached. The cubs and yearlings will sometimes run away with mother, but often they will stop and stare curiously for a few long moments before scurrying up a tree, or running in a different direction. The point is, left alone, wild black bears pose very little danger to hikers who treat them with prudence. Yes, they are big and powerful, and fully capable of harming us. But they virtually never do. My only advice with regard to wild black bears would be to leave them alone. In all likelihood they will reciprocate.

During our third PCT hike, we saw at least one "wild" black bear, with or without cubs, each day from Seiad Valley in northern California, south to Walker Pass. That was a lot of miles, and a lot of bears. And today's PCT hiker is likely to encounter "Blackie" almost anywhere along the full length of the trail.

Late one afternoon we came upon a cinnamon colored back bear and her two cubs. One look at us, and they scattered. One cub scampered up a small tree, not far from the trail, while the mother chaperoned the other cub up the forested slope. Abandoning the first cub, her intent was apparently to safeguard at least one cub, and if the other did not remain with her, then that was its problem. The little guy was quite young and cute. Jenny pleaded in jest, "Get him for a pet." No thanks.

Certain circumstances can cause a black bear to deviate from its normally docile behavior. For example, if a person is hiking or camping with a dog, especially a large dog, then that dog can find and chase a bear. Most frightened bears will climb a tree; but a big male can become enraged and chase the dog – back to the person. An enraged bear of any type is extremely dangerous.

Park Blackie

Inside National Parks, where hunting is usually not permitted, the black bear has an entirely different personality. It is not so afraid of humans. So with keen senses and an opportunistic demeanor, it tends to gravitate to the nearest black hole of humanity – namely the campgrounds. Once there, Park Blackie becomes "habituated" (read: very bold around people) and commences raiding campsites and vehicles for food, or objects resembling or possibly containing food. And being remarkably intelligent and insatiably hungry, the bear devises all manner of clever tactics to get the food, including smashing windows, prying open car trunks, and I have even seen them unlatching locks on coolers and unscrewing lids on jars.

The rangers call this "a bear problem," and rightly so. And when the bear's havoc-wreaking becomes intolerable, they bring out their dart guns and bear traps. Once captured, "bruin" is typically tranquillized, ear-tagged and even body-painted, and relocated to some improbably faraway forest. But the bear does not forget those glorious opportunities of plundering. So using its remarkable homing skills, it will often return to the scene of the crimes, however far away – only to be caught again and tagged on the other ear.

However, bears do not like being darted, caged and driven for miles. Such treatment tends to anger them fiercely. Nor do they ever forget it. So a twice-caught back bear can be as dangerous as a grizzly. And should a double-tagged bear wander into the same campground where it was caught twice before, the rangers take it on yet another drive, this time on the road less traveled, to be disposed of as humanely as possible.

However, the tagged bear might not return to the campground, but more simply descend to the nearest outpost of civilization and resume it's pillaging there. But again, if that bear has ear tags and body paint that mark it as troublemaker, it is likely to be shot on sight. And when the property owner reports the incident to the authorities, the reply is sometimes "shoot, shovel, and shut up."

Park-type bears are also found in a few places outside National Parks in areas of backcountry popular with campers and hikers. These are "wild" bears that exhibit "park" bear behavior. Even though hunted, the food temptation can be so powerful that it may override the animal's fears. If they smell food or rubbish, the park-type bears are likely to find it.

Sadly, human caused habituation usually leads to the bear's demise.

Dangerous to campers?

Rarely, a park black bear will injure a tourist trying to feed it by hand; never mind that the bear does not always know where the food ends and the hand begins. And even though a bear might appear tame, it still requires a certain amount of personal space. Normally it will only growl or behave defensively if someone ventures too close. But instincts can surface lightning fast, for example when a park visitor instructs the children to pet the bear or its cuddly-looking cubs for a photograph.

As with all creatures wild or not so wild, most of the park bear's time is spent in search of food. Yet once again, it normally has no appetite for the flesh of campers. It wants only their food. And when it wanders into a campsite in broad daylight—inside a National Park—only rarely will it meet with resistance. Rather than defend their supplies, most campers will flee, leaving the bear to feast at the picnic table. This reinforces Bruin's bold behavior. Smart campers, however, will quickly load their food into their cars and drive away. And smart hikers would do much the same: quickly stowing their food into their backpacks and hiking on – leaving the bear to try its luck elsewhere.

But should Blackie actually grab one's food at one's camp, the tables are irrevocably turned. In the interests of one's own safety, do not attempt to steal it back.

I have observed that Park Blackie can grow very large and belligerent in the late autumn while preparing to sleep for the winter. By then most hikers will have gone. Nevertheless, as a last resort to persuade a camper to yield his or her food, late-season Blackie might charge. This frightening behavior is well documented, and I have experienced it myself. However, when the matter concerns food, late season black bear aggression is usually a bluff. The bear will likely stop a few meters short. Unsettling to be sure, but once again, I have seen this behavior only during the very late season, bordering on winter.

Protecting food

The National Park authorities have implemented various schemes to solve "bear problems." First, they may instruct us to camp only in designated campsites. This is convenient for the rangers, and for the bears as well.

I do not mean to depreciate backcountry rangers. Only after we have walked a few miles in their moccasins will we begin to appreciate the challenges these hardy souls face. In the more popular Parks, Monuments, and Recreation Areas, the rangers are inundated with unconscionable campers who every night of the summer leave food and trash scattered around their camps. These campers belong in established camps.

Food bags hung from tree limbs

Because the rangers cannot fine the bear when the bear steals the camper's food, the rangers fine the camper when the bear steals the camper's food. And these fines can be stiff.

In the past, official literature and many older how-to

books depicted various methods of suspending bags of food from tree branches, so many feet above the ground, and so many feet out from the tree trunk. Unfortunately for the tree, these methods often damaged the branches, due to the sawing action of the taut cords. And, unfortunately for the campers, this method rarely worked.

It seems that many bears in the National Park backcountry, and beyond, owed their livelihood to well-intentioned hikers who trusted in the food-hanging system. Nocturnal bruin is incredibly resourceful at retrieving food bags, and the nights are long. I have seen the results of scores of bags plucked from remarkable heights. Even lost one myself in Yosemite many years ago, hung so high that the bear would have needed a stepladder to reach it. But reach it the bear did; and the massive branch supporting my erstwhile bag narrowly missed smashing my tent.

Metal lockers, wires, hangers and fences

Finding a suitable tree with a high and strong branch is a time-consuming chore at best. Realizing this, the Park Service began supplying many backcountry campsites with metal storage lockers and overhead wires[19] from which to suspend food bags. In some areas they devised other methods such as "coat hangers" (tall metal poles with angled racks at the top for hanging food bags), fenced-in shelters, such as those found in the Smokies, and bear poles as found in the Canadian Rockies. Recently, however, the authorities have removed some of these contraptions in an attempt to restore the areas to their more natural condition.

Bear-proof canisters

In their place, the Park Service is now recommending personal bear-proof canisters in many areas of the

---

19 Talk about an entertaining three-ring circus: I have seen a bear teach her cub to climb a tree and slither out on a wire to reach a suspended food bag.

National Parks, and in some cases requiring them – such as along the JMT. So the prospective hiker would be well advised to check the regulations beforehand, either online or by phone.

Canisters can keep the bears from getting into the camper's food, granted. But they might not represent the perfect solution. One difficulty lies in the bears' resourcefulness. Once a bear has learned to associate hikers with their food, it will usually search for ways to obtain that food, no matter how many times it meets with failure. If it finds a potential opportunity, it may investigate.

So canisters do not necessarily prevent bears from gravitating to the established camps—tempted by the cooking odors—and once there, prowling through the camps, pawing through any gear, and disrupting peoples' sleep. Especially when many campers leave food out in the open.

For example, when tired and hungry hikers arrive at the established campsite, they may open their canisters, pull out some food, and forget to close the canisters. Or they might empty the canisters altogether and use them for washtubs or laundry tubs. Should a bear suddenly appear, attracted by the smell of food, perfume, sunscreen, deodorants and so forth, these campers are likely to flee, rather than calmly put the food back in the canisters and close the lids. And if the bear is successful in getting a free lunch, it will become even more habituated.

Nevertheless, in areas where the canisters are required, one must use them. That, or avoid the National Parks altogether, and hike and camp in other places across the vast wilderness afield. Given the choice, we would pick the latter. But we also have enjoyed the Parks.

Typical camper behavior

But what of that wilderness afield? The maps show hundreds of thousands of miles of trails in beautifully scenic areas outside the National Parks, from the mountains to the plains to the deserts. Many of these trails also have standard, relatively well-used campsites at places of convenience or special beauty, or merely in strategic locations, for example near a lake or creek. These places naturally attract campers, in the same manner as the established campsites in the Parks usually do.

Unfortunately, every one of those "standard" campsites is likely known by every bear that lives within several miles; for even though the bear's eyesight may be poor, its sense of smell is extraordinary.

When people at these places build campfires, the smoke sends an olfactory signal to the bears clearer than any siren. And when they cook food, they are sending aromas many times more alluring. And when campers hang bags of food at those camps, they might as well be advertising them; same with leaving food and rubbish strewn about.

So while these campsites might be convenient for the people, they are hazardous to the bears in the long term, because of their tendency to human-habituate the bears. And we have already seen where that can lead.

Fortunately, not every standard campsite along every trail has a bear problem – far from it. But the number of hikers and other outdoor enthusiasts who use these campsites is growing each year. And the bear's habitat is shrinking in many areas due to forest fires. So every camper who uses those campsites with the old rulebook camping practices can be the start of a bear problem in that area. When I think of the heavily used established campsites in the National Parks, and what they have become—both to people and bears—I imagine that they must have had their beginnings in like manner.

So it might be time to think a little further down the trail, when future generations of hikers and bears may be confronted with these problems.

Super lightweight bear canisters might be one answer. At present, approved canisters are fairly heavy, weighing from two to three pounds. They are also bulky and have limited capacity. We have seen a few prototype lightweight ones, but the problem for the designers lies in the awesome power of the bears' jaws. Also, the marketing potential may not be sufficient to justify their refinement, especially when hikers might rent rather than buy.

As another solution, hikers might also take some pressure off those standard campsites by spreading out and adopting the principles of stealth camping.

Back bears precautions

At the time of this writing, stealth camping is allowed in most areas of the backcountry, even in many areas of the National Parks but certainty not all.

Jenny and I camp well away from the bear's standard zones of activity, and take definitive measures to decrease the chances of a bear visit to our stealth-sites.

By "well away" I mean several miles from the nearest standard campsite. Also we are extremely careful to preserve the stealth camping legacy by not cooking or building campfires at our impromptu stealth-sites, by not wearing highly-scented deodorant or insect repellent and the like, which might attract a bear, and by leaving our camps in absolutely pristine condition.

We also keep a small flashlight near at hand. Many wild creatures are nocturnal, and a shuffling or scratching could indicate deer, a porcupine, mouse or vole, or another small to medium sized creature. These animals have awakened us many times, and after we have shined a flashlight on them to identity them, they have always brought smiles to our faces. But also that noise could be a bear. We have not heard or seen a bear at one of our stealth-sites, but if and when we do, we would simply rise, pack up, and move on.

Our preference for storing food at our stealth-sites (outside of the National Parks), and it is only that—our personal preference—is to keep our food bags somewhat near our heads but just out of our reach. By sleeping with our food just outside the shelter, we are placing the food more safely between ourselves and any bear. We do not keep our food inside a tent, under our heads, or under our legs. That would be placing ourselves between the food and any bear. People have been seriously injured by a big Blackie ripping into their tents and inadvertently trampling or clawing them to get at their food.

Grizzly Bears

The grizzly bear (Ursus arctos) also called the brown bear, is the California state animal, even though it was last seen there in 1924. Eradicated from its former habitat across the western and southwestern states—ostensibly for sport, but in reality out of fear—the grizzly now roams freely in North America only in Alaska and Canada; and in limited numbers in Glacier and Yellowstone National Parks, and to a lesser extent the Bob Marshall and Scapegoat Wilderness and a few parts farther south.

This powerful, brownish-yellow bear possesses an altogether different disposition, so our discussion about the black bear does not apply here.

Our grizzly sightings

In our 125 or so grizzly bear sightings, about half of them were up-close and dangerous. Most of these encounters occurred on the northwest coast of Alaska, and we recount some them in our book *Siku Kayak*.

While working in Yellowstone NP in 1963, I watched a few grizzlies at a safe distance. But also I hiked a few hundred miles on Yellowstone trails without seeing a bear. During our CDT trekk of 1992 we hiked through Glacier, the Bob, Scapegoat and Yellowstone without seeing a grizzly, although we saw many fresh signs, mainly in Glacier.

To date, we have seen grizzly bears only once while hiking. This was on the Idaho-Montana border, a ways south of Lemhi Pass on our IUA trip. From a distance of thirty yards we caught sight of a big sow and her yearling cub lumbering along, foraging. Being at the top of the food chain, grizzlies are not particularly wary; so these bears did not notice us. We quickly and silently backtracked a hundred yards around the corner, and circumvented the area widely.

Defensive measures

We found Glacier Park utterly spectacular, with beautiful scenery and excellent hiking. But also, it is reputed to have some of the country's most dangerous bears.

On average, Glacier sees about two to three maulings a year. The authorities tend to play down these tragedies by pointing out the even greater risks of falling off trails and over cliffs, getting into auto accidents within the Park sustaining heart attacks, and so forth. Still, I find these bear-related attacks appalling. By my way of thinking, hiking should be about enjoyment, not mortal peril.[20]

For defense, a shotgun loaded with rifled slugs is a perennial favorite with people in the far north. But such a weapon comes with its own dangers. The shooter must have a great deal of training and practice beforehand. If a shot only wounds a grizzly, the enraged animal could become much more dangerous.

Spray canisters of oleoresin capsicum (OC) are becoming more effective with the developing technologies. We carry them on our trips when in grizzly country, along with other measures. Some bear spray manufacturers have very informative websites, so I will not repeat that information here.

Suffice it to say that when in grizzly bear territory, each hiker would be well advised to keep a large spray canister immediately serviceable at all times. It can be worn clipped to the belt or backpack strap by day, and placed close at hand at night. But first one must practice using

---

20 The rangers there who make and enforce the rules live in bear-proof houses themselves, and often when out on "patrol," carry shotguns for bear defense.

it, so that the handling becomes instinctual. Otherwise in a panicked encounter, one may not remember how to use it.

Hiking in grizzly territory

Since the grizzly can be most unpredictable, the hiker must remain alert when in its domain, keeping eyes and ears open. One might consider hiking with companions, the more the better. On the trail, one must be extremely careful not to startle a grizzly. Forewarned, the bear will likely move away. But thick brush and tall vegetation can conceal bears, and they often do not pay attention to what might be coming. If surprised, a bear could charge, even at a distance of 100 feet or more. Making a great deal of noise, then, is the order of the day. In grizzly country (and only in grizzly country) one might consider carrying bear bells, singing loudly, and making regular call-outs. However, we have met a few old-timers who recommend against attracting the bears' attention. So our personal rule is to sing in thick brush and keep silent in the open where a bear is more easily spotted.

Judicious cooking

When hiking in grizzly country, a person might carry the type of food that does not need to be cooked, for the peace of mind if nothing else. Despite the desire for a hot meal and a mug of hot soup, these might not be worth the risk. The food should be packaged in re-sealable plastic bags, and the garbage kept tightly sealed and well away from camp, same with the food and any cooking utensils.

Camping precautions

In the grizzly's domain, Jenny and I are much more cautious as we search for a stealth-site, staying away from dense brush and thickets. Instead we look for open areas where we will have a wide view of our surroundings. And too, we much prefer camping under an open tarp. A tent might attract a curious bear to see what is inside, although they mainly operate by smell rather than by sight.

Many items from home that a camper might consider odorless, or pleasantly perfumed, could be quite attractive to bears, especially to grizzlies. "Signal odors" might include soap, deodorant, toothpaste, body lotion, sunscreen, the perfume of laundry soap in the clothes, and the perfume from the static-free sheets used in the clothes dryer.

Bears can also smell a person's body odor accumulated after hiking for a few days. So on a long trip one might bathe often, but not with scented soap. And bears can smell odors of cooking lingering in one's clothing. So as a precaution, one might consider sealing the hiking clothing, shoes, socks, rain jackets, etc, in a plastic bag at camp, and wearing clean, unscented clothing while sleeping, as we did in Glacier N.P.

A bear's sense of smell is believed to be 100,000 times more acute than a human's.

The most powerful odor of all to a grizzly bear is blood; it may bring them into a killing frenzy. So women in their time of month must keep themselves extra clean. And once again, when in grizzly country, carrying bear spray is probably a good idea.

———————

As majestic as these creatures are, most hikers and campers would rather not see a grizzly, at least up close. By following the precautions outlined above, one can stack the odds in one's favor.

Glacier Peak glinting over the rise, PCT-2.

Cougars

Stealth and survivability

The thought of a cougar strikes fear into the hearts of many hikers; but in the vast majority of cases this fear is completely unjustified. "The only thing we have to fear," said Franklin D. Roosevelt, "is fear itself."

The cougar (Felis concolor) is also commonly called the mountain lion. And depending on location it is also known as the puma, panther, or catamount. It ranges from central Canada to Patagonia, and flourishes in a variety of environments, including swampy terrain, jungles, deserts, and forests – from sea level to the alpine regions.

Some ranchers still consider the cougar "vermin" and poison it. According to them, their livestock—which they import into the cougar's domain—need protection. Fortunately for the cougar and the rest of the intricately balanced natural world connected with this magnificent animal, the cougar's stealth and adaptability have enabled it to endure.

By current estimates, some 5,000 inhabit California, a figure that comprises about a quarter of the cougar population for the western states combined. The Florida panther population is estimated at only 30 to 50 animals.

The cougar has well developed hearing, a keen sense of smell for following scent trails, and excellent vision for hunting both day and night. It can spring twenty feet, and make a running jump the same height into a tree. It can sprint like a cheetah, but prefers to stalk its prey until close enough to leap onto the prey's back and take it down. The cougar feeds mainly on deer and elk, but its diet may also include small mammals, wild turkeys, and when available, domestic livestock.

Risks to hikers

The black bear, the grizzly bear, and the cougar are each fully capable of attacking hikers. They are powerfully built, always hungry, and have large canine teeth designed to deliver lethal bites. Yet only the grizzly poses any real danger to hikers. As such, those who visit the grizzly bears' realms would be wise to carry spray canisters of OC, as described in the previous chapter.

Should a hiker visit Glacier N.P. while disregarding the normal bear-related safety precautions, he or she might be trolling for trouble. On the other hand, this same hiker could visit anywhere else out of grizzly's territory, and thrash in the bush heedlessly for hours, cook just about anywhere, and generally bumble through the woods with little heed for caution, and not worry about being attacked by any animal, large or small, including the black bear, cougar, moose, marmot, or mouse. The black bear might want your food; and the mouse might want some as well. And indeed, the person may see black bears on the trail and mice around camp. But in a lifetime of hiking, that person might never see a cougar. And in that lifetime of hiking, he or she could talk to every hiker met along the way, and virtually none of them would have any personal experiences with cougars, other than maybe a rare and brief sighting.

The cougar is an extremely efficient hunter, sensing its prey at a distance and stalking it with almost otherworldly stealth. But is the cougar dangerous to hikers? I don't think so. If it is inclined to attack hikers, it would have taken us all down long ago. People have a genetic fear of being preyed upon by large animals. For our primordial ancestors, this was a good type of fear. It helped alert them to danger and greatly increased their chances of survival.

But statistically, the cougar might endanger people today only in a few broad scenarios. One: a young, inexperienced cat wanders into an encroaching suburb to see whether it might snatch a family pet or lone child. And two: a cougar lashes out in defense of her kitten when she feels threatened by someone heedlessly running or racing along.

Jenny and I were hiking the PCT in Washington when suddenly we heard a fearsome growl coming from somewhere close. We backed away, and caught sight of a cougar flashing through the thick brush. Then we heard a soft "meow" from a nearby kitten. The mother was apparently warning us to stop, desist, and stay away!

At the time, we were headed in the general direction of her youngster, unknowingly of course. But because we were merely walking, i.e. moving slowly, I think the mother had time to warn us. But suppose someone was moving faster at the kitten, for example jogging or mountain biking. In that case the mother might have no time to issue a warning; her instincts might dictate that she physically stop the threat.

Cougars are wary of people

Cougars, like all big carnivores, are skilled at judging the risks involved with making a kill. And programmed into the cougar's gene memory from primitive times is an innate fear of human hunters. That is why hikers are generally safe among these animals. But on rare occasions—particularly when protecting kittens—the cougar may behave differently when suddenly threatened. It may instinctually panic and leap on a jogger or mountain biker to stop what it might perceive as a threat.

Unfortunately, once this cougar has learned that people are not very good at defending themselves, like deer or elk, this cougar may repeat the behavior. So with the news of this incident, the authorities usually try to find and dispatch this animal to prevent a recurrence.

In the above scenario, the person who is moving faster than a normal walking speed might be at a disadvantage. He or she might not notice subtle movements in the peripheral vision; or might not hear a kitten's meow; and may not be able to react quite as quickly as someone walking. The cougar has a similar dilemma. One moment all is quiet and peaceful; the next moment a threat suddenly appears. Instincts might take over.

I have not heard of a cougar pouncing on sleeping campers. This alone seems to speak volumes about the camper's safety in cougar country.

A juvenile cat, seeking its niche, might test a person as to whether he or she will put up a fight, or merely run away, as would a deer. Again, this situation is extremely unlikely. But in such a case the person might do everything possible to show that he or she is fierce and aggressive, for example by throwing rocks or sticks at the cat. In every incident that I have read about, what few there have been, this tactic frightened away the animal.

In a worst-case scenario, should a cougar attack a person from behind and lock its jaws around the neck, someone else might persuade a release by pounding the animal's snout violently and repeatedly with a hefty rock or big stick. Or the person himself might be able to unlock the jaws by reaching into the mouth, just behind the canines on both sides, and pulling the lower teeth and jaw down.

———————

A few websites give statistics on cougar-related incidents, and can make for interesting reading. Many stories found in the media may have some basis, but might not have been reported accurately or interpreted correctly. And any second-hand stories are subject to exaggeration and over-dramatization. For example, we knew of a hiker on the PCT who put Jim Bridger to shame with the tall tales he spread on the trail and in towns. The second-hand stories we heard from the town folks were sensational: cougars supposedly stalked him during the day, and bears ripped his sleeping bag off of him at night. Yet we were hiking behind this fellow and were having no such problems. So we tend to dismiss such improbable accounts.

Late summer in the Sierra; PCT-3

Part 8

Long-Distance Hiking

CDT

Trail Life

Dreams into Goals

"The way you activate the seeds of your creation
is by making choices about the results you want to create.
When you make a choice, you mobilize vast
human energies and resources
which otherwise go untapped."
— *Robert Fritz*

A person is never more than two feet from freedom

Human life is a dichotomy, encompassing the new and the old. Our new science and technology are accelerating us into the future, but our genetic make-up is anchored in the past. For indeed, as Homo Sapiens we have built-in traits and instincts designed to insure our survival back in prehistoric times.

So while striving to create an ever more sophisticated society, where progress is determined by how far we have bulldozed away nature, we were designed to function in the natural world, where physical exertion and exposure to the elements were a part of life.

Technology has freed us from those pressures of raw survival. So physical challenges are rarely imposed on us. But this freedom is not without cost. The industrialization and luxuries that shelter us from labor and discomfort also prevent us from experiencing the natural world and exploring new realms – both on a geographical level and a personal one.

I think these primitive instincts are ingrained in each of us. And it seems to me that if we address them every now and then, our lives would become more sharply focused. But about the only way we can do that, in this day and age, is to invent goals for ourselves – goals which involve sweat-induced labor and a measure of discomfort, and which reintroduce us to uncertainty and risk. For it is only by confronting these challenges that we can even begin to experience our full capabilities as human beings.

How so? We are subject to a disordering of life, an all pervading force acting on us the way gravity would act on a rock lying tenuously upon a steep hillside. Left alone, the rock's only future would be to skid slowly downward, as nudged by storms, earthquakes or erosion.

In certain ways we are like this rock; and civilization is sapping the lives out of us, regardless of how well acclaimed a person might be, or how well clothed, automobiled, housed, and entertained.

Many people feel a longing to escape the endless treadmill, the increasing crowding together, the world foul with pollution and crime, and the corporations who might prey upon us – and instead to experience something new and more fulfilling.

This longing is our genetic programming speaking to us.

In his book *Personal Best*, George Sheehan draws a compelling likeness between recovering alcoholics and runners (or perhaps backpackers, mountain climbers, ocean voyagers, et al) in that people in each group seem to have an innate urge to strive against what evils would consume their lives. The ruinous agent the recovering alcoholic battles is of course liquor, and that which the athlete or adventurer strives against is languor.

Dreams

The goals we invent for ourselves have to be contrived.

Of themselves, they do not exist. What may exist are our dreams. But dreams are like electricity with no wires. They have nowhere to flow despite their tremendous potential.

Most of us have dreams, but not all of us forge them into goals. Like electricity with no wires, most people simply await the right opportunities.

Even if the right opportunities were to happen along, they might only ensnare a person to the wills of the

> As Thomas la Mance quipped: "Life is what happens while you are making other plans."

people who created them. Self-wrought goals, on the other hand, beckon us ahead of our own volition.

Dispersed campfire coals extinguish themselves. But scooped together they can ignite the kindling to produce a heartening blaze. And so it is with dreams. Scoop them carefully and purposefully together, fan some life into them, and they can engender a blaze of resolve and purpose. And scoop together the disparate but glowing fragments of our lives – the innate talents, abilities and courage within us all, and we become far more capable.

Expression of life

The dreams and goals that are most interesting to Jenny and me are those that take us back into the natural world where we can test our mettle, exercise our bodies, and yes, perhaps experience a measure of discomfort, and even at times come face to face with uncertainty and risk.

Society would view these as personal indignities, to be avoided at all costs. But during our trips and expeditions we feel more alive than ever. For us, our trips are an expression of life itself.

Introducing ideas

Not everyone has clear pictures of the fun and exciting challenges that might be awaiting them. Ideas can come from almost anywhere. For example, from books. Reading can introduce a person to a whole world full of possibilities.

A sailing book

As a young man, one of my favorite pastimes was reading adventure books, including those of sailing the high seas. Emulating those hardy souls vicariously, I envisioned that one day I would undertake an around-the-world journey of my own. But because I lived nearly mid-continent, my seafaring had to take place solely between the covers of those books. Then in 1980 I determined to get closer to those dreams by moving to San Diego. One evening I was reading Maurice and Katie Cloughley's *A World to the West*, a lustrous account of their sailing circumnavigation. At one point Maurice wrote that after a particularly grisly passage between landfalls, he and Katie sailed their ketch into some tranquil lagoon—out there in never-never land, it seemed to me— and anchored in its crystal, warm waters. "How good it was to be in," he wrote, "we felt fabulous."

Those words struck me.

The next day I found myself seated in my flashy new sports car waiting interminably for a traffic light to change at a frenzied intersection. Like a hostage, I sat listening to the high-tech stereo blaring interminable advertisements in quadraphonic sound. Despite the air-conditioned comfort, "I felt frustrated" would have been about all that I could report.

The contrast between the vibrant lifestyle I was reading about, and the lackluster one I was actually living, hit me hard. My business (distributing *Friends*) was bristling, but the unbounded struggle for financial success and security, I had to admit, was not fulfilling any deeper needs. The next day I began searching for a sailboat.

A bicycling book

As another example of a book planting an idea, many years back Jenny and I read a book by a couple who had undertaken a long bicycle trip. They wrote about the pain and sometimes the agony, for example when one of them crashed headlong onto the pavement. They wrote about the insects, rain, and all sorts of things that would dissuade the average person from even attempting such a trip. But reading between the lines, we could see that they were extremely proud of their ride, and that they considered it well worth their while, in terms of what they had gained. So we thought: "what if?"

We carried that dream in our hearts for years. Meanwhile we read several more books on the subject, during which time those dreams began to coalesce.

Moving ahead

A person's goal does not have to be grand or impressive. But when the dreamer has decided on an immediate goal, his or her life becomes more dynamic and meaningful. The free time will be filled, not with watching useless TV programs, browsing the internet, or text-messaging various people who lack plans of their own, but with the preparations, physical conditioning, and the moving ahead with the plan.

I think each one of us tends to pattern our lives according to our highest wishes. Those people who enjoy watching TV more than anything else, do that. Those who want impressive cars and luxurious homes, expend their lives getting those. But those who dream of hiking a long trail, for example, or sailing the high seas, or peddling or paddling a long journey, and who want to do this so seriously that they are willing to make the required sacrifices, then that is what they will do. This is true regardless of a person's physical make-up, job, financial situation, age, and level of experience. Whatever this person focuses upon, will become his or her reality.

So give yourself something special to be excited about, to plan for, and to live for. And do not limit yourself. Your only genuine limits are the ones you place upon yourself.

As a reader once confided: "Having been lazy and laid-back most of my life, I was amazed at my ability to set an objective and totally commit myself to it."

I think Sir Arthur Conan Doyle said it best in one of his dialogues: "My life is spent in one long effort to escape from the commonplaces of existence."

PCT-2

Financing the Journey

"There is no more fatal blunderer than he who
consumes the greater part of his life
getting his living."

— *Thoreau*

In-come versus out-flow

For the hiker who dreams of a summer on the trail, the chances of a successful journey can be quite good. This is true regardless of the person's finances, be they lavish or negligible. To succeed at long-distance hiking, the adventurer needs to have an uncompromising sense of motivation and focus. Without these, a checkmate is likely. But with them, the adventurer will make whatever compromises are necessary.

Regardless of income, a person's financial situation depends mostly on the rate of spending. Case in point: High-salaried individuals may seem well-off, but they might be practically broke if they spend most of what they earn. And if they have gone deeply into debt, their situation often becomes desperate. Debt is rampant these days, and while it allows for a so-called higher standard of living, it also deprives people of their freedom – freedom to spend more time enjoying the wilds, in this case.

People often consider their luxury possessions essentials, and accept the recurring payments as necessary. In reality, the payments are necessary only because of the debts entered into. And the reason that modern life is so expensive is because of the size and number of a person's expenditures. These might include house payments or apartment rent, furniture payments, insurance payments, repair bills and property taxes, utility and telephone bills, memberships, subscriptions, high-speed internet services, health and life insurance, new car installments and the associated insurance premiums, licensing fees, gas and maintenance costs. A person might have frequent entertainment expenses, a few lavish vacations to pay for, along with high credit card and loan interest, and so forth. Money in the bank equals deposits *minus* all of these expenditures. Little wonder that money can be such a problem.

Most of us could easily afford a summer's backpacking journey by eliminating, or at least minimizing some of these expenses. Rather than drive a new car, a person could drive an older one. Consider that the monthly payments and insurance premiums on a new car could easily grubstake a thru-hiker all summer long, year after year for the duration of the debt. One way to cut expenses might be to relocate to a less expensive town. Granted, the standard of living might not be upscale, and the job might not pay as well, but the costs of living could be far less. The prospective adventurer with sights set beyond the ostentatious might be just as content, and his or her savings might grow.

Many distance hikers finance their multi-month excursions by working long hours during the winter months, while spending the absolute minimum. Even though their income may not be great, their expenses are relatively few, so their savings increase.

Some of my happiest times were those early years in Yosemite when I lived either in a tent or an old car. Every summer I saved just enough money from three months of wilderness instructing to allow me to focus the remaining nine months on rock climbing and sea

Resupplies

"I journeyed fur, I journeyed fas';
I glad I foun' de place at las'!"
— *Joel Chandler Harris;*
Nights with Uncle Remus

Turning our backs on the distractions of urban life, Jenny and I follow our chosen trail deep into the wilds. And there we may remain for days on end, reveling in the freedom and the purity; the "tonic of the wilderness" as Thoreau so aptly put it. Until we run out of food.

But running out of food does not mean that we have to return home. Nor does it mean that we need airdrops, at least here in the Lower 48. Our wilderness areas are conveniently situated, giving us walkable access to places that sell food, or places to which we can receive food mailed to us. Along the more well-traveled trails, these "resupply" opportunities are spaced usually no more than four to six hiking days apart. And when we reach one, we can load our backpacks with provisions, and then set off again into another stretch of backcountry. On a longer trip we can repeat the process for weeks or even months at a time.

The resupply opportunities normally consist of stores, post offices, or resorts. Seldom are they in the wilderness, or even close to our chosen trails. Most often we must hike out a ways to reach them. Maybe a mile, sometimes much more. But since we are carrying reasonably light packs, the extra walking should entail little extra trouble. And if we have been in the woods a while, we may be looking forward to fresh food, hot showers, laundromat,

restaurant, telephone, post office, and perhaps even a motel room or hostel for the night. Some trail towns offer all these amenities and more, while the little outposts might offer only the bare minimum.

Food for the next stretch of hiking will usually be our greatest need. But many of the small stores and resorts may not sell the types of nutritious foods we prefer; particularly as our hard working bodies require quality food, and lots of it. Also, we might need new shoes or a few items of equipment or clothing to replace things worn out.

For these reasons, we may decide ahead of time, while in the planning stages of our hike, to amass most of our supplies at home, and then arrange to have someone mail them to the resupply "stations" so that they will be there when we arrive.

The resupply station

I use the term "station" to suggest, not a large building of brick and stone, like a train station, but an ordinary post office, a small store, or a resort with postal facilities. It is a station in the sense that, during the course of a long journey, we stop there for a short while before moving on. However nondescript, it is a place where a friendly postal worker or proprietor of a small store or resort will receive our box of supplies and hold it for us until we arrive.

Station types

The types of resupply stations available vary from place to place. And each has its own way of operating, with different hours, availability of services, and restrictions on holding parcels. Based on these differences, we can group the stations in three types:

▶ Post Office: offering the usual postal receiving and sending services. Typically post offices are housed in their own buildings. They do not accept parcels sent by other parcel delivery services like United Parcel Service (UPS) or FedEx. Most post offices are closed on weekends, though some have limited hours on Saturdays. And they are normally closed during national holidays. In the three-season trekking season these holidays are: Memorial Day (the last Monday of May), Independence Day (July 4), Labor Day (the first Monday of September), and Columbus Day (the second Monday of October).

▶ Resort or store with a small post office inside the building: These offer hikers the best of both worlds. They accept parcels sent via U.S. Postal Service, UPS, FedEx, and most other delivery services. They will usually hand over parcels anytime they are open, which is typically seven days a week throughout the summer season. And they can handle outgoing parcels, at least during their postal hours.

▶ Resort or store with no post office: These are commercial enterprises that might receive and hold parcels, sometimes for a fee. On the plus side, they will normally hand over a hiker's parcel anytime they are open, usually seven days a week. And this is a big plus. On the minus side, they can rarely handle outgoing packages or mail. These resorts or stores tend to be fairly remote, so they are out of range of the postal delivery service. Instead, they must send an employee to the post office in the nearest town. As such, they usually prefer that hikers send their boxes to them via United Parcel Service. UPS might deliver the packages to their door, whereas the Postal Service delivers only to their nearest post office. If sending a box via UPS, you might save money if you let the clerk know that you are sending the package to a commercial address rather than a residential one.

Handling dozens of hikers' boxes is a big job for the people running the more heavily used resupply stations. Naturally, some of the private concerns charge handling fees. Those that do not are acting out of generosity. Either way, it is always a good idea to express one's appreciation for their services. Without them, our journeys would be far more problematic.

Selecting resupply stations

To determine the various resupply stations available along our intended route, Jenny and I study a relevant guidebook, if any. Often it will list towns or resorts near the trail. In addition, we examine the appropriate maps, starting with a state highway map for an overview of the area. Also, a person might contact other hikers who have traveled the same route, and ask them for information about resupply stations and services.

Ready for resupply day

Depending on the trail and the remoteness of the region it passes through, we might have to walk a considerable distance between resupplies. We have hiked a number of 200-mile stretches between resupply stations. Along the CDT we hiked a 300-mile stretch along the Idaho-Montana border, bypassing one far-off-trail possibility. We did this twice on different trips. On the other hand, in some cases we have found the resupply stations so numerous and close together that we skipped a few, in order to save the off-trail time and expense. This is what trip planning is all about, and in many ways it can be a challenge in its own right. The idea is to plan ahead so well that during the journey we encounter the minimum of difficulties and disappointments.

Once we have located the stations and selected them as pertinent to our trip, we contact each one and ask whether they will accept and hold our supply parcel. And if so, then what are their hours and fees. We ask how far in advance they recommend we send the package, and we find out whether they have any restrictions or other requirements. Once they have responded, we can start planning our itinerary.

The spreadsheet itinerary

The trip itinerary helps us determine what supplies to send where, and when. We use a computer spreadsheet for this, but a person could tabulate his or her plans with pencil and paper. Either way, we begin by entering our list of chosen resupply stations into our spreadsheet (or list). Next, we determine the trail miles between each station. If this information is not given in the appropriate guidebooks, then we measure it on our maps. We then enter this mileage data into our itinerary. For example, our list will show Station A, then x miles to Station B, then x miles to Station C, and so forth.

Next, we estimate the number of hiking days between each station. To do this, we divide the between-station trail mileages by our estimated daily mileage. For example, if Station A and Station B are 100 miles apart, and we are planning to hike 20 miles a day, then we would cover the distance in 5 days. This tells us that we need to place five days worth of food and provisions in the resupply box going to Station A.

Obviously, a higher daily mileage will reduce the amount of food we will need to carry between resupply stations, and therefore it will lighten our packs. If the trail is extremely long and the hiking season comparatively short, then a higher daily mileage is beneficial and perhaps even necessary. But on shorter journeys, when we might be more interested in exploring, climbing peaks, or relaxing around camp, the daily mileage may not be so important. Whatever the case, we simply plan that into our spreadsheet by adjusting our daily mileage figures.

Estimating layover days

When reaching a resupply station, we may want to spend a bit of time there, showering, laundering clothes, and enjoying a couple of restaurant meals. So we plan ahead for this layover time. In terms of the spreadsheet itinerary, the moment we leave the trail to head for a station, we are effectively beginning a "layover." If we plan on backtracking to the trail, rather than short-cutting ahead, then while hiking out to the station, and hiking back to it, we are not gaining trail mileage. Technically, then, if we spend half a day walking or hitchhiking out, and the same amount of time returning to the trail, then we are expending a full layover day. How long a person spends off the trail is up to him or her. But we try to anticipate this, by figuring it into our itinerary. It works like this:

Let's say that we plan to start hiking on the morning of Day 1, and that we will hike for five days and arrive at Station A in the evening of Day 5. We plan to spend that night there, at Station A, and we plan to spend the next day and night there as well. This means that we would depart Station A the morning of Day 7. The idea is to specify this in our spreadsheet, detailing not only our hiking time, but our layover time as well.

This type of spreadsheet is simple to create, and should work for any trail. Engineering types like myself can take the process further by formulating various mathematical algorithms, and programming them as modules in the spreadsheets.

With our spreadsheet information in hand, it's time to

fill our resupply boxes with food and other supplies for each trail segment.

Preparing the resupply parcels

Once we have determined the number of resupply stations we will use, we know how many shipping boxes we will need. For this we could buy cardboard boxes commercially, but usually we can find equally suitable boxes salvaged from recycling bins. We might check behind stores, or ask the store managers for their discarded boxes. Bookstores often have particularly strong and durable boxes. This is important because the resupply parcels might be subject to rough handling en route to their destinations. And unfortunately, paying extra for "Special Handling" is unlikely to help. So we use sturdy boxes. We also double-tape all the joints, including those across the tops and the bottoms, and carefully remove any previous address labels to reduce the chances of the box heading to the wrong place.

At this point, we have a number of boxes and sacks of food taking up floor space. So we line the boxes along a wall. If our journey will be long, then so will our line of boxes. In fact they might extend the full length of one wall, head out the doorway and run part way along a wall of an adjacent room.

Onto each box we affix a temporary label specifying its destination. The order of these boxes is specified in our itinerary. Then, we fill each box with its designated number of days' supplies. These supplies would include food—both for meals during the hiking and possibly for eating at that particular resupply station—camera chips for the next section of trail, the appropriate section of the guide book, (cut from the book and re-bound into the appropriate trail segments using staples and adhesive tape) any additional maps, journal paper, flashlight batteries, first aid items, and any replacement or additional articles of clothing and footwear. If the parcel weighs more than fifty pounds, for example if a person is boxing

up supplies for more than two people, then it might be better to repackage it into two smaller boxes.

Other than potatoes, we are careful about adding fresh produce. As it rots, it gives off a terribly foul odor that can spoil much of the box's contents, as well as relations with the resupply station managers. We are careful, too, about how we pack the boxes. A mistake that I made only once was to pack soap next to food. The essence of soap permeated its plastic bag into those of its neighbors. The resulting soap-flavored corn chips had little to recommend them.

The shipping label

The ship-to label needs to be easy to read. A neatly printed name and address written with a large, black marking pen will stand out. This will help the clerk find and recognize the package. A hastily scribbled name and address written with a ball point pen might be overlooked in a stack of many boxes.

We also write our expected arrival date on the shipping label. This helps station managers organize the hikers' parcels. And in the unlikely event of a missing hiker, it could provide useful information for the authorities.

If a box contains supplies for two or more hikers, then the shipping label should include all names, rather than that of only one person in the group. Someone from this group might reach the supply station well ahead of the designated "leader." Or someone might be elected to detour to the station to collect the parcel. Or, as sometimes happens, someone might drop out. Whatever the case, postal regulations forbid handing over a box to someone whose name is not on the address label. And regulations require that this hiker show photo identification: a driver's license or other form of picture ID. That means, of course, the address label must show real names, rather than trail names.

Mailing the parcels

Most distance hikers enlist the services of a relative or close friend, who "volunteers" to mail the resupply parcels according to the itinerary schedule. Mailing them all at once might seem like a good idea, but postal regulations state that parcels sent to a General Delivery address—the usual method for hiker's resupply boxes—must be returned if not picked up within four weeks. In more realistic terms, if a box has been in residence for more than two or three weeks, the station manager may be less congenial, since they are usually cramped for storage space.

We leave a copy of our shipping schedule with our home-base person, and carry a copy for our own reference as well. During the actual journey we telephone home-base occasionally to relate news of our progress, to adjust the shipping schedule if necessary, and most importantly to encourage our helper and express our ongoing appreciation. Theirs is a lackluster job, driving repeatedly to the post office or UPS center, lugging ponderous boxes inside, and standing in line with them. But the arrangement has decided advantages for us. For example, we can leave the boxes open so that our helper can add things prior to sending them. These might include home-baked goodies, fresh potatoes, and any items of clothing or equipment that we might request by telephone.

During the course of the summer, should a hiker change his or her mind about continuing the trek, he or she should arrange for the parcels to be returned. If sent "Priority," then they will be returned at no extra charge. If sent "Parcel Post" then they will be sent back with postage due. In that case, one can save money by using the "Change of Address" forms, available at a post office. The hiker would fill these out and mail them to each postal-type resupply station, along with a request for the return of the parcel. The private, parcel-holding establishments work differently. These would need to be called or written

to with the request. And the hiker would of course send them any money required for holding the parcels, in addition to the return postage. That, or instruct them to throw out the parcel. A hiker who "forgets" this important step might have the search and rescue team looking for him or her. Not a good idea.

The return parcel

At many of our resupply stations, we might want to send items back home; items from our packs that we have deemed unnecessary or no longer need such as journal pages from the previous section's hike, and so forth. We facilitate this by including a shipping label and a small roll of boxing tape in each resupply parcel. To fashion a small roll of tape, we simply wrap a long length of tape around a cylindrical object – such as the cardboard insert from a roll of toilet paper. There at the station, we can recycle our resupply box by cutting it down to the appropriate size for the items we wish to send home. After filling this modified box with the unneeded items, we tape it closed, remove the old label, tape on the new shipping label, and mail the parcel home.

The drift box

On our longer hikes, Jenny and I have used what we referred to as a "running resupply box," also known as the drift box, or sometimes the bounce box. This is a small parcel that we send ahead rather than home. It contains items that we might need later, but not presently, such as spare shoes and fresh insoles, extra socks, a spare water filter cartridge, extra camera batteries and chips, a small whetstone, a utility knife with disposable blades, a tube of seam-sealing compound, a spare spoon, an extra sweater, and a roll of boxing tape. The drift box gives us occasional access to these items without the need to carry them. We send it Priority to a station approximately two weeks ahead. And we write forwarding instructions beneath the mailing address, in case the parcel is delayed and we reached the station first. We also keep with us a list of the drift box's contents, along with such information as the date we mailed it, and where we mailed it to. This reminds us of what we sent, and from where. Coming into a resupply station, it is always nice to know what supplies should be waiting.

However, as we became more experienced with long-distance hiking, we outgrew the need for the drift box. We did this by minimizing the needed items, and anticipating the rest and packing them into our resupply boxes from the start.

Hikers lacking a home base

Hikers who must be extra thrifty, or who are visiting from other countries, or who lack a home-base helper, could use one of the following methods for resupplying:

1) Skip the resupply parcels and hitchhike out to towns at frequent intervals and buy food there. Many hikers use this method. But while saving money on resupply postage, they tend to spend even more money in the trail towns.

Jenny and I have given rides to many hikers, and have even bought some of them lunch. However, when on journey we enjoy spending most of our time in the wilds, so we shape our itineraries with an eye toward minimizing hitchhiking. And too, we have never been comfortable hitchhiking, so we use this method only rarely. Mainly, we do not care for relinquishing our control, nor the feeling of standing alongside a road imposing ourselves on the motorists flying by, especially because we know that most motorists do not appreciate hitchhikers. Nevertheless, when a ride finally does come along, we enjoy meeting the people who kindly gave us a lift, and we appreciate the quick transport from trail to town.

For us, the hitchhike method has other drawbacks. The grocery stores rarely sell our preferred trail foods: corn spaghetti for example. And if we need other items,

new shoes, etc., our chances of finding them in that town are slim. That is mainly why we use the resupply parcels method: so we will have the things we need without extra trouble. On the plus side, most grocery stores sell fresh fruits and vegetables. To us this is big plus, although the produce will not last long without refrigeration, so we cannot carry much back to the trail with us.

2) The second option is to take the parcels en masse to a professional mail forwarding service. Be sure they understand your plans and your high degree of dependency on those parcels. Also, leave with them your mailing schedule. We have used mail-forwarding services twice. The first time, the proprietor was so disorganized that we had to return to collect our parcels and mail them to a friend who agreed to handle them. The second service, in a different state and year, was a resounding success. So if you decide to use a mail forwarding service, select it with great care, and plan for contingencies.

3) The third option is more complicated, but it might give a person more independence. The variations are practically unlimited, but the general plan is this: Every six weeks, head out to a town and buy food and whatever else you will need for the next six weeks. Load your pack with a two-week supply. Send a second two-week supply two weeks ahead. And send a third two-week supply four weeks ahead.

One can shorten the two-week interval by loading two or three larger drift boxes with more than ample supplies, then leap-frogging them ahead. Remember, too, that certain resupply stations might have at least a modest selection of groceries. A person could use these opportunities to stockpile extra food for the next section of trail, or for sending ahead to other stations.

Lost in space

After all the time and energy involved in packing the resupply boxes and the expense of shipping them, you might arrive at a resupply station to find a box is not there. What do you do? Most importantly do not get angry with the clerk; it is not their fault. Instead, describe your box and ask the clerk to check again. The box could well be there; they might not have found it yet. Failing that, ask the clerk to forward your box (when it does arrive) to somewhere ahead, along your route. Then purchase whatever supplies you need to get by.

Layover day philosophy

When it comes to making the most of the summer's journey, each hiker will have his or her preferences. Some like to spend a fair amount of time in towns, sampling the culture, socializing with other hikers, and relaxing in the company of services such as restaurants, libraries and hostels. Others prefer to minimize the distractions of society, and spend most of their time in the woods.

Depending on how far away from home you have traveled, and how new you are to the region, you might find the cultural differences quite interesting. The locals are often eager to talk about the town's history and some of its finer points. The town itself might have historic buildings or monuments, or sites that would be well worth a visit.

The enigma with layover time is that it can be extremely volatile. On the trail the clock seems to run at its normal rate, but at the resupplies it races. Hours and even days can evaporate at these stops.

Another consideration is that even several extra days of layover time will do little to restore one's vigor. A hiker hauls into a resupply town feeling pretty beat, and after three to five days of rest he or she sets off again – only to feel that same old deep-seated fatigue creeping back into the bones within the first hour of hiking. The solution to this is simple: condition the body properly ahead of time, carry lightweight gear, eat nutritiously and drink plenty of water, and very importantly, stay off the feet while at camp and at a resupply stop. These measures can virtually eliminate one's need for excessive layover days. But again, each person will have his or her preferences.

Minimum impact resupplying

Life in the wilds is largely free of urban responsibilities, so of course after we have been out there a while, we might tend to forgo some of the social refinements. But appearances aside, we may fail to realize how strong our body odor might be, and how offensive it can be to the townsfolk. This suggests the importance of bathing in the wilds ahead of time using the dundo method and a bit of soap. Also we could wash a shirt. And once in town, we would head straight for the laundromat and showers.

Resupply station managers and most residents of the trail towns are friendly to hikers. But when a group of hikers arrive, they can become annoying to some people if they fail to exercise consideration, leaving dirty clothes and grimy gear strewn about the city park, in front of the post office on Main Street, or in the laundromats. These scenes of hiker "anarchy" can be avoided by practicing minimum-impact resupplying.

Supercharging Mileage

"'Come to the edge,' he said.
They said, 'We are afraid.'
'Come to the edge,' he said.
They came.
He pushed them…
And they flew."
— *Guillaume Apollinaire*

**Hiking greater distances
with no extra effort**

To this point we have examined ways of reducing the exertions of hiking, ways that are applicable to virtually any trail, be it long or short. And while most wilderness enthusiasts are not interested in covering 20 or 30 miles every day, those dreaming of thru-hiking a trail of a thousand miles or more, in a single season, might want to give the matter some thought. So in this chapter I detail a few techniques that we have used to boost mileage. These techniques are not only for thru-hikers; they might be of help to almost anyone heading out for more than a few days.

The Pyramid of Hiking Style

In order for the miles to come more easily, Jenny and I have learned to take a more critical look at our wants, and distinguish them from our needs.

The following scenarios illustrate how strongly such choices in hiking "style" can affect the course of the jour-ney. I am not suggesting that one choice is better than the other, but simply that they produce different results.

Imagine a hypothetical pyramid, with steps leading up its flanks representing various levels of hiking style. The step at the bottom typifies a nonchalant, carefree, and unhurried approach; while the top-most step suggests the peak of efficiency and drive. Most of us adopt a hiking approach, or style, that is somewhere between the bottom and the top.

When we want to cover more miles with less effort, we can take a few steps up the pyramid to a more efficient style. On the other hand, if not careful we can take a few steps down. Any step we take, either up or down, starts with a shift in attitude, an adjustment in equipment, or both.

A descent – more work, fewer miles

Let's start midway on the pyramid's flank and begin an unfavorable descent. Usually such descents are unintentional, but they happen with regularity. I will exaggerate this descent to give a better idea of the concepts.

Imagine that we are planning a wilderness trek in which we will follow an established trail, say, 200 hundred miles long. Along the way we will detour to a few towns near our route, to replenish food and stove fuel. And because we have set aside plenty of time for the trip, we are in no hurry. We intend for this hike to be a vacation.

The trail distance to our first resupply point (Station A) is 48 miles. At a modest pace of 12 miles a day, this

> Please note that my pyramid analogy is not meant to suggest that one hiking style is superior to another. Far from it. I mean to suggest only that a person can take the pyramid principle into account, if desired. On most of our hiking trips we do not care for maximum mileage. But on a thru-hike we do, and that is what this chapter is all about.

initial section will take us four days. Intent on taking our time and enjoying life, we decide to include a considerable quantity of food, along with a few camp luxuries such as a thick paperback, a backgammon set, and a few more even heavier and bulkier items. Our existing backpack would be crammed with all this, so we decide to buy a larger one.

While carrying this new and heavier backpack loaded with all these extra goodies, we will have to exert ourselves more, granted. But we will allow plenty of rests along the way, and sleep in late whenever we feel like it. For after all, we are in no hurry. So we might as well plan a fifth day to hike the 48 miles. Of course, in order to accommodate that extra day we will need to pack another day's food and stove fuel. These will increase our load once again; but not to worry: the new backpack has plenty of room. The pack is so large, in fact, that we might as well throw in a frying pan. We will never know it is there because the pack is advertised to carry heavy loads in comfort.

> As we increase our loads, we become more susceptible to injury. And contrary to our intentions, our hiking enjoyment diminishes. Heavier loads also shrink our daily mileage capabilities, while lessening our agility, making us more prone to stumbling and sustaining injuries of impact. And of course they increase our chances of feet and leg problems.

Originally the plan was to take life easy; this hike is supposed to be enjoyable. So maybe we should divide this first trail segment in half by hitchhiking out to another town for supplies. This will lighten our load by reducing the amount of food and fuel we will have to carry. To reach this intervening town from our trail route, we will have to hike a side trail six miles out. And after an uncertain hitchhike into town, and another one back to the trailhead, we will have to backtrack the six miles to the main trail. So we are adding two more days – one to accommodate the extra hiking and hitching, and the other for relaxing and enjoying town life.

Adding these two days to the five, we will now spend seven days reaching our original objective at Station A. But during each of the two segments we need carry only three days of food and fuel. This leaves us plenty of room for extras. Let's bring along a backpacker's chair and a zoom lens for the big camera. And since we have wanted to try out that nifty baking device, we can bring a few special dessert mixes.

I think you can see the trend. As we sink into the planning morass, we are turning the trek into an ordeal. Ostensibly, we are catering to our sense of comfort and enjoyment. But in the process we are also lengthening our journey in time and distance. We are also imposing heavier loads on ourselves, taken as a whole.

We have attempted to reduce our packweight by dividing the section, resupplying at an intervening and trail-distant station. In theory we are lightening our packs somewhat, but in truth we are only carrying more weight over a longer distance.

All this benefits us nothing in terms of comfort and enjoyment. And everything we try to do to make the hike more convenient only compounds the difficulties. We are, in short, descending the Pyramid of Hiking Style.

Fortunately, we can reverse this trend with only a few minor adjustments in mindset.

An ascent – less work, more miles

Let's return to the starting point, midway up the pyramid's flanks, and re-plan this hike with a fresh approach.

We want to hike the original 48 miles to Station A in 4 days. And it would be nice if we could enjoy the hiking, rather than endure the heavy load and its associated toil. Since we would like to hike the full trail, all 200 hundred miles of it, we can now see how a bit of discipline would prove beneficial. Originally we had planned to hike 12 miles a day. At a modest pace of 2.75 miles an hour, we would need to hike 4.4 hours each day, not including rest stops. Surely we can hike longer that that. Let's get going an hour earlier.

Disciplining ourselves into hiking 5.4 hours each day, and still allowing 8 hours of sleep each night, we leave ourselves a prodigious 10.6 hours of resting and relaxing every day. So maybe we can hike an additional hour in the afternoon. Assuming we travel at the same 2.75 mph, our daily mileage will jump from 12 miles to 17.6. That extra 2 hours on the trail makes a huge difference. At 17.6 miles a day, we can travel the 48 miles not in 4 days, but in a mere 2.7. We just saved ourselves 1.3 days of hiking. So we can remove that much food and fuel from our backpacks. This reduces our load by several pounds. And we might as well eliminate a few luxury items from our pack, lightening it even further.

And here is where the "magic" in the more disciplined approach begins to take effect. Because our pack is less heavy, we will hike—not faster—but with less fatigue. So in terms of endurance, the reduced pack weight offsets the extra time spent hiking. Covering the 17.6 miles a day while carrying a lighter pack, we will arrive at the evening camps no more fatigued than had we hiked only 12 miles while carrying the heavier load. We gain extra mileage at no additional cost in effort.

Distance hikers who grasp this principle are well on their way up the pyramid. Let's look at a few more techniques:

Once we reach Station A, we might decide to send home a few more items that we do not need. Some of these we have not been using; others only infrequently and with no real advantage. None of this extra gear is facilitating our trip, so why lug it for nothing, six or seven hours a day, every step of the way? Let's rid ourselves of the extra fleece sweater, the cotton t-shirt worn only at camp, the extra nylon pants, two pairs of the most worn (and dirtiest) socks, the down booties, four pads of the moleskin, the two extra tent stakes, the carabiner dangling affectatiously off the pack, the salt and pepper shakers, the candle lantern (saving a few pieces of one of the candles for emergency fire-starting), and the electronic pedometer.

I am not condemning any of this gear, or discouraging anyone from using it; these are only examples. But they do make quite a pile; and ridding our pack of them will make the hiking that much easier. With better maneuverability, we will not have such a hard time tromping through lingering snow fields, climbing over blowdowns, and wading creeks. Also with less weight on our backs we can move ahead with less strain, meaning that we will be less prone to injury.

We are not compromising the hike's enjoyment. On the contrary: the aesthetics of the journey will increase as we travel less encumbered. And once again, we are *not* striving to increase our hiking speed. Trying to hike fast only reduces our long-term mileage and increases the chances of an injury.

As we ponder the pile of things on their way home, we have to admit that they were not helping us enjoy the trip. The pile weighs close to 5 pounds, and if we subtract that from our original load, the weight reduction will enable us to hike an additional 2 miles a day with no extra effort (see the chart in the "Slashing Packweight" chapter).

Our daily mileage is now up to 19.6, while still ambling along at an easy 2.75 miles an hour.

> Speed is not the issue here. Trying to hike fast only reduces our long-term mileage and increases the chances of an injury.

With the extra 2 miles per day gain, we no longer need as much food to reach our next resupply at Station B. And when we remove that food, we are lightening our pack again, and enabling ourselves to hike a little farther each day – still with no additional effort.

We are making some big gains here, but we are not finished.

We have seen other hikers wearing running shoes, and they seemed to be doing very well in them. At home we wear running shoes for kicking around town, and for the daily jogs. Maybe we can hike in them as well. Let's send home our boots in favor of running shoes. The running shoes will allow us to hike not faster, but with less fatigue. Switching from heavy boots to light-weight running shoes gains us another 7½ miles a day (see the "Footwear" chapter) again with no more effort. Our daily mileage capability has risen to 27 miles. We have more than doubled our original figure, and are now hiking marathon mileages.

PCT-3

And of course, this additional 7½ miles a day allows us to remove even more food and fuel from our pack, lessening its weight further, and increasing once again our mileage capabilities.

Let's take yet another step up the pyramid.

Since we are improving our capabilities, we might as well use them to best effect. Let's skip resupply station B altogether and press on to Station C. This will save us from hiking out to Station B, and squandering the time while tending to logistics. And by planning to skip the resupply station, we eliminate the chances of arriving there on a weekend when the post office is closed and our resupply parcel would be unavailable. Skipping Station B saves us at least a full day of hassles, maybe two. And it saves us the money we would have spent there, and the postage on that resupply box.

In skipping resupply station B and continuing on to C, we will need to include more food. How much depends on the distance between B and C. Let's say that this distance is 67 miles. This may sound like a lot, but at our new rate of travel it is only 2½ days. That many days' food at 2½ pounds per day weighs 6¼ pounds. However, that last day of hiking will be quick and easy, since our pack will be down to its baseline weight, which is not much. And we will not need to carry the final day's dinner, because we would arrive at resupply C in time for a hearty dinner there. So out of our pack comes that dinner.

All said and done, we arrive at station C literally weeks

ahead of when we would have, had we stuck with our initial planning. And we did it with no extra effort.

Dividing the day into thirds

Now that we have supercharged our mileage, we need a method that better regulates the day's hiking and lets us know how we are doing.

A technique that Jenny and I often use—when we want to extend the day's travel—is to divide the day in thirds. For example if we want to hike a 33-mile day, we hike 11 miles in each third. Let's look at how this works.

On reasonably graded trails we tend to hike at 2.75 mph, which is a very moderate pace. Let's say that on average we hike for 45 minutes then stop for a 15-minute rest break. Nothing difficult about that. Each hour we cover 2 miles. So our average pace is 2 mph. We want to hike 11 miles, so this will take 5.5 hours.

We start hiking at 5:30 in the morning, intent on covering the eleven miles by 11:00 that same morning. Then we hike eleven more miles by 4:30 that afternoon, and the final eleven miles by 10:00 pm.

Here is how we do this. After studying the map we know about where the 11-mile point is, and the 22-mile point and the 33-mile point. If we reach the 11-mile point by 11 am, then we know that we are doing well. If we do not reach it in time, then we know that we need to shorten the rest breaks. What usually happens with Jenny and me, though, is that we reach the 11-mile mark by 10:00 am, an hour early. This allows us to cruise through the remainder of the day in an even more relaxed fashion, taking longer rests and stopping more often to chat with other hikers.

So although at first glance this system might seem restrictive, actually it is a great way to help regulate the pace. At the end of the day we have spent 12 hours hiking, and 4½ hours resting. So, yes, the 33 miles may be a considerable distance, but by taking regular and fairly

Daily Mileage	Segment Mileage	Morning	Midday	Evening
24	8	6 am - 10 am	10 am - 2 pm	2 pm - 6 pm
27	9	6 am - 10:30	10:30 - 3 pm	3 pm - 7:30
30	10	6 am - 11 am	11 am - 4 pm	4 pm - 9 pm
33	11	5:30 - 11 am	11 am - 4:30	4:30 - 10 pm

lengthy breaks, we are left with plenty of time to snack and drink water, and cook a meal to maintain the needed energy. The beauty of this system is that virtually any well-trained hiker can take a 15-minute break every hour of the day and still pull off some big miles. The secret is to start early and finish late. We do this comfortably by conditioning our bodies ahead of time, carrying lightweight gear on the actual journey, wearing running shoes, eating nourishing foods, and staying well hydrated.

The table summarizes the triple-segmented day for various daily mileages, at an average hiking rate of 2.0 mph. Select a daily mileage and divide it into thirds. Then divide your day in thirds, and you will be well on your way toward higher mileages.

Seize the day

A good night's sleep brings the dawn of a new day. The birds bestir themselves at the first hint of daylight; and like them, when distance hiking we like to rise at dawn. This is because the early morning hours are our favorite for hiking. In pilot training I learned to take off from the beginning of the runway. "The runway behind you does you no good," as the flight instructor said. And so it is with the hiker's day.

An early start and a late stop helps us make the most of each day. And we like to make the most of our rest stops also. We do this by staying off our feet, drinking lots of water, and eating hearty snacks. The higher mileage hiker needs to be careful not to spend too much time standing, for example while talking with other hikers. Not because of the delays, but because of the blood pooling into the legs and feet. If we feel like chatting at some length, then we might consider declaring a rest stop, taking off our packs, and getting off our feet.

Another technique that can help extend the miles is to use waypoints as springboards. Shelters, creek crossings, lakes, and trail junctions can serve to urge us several more miles. But the temptation might be to say to ourselves, "four more miles to Green Lake Shelter; I think we will stop there for the night." This is letting the waypoint dictate progress. Instead, we could say to ourselves: "once we reach the Green Lake Shelter, we will continue for one more hour before making camp." The idea is to use the waypoints as incentives, rather than as destinations.

In the late afternoons, fatigue may prompt us to stop and make camp. But much of that tiredness does not stem from the hiking, per se, but from a lack of food. If we are in shape and traveling lightly, then at this point in our day we probably need a hearty meal. So we stop near a water source and cook and eat dinner. We collect and filter a supply of drinking water, and we clean the pot and spoons. Then we might enjoy a dundo bath, or at least a sponging off of the day's dust and grime. But rather than pitching our tarp or tent there, we re-load the backpacks and press on. If the meal is high in nutrition, then it will re-energize us, and we will probably find ourselves hiking buoyantly for several more enjoyable hours. Much farther along, we would leave the trail and establish a stealth-camp. Our arrival there can be quite late because the camp chores will be mostly done. About all we will have to do is pitch our shelter and crawl gratefully into the sack.

For many backpackers, the notion of distance hiking according to a schedule might seem the antithesis of a wilderness experience. High-mileage thru-hikers are often accused of not seeing anything along the way; that they are left with nothing but hazy memories of rushed trail experiences. Our own thru-hiking has not borne this out. We walk no faster than most day hikers; and generally we stop and rest every hour or so, which is not always the case with most day-hikers. We find that we can connect with the natural world very profoundly while hiking 30-plus miles a day, week after week. At such times the journey tends to expand in many dimensions as it reaches ahead. In addition to our higher mileage trekking, we have been on plenty of trips lasting a week or more while covering very little mileage. My conclusion is that as long as a person is traveling on foot, his or her ability to observe, experience and connect with nature has nothing to do with the number of miles hiked each day.

Northern California; PCT-1

Trail Shock

"For you never can tell
if it's heaven or hell,
And I'm taking the trail on trust;
But I haven't a doubt
that my soul will leap out
On its Wan-der-lust."

— *Robert Service*

Learning to recognize it
Projecting through it

Long-distance hikers starting out on their journeys tend to undergo a number of abrupt changes in lifestyle. From Day One their exertion levels skyrocket, launching their nutritional needs practically into orbit. Yet the types of foods they eat often default to the traditional trail-foods variety, causing a decline in nutritional intake. The excitement of having finally begun the trek, coupled with the anxieties of confronting the great unknown, tends to suppress the appetite. So rather than eat greater portions of higher quality foods to satisfy their soaring needs for energy and nutrition, they tend to eat less food of lower quality.

Additionally, the hikers' fluid needs and intake will change abruptly once they start their journey. Full of enthusiasm and ambition, these hikers may travel at an uncontrolled pace for the first few days, despite their loads and any steep hills and mountains along the way. The overexertion causes them to sweat, often profusely, and soon they become dehydrated, often very deeply.

Water sources may be somewhat sparse, the job of treating the water in the quantities they need might be too bothersome, and their suspicions about the quality of the water may discourage their drinking much. And during those first few days, the trail may lead to higher elevations where the atmosphere may be a little thinner than what the hikers are used to. This further upsets their fluid balances by increasing the rate of sensible and insensible perspiration.

Blend in the preexisting fatigue of hectic, last-minute preparations, the weariness of traveling from home to trail, the exhaustion of the overly rambunctious hiking with an assortment of stiff, aching muscles, and maybe a growing collection of blisters, and the result, as many have discovered, is the standard early-trip breakdown.

One moment things seem only miserable; the next moment the journey loses every hint of its former luster and the prospects of continuing seems utterly implausible.

At this point depression sets in, as the mind struggles to accept the new reality of "failure" and its myriad and practically unthinkable consequences.

I call this "trail shock," and recommend that every prospective long-distance hiker plan for it. Basically, the newer the person is to distance hiking, and the newer to the particular environment, the sooner trail shock may hit. And the more out-of-shape, and the more overly ambitious, the harder it will hit. But take heart. Trail shock is not a sign of failure – but of adaptation. In all likelihood the journey is not at risk; the hiker is merely going at it too hard. The solution is to throttle back for the initial few weeks, and allow both body and mind the time they need to make the necessary adjustments.

Jenny and I have experienced trail shock in the initial stages in most of our long backpacking journeys, to greater or lesser degrees. When it happened on our first two treks, we suffered the usual misgivings. But after that we learned to recognize trail shock for what it was; so we were able to minimize it. We did this by taking things relatively easy during the first few weeks, paying careful attention to our nutrition and fluid intake, and by keeping our minds focused on the positive aspects all around us, of which there were a great many.

A variation of trail shock can strike at other times during a long hike. In these instances it is not so much the body trying to adapt to a new lifestyle, but the mind attempting to deal with a goal that it perceives as impossibly distant. Here again, proper nutrition and adequate intake of water play key roles in preventing and treating these little hit-the-wall type burn-outs. If all else fails, one might give oneself a few days' "vacation" from the trail. This will in all likelihood refresh the body and mind, and can usually bring the original goal back into focus.

Pacific Northwest; PCT-3

Part 9

FURTHER INFO

PCT-1

Trail Life

Sewing Your Own Gear

"No one knows what he can do till he tries."
— *Publilius Syrus, 1ˢᵗ century BC*

The machine pays for itself in the first season of use

Picture the illustrious garments in the backpacking stores and catalogs. These garments began as rolls of fabrics. In most cases these fabrics are available directly to the consumer. With these materials, active people everywhere are discovering the benefits of sewing their own performance clothing and gear.

In this chapter I describe how to sew your own hats and mittens, ditty bags, stuff sacks, thermal shirts and pants, rain jacket, tarp, and several other items. Granted, sewing them yourself will take some time. Perhaps you could borrow that time from some television watching or internet browsing. Sewing is at least as absorbing, and far more productive and rewarding. And it can save you money otherwise spent on commercial items. You can customize the designs to suit your particular body size and style preferences. You can choose your colors and fabric types, add pockets, zippers, drawstring closures. And you can reinforce stress points to make sure the item will stand up to heavy use. The possibilities are endless. And I like to think that the skills of "sewing your own" foster a more independent attitude, taking you a step beyond the usual consumerism. That is, something bought commercially is a mere possession, while something you make yourself becomes an extension of your own energies, and a meaningful part of your life.

A suitable sewing machine

Many older sewing machines are actually more robust and powerful than those of our modern, plastic genre. And they are more than capable of sewing the projects in this chapter. Whatever type of machine you choose, it does not need the confusion of computerized stitches. A second-hand machine will do fine, and it need have only the three basic stitches:

▶ The straight stitch – for joining fabrics that do not stretch appreciably.

▶ The zig-zag stitch – for sewing stretch fabrics. By nature of its geometry, this back-and-forth stitch gives like an accordion when the material is stretched.

▶ The reverse stitch – for finishing each row of stitching by sewing backward a short ways, preventing the stitching from raveling.

Most sewing machines have mechanisms for adjusting the upper and lower thread tensions, allowing the machine to accommodate fabrics of differing weights and thickness.

If you are new to sewing, ask someone to show you how to operate your machine. Ask them to show you how to thread the machine, and how to adjust the thread tensioning. Then practice on scraps similar to the materials you will be sewing. Sew two scraps together and examine both sides. Are the stitches reasonably similar on both sides? If not, adjust the upper and lower tensions, sew another row of stitching, and check again. Once you can balance the stitching, you have become fully capable of making an entire line of backcountry gear.

Needles

Use high quality needles and replace them often. Synthetic fabrics are more abrasive than cotton ones, and will dull the needles faster. A dull needle will skip stitches and break thread.

For the projects detailed in this chapter, you will need three sizes of needles: size 80 for most medium weight fabrics, size 70 for the very lightweight, and size 100 for sewing through many layers of heavier fabrics and webbing, as in the backpack project. Buy one package of each size.

Thread

None of the projects require heavy thread. Ordinary 100% long-fiber polyester thread, medium weight, will suffice. You can also use cotton-covered polyester thread; the cotton content is miniscule, and it helps protect the fabric from thread abrasion.

Fabrics and patterns

Well-stocked fabric stores may sell some of the materials needed for these projects. For instance, they might have lightweight nylons, polyesters, perhaps fleece, thermal fabrics such as polypropylene, and maybe even water-proof-breathable fabrics. Otherwise, you can mail-order your fabrics, sewing supplies and patterns.

When purchasing your fabrics, check to see what weight they are. For example, the 1.9 ounce coated rip-stop nylon is quite light, but there are even lighter nylons available. The number refers to ounces per square yard. No-see-um netting is about 0.8 ounces per square yard.

All of the sewing projects described in this chapter are relatively easy to complete. Some require more materials and more time than others, and I have arranged the projects with this in mind, starting with the most basic. As with hiking, focus on the task at hand, and proceed ahead, one step at a time.

Fleece hat

Let's begin by making a simple skull-cap for use while hiking on a blustery day, and while sleeping. I take one

of these on every trip. The first step is to select a fabric. You will need two pieces, both 12" by 14". Use thin fleece, sweatshirt fleece, brushed tricot, or any other synthetic with some stretch and a bit of loft for warmth.

Now, check which way the fabric stretches. Most fleece and jersey knits stretch more in one direction than the other. When making an item from stretchy material, even slightly stretchy like fleece, align the direction of the most stretch to cover the body part girth-wise, rather than length-wise. For the hat, the stretch would be around the head, not top to bottom.

Lay the two pieces together with their fuzzy sides facing away from each other. You will be sewing the hat together inside-out. In fact, you will sew all of your projects inside-out. Then when you turn the finished products right-side out, the seams will be neatly hidden inside. Pin the pieces together, and cut them into a dome shape, leaving the bottom open. Also, make the hat extra long, so that it covers the face for sleeping, and folds up over the forehead for wearing during the day.

Using a narrow zig-zag stitch, sew the two pieces together – up one side, arching over the top, and back down the other side. Keep the row of stitching about 1/2" away from the edge. This space is called the "seam allowance." Try the hat on for fit, then if necessary make it smaller, or start over and make a larger one.

Neither the sewing novice nor the expert should expect their projects to turn out perfectly the first time. The seam-ripping tool is the tailor's best friend. And as George Bernard Shaw said: "Success covers a multitude of blunders."

Once your skull-cap fits snugly and to your satisfaction, trim away the excess seam allowance, leaving about a quarter inch of material outside the stitching. Turn the hat right-side out, and voilà! You have taken your first step to commercial independence.

Mittens

Making a pair of mittens is almost as easy as making a skull-cap. Use the same material as for the skull-cap, and also make a second pair from thicker, warmer fleece.

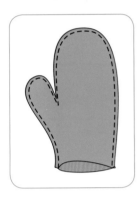

Start by drawing your pattern. To do this, lay the palm of your hand down flat on a piece of paper in the mitt position – fingers loosely together, thumb at a 45° angle. Then trace around your hand and along the wrist a few inches. Cut the paper pattern out, not on the line but half-an-inch outside of it, allowing for a looser fit. Trace the pattern onto a suitable piece of fabric, with the stretch of the fabric running the width of the hand, not from fingertip to wrist.

Cut the material on the line, using scissors or a rotary blade and mat. If your fabric looks the same on either side, like most fleeces, you can cut out three additional pieces. However, if your fabric has a fuzzy side and a smooth side, you need to cut out only two pieces the same, then flip your paper pattern over and cut out the other two pieces.

Match two pieces, pin them together, and sew around the outside, leaving the opening for the hand. Use a straight stitch or a very narrow zig-zag, with a 3/8" seam allowance. Before you turn the mitten right-side out, try it on. If it fits well, you can trim the seam allowance closer to your stitching to minimize seam bulk. Now

re-size the pattern here and there for the best possible fit, then save the pattern. Jenny and I re-use our patterns year after year. In fact, we make patterns for all our projects, and keep them in a special box. They are important to us, because we know that whatever we make from them will fit us just right.

Ditty bag

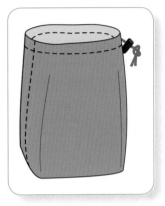

I like to carry my small, personal items in a ditty bag, one that closes with a drawstring and small cord-lock. Generally this bag measures 7" by 5½" with a flat bottom (or 6" by 3" with a square bottom, description to follow). I usually make the bag from silicone nylon, or sometimes netting so that I can see the contents; but the choices of suitable fabrics are many.

Whatever the fabric, cut a piece 11½" wide by 8½" tall. Sear the edges lightly with a flame to prevent fraying. Fold the material in half to form a smaller rectangle, 5¾" wide by 8½" tall. The fold will be along one edge of your bag. Using a straight stitch with a ¼" seam allowance,

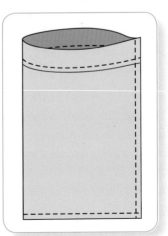

stitch along the other edge and across the bottom. You should now have a small, flat bag, 8¼" by 5½" open at the top. Its seam runs down one side and across the bottom. Now we will make the drawstring casing. With a hot nail held in a pair of pliers, melt a hole through one layer of the fabric, opposite the side seam and 1½" down from the top edge. Size the hole so that a small safety pin secured to the end of your drawstring will just fit through it.

Fold the top edge down to form a 1¼" wide drawstring casing. Stitch along the edge with a ¼" seam allowance, making a 1" casing. Then turn the bag right-side out. Cut a piece of nylon drawstring 15" long, attach the safety pin to one end, and feed it into the hole, around the bag inside the casing, and back out the hole. The safety pin facilitates this feeding process. Remove the safety pin, attach a cord-lock to both ends of the drawstring, and tie a keeper knot in the ends of the cord.

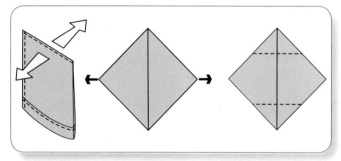

To make a square bottom, begin by turning the ditty bag inside-out. Holding it upside down, pull the sides apart, forming a square bottom. Lay this square bottom flat, and stitch as shown.

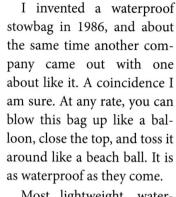

Waterproof stowbag

You can test a fabric for waterproofness by pressing it to your lips and trying to suck air through it. If any air passes through the fabric whatsoever, then for our purposes the fabric is not waterproof. Contrary to what one might expect, a person cannot suck air through waterproof-breathable or vapor-permeable fabrics. This tells us that these fabrics are only infinitesimally breathable.

I invented a waterproof stowbag in 1986, and about the same time another company came out with one about like it. A coincidence I am sure. At any rate, you can blow this bag up like a balloon, close the top, and toss it around like a beach ball. It is as waterproof as they come.

Most lightweight, waterproof fabrics are suitable for this project. My preference is 1.3-ounce silicone-coated nylon. Start with a piece 26" wide by 39" tall. Fold this in half, coated-side out (if any) to produce a rectangle 13" wide by 39" tall. Lightly sear the long edges.

With this project we will use a stronger, two-step seam known as the felled seam. Start by sewing with a straight stitch the length of the long edge with a ⅜" seam allowance. Lay the bag—which is actually a long tube at this point—on the table with this side seam centered and running down the middle. Using your fingertips, press the seam allowances down to one side. This is where the term "felled" comes

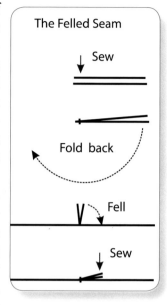

The Felled Seam

Sew

Fold back

Fell

Sew

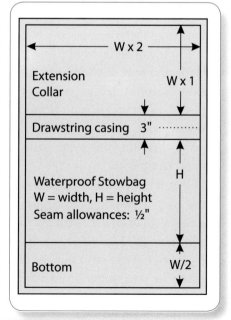

W x 2
Extension Collar
W x 1
Drawstring casing   3"
Waterproof Stowbag
W = width, H = height
Seam allowances: ½"
H
Bottom
W/2

from. Feed the tube back through the machine, stitching this felled seam allowance down to one layer of the bag, leaving the other side under the machine's free arm, or bunched up, out of the way. So, you have just sewed a long tube, and also sewed the seam allowances down. When you turn the tube right-side out, you should see two parallel rows of stitching, about a quarter inch apart.

Next you will sew the bottom seam. With the bag turned inside-out, lay the tube flat. Rather than sewing the bottom closed using a felled seam, simply fold the bottom over twice, and stitch – like making a hem. This clothing bag will have a rectangular bottom, as described in the ditty bag project, so measure down about three inches from the triangles' corners for the stitching line.

After sewing the bottom corners, turn the bag right-side out, lay it flat, and draw two parallel lines around the bag's circumference: one 14¾" from the top opening, and the other 16¼" (in other words, 1½" apart). These lines show where the drawstring casing will be. Fold the top "collar" of the bag in on itself, and crease it along the 14¾" line so that the raw-edged opening is inside the bag. Sew two parallel lines, 1/8 inch apart, around the bag on the 16¼" line. Stitch back and forth across the side seam several times to reinforce that intersection of stitching. We have now made a drawstring casing 1½" wide. Instead of melting a hole for the drawstring as you did with the ditty bag, use a seam ripper to carefully remove ½" of the side seam stitching near the top of the casing. Cut a length of drawstring 33" long and feed it through the casing. Add the toggle, knot the drawstring, trim the excess cord, and sear their ends to prevent fraying.

After waterproofing the seams (refer to the next chapter, "Seam Sealing") you can test them by inflating the stowbag like a balloon, twisting its top closed, and squeezing the bag. Listen for air leaking out a seam.

Load the stowbag with your hiking clothes, then squeeze out some of the air to reduce its size. Close the bag by twisting the collar tightly. Pull the drawstring half-way, tuck the twisted collar beneath the casing, then cinch the drawstring tight.

Spandex hiking shorts or pants

Look for fabrics and patterns at your local sewing store. You can use a pattern for long sweatpants and make mid-thigh shorts instead. The many different kinds of synthetic materials and weights all have different stretch characteristics. For spandex shorts and pants, choose a lightweight nylon spandex with good stretch in both directions. Remember that the direction of the greatest stretch runs around the body. When sewing spandex, use a size 70 needle and a narrow, short zig-zag stitch with a quarter inch seam allowance. To hem the legs, I fold the material once and zig-zag stitch it. I also make a ½" wide waistband casing fitted with a length of ⅜" wide elastic.

Thermal shirts and pants

Today's thermal fabrics include polypropylene, Thermax, Coolmax, Poly Lycra Jersey, and the polypropylene-fleece blends, to name but a few. Each has its own weight, thickness and stretch, and you will need to make sure that the type you select for shirts and pants has the appropriate characteristics. For making thermal pants and shirts, you might look for a pattern for long underwear, and omit the fly on the pants in order to reduce bulk. When sewing thermal fabrics, use a size 80 needle and a short zig-zag stitch set to medium width.

Fleece jacket

A fleece jacket is rather heavy and bulky, nevertheless it is fun to make. The patterns for these are many. I omit the waistband and the sleeve cuffs. Instead, I make the jacket and sleeves longer, and finish off the bottom edges and sleeve cuffs with a spandex binding. (For an example, see the book *Sewing Activewear*, published by the Singer Company.) I also reduce the bulk in the collar by using a lighter-weight material for the collar facing, for example a thermal fabric. For the front zipper I have found the 1-way separating—rather than the 2-way separating—to be the best. The 1-way zipper is easier to start and more durable. I use a 29" zipper and Jenny, a 27". For our clothing and gear projects we use either the plastic molded tooth or the nylon coil types. On pockets I prefer lighter-weight coil zippers.

When sewing non-stretch fleece, use a straight stitch. When sewing stretch fleece, use a zig-zag stitch with a short length and width.

On these jackets I like front pockets for warming the hands, and zippers on those pockets to keep from losing things. To install a pocket zipper, slit the front of the jacket where you want the pocket opening. Sew on a 6" or 7" coil zipper, following the directions on the zipper package. Cut a piece of thermal fabric for the pocket liner. Hem all the edges, pin the liner to the inside of the jacket against the zipper, and stitch it around its perimeter.

Shell jacket

The shell jacket is an invaluable addition to the hiking wardrobe, protecting us from mosquitoes, blackflies and no-see-ums, and from sunburn, cold wind, and brush. Jenny and I carry shell jackets and pants on most of our outings, even in the Arctic. These are made quite easily from tightly-woven, uncoated nylon. The material should be breathable, but not overly so. You can test the breathability of a fabric the same way you tested for waterproofness: by pressing it to your lips and sucking air through it. If you can breathe through it quite easily then it is probably not mosquito-proof. On the other hand, if sucking air through it is difficult, then you are likely to sweat in it. I prefer the lighter colors for these garments because they are cooler while hiking under direct sunshine, and they are less attractive to flying insects.

Patterns for shell jackets and pants abound. Be sure that the pattern you choose has a hood. And consider

adding zippered front pockets. Remember that the emphasis with all your sewing projects should be on simplicity and lightness.

Shell pants

For shell pants, I omit any side zippers which only add unnecessary weight and bulk. However, you might want to add a chafe patch, approximately 6" wide by 5" tall, stitched to the bottom of the pant legs where your shoes brush against the pants every now and then. I also use a narrower (half-inch wide) elastic waistband and elastic in the leg cuffs to keep the mosquitoes out. The fabric for the shell pants should be breathable yet bug-proof, same as with the shell jacket.

Mosquito mitts & booties, and sun mitts

Mosquito mitts and booties weigh almost nothing, and they take up very little space in one's backpack. They provide welcome relief when mosquitoes or blackflies are swarming. I prefer to use them in lieu of chemical repellent. I wear the mitts while hiking, and both the mitts and booties while resting alongside the trail. The booties are for when I remove my shoes for airing.

Make the mitts pattern by tracing around the hand in the same way as you did for the fleece mittens, except make them one inch bigger all around. The mosquito mitts fit very loosely, so this needs to be a separate pattern. To keep the bugs from crawling in at the wrists, make the mitt wrists several inches longer so that you can tuck them up inside the sleeves of your shell jacket. For fabric, use scraps left over from your shell jacket and pants projects. Do not be tempted to use no-see-um netting; mosquitoes can reach through this fabric wherever it presses against the skin. For the booties we use an age-old Inuit mukluks pattern, but a much simpler design, and just as useable, is to sew a couple of loose-fitting stowbags, without the draw-cord casing, large enough to fit a foot into, and long enough to tuck up into the pant legs.

Although the bug mitts will also protect the backs of your hands and fingers from strong UV, I find them too hot in intense sun. And I like to have my fingertips free of any covering. For sun mitts, I prefer a simple tube made of breathable nylon that fits over the hand, open at the fingers but still providing effective cover for the backs of the hands. Jenny prefers a more snug-fitting, tube-style sun mitt made from spandex.

Mosquito head-net

A mosquito head-net completes the bug-proof ensemble. This we make out of no-see-um netting, which is a much finer weave than mosquito netting. No-see-um netting comes in white, black or gray; black absorbs more of the sun's heat, but it is the easiest to see through.

Start with a round piece of netting 15" in diameter. This will be the top of the head-net. Make the side walls from two pieces, 30" wide by 24" tall. Lay out these rectangles, and along the 30" edge make a mark 3" in from each end. Place the round top piece on top of one of the rectangles,

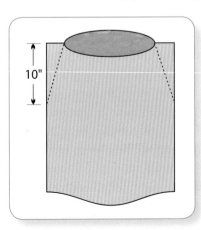

and with a ⅜" seam allowance, sew the two together between the two marks. The result looks like the accompanying illustration. Then sew the second rectangle to the other side of the circle. The 3" marks that you made should meet up at the sides of the head-net. You will

eventually trim away the excess seam allowance, but first sew the two side seams, starting at the round top edge and stitching 10" down. Stop at 10" and stitch back and forth several times to keep that stress point from tearing out. That 10" point will sit on top of your shoulder, and the remainder of the material will hang down inside your shell jacket, one flap in front, the other flap in back. Now you can trim off the excess 3" from both sides, leaving a nice ⅜" seam allowance down both sides of the head-net.

A broad-rimmed hat, or baseball cap worn underneath the head-net will keep the netting off the top of your head and away from your face.

Rain jacket

Jenny and I make our rain jackets usually of 2-ply Gore-Tex or other waterproof-breathable fabrics, as opposed to coated waterproof fabrics that do not breathe. We make these jackets from the same patterns as the shell jacket, but we make them somewhat larger to accommodate a few more layers underneath. You can skip the hand pockets unless you also want to sew protective covers over the zippers. Again, make sure you start with a new needle, size 70 or 80. Use the felled seam where possible, since it is stronger and easier to seal. See the following chapter on "Seam Sealing."

Tent awning

(See illustration in "Tarp and Tent" chapter). To make a tent awning, choose a lightweight, waterproof fabric such as urethane-coated nylon. The awning's shape and attachment will depend on the shape of your tent fly and its doorway configuration. The idea is to shelter that doorway to prevent rain from entering when the doorway is wide open, which it normally should be for the most ventilation.

I will describe how I make an awning for a tent that is symmetrical about its long axes, head to foot. To ensure a proper fit, make the awning from two pieces: a left and a right, each piece measuring approximately 35" by 45". You can customize this for your own tent. After pitching the tent and fitting its fly, tape each awning-half along the 35" edge onto the fly above the doorway, and overlapping half an inch where the two pieces meet in the middle. This overlap will become the seam allowance, although you will need to trim it to the right shape before sewing that seam. When you lift the two pieces and hold them outstretched and slightly downward in the finished awning position, you can see how the pieces will overlap. Mark where the two halves cross each other at the front edge, then remove the pieces from the fly. Trim appropriately, and stitch them together using the felled seam. The awning is now one piece, and ready to sew onto the tent fly. Mark the fly where the awning will attach to it, then remove the fly from the tent and sew the awning to it. And then seal the seams.

Next, sew three guy-line attachment loops and reinforcement patches, one at each front corner and one in the center along the front edge. When the awning is not needed, you can fold it back over the tent, or you can roll it up and secure it with webbing ties sewn through the fly and seam sealed.

Tarp

The tarps that my students and I used for many summers of wilderness travel back in the 1970's were made of ordinary clear polyethylene plastic, 3 mil or 4 mil thick. We hung them over ridge-lines strung tightly between two trees, and fastened lines to their corners with sheet bend knots.

The tarp that Jenny and I used on our third PCT hike, and many years thereafter, is made of 1.9 ounce coated nylon. This material is quite strong and reasonably light in weight, and it is a good step up from clear plastic. Today we use 1.3-ounce silicone-coated nylon, which is

the lightest and most waterproof for its weight, but at a slight sacrifice in strength – meaning only that it requires handling with a bit more care. For the reinforcement patches at the guy points, we use scraps of tarp material. And for the guyline attachment loops (pulls) we use very thin nylon webbing.

My two-person tarp is 106" (8'10") square (not including the beaks) when flat on the ground. To make a one-person tarp, you would reduce the width. But you can customize both length and width to suit your needs.

The tarp body requires two pieces of material. For my

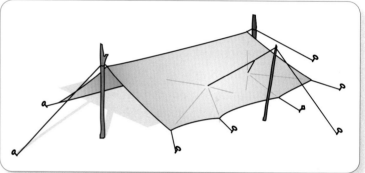

two-person tarp the dimensions are 106" long by 54" wide, which includes the seam allowances. Sew these two pieces together length-wise, using a flat-felled seam, creating one large piece. The center seam becomes the tarp's ridgeline. If adding beaks (see illustration) add them now. Then sew a doubled ⅜" hem around all edges. Refer to the accompanying illustrations for the arrangement of the various reinforcements and attachment loops.

People have asked about using Tyvek for tarps, ground sheets, and so forth. I think the interest in this material is based more on the name, which has sort of an exotic appeal to those unfamiliar with it. But Tyvek is a very common material that has been around for decades. Personally, I find it unsuitable for hiking and camping – mainly because it is not waterproof. People have tried

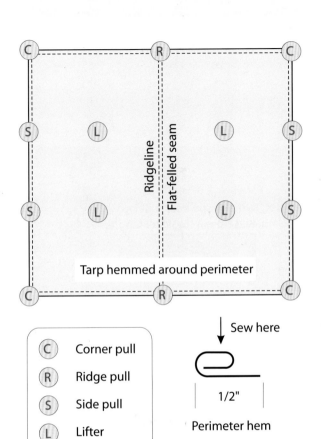

Tarp hemmed around perimeter

C	Corner pull
R	Ridge pull
S	Side pull
L	Lifter

Sew here

1/2"

Perimeter hem

Flat-Felled Seam

Strong, and nice looking because it hides the raw edges. Used for waterproof stuff-sacks, tarp ridgelines, etc.

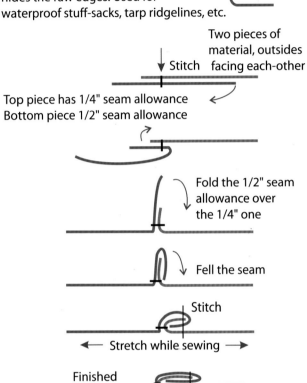

Two pieces of material, outsides facing each-other

Stitch

Top piece has 1/4" seam allowance
Bottom piece 1/2" seam allowance

Fold the 1/2" seam allowance over the 1/4" one

Fell the seam

Stitch

← Stretch while sewing →

Finished

Seam-seal this side

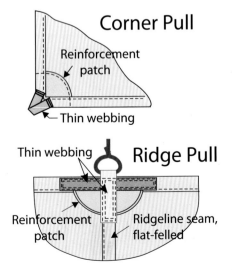

Corner Pull

Reinforcement patch

Thin webbing

Ridge Pull

Thin webbing

Reinforcement patch

Ridgeline seam, flat-felled

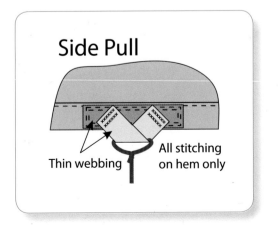

Side Pull

Thin webbing

All stitching on hem only

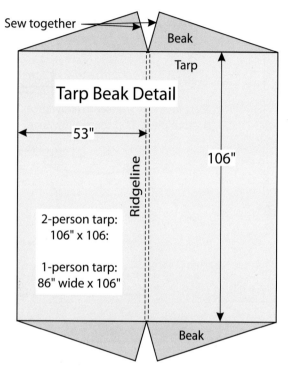

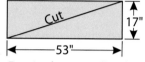

Tarp Beak Detail

Sew together

Beak

Tarp

Ridgeline

53"

106"

2-person tarp:
106" x 106:

1-person tarp:
86" wide x 106"

Beak

To make one beak, cut two
halves from a single rectangle.

Cut

17"

53"

For single tarp 86" wide,
beak rectangle would
measure 43" x 17"

Lifter Patch

Material: 500 denier,
coated Cordura

2" diameter

2 lifter line attachment slits,
3/4" long, 1/2" apart

Sew Lifter Patch to tarp around
perimeter, two rows stitching

Tie lifter-line through loop
formed by the two slits

applying various coatings to the Tyvek to make it water-proof, but I think the problems outweigh any advantages. For an inexpensive and far more workable alternative, I recommend ordinary 3-mil polyethylene. It is available at most hardware stores, perfectly waterproof, and sur-prisingly durable when properly used.

Quilt or sleeping bag

If you are thinking of trying a quilt, you can save money by making your own. Or you can make a sleeping bag by following the steps listed below. Manufacturers tend to complicate the designs of their sleeping bags in order to attract sales, but we hikers need only a simple quilt or bag. Making these at home is easy and straightforward, particularly with today's synthetic insulation that does not require internal baffles built into the quilt or bag, as goose down does.

The quilt simply drapes over a person like a blanket. It consists of two sheets of thin, nylon fabric sandwiching the insulation. To make a sleeping bag out of it, simply fit both edges with a zipper, and fold it in half.

Inexpensive insulation will usually result in a much heavier and bulkier product. For best results, use the newer brands of insulation. To achieve the desired thick-ness, simply double or triple the layers. See the "Quilt and Sleeping Bag" chapter for temperature rating details. Our two-person quilt is 64" wide and 80" long. A one-person quilt would be about 45" wide, and would exclude the insulated flap (see below) between the heads. I am 70" tall, so we make our quilts 10" longer than me. To cus-tomize the length of your quilt, add 10" to your height. To determine the width, lie on the floor, drape a small blanket over you with about 6 inches (or more if desired) of overlap lying on the floor on both sides. This will give an idea of your quilt's width.

Follow these steps, and you will have a quilt that is as effective as any sleeping bag on the market:

▶ Think of the quilt as a 2" thick blanket. Cut out two pieces of 1.1 ounce breathable nylon to the desired shape of this "blanket," as it would appear when laid flat on the floor. Remember that you start by sewing the pieces together inside-out, then later turn the finished product right-side out so that the seam allowances are inside. Sew the two pieces together around their edges, but leave the head end open like a giant pillowcase. Consider a lighter-colored nylon for the upper layer, to minimize radiation heat loss, and darker-colored for the lower layer, which when exposed to the sun will dry the quilt much faster.

▶ While the "pillow case" is inside-out, lay it on top of your layers of insulation. Cut the insulation to the same

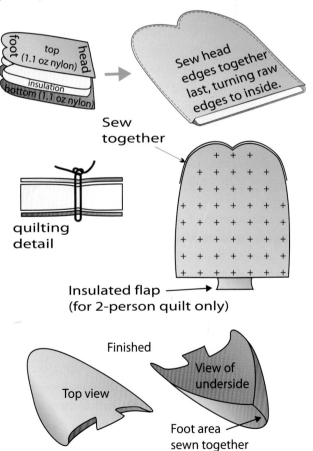

foot · top (1.1 oz nylon) · head

insulation

bottom (1.1 oz nylon)

Sew together

Sew head edges together last, turning raw edges to inside.

quilting detail

Insulated flap → (for 2-person quilt only)

Finished

Top view

View of underside

Foot area sewn together

size and shape as your "pillow case," then pin them in place.

▶ Following your line of stitching on the nylon as a guide, sew the insulation to the pillow case around its perimeter – except along the open edge at the head of the quilt. Use a long straight stitch.

▶ At the head end, separate the two layers of nylon, and sew the insulation only to the nylon layer next to it. This will allow you to turn the entire quilt right-side out without having the insulation shift out of position. It also makes the next step easier.

▶ Turn the quilt right-side out, and stitch the top edge closed, tucking in the raw edge of nylon to the inside.

▶ Continue stitching around the perimeter of the quilt, through all the layers, ⅛" from the edge. As you stitch, keep the original seam visible.

▶ The quilting stabilizes the insulation, keeping it from shifting and being pulled apart as you pull the quilt out of its stowbag. Grid the bag off in 18" squares if using continuous-filament insulation, or 12" squares if using discontinuous filament. Do this using a tape measure and smalls pieces of tape to mark each grid intersection. Insert a 20" length of synthetic yarn into the eye of a large hand-sewing needle (known as a tailor's or leather-craft needle). Poke the needle through the quilt at one of the grid-points. An eighth-inch from where the needle emerges, poke it back through the quilt the other way. The yarn now runs through the quilt rather like a staple, with its two ends sticking out one side. If the quilt is 2" thick, use a mandrel that is 2" wide – such as a yardstick or piece of cardboard. Lay the mandrel on the quilt upright between the two yarns. On top of the mandrel tie a square knot, and snug it up tight. When you pull out the mandrel, you have a perfect 2" loop in the yarn – matching the thickness of the quilt. Repeat the process at each grid mark.

▶ Sew on a full-length zipper if you want to make

a sleeping bag, or simply sew the bottom 26" of the quilt together, starting at the foot and running up toward the head, to make a pocket for the feet.

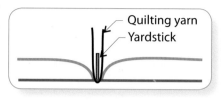

Quilting yarn
Yardstick

Before we figured out how to shape our quilts in certain ways, a gap would form between Jenny's and my necks and shoulders, permitting an undesirable draft. Our solution was to make an insulated flap of the same materials as the quilt itself, and about 12" wide by 8" tall. We sewed this to the quilt, such that the flap hung down between our necks and blocked the draft. Also, we sometimes sewed a couple of Velcro patches along the sides of our quilts, and we glued the opposite patches to our foam pads. This helped secure the quilt over us.

The backpack

The accompanying illustrations show the construction details of my backpack. To begin, you could take measurements from a commercial pack of the size you are interested in, and transfer those measurements to paper, creating your own pattern. Or you could start with a commercial pattern. As mentioned in the "Backpack" chapter, my pack is 11½" wide, 9⅓" deep, and 20½" tall, not taking into account its extension collar.

Whether using a commercial pattern or creating your own,

you can customize the pack to suit your needs. You can omit most of the straps and fancy accessories. You can add a water bottle pocket made of mesh on one side, a fuel bottle pocket on the other, and a large pocket on the back for stowing a wet tent fly or tarp. Along the top of the pockets you could make a small casing and run elastic through it to prevent the loss of the pocket contents. If your load will generally be below 20 pounds, you could dispense with the internal stays and hip belt.

Reinforce all stress points with small patches of material in order to spread the load over a wider area and to reduce the chances of the stitching pulling out. The great-

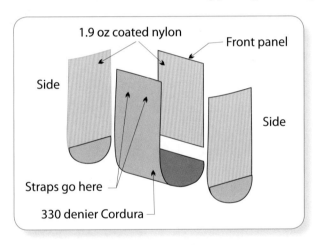

1.9 oz coated nylon

Front panel

Side

Side

Straps go here

330 denier Cordura

est stress occurs where the shoulder straps attach to the upper part of the pack. The reinforcement patches there need to be quite large. Another stress point is where the shoulder straps attach to the bottom of the pack. In this area, do not attach the nylon webbing straps directly to the body of the pack. Rather, attach the webbing to a doubled layer of material, triangular in shape, and attach that to the pack.

For our home-made backpacks that we carried on the AT, PCT-3 and IUA, we used 330 denier coated Cordura® for both the bottom and the panel that rests against the

back, and 1.9 ounce coated nylon for most of the remainder. We used the same kind of thread as with the previous projects. Triple-stitch everything, using a straight stitch.

Shoulder strap construction

The construction of the shoulder straps is not difficult. Use a heavy-duty size 100 needle, and ask your mail-order suppliers what they sell for pack strap foam.

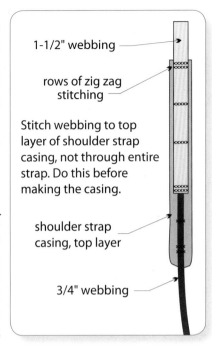

1-1/2" webbing

rows of zig zag stitching

Stitch webbing to top layer of shoulder strap casing, not through entire strap. Do this before making the casing.

shoulder strap casing, top layer

3/4" webbing

To begin the shoulder strap, cut out four pieces of 330 denier Cordura, 13" by 3". These will become the casings into which you will insert the foam pieces. Before sewing the top and bottom halves of the casing together, stitch the nylon webbing to the top piece. Use 9 inches of 1½" flat nylon webbing at the top, and 20 inches of ¾" flat nylon webbing at the bottom. The top is wider because it secures directly to the pack. The bottom is narrower because it must feed into an adjusting buckle, and a 1½" buckle would be far too large. Leave 2½" of the wide webbing extending beyond the raw edge of the casing. Position the narrow webbing so that it overlaps the wide webbing by ¾". Sew the webbing to the top layer of the casing, as illustrated.

With the webbing now in place you can proceed with the rest of the shoulder strap. Use a straight stitch and sew the top casing to the bottom casing, along both edges, inside-out, with a 3/8" seam allowance. Leave the top and bottom open. Double-stitch these edges for a stronger

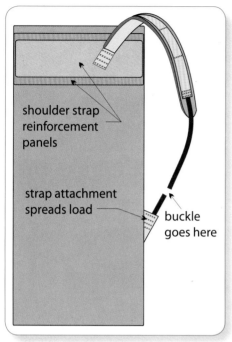

shoulder strap reinforcement panels

strap attachment spreads load

buckle goes here

seam, then sear the raw edges of the casing all the way around. Now you can turn the casing right-side out, so that the webbing is on the outside and the side seams are hidden.

Cut the foam to the size of the casing, round off the corners slightly, and insert it into the casing. The foam should fit reasonably tightly, so you might find it a bit of a wrestling match to situate it correctly. Finish the top and bottom of the shoulder strap by tucking the raw edges of the Cordura inside, and sewing the ends closed.

Now you can stitch the free end of the 1½" webbing to the pack. Use large safety pins to position the strap to the pack temporarily. Try the pack on for fit, and adjust the placement of the straps to suit. Stitch the straps to the pack using four rows of zig-zag stitches, half an inch apart. Be sure that you have at least two layers of reinforcing material underneath this high stress point.

You can finish off the collar extension with a 1" wide casing, drawstring and toggle. You can even add a second casing and drawstring at the bottom of the extension collar so that you can cinch the pack closed when the collar is not loaded. There are many other additional features you can add: a narrow webbing strap across the sides to hang socks for drying, a haul loop at the top

between the shoulder straps for lifting the pack. And an ice-axe loop. Be careful not to add too many extraneous features; keep it as simple and as light as possible.

Hiker's Friend Water Filter System

I designed the Hiker's Friend water filter system in 1986 for our first thru-hike, and Jenny and I have used it during many thousands of miles of hiking, Arctic sea-kayaking, and canoeing. I first described the system in the first edition of this book. It is so simple in construction that just about anyone can make their own. So let's start with an overview of how this filter system works; then I will describe how to make one for yourself.

The Hiker's Friend system is gravity-fed, and therefore it requires no effort to operate, other than what is needed to hang it from a tree branch or other support. Once we start the filtering, it works unattended, meaning that we are not slaves to the pump. As a package, it is considerably smaller and lighter than most filter units on the market.

It consists of only four parts: a circular sheet of waterproof nylon that forms a water bag, a filter cartridge, a suspension cord, and a 7½ foot length of clear tubing. The water bag is suspended at head height, and

Hiker's Friend water filtration system hanging from a sapling.

the tubing runs from the cartridge down to a water bottle at ground level.

Many types of filter cartridges will work in the Hiker's Friend, as long as the cartridge has a tubing nipple at one end on which to attach a length of tubing. The tubing itself is available at most hardware stores.

The water bag is easy to make, even without access to a sewing machine. It looks like an upside-down round parachute, but with a difference in the sus-pension. To make the bag, cut out a 30" diam-eter circle from a piece of lightweight, coated nylon fabric. Fold the circle of fabric in half three times to make a pie-shaped wedge, one-eighth of a pie. Mark each of the eight creases at the edge – these will

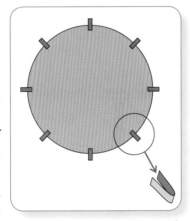

be the equally-spaced suspension points around the cir-cle's perimeter. As you did for the small ditty bag, you could melt a small hole at each suspension point, about an inch from the edge, and thread a 6-foot long cord through them. The stronger method is to sew a tab of webbing at each attachment point. Use ⅜" wide nylon webbing 3" long. Sear the ends to prevent fraying. You will need eight of these. Fold each piece of webbing in half to make doubled pieces 1½" long. Position one piece of webbing at each of the eight suspension points. The folded-in-half webbing should straddle the fabric, and should extend beyond the fabric ¾" to accommodate the suspension cord. Note that I do not hem the edge of the bag. After sewing all eight tabs, feed the suspension cord through them.

You now have a water bag for use with the Hiker's

Friend filtration system, or by itself at camp for storing water. You can also use this bag as a shower by fitting it with a siphon tube and a small, plastic shower-head.

To continue with the Hiker's Friend project, you need to attach the filter cartridge to the inside bottom of the bag, so that the cartridge does not float to the top and suck air. To keep the filter cartridge at the bottom of the bag, tie an overhand knot in the middle of a 16" length of cord, open the water bag and locate its center, lay the knot on the center, then reach under the bag to the out-side and pinch the knot with the fabric. Use a piece of twine to wrap several times around this pinch, from the outside. Tie off the twine with a secure knot. Open the water bag and tie the filter cartridge in place, using the fixed cord. The tubing attaches to the cartridge inside the bag. The tubing then comes up and over the bag's rim, and descends to the water bottle at ground level.

Attach the tubing to the cartridge, then fill the bag by dragging it through the water like a parachute, or by holding it under running water, or by pouring water into it from a cookpot. Hang the bag from a tree branch, and start the siphoning flow by sucking on the free end of the tubing. Until the cartridge becomes saturated, it will expel air bubbles into the siphoning tube. These bubbles reduce the siphoning pressure and you need to get rid of them. To do this, simply raise the tube and permit the bubbles to float upward toward the tube's free end, and escape. When the tube contains only water, lower its free end into a water bottle. Note in the photo that the tubing should J-bend upward before entering the collec-tion receptacle. The J-bend prevents any drips of unfil-tered water running down the outside of the tube, from contaminating the filtered water inside the water bottle. To stop the filtering, simply raise the tubing. To keep it raised when not in use, tuck the free end behind a sus-pension loop.

To change a clogged cartridge, simply untie it and replace it with a new one.

You can speed the filtering process by running the tubing directly through the bottom of the water bag. To do this, cut a hole in the bottom center of the water bag, the same diameter as the connection nipple of the cartridge you will be using. Wrap a thick rubber band (I use a "broccoli band" from the grocery store) around the bottom end of the cartridge to help seal the joint; the rubber band acts as a gasket. Then place the cartridge tip through the hole and lash the bag to the cartridge around the rubber band. Lash tightly using waxed artificial sinew, available at leather-craft supplies stores. To change the cartridge, carefully cut away the lashing, and then use a new rubber band and a new length of sinew to lash a new cartridge in place.

Modifying a commercial umbrella

Most commercial umbrellas are constructed with various pieces that are not necessary to the umbrella's function. When I modify one of these umbrellas, these superfluous pieces are what I am after.

I begin by sawing off the J-shaped plastic handle, leaving a 3½" stub. This is just long enough to hold on to. Next, I pull off the plastic top-cap and discard it. And after hack-sawing the excess metal shaft above the canopy to within ¼" of the top of the fabric, I file the shaft's new top end smooth.

I then remove the springs and other non-essential components. Here is how: Each tine has a plastic end-cap, to which the fabric is tied. I pull three adjacent end-caps off their tines, then cut the thread holding the canopy

to these tines. I do not cut off the end-caps. I am now able to slip the canopy over the top of the umbrella framework, just far enough to expose a small nail running through the top of the uppermost plastic assembly. This nail secures the assembly to the shaft. I carefully pry out the nail, and save it for later replacement. I then lift the assembly off the shaft and set it temporarily aside.

At the bottom of the shaft, just above the plastic handle, is a slot containing the thumb release piece. Pressing this trigger will deploy the umbrella, but actually this trigger

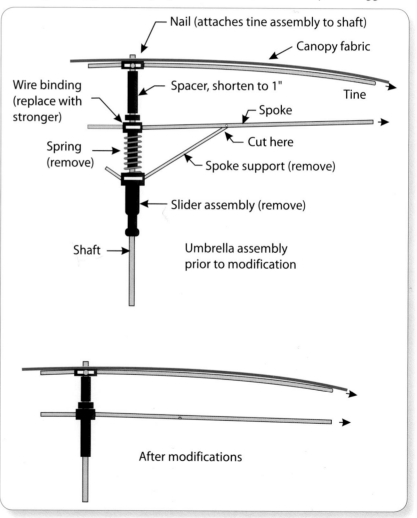

Nail (attaches tine assembly to shaft)

Canopy fabric

Wire binding (replace with stronger)

Spacer, shorten to 1"

Tine

Spoke

Spring (remove)

Cut here

Spoke support (remove)

Slider assembly (remove)

Shaft

Umbrella assembly prior to modification

After modifications

is unnecessary after my modification. A few inches above the slot is the trigger's anchor point, and if I use a small screwdriver to depress the anchor, I can remove the trigger piece and discard it.

The illustration shows what other components I remove for the umbrella modification. At the center of the canopy, on the outside, I sew or glue on a reinforcement patch of coated fabric, 1½" in diameter. I then reassemble the unit, replace the nail, carefully pull the canopy back over, and pop the plastic end caps back over the ends of the tines.

Seam Sealing

Sealing the seams is usually the last step when making your own waterproof gear. And the job is best done correctly the first time. This means using the right compounds in the right ways.

Unfortunately, some widely distributed seam sealing compounds harden and begin flaking away within a few weeks of application, especially when exposed to strong sunlight. Even some of the more reputable tent manufacturers supply these inferior sealers with their products. Why? Probably because these particular compounds are easier to apply. However, seeing the results of your work exfoliating away is not a pretty sight. And speaking from experience, the act of removing the inglorious mess in order to repeat the job can be even more dispiriting. Here is what I recommend:

On urethane-coated fabrics, use SeamGrip or AquaSeal, both from the McNett Corporation. These two products work especially well when mixed with their accelerators (see manufacturer's instructions). The accelerator adds a bit of strength, and greatly shortens setting time.

On silicone-coated fabrics, use clear 100% silicone sealant, available at hardware stores. You can dilute the silicone sealer with mineral spirits, MEK, unleaded gasoline, or Coleman type white gas, then paint the mixture on the seams with a small brush. The diluting agent allows the sealer to work into the seams better, and yields a thinner and lighter layer.

Before seam sealing any item of gear, wipe away any dust or residues of manufacture using a damp cloth, or a cloth wetted with a mild degreasing solvent such as rubbing or denatured alcohol. These precautions will ensure that the sealant bonds to the fabric properly. After applying the sealant be sure to let it dry thoroughly. Also, avoid using the sealing compounds indoors; the vapors can make a person ill. Even outside, work only in 10 or 15-minute intervals, allowing your respiratory system to recover and the compound's solvents to evaporate. The more "footage" you try to seal in a single session, the more likely the newly-sealed seams will fold back on the material. This can smear the compound unattractively onto the main body of your project. So split the job into several short sessions, and allow several hours of drying time in between each one.

Stretching the seams exposes more of the stitching to the compound brush. If sealing a tarp, pitch the tarp tightly, then paint the seams. Or if sealing other items, you might be able to enlist a helper. As one person stretches the seam apart, the other applies the sealing compound. If working alone, you can lay the piece down on a clean, hard surface and place a knee or a heavy weight on one side of it, then stretch the seam with one hand while applying compound with the other.

Use a small bristle brush to apply the compound. If the bristles are insufficiently stiff, trim them shorter. And do not try to make a neat job. Neat jobs are far more prone to leaking, because they tend to lack sufficient coverage. Smear the compound on the seam half-an-inch wide to prevent water from wicking laterally through the fabric. Sealing the seams on one side of the item is usually sufficient. When the job is complete, allow the sealant to cure undisturbed for a day or two.

Finally, test the gear under a garden hose, or in the shower if you are working with clothing, and correct any leaks. On humid days, however, be aware that the cold water from a hose could cause condensation to form inside a tarp or tent fly, making it appear to be leaking. Look carefully for beads of water actually coming through the seams.

In camp, you can improvise sealing compound with lip balm, tree sap, or even peanut butter. For more lasting repairs, of course, use seam sealing compound. On longer outings you could place a small tube of compound in your drift box (as described in the "Resupply" chapter). Use it to repair small tears also. Tape the tears closed from one side, and apply compound to the other side.

Sewing projects for a winter's day

Sewing hiking gear is an extremely effective way to save money, and it can be very rewarding. And once you gain more skill and experience, you may think of all sorts of other interesting projects. Here are a few more suggestions:

▶ Sew an eyeglasses loop inside your tarp or tent, to keep the glasses handy yet out of harm's way at night. Sew on a second loop for your wristwatch.

▶ Pack cover: Most commercial ones do not fit well, and they tend to leak profusely. Design one to fit your pack. Or, make a pack liner.

▶ Waterproof pack liner: This is a large waterproof stowbag, custom-fitted to the inside of your backpack.

▶ Hiking shirt: Chose a pattern for a loose fit, with a collar and button up front. Use a lightweight, breathable, synthetic fabric, like polyester.

▶ Eyeglasses bag: Make it from soft fleece.

▶ Watch band: Make it with webbing and Velcro.

▶ Tent peg stowbag

▶ Camera stowbag

▶ Cookpot stowbag: Use in conjunction with cookfires, which blacken the pot.

▶ Food bags

▶ Shower booties: These are easily made of lightweight coated nylon, with elastic around the top edges. The final product looks much like a pair of inverted shower caps.

▶ Stowbag for the Hiker's Friend water filter.

Lupine

Ray & Jenny's 1994 Gear List for PCT-3

In the interests of comfort and safety, please note that we are not recommending this equipment. Always compile your own gear based on personal experience and needs.

Ray's Gear

Backpack	13.5 oz
Umbrella	9.0 oz
Reflective film umbrella covering, with rubber bands and tape for attaching film to umbrella	0.8 oz
Sleeping quilt: synthetic fill, includes mosquito netting. 79" long, 58" chest, 44" foot	49.0 oz
Sleeping bag stowbag, 2 ply W/B	2.5 oz
Stove, fuel, windscreen, in coated nylon stowbag	24.8 oz
Water bottle (empty soda bottle)	1.6 oz
Hat: fleece	1.2 oz
Shell jacket: breathable nylon	6.0 oz
Mittens: fleece	1.0 oz
Shell pants: breathable nylon	3.0 oz
Socks: 2 pair thin nylon	1.2 oz
Shower booties, coated nylon	0.8 oz
Face towel: cotton, 12" square	1.8 oz
Clothing stowbag (plastic garbage sack)	1.3 oz
Ditty Bag #1, nylon mesh	0.2 oz
Windex for cleaning eyeglasses and camera lens	0.8 oz
Half a cotton bandana for cleaning eyeglasses and camera lens	0.1 oz
Compass	0.8 oz
Spoon: Lexan	0.2 oz
Prescription dark glasses	1.2 oz

Eyeglasses bag: fleece with velcro	0.2 oz
Flashlight with single AAA battery and spare bulb	1.0 oz
Pocket knife	0.8 oz
Toothbrush	0.1 oz
Dental floss	0.1 oz
Hydrogen peroxide (antiseptic)	0.5 oz
Cord	0.5 oz
Ditty Bag #2, nylon	0.6 oz
Medical kit: Betadine, Metronidazol, Diasorb, Amoxicillin, Campho-Phenique Antibiotic, zinc oxide, Mycelex (for athlete's foot), 1 T. salt in tiny resealable plastic bag	4.0 oz
Sewing kit: heavy thread, 3 safety pins, 3 needles	0.1 oz
Emergency fire starter kit in resealable plastic bag: small lighter, stick matches, birthday candles	0.9 oz
Spare flashlight battery, size AAA	0.5 oz
Valuables: traveler's checks, cash, credit card, driver's licenses, in resealable plastic bag	1.0 oz
Toilet kit: toilet paper & Dr. Bronner's soap in plastic vial	2.0 oz
Journal pad, maps & pen	2.0 oz
Ray's Baseline Pack Weight	**8.44 lb**

Jenny's Gear

Backack	11.5 oz
Umbrella	6.0 oz
Reflective film umbrella covering, with rubber bands and tape for attaching film to umbrella	0.8 oz
Tarp: 1.9 oz coated ripstop nylon, 8'8" square	28.0 oz
Tent stakes: 8 aluminum, 7" long	2.5 oz
Tent stakes stowbag: nylon	0.1 oz
Ground sheet: 81.5" long. 48" wide at head, 34" at foot	6.5 oz
Foam pads: two 3/8 inch thick closed cell polyethylene. 19.5" wide at shoulders; 17.5" at hips; 36.5" long	9.5 oz
Camera with 1 roll film	6.0 oz
Camera stowbag: coated nylon	0.5 oz
Camera kit: 1 roll of film, spare battery, and bulb brush	1.4 oz
Water bottle (empty soda bottle)	1.6 oz
Water scoop: breakfast cereal cup, plastic	0.1 oz
Water trough: cookie package, aluminum foil	0.2 oz
Hat: fleece	1.0 oz
Shirt: Thermax, long sleeve	3.0 oz
Shell jacket: breathable nylon	6.0 oz
Mittens: fleece	1.5 oz
Shell pants: breathable nylon	4.0 oz
Socks: 3 pair, thin nylon	1.8 oz

Shower booties: coated nylon	0.8 oz
Half of a cotton bandana as towel	0.3 oz
Clothing stowbag (plastic garbage sack)	1.3 oz
Jenny's Ditty Bag, nylon	0.2 oz
Flashlight with single AAA battery & spare bulb	1.0 oz
Lighter	0.5 oz
Comb	0.3 oz
Toothbrush	0.3 oz
Spoon: Lexan	0.2 oz
Can opener: P-51	0.2 oz
Repellent in pump spray bottle	1.8 oz
Sunscreen	0.8 oz
Note pad & pencil	0.3 oz
Prescription dark glasses	1.2 oz
Eyeglasses bag: fleece with velcro	0.2 oz
Lip balm	0.5 oz
Aspirin & vitamins together in small resealable bag	0.3 oz
Foot Care in resealable bag: 12 adhesive strips, full pack of 2nd Skin & dressing, superglue, rubbing alcohol, padded adhesive strips, athletic tape.	3.5 oz
Cookpot with lid: aluminum, 2 quart capacity	7.8 oz
Cookpot stowbag: coated nylon	0.5 oz
Jenny's Baseline Pack Weight	**7.12 lb**

Ray's clothing worn

Sun hat with wire rim	2.0 oz
Shirt: polyester	4.0 oz
Watch	1.5 oz
Shorts: spandex	4.3 oz
Socks: 2 pair, thin nylon	1.2 oz
Shoes	22.0 oz

Jenny's clothing worn

Sun hat	2.0 oz
Shirt: polyester	2.0 oz
Underwear	0.5 oz
Shorts: nylon/spandex	3.0 oz
Socks: nylon	0.6 oz
Shoes	21.0 oz

Ray's Additional Gear

Head net: no-see-um netting (used in central OR only)	1.2 oz
Hat: fleece & 2-ply W/B covering (used in northern WA only)	2.5 oz
Jacket: 2-ply W/B (used first few days only)	6.0 oz
Sweater: lightweight fleece (carried through northern WA, rarely needed)	14.3 oz
Wicking shirt: Thermax, long sleeve (used in WA only)	8.0 oz
Shell mittens: breathable nylon (used in central OR only, for mosquitoes)	0.2 oz
Wicking pants: Thermax (used in northern WA only)	7.5 oz
Snow boots: Avia N'yati (used in WA only)	26.5 oz
Socks: 2 pair, polyester & wool blend (used in WA only)	2.2 oz

Shell booties: breathable nylon (used in central OR only, for mosquitoes)	0.2 oz
No-Fog cloth in resealable plastic bag (used in northern WA only)	0.2 oz
Water bag: 2.5 gal (used in southern CA only)	3.5 oz
Ice axe, modified (used in northern WA only)	12.8 oz

Jenny's Additional Gear

Hat: fleece (used in WA only)	3.0 oz
Sweater: lightweight fleece (used in northern WA only)	14.0 oz
Jacket: 2-ply W/B (used first few days only)	8.3 oz
Shell mittens: breathable nylon (used in central OR for bugs and southern CA for sun)	0.2 oz
Wicking pants: Thermax (used in WA only)	7.0 oz
Snow boots: Avia N'yati (used in WA only)	25.0 oz
Socks: 2 pair, polyester & wool blend (used in WA only)	4.0 oz
Socks: 1 pair, ragg wool (used in northern WA only)	3.8 oz
Shell booties: breathable nylon (used in central OR for mosquitoes only)	0.2 oz
Water bag: 2.5 gal (used in southern CA only)	3.5 oz
Ice axe, modified (used in northern WA only)	12.5 oz

A Few Quotes

"Books are ships which pass through the vast seas of time." – Francis Bacon

"Any jackass can kick down a barn, but it takes a good carpenter to build one." – Sam Rayburn

"You cannot dream yourself into a character; you must hammer and forge yourself one." – James A. Froude

"No one knows what he can do till he tries."
– Publilius Syrus

"If you think education is expensive - try ignorance."
– Derek Bok

"When dealing with people remember you are not dealing with creatures of logic, but with creatures of emotion, creatures bristling with prejudice, and motivated by pride and vanity." – Dale Carnegie

"Never discourage anyone who continually makes progress, no matter how slow." – Plato

"Good judgment comes from experience, and experience - well, that comes from poor judgment."
– Anonymous

"I cannot give you the formula for success, but I can give you the formula for failure - which is: try to please everybody." – Herbert B. Swope

"A vigorous five-mile walk will do more good for an unhappy but otherwise healthy adult than all the medicine and psychology in the world." – Paul Dudley White

"Some people think they have an open mind when it is really their mouth." – Anonymous

"When you have a taste for exceptional people you always end up meeting them everywhere."
– Pierre Mac Orlan

"Its name is Public Opinion. It is held in reverence. It settles everything. Some think it is the voice of God."
– Mark Twain

"To bring up a child in the way he should go, travel that way yourself once in a while." – Josh Billings

"Never, never, never, never give up."
– Winston Churchill

"To read without reflecting is like eating without digesting." – Edmund Burke

"A ship in harbor is safe, but that is not what ships are built for." – John A. Shedd

"Life is either a daring adventure, or nothing."
– Helen Keller

"You are today where your thoughts have brought you; you will be tomorrow where your thoughts take you."
– James Allen

"Any fool can criticize, condemn and complain - and most do." – Dale Carnegie

"Idleness wastes the sluggish body, as water is corrupted unless it moves." – Ovid

"Life should not be a journey to the grave with the intention of arriving safely in a pretty and well pre-served body, but rather to skid in broadside, thoroughly used up, totally worn out, and loudly proclaiming, 'Wow, what a Ride!'" – Unknown

"Heaven is under our feet as well as over our heads."
– Henry David Thoreau

"I hear the 'Call of the Wild' and it's starting to sound personal." – Frank Poole

"You are never given a wish without also being given the power to make it true." – Richard Bach

"Now my soul hath elbow room." – William Shakespeare

"The human mind treats a new idea the way the body treats a strange protein; it rejects it."
– Biologist P.B. Medawar

"People do not lack strength; they lack will."
– Victor Hugo

"What is the use of running, when you're on the wrong road?" – Anonymous

"If you always live with those who are lame, you will yourself learn to limp." – Latin proverb

"Each one sees what he carries in his heart."
– Johann Goethe

"We find after years of struggle, that we do not take a trip; a trip takes us." – John Steinbeck

"Men go abroad to admire the heights of mountains, the mighty billows of the sea, the long courses of rivers, the vast compass of the stars,…and yet they pass themselves by." – St. Augustine

"They are able because they think they are able." – Virgil

"Don't let what you cannot do interfere with what you can do." – John Wooden

"Adversity introduces a man to himself." – Anonymous

"Advertising is the rattling of a stick inside a swill bucket." – George Orwell

"If you're looking for a big opportunity, seek out a big problem." – Anonymous

"Everyone thinks of changing the world, but no one thinks of changing himself." – Leo Tolstoy

"Life is not so short but that there is always time enough for courtesy." – Ralph Waldo Emerson

"Your living is determined not so much by what life brings to you as by the attitude you bring to life."
– John Homer Miller

"To accomplish great things, we must dream as well as act." – Anatole France

"Half the work that is done in this world is to make things appear what they are not." – Elias Root Beadle

"The fool who proclaims the general folly first and loud-est passes for a prophet." – Carl Jung

"If I had to do it all over, I'd start again next week."
– Walkin' Jim Stoltz

The Book's History

"All truth passes through three stages.
First it is ridiculed,
second it is violently opposed,
and third, it is accepted as self-evident."
— *Arthur Schopenhauer, German Philosopher 1788-1860*

The evolving book

Before 1991, almost every backpacker on an overnight trip carried more than forty pounds. Even loads of fifty and sixty pounds were common. So prior to the early 1990's, the lightweight hiking movement, as we know it today, did not exist. Granted, a few hikers practiced the minimalist approach; but the methods these hardy souls used did not catch on, mainly as they did not work well for other people. There were no popular books on the subject of lightweight hiking, nor any books or articles that described a workable lightweight hiking system. So for our first PCT hike I had to come up with my own ideas on how to make lightweight gear, and how to make this gear work for us.

These ideas proved so successful during our first two thru-hikes in 1987 and 1991 that I decided to write the *PCT Hiker's Handbook*. Although the book was slanted toward thru-hiking that trail, it also chronicled the initial phases of my gear and associated techniques for long-distance, lightweight hiking.

From December 1991 to April 1992 we sold several dozen beta-copies of the *Handbook* to PCT hikers in planning. In April of 1992 we published the first commercial edition. With the advent of the *Handbook*, the concepts of a workable and safe lightweight approach to hiking slowly spread throughout the backpacking community.

An idea whose time had come

With subsequent printings in the first half of the 1990's, more hikers learned about lightweight gear and techniques; some by reading the *Handbook*, but even more hikers learned of the methods by seeing other people use them – in many or most cases without learning of the source of these ideas.

Only the beginning

For Jenny and me, the *Handbook* and its ideas were only the beginning. We went on to thru-hike the Continental Divide Trail in 1992, and the Appalachian Trail in 1993, at which time I coined the term Triple Crown in reference to all three of these long distance trails. The following year we returned for our third PCT thru-hike in 1994.

During these three hikes I continued to refine our pack-weights and to develop even more effective techniques. By the end of 1995 my gear and methods had taken a quantum leap. So in order to chronicle these refinements, in the spring of 1996 I rewrote the *Handbook* and called it the *Pacific Crest Trail Hiker's Handbook, Second Edition*.

Beyond the ordinary

As the book grew and matured, the feedback indicated that our type of gear and our hiking and camping methods were working for a much wider audience: backpackers with varying levels of experience and skill, and who hiked in many different regions on trails both long and short.

So in 1999 I peeled back the book's original skin and took the subject to new level. I kept the information pertaining to my gear and clothing, the associated techniques, and our hiking and camping methods in general.

But I removed the PCT specific material and made the book into an all-trails version. The book went into its eighth printing with fresh content and a new title: *Beyond Backpacking*.

Not only was its subject matter "beyond" the standard backpacking method, but also I wished to convey an equally important idea of personal philosophy. That is, I felt that there should be more to backpacking then just tromping along a trail. I wished to take the reader *beyond* all that, into a world of greater awareness of the natural world and deeper meaning.

Test of time

By now the backpacking community has accepted the benefits of lightweight gear as self-evident, at least for the most part. Yet the book needed another metamorphosis. Over the years my lightweight systems have evolved further because I have never stopped refining them. Also, a new generation of backpackers are eager to set out with lighter packs. And to do so, a solid understanding of a good, safe, lightweight system is important.

In the Fall of 2008, *Trail Life* emerged as a reflection of the evolution of my thought and techniques. A lightweight approach to backpacking is here to stay; yet the gear I developed, the techniques for using that gear safely, and the quiet philosophy behind it all may be new to many hikers. It is the enthusiasm of today's hikers and campers that continues to keep this book fresh and young.

From the humble beta version of the *Handbook* to the current rendition and on into the future, the book's history confirms that backpacking can be enjoyable and relatively safe with a lighter-weight approach.

The book's
10th printing

The Book's Publication History
PCT Hiker's Handbook
Beta printing – Dec 1991 (Several dozen copies sold to PCT hikers in planning.)
2nd printing (1st commercial printing) – Apr 1992
3rd printing – Sep 1992
4th printing – Oct 1994
Second Edition Handbook
5th printing – Feb 1996
6th printing – Mar 1997
7th printing – Feb 1998
Beyond Backpacking
8th printing – July 1999
9th printing – Mar 2000
10th printing – Oct 2001
11th printing – Sep 2002
Trail Life
12th printing – Oct 2008

Coined terms used in this book: Beaks, Brain Lock, Bug Mitts, Butterfly Clove Hitch, Coalescence, Cookfire, Draft Stopper, Dura-dirt, Monster Mash, Park Bear, Power Hiking, Power Resting, Quilt, Resupply Station, Shell Jacket, Shell Pants, Signal Odors, Split Zip, Stealth Camping, Sun Mitts, Tent Awning, Trail Shock, Triple Crown.

Author's Notes

The photographs I used in this book were taken during our long-distance hikes. For the first three hikes (PCT-1, PCT-2, CDT) we carried fairly heavy loads, as described in the first part of the book. So the photos from those hikes reflect that. Nevertheless, those hikes were a lot of fun. Our second three distance-hikes (AT, PCT-3, IUA) were even more fun with our lightweight gear. And granted, this book is based on our lightweight approach. But over-all, it is about enjoying the wilds – regardless of the type of gear carried. I hope that the photographs reflect that too.

As this photo shows, lightweight long-distance hiking is not always lightweight. Faced with a long waterless stretch, our home-made backpacks can still handle a load of water. Here we are leaving Kennedy Meadows during our southbound trek (PCT-3).

Finally, I hope this book will inspire you to spend more time in the wilds; doing so is bound to enrich your life, as it has ours.

Index

Author's Profile

*"By the trails my feet have broken,
The dizzy peaks I've scaled, the campfire's glow;
By the lonely seas I've sailed in…
I am signed and sealed to nature – be it so."*
— *Robert Service*

Ray Jardine graduated from Northrop University with a degree in Aeronautical and Astronautical Engineering, and worked in the aerospace industry as a specialist in computer-simulated space-flight mechanics. He retired at an early age to pursue his outdoor interests.

A mountaineer, he climbed most of Colorado's fourteeners, many in winter; and he climbed extensively across western North America. His highest peak has been Peru's Huascarán, at 22,205 feet.

Ray worked as a winter mountaineering instructor for two seasons, and as a wilderness instructor for seven. In the process he backpacked several thousand miles. He also held an EMT certificate from St. Anthony's Hospital in Denver.

A rock climber for 19 years, Ray established some of the era's toughest climbs, including the world's first 5.12 graded climb: The Crimson Cringe, and the first 5.13: The Phoenix. He climbed extensively in Great Britain and across western America. His ascents in Colorado include seven Diamond routes. In Yosemite Valley he pioneered 50 first or first-free ascents, and was the first to free climb a grade VI.

Ray developed the protection and anchoring device known as the "Friend" which revolutionized the sport.

And he originated the style of climbing used today that enables more challenging routes to be climbed. According to Rock & Ice magazine, "The brilliance of his routes, the undeniable contributions of his designs, and his yet-unrealized visions of the future of the sport place Ray Jardine among the rarest of climbing revolutionaries."

In the early 1980's Ray and his wife Jenny sailed around the world aboard their ketch SUKA, an acronym for "Seeking UnKnown Adventures." During the voyage they spent 6 months scuba diving and snorkeling in the Caribbean. Ray is a PADI certified diver.

Ray is also an avid hang glider pilot. He has logged some 400 hours aloft, flown to 16,000 feet, cross-country 50 miles, and thermal gained 9,100 feet (nearly two miles straight up). He has flown sailplanes and small powered craft, and he held an Australian Restricted Private Pilot's License.

Ray and Jenny have completed five long-distance hikes:
* Hike #1: Mexico to Canada, generally along the Pacific Crest Trail, 2,500 miles in 4-1/2 months, 1987.
* Hike #2: The PCT, 2,700 miles in 3 months 3 weeks, 1991.
* Hike #3: The Continental Divide Trail, 2,500 miles in 3 months 3-1/2 weeks, 1992.
* Hike #4: The Appalachian Trail, 2,100 miles in 2 months 28 days, 1993.
* Hike #5: The PCT southbound, 2,700 miles in 3 months 4 days, 1994.
* And another long-distance trip: the IUA Hike & Bike, Canada to Mexico, 2,000 miles in 63 days, 2003.

In 1991 Ray wrote the First Edition of *The PCT Hiker's Handbook*, which described his new system of lightweight hiking. In 1996 he re-wrote the book and called it the Second Edition. And in 1999 he wrote the all-trails version, and titled it *Beyond Backpacking*.

Ray has also written *The Ray-Way Tarp Book*, and *Siku Kayak*.

Sea kayaking has also been a favorite pursuit. Ray and Jenny have paddled several thousand miles in areas such as offshore California, the Sea of Cortez, French Polynesia, Australia, Alaska and Canada.

His Baja Sea-Kayaking trips include: Baja #1: 1974, kayak 200 miles in 2 weeks, San Felipe to Bahia LA. Baja #3: 1976, kayak 24 days San Felipe to Bahia Animas. Baja #4: 1977, kayak 26 days Bahia LA to La Paz. Baja #8: 1981, kayak 23 days San Felipe to La Paz. Baja #9: 1989, kayak 34 days San Felipe to La Paz with Jenny.

Ray & Jenny's Arctic Sea-Kayaking trips include:

* "Arctic" Trip #1: Anacortes WA, Inside Passage, Chilkoot Trail by portage, Yukon River to the Bering Sea. 3,392 mi, 100 days, 1988.

* Arctic Trip #2: in kayak #2, west coast of Arctic Alaska from the Yukon River north to the Inuit village of Shishmaref. 600 mi, 48 days, 1995.

* Arctic Trip #3: Siku Kayak. Shishmaref to Point Barrow and across the top of Alaska. 1,400 mi, 78 days, 1996.

* Arctic Trip #4 Mackenzie River (Canada's largest) 975 mi, 18 days, with an additional 200 mi, 12 days along Arctic coastline until stopped by polar pack ice, 1997.

For these trips they built kayaks: Kayak #1: Solo fiberglass (built on Catalina Island). Kayak #2: "Headwind Magnet," a two-person kayak of carbon fiber, Airex and epoxy, designed by Ray on a CAD program that he wrote himself, 1994. Kayak #3: Siku, 1995. Kayak #4: Nunaluk, 1996.

Ray & Jenny particularly enjoy Canoe Tripping. Their long trips have included:

* Canoe Trip #1: Fulton Chain of Lakes, Adirondacks, 125 mi, 12 days, 1996.

* Subarctic Canoe Trip #2: Thelon River, 575 mi, 24 days, from Lynx Lake to the Inuit hamlet of Baker Lake near Hudson Bay, 1997.

* Subarctic Canoe Trip #3: Back & Meadowbank Rivers. Across the Barrenlands of sub-arctic Canada, from Sussex Lake traveling down the Back River, up the Meadowbank River, over the Divide and down to the hamlet of Baker Lake, 736 mi, 40 days, 1999.

* Subarctic Canoe Trip #4: Kazan River. 560 mi, 24 days across the Barrenlands of sub-arctic Canada, 2001.

* Subarctic Canoe Trip #5: Great Slave Lake and the Coppermine River starting from Yellowknife via Pike's Portage, to the Arctic Ocean, 960 mi, 38 days, 2005.

In 1998 Ray and Jenny were featured guests in the BBC television series Wilderness Walks, filmed during a six-day trek through the Three Sisters Wilderness of Oregon, 1998.

For nearly 2½ years, from Sept 2000 to Feb 2003, Ray and Jenny were full-time skydivers. Altogether Ray jumped 2,591 times, and Jenny 1,850.

Part way through their skydiving career they took a 2-month vacation from jumping to row a boat across the Atlantic Ocean, 3,000 miles in 53 days, 2002.

Back on terra firma, they peddled their tandem bicycle in a grand loop across the U.S., coast to coast – twice. This was their "Hello America Bicycle Tour" 6,700 mil, 92 days, 2004.

For something new and adventurous, Ray and Jenny spent two weeks snowkiting on the ice cap of Greenland, 2006.

Perhaps one of Ray and Jenny's most extreme adventures was skiing to the South Pole, 750 mi, 57 days. On that same trip Ray also summited Vinson Massif, the highest peak in Antarctica, 2006-07.

Most recently, he and Jenny spent two months mountain climbing in the Andes, 2008.

For stories and photos about these adventures and others, see Ray's web site: www.RayJardine.com